THE ORIGINS OF THE SECOND WORLD WAR IN EUROPE

ORIGINS OF MODERN WARS
General editor: *Harry Hearder*

Titles already published:

THE ORIGINS OF THE FRENCH REVOLUTIONARY WARS
T. C. W. Blanning

THE ORIGINS OF THE ITALIAN WARS OF INDEPENDENCE
Frank J. Coppa

THE ORIGINS OF THE WARS OF GERMAN UNIFICATION
William Carr

THE ORIGINS OF THE RUSSO–JAPANESE WAR
Ian Nish

THE ORIGINS OF THE FIRST WORLD WAR (Second Edition)
James Joll

THE ORIGINS OF THE SECOND WORLD WAR IN EUROPE
P. M. H. Bell

THE ORIGINS OF THE SECOND WORLD WAR IN ASIA
AND THE PACIFIC
Akira Iriye

THE ORIGINS OF THE KOREAN WAR
Peter Lowe

THE ORIGINS OF THE VIETNAM WAR
Anthony Short

THE ORIGINS OF THE ARAB–ISRAELI WARS (Second Edition)
Ritchie Ovendale

THE ORIGINS OF THE SECOND WORLD WAR IN EUROPE

P. M. H. Bell

LONGMAN
London and New York

Longman Group UK Limited
Longman House, Burnt Mill, Harlow
Essex CM20 2JE, England
and Associated Companies throughout the world

*Published in the United States of America
by Longman Inc., New York*

First published 1986
Tenth impression 1993

BRITISH LIBRARY CATALOGUING IN PUBLICATION DATA

Bell, P.M.H.
  The origins of the Second World War in Europe.
  I. Europe—History—1918–1945
  I. Title
  940.5'1   D720

ISBN 0 582 49112 6

LIBRARY OF CONGRESS CATALOGING IN PUBLICATION DATA

Bell, P.M.H. (Philip Michael Hett), 1930-
  The origins of the Second World War in Europe.

  (Origins of modern wars)
  Bibliography: p.
  Includes index
    1. World War, 1939–1945——Causes. 2. Europe–
Politics and government——1918–1945. I. Title.
II. Series.
D741.B38   1986   940.53'112   85-23103
ISBN 0-582-49112-6

Set in 10/11pt Linoterm Times
Printed in Malaysia by VP

CONTENTS

LIST OF MAPS

EDITOR'S FOREWORD

Mr Philip Bell's interpretation of the origins of the Second World War is dispassionate, uncommitted, and perhaps for that reason brilliantly unanswerable. His basic point that 'some theories wide enough to explain everything, end by explaining nothing', is made in the context of a consideration of the argument that the existence of sovereign states is a cause of wars, an argument that Mr Bell considers to be 'true but unhelpful'. It we apply the point on the long debate on the 'appeasement' of nazi Germany in the 1930s we can see that a blanket condemnation of 'appeasement' is too imprecise to be tenable, and, indeed, explains nothing. The trouble is that vague, sweeping generalizations tend to be accepted by an ill-informed public, and build themselves up into powerful myths. Such generalizations may be accepted by the media and the public for several decades after they have been discarded by most professional historians. Most journalists seem still to think that the policy of appeasing Hitler was, in each of the relevant crises, cowardly and mistaken. They do not distinguish between the factors which were operative in 1936 from those operative in 1938, or, again, in 1939. Mr Bell shows that the British government's policy had a cowardly side to it during the Spanish Civil War, but that Chamberlain's policy in 1939 was extremely courageous. When Stalin preferred to negotiate with Hitler, Chamberlain preferred to resist Hitler by a declaration of war, encouraged, it is true, by an impatient House of Commons.

There is no space in an editor's foreword to say more on the appeasement debate. Bell's lucid account and interpretation of the diplomatic history of the 1930s demolishes many familiar fallacies, without ever becoming polemical in tone. One point on Munich is worth mentioning here: in agreement with Professor D. C. Watt and other recent authorities, Mr Bell shows that Hitler regarded the settlement as a disaster, because he wanted a short, successful war against Czechoslovakia in the teeth of the passive disapproval of Britain and France. He was not content with success at the conference table. As Bell says, he wanted war for its own sake, and with such an outlook was perhaps unique in modern history. Ciano noted in his diary that if you offered Hitler more territory than he was demanding, he would still be disappointed, because what he wanted was war. But even this was not always true, so that even about Hitler generalizations can be dangerous.

In wanting victorious wars rather than diplomatic victories Hitler was acting not only immorally, but also irrationally. Sometimes he attacked another country because he wanted to secure resources from it, but sometimes he was already securing the resources he needed from that country without going to war. The classic example of this is his decision not to wait to eliminate Britain before invading the USSR, even though Stalin was already generously supplying him with both raw materials and manufactured products. Yet it remains true that Hitler sometimes made war pay, and while he was actually waging it, not merely after victory. Mr Bell points out that the acquisition of the vast resources of western Europe made war immensely profitable for Germany, at least in the short run. Here there is a parallel with a picture given by Dr T. C. W. Blanning in a companion volume recently published in the series, a volume on the origins of the French Revolutionary Wars. The French Directory and Napoleon, like Hitler, lived off a diet of warfare. For a country to acquire profits which could be used during the war is less common in the decades between Napoleon and Hitler. More often warfare is greedy of resources, even if victory is to bring profits after the end of hostilities. Often even a victorious power is permanently poorer after the war than it was before – as Britain has been after the two world wars. But surviving on the immediate conquests of wars had its dangers for Hitler, as Mr Bell shows. It created a 'vicious circle in which armaments were built up to make conquests and then more conquests were necessary to expand armaments', a process which 'reached an explosive stage in 1939, when raw materials, labour and food were all needed to sustain the pace'.

Bell makes an important distinction between Hitler's policy in western Europe and his policy in eastern Europe. In western Europe he seemed to be living in an antiquated world of power politics, thinking, for example, of a possible alliance with Britain against France, without realizing that the time was long past when the Western democracies would make war against each other. He considered also the rather more plausible idea of an Anglo-German alliance against the USSR. But his attitude to the war in western Europe, as Bell says, was one 'which would have been easily recognizable to Bethmann-Hollweg and the German General Staff of 1914'.

In eastern Europe a far more terrible feature of nazi policy emerged already in 1940 and 1941 – a racist policy against the Poles and the Russians which anticipated the 1942–45 holocaust of Poles and Jews. In the discussion of the relationship between ideology and *realpolitik* with which this series has often been concerned, nazism must presumably be considered as some monstrous kind of ideology. And if a choice must be made between two evils it must surely be concluded that the *realpolitik* of the pre-1914 world was preferable to the nazi 'philosophy' which resulted in the death camps.

HARRY HEARDER

ACKNOWLEDGEMENTS

In writing this book I have incurred many obligations, and I am happy to take this opportunity to thank those who have helped in its preparation. I am particularly grateful to Harry Hearder, the General Editor, for his invitation to contribute this volume to the series on the origins of modern wars, and for his help and encouragement in its writing. The University of Liverpool has provided research grants which have assisted my visits to various libraries.

I owe a great debt to my friends Edward Acton, David Dutton, John Gooch, and Ralph White, who read a long draft with sharp eyes and immense patience. Their wise and tactful comments have saved me from a number of errors and wrought many improvements in the text, though they bear no responsibility for the imperfections which remain. Betty Plummer, despite adverse circumstances, typed and retyped the whole book with her customary calm efficiency.

In attempting a general survey of so wide a subject as the origins of the Second World War in Europe, I am acutely conscious of my dependence on the multitude of scholars who have increased our knowledge and enlarged our understanding of the events under discussion. Some of my debts are acknowledged in the notes and reading list. My gratitude to the many other writers whose work I have absorbed over the years is no less real, even though they may not be specifically mentioned.

As always, my deepest thanks go to my wife for her help and support in all that has gone to the making of this book.

Department of History,   P.M.H. BELL
University of Liverpool   April 1985

ABBREVIATIONS

AO: Auslandsorganisation (Foreign Countries Organization)
DGFP: Documents on German Foreign Policy
NKVD: Narodny Komissariat Vnutrennikh Del (People's Commissariat for Internal Affairs)
NSDAP: Nationalsozialistische Deutsche Arbeiterpartei
OKW: Oberkommando der Wehrmacht (High Command of the Armed Forces)
PPF: Parti Populaire Français
SA: Sturm Abteilung (Nazi storm-troopers)
SS: Schutz Staffeln

Part One

INTRODUCTION: PROBLEMS OF INTERPRETATION

Chapter 1
ON WAR AND THE CAUSES OF WAR

On 3 September 1939 the Foreign Minister of the Third Reich, Joachim von Ribbentrop, received the British Ambassador in Berlin, Sir Nevile Henderson. War had just been declared between their two countries; and the Ambassador remarked that 'it would be left to history to judge where the blame really lay'. Ribbentrop replied that 'history had already proved the facts'. An hour later, it was the turn of the French Ambassador, Robert Coulondre, who was told that when war came France would be the aggressor, and replied: 'Of that history will be the judge.' Noting these exchanges, Sir Lewis Namier commented: 'The judgement of history was invoked by all alike.'[1]

History has not let them down. The origins of the Second World War have exercised the minds of generations of historians, and have filled thousands of pages, without exhausting either the fascination of the subject or the stamina of their readers. Many still remember the war vividly and were directly affected by it. Others, born after it ended, remain responsive to its echoes, as novels, films, television, and children's comics all bear witness. The history of that time is still invoked in the political debates of the present day. 'Appeasement' and 'Munich' are still words of power in the speeches of politicians and the columns of newspapers. Nazism and fascism remain current terms of political abuse. The spectre of the holocaust of Jewish lives is ever-present to twentieth-century European man.

We live still in the shadow of the Second World War. Its casualties, variously estimated at between 40 and 50 million dead, have left a lasting scar upon the populations of the world, and especially of Europe. Movements of populations in eastern Europe broke patterns of settlement established since the Middle Ages, so that Poles and Russians now live in territories which previously had been German for centuries. The physical ruins which littered Europe were fairly quickly repaired; but the destruction has left its mark on many great cities. Even countries which managed to remain outside the storm of hostilities were deeply disturbed by its passage, as the history of Sweden or Switzerland demonstrates.

Events of this magnitude continue to command attention and

demand explanation: and to embark upon a fresh review of the origins of the Second World War in Europe needs no apology. The scope of the enquiry is limited to Europe – a large enough arena, in all conscience, but more manageable than an attempt to comprehend the whole globe.[2] But Europe was not self-contained. Britain and France were great imperial powers, with possessions and commitments all over the world. The Soviet Union, equally an imperial power, included vast territories in central and eastern Asia only secured since the mid-nineteenth century. Nearly 8,000 kilometers of its land frontiers lay in Asia, compared with some 2,400 kilometres in Europe. All three powers were much concerned by the growth of Japanese power in the Far East. All three were faced by the recurrent imperial problem of the twentieth century, nationalist movements among their subject peoples – the British in India and the Middle East, the French in Syria and North Africa, the Soviets in the Caucasus and the Ukraine. For none of the three is it possible to consider their European problems, and their role in the origins of the war, without an eye on the global context.

Across the Atlantic from Europe, the USA sought for much of the 1920s and 1930s to withdraw into semi-isolation, hoping to return to the apparently secure haven of a pre-1914 normality. In the 1930s, successive Neutrality Acts were specifically designed to insulate the USA from European conflicts, and to ensure that there should be no repetition of the events of 1917, when she was drawn into the First World War. Yet Europeans could never forget or ignore the American presence over the western horizon. The activity (or otherwise) of the American economy, and the shape of American foreign policy, had profound effects in Europe. If at some point the economic and military strength of the USA were again to be mobilized, as in 1917–18, for participation in a European war, the consequences would be far-reaching. European powers held the centre of the international stage in the 1930s, but this was largely because the Americans chose to remain in the wings: and the American dimension of European affairs must constantly be allowed for.

Other complications arise from that deceptively simple name, 'the Second World War', which reveals problems on even a cursory inspection. It is conventional in western Europe to refer to the conflict as the war of 1939–45, just as we speak of the war of 1914–18; but the cases are very different. In 1914, Austria-Hungary declared war on Serbia on 28 July, and within a week five of the six European great powers were at war. While it is true that the Ottoman Empire came in later in the year, and Italy not until 1915, the main war crisis was short, concentrated, and decisive. One day Europe was at peace; and then a week later most of Europe was at war, in proper form, with ultimatums and declarations of war duly delivered.[3] By contrast, it is far from easy to say precisely when the Second World War in Europe began. It has appeared to many observers, both at the time and since, that the conflict began in 1936, with the Spanish Civil War, which seemed to mark the outbreak of an ideological war which was already latent over most of Europe. Volunteers flocked to Spain in this belief, often projecting their own passions and hatreds on to the fierce internal antagonisms of the Spanish people. Regular forces from Germany and Italy, and 'advisers' from the Soviet Union were involved, as well as the International Brigades recruited through the Communist International. Spain became the battleground for what seemed to be a European war fought by proxy.

While the Spanish Civil War was in progress, there occurred elsewhere the German occupation of Austria in March 1938; the Czechoslovakian crisis of September 1938, when the French army was mobilized and war seemed imminent; the German seizure of Bohemia and Memel in March 1939; and the Italian invasion of Albania in April 1939. Could this properly be called a time of peace, or war? The threat of force was ever-present, even if its use was only sporadic; and it is doubtful whether a tank has to open fire for its presence to constitute a warlike act. Undeclared war is a fair description of the state of Europe in 1938–39; until finally open war broke out when Germany attacked Poland on 1 September 1939, and found an opponent willing, and even eager, to fight rather than surrender. On 3 September Britain and France declared war on Germany; though their formal declarations made remarkably little immediate difference to the situation. Their armies and air forces remained inactive in the west; while in the east Germany (assisted after a time by the Soviet Union) conquered Poland unhindered. There followed the period of the phoney war, from October 1939 to April 1940; so that a time of undeclared war was followed by a period when war was declared but not waged. There was not very much difference between the two.

War was waged in earnest in April 1940, with German attacks on Denmark and Norway; in May, with the German invasion of the Low Countries and France; and in June, with the entry of Italy, which extended the conflict to the Mediterranean. In October 1940 Italy attacked Greece; in April 1941 the Germans conquered Yugoslavia and Greece; and finally in June 1941 they invaded the Soviet Union, the final extension of the war in Europe, which by then engulfed almost the entire Continent.

There was thus a movement from civil war and war by proxy in Spain, to local war (Germany and Poland), then to regional war (Scandinavia and western Europe), and finally to Continental war. There were spells of peace which was no peace, and of war which was remarkably unwarlike. Contemporaries were well aware that the line between peace and war, far from being sharp and clear-cut, was so blurred as to be almost invisible. On 10 November 1938, Adolf Hitler congratulated himself (and representatives of the German press, to whom he was speaking) on the tactics of propaganda, political pressure, and threat of force, which had been successfully used to 'wreck the nerves of those gentlemen in Prague . . . '[4] At almost exactly the same time, in comparatively peaceful England, Stephen Tallents, the Director-General of the shadow Ministry of Information which was being set up in the expectation of war, wrote of the 'present continental conditions, in which the boundaries between peace and war are so largely obliterated'.[5] Europe thus witnessed a process of change, not a sudden leap from peace to war; and an explanation ot the origins of the Second World War in Europe must examine the forces which lay behind the change, as well as the events which marked the different phases of its development.

War came by stages; and as it came, it was not one single war, unitary and simple in its nature, but a number of wars, different in kind, in aims, and in methods. The war in Spain was at once a civil war between Spaniards, a war between individuals from many parts of the world, and a war involving European states. The war fought by Germany against Poland in 1939 was, in German eyes, not just a war to shift their boundary with Poland from one line to another, but was aimed at the destruction of the Polish state and the subjugation of its people; and as such it went on for several years, because this process was fiercely though clandestinely resisted. The war in western Europe in 1940, on the other hand, was more in the style of 1914 and other 'orthodox' wars between states, waged between uniformed armed forces, using recognized military methods and exercising considerable forbearance towards the civilian population, and ending in the case of France in an armistice which showed a calculated restraint on the German side. The label 'Second World War in Europe' is used to denote not one event, but a number of separate conflicts, different in kind as well as in date. An explanation of origins must deal with these differences.

These are the tasks which a consideration of the origins of the war (or rather, wars) must face. But what is meant by 'origins' in this context? It is possible to seek the origins of the war in the events of diplomatic relations – the alliances and alignments of states, the activities of ambassadors and foreign ministers, conferences between statesmen. It may be, however, that such matters were merely superficial, eddies on the surface of a deep-running stream, whose course was determined by more profound forces. If so, what were these forces? Obvious possibilities may be found in the movement of ideas and the clash of ideologies; in economic pressures and opportunities; and in changes in military technology and strategic thought. If we accept the importance of such developments, what were the links between them and the decisions of individual statesmen and the sentiments of peoples?

Tolstoy, in *War and Peace*, wrote that historians had produced various diplomatic explanations of the war of 1812 – 'the wrongs inflicted on the Duke of Oldenburg, the non-observance of the Continental System . . . the ambitions of Napoleon, the firmness of Alexander, the mistakes of the diplomats, and so on'. If this were so, then more care on the part of the diplomats, different phrasing in a note, a minor concession on the part of Napoleon – and there would have been no war. Tolstoy rejected such explanations. For Napoleon and Alexander to be able to act as they did, he believed, 'a combination of innumerable circumstances was essential. . . . It was necessary that millions of men in whose hands the real power lay – the soldiers who fired the guns or transported provisions and cannon – should consent to carry out the will of those weak individuals, and should have been induced to do so by an infinite number of diverse and complex causes.'[6] Substitute Hitler and Chamberlain for Napoleon and Alexander, and Tolstoy's assertion is easily transposed from the war of 1812 to the Second World War. But were Hitler and Chamberlain merely weak individuals, controlled by circumstances and waiting on the consent of the millions who seemed to be their puppets, but in whose hands the real power lay? How can we decide?

Different approaches to the problem produce different explanations. It is possible to start by trying to explain, not one single war, but the phenomenon of war in general; and much effort has been put into this search. Ever since war ceased to be regarded as a scourge sent by God as a punishment for man's sins, men have sought the causes of war, so that, once identified, they might be eliminated. In the eighteenth century it was argued that war was produced by the ambitions (or even the mere whims) of monarchs and their courtiers; but this view foundered in the French Revolutionary Wars, fought by a republic and peoples' armies. In the nineteenth century, Richard Cobden and the Manchester school of liberalism held that universal peace would come through the railway, the steamship, the penny post, and free trade: when all had enough of this world's goods, none would wish to waste them in warfare, nor would there be any point in fighting to obtain a larger share. But events belied these hopes. In 1914 the postal services carried mobilization notices, and the railways transported armies to battle. The twentieth century proceeded to provide at least its fair ration of wars, and perhaps more – one observer listed thirty between 1900 and 1964.[7]

Among these conflicts, it was particularly the First World War of 1914–18 which stimulated the search for the causes of war into even greater activity. Shocked by the catastrophe and determined to avoid its repetition, men scanned the period before 1914 in search of the causes of war. They found them in plenty; and for each cause of war there was a remedy. Wars – and particularly that of 1914 – were caused by armaments and arms races. The remedy, therefore, was disarmament. Wars were caused by alliances and secret diplomacy, which bound states together without the knowledge of their peoples, and turned a small quarrel into a European war. The solutions here were to avoid alliances, and to practise open diplomacy, so that peoples could restrain their governments from dangerous commitments and warlike acts. Wars were caused by the very existence of sovereign states, free (and indeed accustomed) to fight one another from time to time. Here, the answers were to create some international organization to restrict the right to go to war, and to develop the role of international law. For socialists, wars were caused by capitalism, and by imperialism which was the latest form of capitalism; so that capitalist states, under the influence of bankers and great industrialists, fought for markets, raw materials, and fields for investment. In the long run, the answer was to do away with capitalism, for in a socialist world there would be no war; in the short run, means might be found to share markets, investment opportunities, and resources. There were widespread theories about 'scapegoat wars' – wars to relieve conflicts within a country by turning upon an external enemy. Here the answer seemed to be that after 1914–18 anyone could see that the remedy was worse than the disease – if Russia or Germany had gone to war in 1914 as a way out of internal conflicts, they had instead landed themselves in defeat and revolution. There were theories of war by accident – that in 1914, and doubtless on other occasions, the powers blundered into a war which none of them really wanted. For this the remedy was to improve the mechanism of international relations, so that time and opportunity were given to avoid accidents and allow good sense to prevail.

There are many difficulties with such general explanations of war. They tend to fall uneasily between determinism and free will. If wars were *really* caused by capitalism, and arose from its very nature, then how could they be avoided by creating a League of (mainly capitalist) Nations, or by merely adjusting the mechanism of the international system? Some socialists, indeed, argued with strict logic that they could not be so avoided; but most acted as though they could, partly because that was what they wanted to believe, and partly because all but the most rigid determinists recognized some scope for choice and action. Again, some theories, wide enough to explain everything, ended by explaining nothing – the argument that wars were the result of the existence of sovereign states fell into this difficulty. It was like saying that car accidents are the result of the existence of cars – which is true, but unhelpful. As an approach to the problem of the origins of the Second World War, such theories are too general to be very useful; though they should not be entirely disregarded, if only because in the 1920s and 1930s they were often taken very seriously, and so form part of the fabric of the period which we are examining.

Historians have tended to deal more in particular than in general explanations; with the causes of individual wars rather than with the causes of war. But even within this pragmatic approach, there is usually to be found a pattern. Historians seek long-term causes (often called origins), creating conditions in which war is likely or probable – long-standing territorial disputes, conflicts of interest, psychological tensions between peoples. To these they add short-term causes – specific events which bring these disputes and tensions to a head; and finally occasions of war – events which are not in themselves of decisive significance, but in particular circumstances tip the balance, or perhaps just provide an excuse for going to war. In making such analyses, historians make repeated use of analogies: the accumulation of inflammable materials, finally lit by a single spark; or a dam subjected to an increasing weight of water, and finally broken by some comparatively minor crack in the concrete; or explosive forces built up over a period of time and then touched off by the mere movement of a trigger. Behind the analogies lies a standard pattern of explanation, though with varying emphasis being placed on long-term and short-term causes. It is possible to find, for example, discussions of the coming of the First World War which deal mainly with the long term (the growth of internal tensions in Germany, or imperial rivalry between the powers, or nationalist aspirations in the Balkans); and others which deal almost exclusively with the short term, examining exhaustively the events of July 1914. There is frequently room for dispute as to whether a particular event was a genuine cause of conflict, or merely the occasion: again looking at 1914, was the German invasion of Belgium the cause of British entry into the European conflict, or only the occasion for a step which was bound to be taken anyway?

General theories of the causes of war, and the patterns of causation woven by historians, may be very logical and intellectually coherent. But participants in events have a different perspective. Those in positions of authority or influence are profoundly conscious that they must take decisions. At specific moments they must declare war – or not; issue an order to attack another country – or not; order resistance to an attack – or not. Even those who are firmly convinced of a determinist view of life find in practice that they must choose; and do not appear to think that they are in the grip of forces outside their control. Lenin, whose theoretical works demonstrated that war was a function of capitalism and imperialism, had to choose early in 1918 whether his new Bolshevik state should launch a revolutionary war against the Germans (which was what some of his colleagues wanted) or make peace, at great cost· in territory and resources. He chose peace, not on any grounds of historical determinism, but because he knew that Russia did not have the means to resist the German Army. Obviously he did not abandon his view of life and of history; and he believed he was acting to save the Revolution; but the actual decision was based on a calculation about power, and an estimate of the long-term interests of the Bolshevik cause.[8]

Most such decisions, indeed, involve important elements of calculation: about the balance of power; about the security and material interests of the state and its people; about prestige (which is often not just pretence or vainglory, but involves the crucial question of whether other states believe that you mean what you say); and not least about power to achieve the object in view. A vital element in choices about war and peace is usually the calculation, or at least the hope, that victory is possible. Only in the most dire of circumstances do states go to war in the face of certain defeat; and examples are hard to find. It is more usual, in hopeless circumstances, to bow to the inevitable.

Statesmen make their choices out of calculation. War is an instrument of policy. It will be used, in the crudest terms, if it seems likely to pay, in terms of material interest, profit, power, or prestige. In the 1920s and 1930s, it appeared to most statesmen in Britain and France that war was highly unlikely to pay. They had come to regard the last war, of 1914–18, as a calamity, involving human, material, and financial losses which should not again be incurred short of the utmost necessity. They were satisfied powers, anxious to preserve the status quo; but they also wanted peace and quiet. They would eventually fight in self-defence and to prevent the status quo being completely overthrown; but their optimism about the outcome of war was at a low ebb, and their belief in war as an instrument of policy was weak. The rulers of Germany and Italy, on the other hand, represented dissatisfied powers; they wanted to disrupt the status quo; and they were perfectly prepared to use war to achieve that end. Moreover, the Germans believed that war would pay in the simplest sense, by securing economic gains – raw materials, foodstuffs, cheap labour, favourable terms of trade and rates of exchange; and in some parts of their conquests, they were not mistaken. Their optimism about the outcome of war was high; and their belief in war as an instrument of policy strong.

This is not the whole story. Statesmen make calculations of interest, advantage, and power; but they respond also to emotions, to prejudices, to the assumptions which they have absorbed from their upbringing, their way of life, and their friends. They are men, not calculating machines; and this means that sometimes they respond as much by instinct as from calculation. The Belgian Crown Council, meeting all night on 2/3 August 1914 to decide how to reply to the German ultimatum demanding passage through their country to attack France, debated Belgian interests, which gave no absolutely clear guide to action, but then seem to have reached their final unanimous decision to reject the ultimatum mainly out of anger at being bullied, a sense of the country's self-respect, and (on the part of the strong pro-German group) resentment at being let down by one's friends. Again, in 1940, Churchill's resolve to continue the war against Germany despite the fall of France arose primarily from patriotic fighting instincts, which were supported by rather shaky calculations about Britain's capacity to survive and win.

When politicians take the path to war they must then assume that the people whom they claim to lead, the millions who must fire the guns and sustain the war effort, will accept their decision. What then moves the people whose role is in the long run vital for the conduct and continuance of war?

There are those who return a very simple answer to this question: the people respond to a mixture of propaganda and coercion on the part of governments, and have little choice or free will in the matter. This is in most cases too simple to correspond to reality. It is perfectly possible for a country to be taken into war against the wishes of the majority of its people: this was almost certainly the case when Italy entered the Second World War in 1940; and the results were observable in the lack of enthusiasm and determination in the Italian campaigns and war effort from 1940 to 1943, when the whole process culminated in Italy first dropping out of the conflict, and then joining in again on the opposite side. At the other end of the scale, it was also possible for large numbers of the Polish people to continue by clandestine means a struggle against Germany which their armies had decisively lost, at a time when their government was in exile and had no powers of coercion whatsoever, and very little means of propaganda. There are many cases which fall between these two extremes; but by and large governments are conscious that in war they need at least the consent, and preferably the active support, of their peoples; and this support has often been given willingly, and sometimes enthusiastically.

What motivation, then, lies behind such willingness to accept war? How have Tolstoy's all-important millions seen the question of war and its origins? If we turn to 1914 for guidance, we find in Oxford the young Llewellyn Woodward (later an eminent historian of the war) volunteering at once for the army. He did not enjoy his military training, and he was less than certain of the British case for entering the war; but he persisted because he was convinced by the argument of Socrates, that having accepted the benefit of his country's laws he had a duty to do what the state asked of him. Reflecting after fifty years, he saw no reason to have done otherwise. On the other side of Europe, far removed from the refinements of Oxford and the influence of a classical education, we find the inhabitants of a village in Montenegro, men and women alike, pouring from their houses to resist the invading Austrians, not when they crossed the newfangled boundary which had only been there since some recent Balkan war, but when they reached a bridge which had marked Montenegrin territory for centuries – the simple defence of long-held territory by a people with a strong sense of identity. Beween these two responses, the one intellectual and rarefied, the other instinctive and primitive, there lay the reactions of the

11

millions in Europe who answered their mobilization notices, some-times with resignation, sometimes enthusiastically, but in any case with a degree of unanimity which surprised the military authorities, which had expected widespread opposition or evasion.

When we turn from the First World War to the Second, one point stands out clearly. There was a widespread expectation that the reactions of 1914 would *not* be repeated. With the sombre memorials to the dead of 1914–18 all over Europe, 'never again' was the natural and deep-seated response. 'I *will* not have another war. I *will not*' was not the remark of a left-wing pacifist but of King George V, trained as a sailor and deeply imbued with the military virtues.[9] It was true that in the belligerent capitals in 1939 there was little enthusiasm, no cheering crowds in the main squares, no flowers for the troops at railway stations. But, however reluctantly, the peoples of Europe went to war again. They endured, quietly but with immense determination and tenacity, a war which was in many ways more terrible than that of 1914–18. To explain, even in part, why they did so must be one of the tasks of an explanation of the origins of the war; because if the instinct of 'never again' had prevailed in any large section of the European population, either there would have been no Second World War, or at least it would have been a different kind of war, probably at a different time.

At the end of this review of explanations of war and wars, it is interesting to see what professionals in the craft of foreign policy made of the question about half-way through what we now know to have been the period between the wars. In 1919, Lloyd George's Cabinet in Britain decided that defence expenditure should be governed by the assumption that the country would not be involved in any major war for ten years. When this 'ten-year rule' was begun, and for most of its life until it was abandoned in 1932, it was meant only as a working assumption for economies in the defence budget, and did not rest on serious analysis of the international or military situation. However, in June 1931 a Foreign Office memorandum examined the assumptions on which the validity of the 'rule' rested; and its conclusions, though intended as a guide to the circumstances in which war would *not* break out, made in practice a guide to Foreign Office thinking on the conditions in which war could be expected.[10]

The memorandum concluded that there would be no major war on the following conditions:

1. That during the next ten years no two states would be involved in a dispute over a vital interest which peaceful means had failed to resolve.
2. That if two states were involved in such a dispute, one of them would be so averse to war as to abandon its vital interest rather than fight.
3. That, if both states were willing to fight, one of them would be so

weak as to be unable to fight with any hope of success.
4. That an organization existed which was willing and able to restrain the intending belligerents (i.e. the League of Nations).
5. That no situation arose which would create a war psychology.

This admirable summary included many of the points raised in more theoretical discussions: the concept of vital interest; the need for some expectation of success; the need for a general acceptance of war as an instrument of policy, or of necessity; the question of whether an international body would restrain individual states; and the question of war psychology. If all the Foreign Office's conditions of peace were reversed, the result would be a prescription for the causes of war.

These general considerations provide a sketch-map for the journey ahead. We must look at the broad explanations which have been adduced for the Second World War, amounting sometimes to theories of inevitability. We must examine the underlying forces which were at work, shaping and constraining the calculations of statesmen and the feelings of peoples, and building up a momentum towards war. Finally, we must review the circumstances in which conflict became likely, and in which specific decisions for war were taken.

REFERENCES AND NOTES

1. L. B. Namier, *Diplomatic Prelude* (London 1950), pp. 399–402.
2. A companion volume deals with the Pacific and Far East: see A. Iriye, *The Second World War in Asia and the Pacific* (London, 1986).
3. Cf. a companion volume in this series: James Joll, *The Origins of the First World War* (London 1984).
4. Hitler's secret speech to representatives of the German press, 10 November 1938, in Jeremy Noakes and Geoffrey Pridham (eds.), *Documents on Nazism, 1919–1945* (London 1974), pp. 549–50.
5. Memorandum by Tallents, 7 November 1938, quoted in P. M. Taylor, *The Projection of Britain. British overseas publicity and propaganda, 1919–1939* (London 1981), p. 278.
6. L. N. Tolstoy, *War and Peace*, trans. by Rosemary Edmonds (London: Penguin Books 1957), vol. II, pp. 715–17.
7. Quincy Wright, *A Study of War*, abridged by Louise Leonard Wright (Chicago 1964), p. 10.
8. This example is drawn from Geoffrey Blainey, *The Causes of War* (London 1973), pp. 153–6.
9. A. J. P. Taylor (ed.), *Lloyd George: a diary by Frances Stevenson* (London 1971), p. 309.
10. P. J. Dennis, *Decision by Default: peacetime conscription and British defence, 1919–39* (London 1972), p. 28.

Chapter 2

A THIRTY YEARS WAR? THE DISINTEGRATION OF EUROPE

In 1939 and the following years there was a powerful and general sense that men were engaged, not in a second war, but rather in the second phase of a Thirty Years War, another round in a struggle against the German domination of Europe. Since 1919 Europe had moved so rapidly through an attempt at reconstruction and stabilization into a time of renewed tension and conflict that it was hard to recognize anything which could properly be called peace. The mood was caught, lightly but exactly, by Nancy Mitford in her novel *The Pursuit of Love*, when she made her heroine Linda remark: 'It's rather sad to belong, as we do, to a lost generation. I'm sure in history the two wars will count as one war and that we shall be squashed out of it altogether, and people will forget that we ever existed.'[1] The somewhat feather-brained Linda was in some very weighty company. The formidable Marshal Foch, generalissimo of the allied armies in France in 1918, had said of the Treaty of Versailles, 'This is not peace. It is an armistice for twenty years.' Churchill, in the preface to the first volume of his memoirs of the Second World War, wrote: 'I must regard these volumes as a continuation of the story of the First World War which I set out in *The World Crisis*. . . . Together . . . they will cover an account of another Thirty Years War.'[2] General de Gaulle, Eduard Benes, and other notables could be added to the list, In a more straightforward way, any Belgian over the age of twenty-six in 1940, seeing the German Army marching past his doorstep for the second time in his life, could have had little doubt that a nightmarish film had got stuck, and the same events were coming round once more.

In retrospect, such views have continued to carry a good deal of conviction. Europe was indeed wrecked by the First World War. The peace settlement which followed it had grave defects. Germany did try twice in thirty years for the domination of Europe. Taking all this into account, a school of thought has developed which regards the Second World War as the culmination of a disintegration of the European order, begun by the First World War and continued by the abortive peace, which left the Continent in a state of chronic instability. The main lines of this interpretation will be set out in this chapter, before turning to examine a rival explanation.

The basic premiss of the 'Thirty Years War' thesis lies in the disruptive impact of the First World War, which shook the political, economic, and social systems of Europe to their foundations. The political and psychological damage was probably greater than the physical. It is true that casualties were very heavy: 8.5 million dead among the armed services is a generally accepted estimate, without trying to count the civilian casualties, direct and indirect. Yet, except in France, where the war losses struck a population which was already barely reproducing itself, the blow in purely demographic terms was absorbed and recovered from with less difficulty than was expected. The more lasting damage was to the mind and spirit. Many old certainties, traditional beliefs, and habits fell casualties in 1914–18. It was well said of the Kitchener armies raised in Britain that it took generations of stability and certainty to produce such a body of men; and their like would not be seen again. By 1918, there was a profound weariness and disillusionment pervading the armies of Europe which was a far cry from the fire and enthusiasm of 1914. The question repeatedly asked in German units by August 1918 was '*Wozu?*' – What's it all for? – and this found its echo everywhere.[3]

The economic disruption caused by the war was also severe. There was material devastation in the areas of heavy fighting, especially in the battle zones of north-east France and Belgium. All over Europe there was unusual wear and tear, arising from the working of industry, agriculture, and transport under heavy pressure and without adequate maintenance. The men and women who did the work, often for long hours and with insufficient food, were also worn out – the European influenza epidemic of 1919 told its tale of exhaustion and lowered resistance. The end of the war saw the breakdown of transport over much of central and eastern Europe, and shortages of both coal and food, caused partly by falling production and partly by problems of distribution. Financial and monetary problems were less immediately obvious than the material destruction, but were more lasting and insidious in their effects. Britain and France were forced to sell substantial quantities of their foreign investments to pay for the war; and other investments (notably French) were lost in the Bolshevik revolution in Russia. The Germans had their investments in enemy countries confiscated, and lost the rest of their foreign holdings at the peace. Britain borrowed heavily from the USA, and France and Italy from the USA and Britain; all ended the war with a new and heavy burden of foreign debt. There was also a great increase in internal government debts, because most war expenditure was met by loans rather than taxation. In many ways the most profound economic problem was that of inflation, the dramatic rise in prices and fall in the value of money which took place all over Europe during the war years.

(In Britain, retail prices rather more than doubled between 1914 and 1918; and the position in some other countries was worse.) The confusion caused by this was the more marked after a period of generally stable prices before 1914; and the social effects spread out in all directions, to the benefit of those who could keep pace with or profit from inflation, and to the severe detriment of those who had to live on fixed incomes. In all this, it was the material damage which proved easiest to repair. Even the great scar across France and Flanders, where the battle-line had run for four years, was patched over by 1925–26 with towns and villages rebuilt and land brought back into cultivation. It was the removal of the landmark of a stable currency which had the most lasting effects, psychological as much as material.

The political effects of the war were similarly far-reaching; and again were the more shocking because they came after a long period of comparative stability. In the whole of central and eastern Europe at the end of 1918, no government remained as it had been in 1914; and over large areas there was no effective government at all. The dynasties and empires of the Habsburgs in Austria-Hungary, the Hohenzollerns in Germany, and the Romanovs in Russia had all fallen; and the regimes and states which sought to replace them were struggling to come into being amid sporadic fighting and a fog of uncertainty. Three great autocratic empires had collapsed, and the parliamentary democracies of western Europe, along with the greatest of democratic powers, the USA, were intact and victorious. But if in this sense the democracies had won, the liberalism and individualism of the nineteenth century had clearly lost during the war years. The whole nature of the war meant that state control, state initiative, and state interests, had all had a field day. The individual had been subordinated to the state – in Britain, the greatest symbol of this was the introduction of conscription for the armed forces, for the first time in British history. Paradoxically, this process was accompanied by a revulsion felt by many people against their own state, caused often by disillusionment, in some cases with the war and its pretences, in others with defeat or the inadequate rewards of victory. In either event, men turned away from their own state or form of government and looked elsewhere – often to communism on the one hand or fascism on the other.

By the end of the war, Europe seemed on the verge not only of political chaos but of revolution. In Russia in 1917 there were two revolutions, with the Bolsheviks precariously established in power by the end of the year. There was a revolution of sorts in Germany at the end of 1918. The hope of revolution for some, the fear of it for others, were widespread in Europe, with Bolshevik Russia as a beacon light or a menacing glare according to one's viewpoint. In the event, both hopes and fears proved much exaggerated. The new German republic turned out to be a mild form of social democracy, with large chunks of the old regime firmly embedded within it. Elections in Britain in 1918 and France in 1919 produced substantial right-wing majorities. Yet the revolutionary atmosphere had been real enough; it was not forgotten; and it had its effects later.

On this view, the war shook the foundations of Europe to an extent which was virtually irreparable. When the peacemakers gathered in Paris in 1919, they faced an impossible task; and in the event, it is widely argued, they proceeded to make the situation worse rather than better. The 1919 settlement, and particularly its centre-piece, the Treaty of Versailles with Germany, was criticized at the time and for the next twenty years for its harshness, its economic errors, and its inherent instability.

The accusations of harshness referred both to the terms imposed upon Germany and to the manner of their imposition. Germany lost territory. In the west Alsace and Lorraine were annexed by France (or, as the French said, were restored after wrongful seizure in 1871) and the districts of Eupen and Malmédy went to Belgium. In the east, Germany lost Posnania and parts of East Prussia to Poland; and the port of Danzig became a free city under League of Nations administration, with special rights for Poland. Plebiscites were to be held in various other areas to determine whether or not they should remain part of Germany. These resulted in part of Schleswig going to Denmark; two districts of West and East Prussia (Marienwerder and Allenstein) voting overwhelmingly to stay in Germany, which they were allowed to do; and an inconclusive vote in Upper Silesia which ended in the Council of the League of Nations allotting to Poland rather more than the plebiscite would have allowed, and certainly more than the Germans thought due. The port of Memel was ceded by Germany for transfer to Lithuania. In all, Germany lost about 65,000 square kilometres of territory and nearly 7 million inhabitants. She also lost all her colonies, which were handed over to various of the victorious powers under the cover of League of Nations mandates. All this was not unexpected after a country had lost a long and bitter war; and it compared quite favourably with the treatment meted out by Germany to the defeated Russia in March 1918. But the Germans found it harsh. They resented handing over any territory to the Poles; and they claimed that plebiscites were used arbitrarily, and usually when there was a chance of them going against Germany; they were not used at all in Alsace-Lorraine or in most of the territory lost to Poland. Moreover, when in Austria a series of unofficial plebiscites showed overwhelming majorities in favour of union with Germany, the treaty laid it down firmly that such a union was forbidden. The victorious Allies had claimed loudly that they were fighting for democracy and self-determination, but they applied these great principles selectively, or even cynically. The Germans could thus claim unfair treatment; and after a time their claims found an attentive audience in western Europe.

The harshness was also claimed to lie in the severity of the disarmament provisions imposed upon Germany. The army was limited to 100,000 men, with no tanks or heavy artillery; the navy was to have no warships of over 10,000 tons, and no submarines; there was to be no military or naval aviation. Not least, the German General Staff, the brain and nerve centre of the army, and for long a separate centre of power within the state, was to be dissolved. These were unusual provisions in a peace treaty, specifically designed to paralyse German strength and to break the customs and attitudes which the victors called 'Prussian militarism'. The ostensible purpose of the disarmament clauses was 'to render possible the initiation of a general limitation of the armaments of all nations'; and when no such limitation followed, the Germans could again claim to have been unfairly treated.

The same was true of two other aspects of the treaty whose impact was more psychological than practical. The first was the clause put at the head of the reparations section of the treaty, by which Germany was compelled to accept 'the responsibility of Germany and her allies for causing all the loss and damage to which the Allied and Associated Governments and their nationals have been subjected as a consequence of the war imposed upon them by the aggression of Germany and her allies'.[4] This was almost universally referred to as the 'war guilt' clause of the treaty; though it does not use the word guilt, and it may be that its drafters did not intend to convey a moral judgement on Germany. Such niceties were of no importance. The clause aroused deep resentment in Germany, where it was thought that equal (or greater) responsibility for the outbreak of war could be found in the actions of other countries. German historians worked hard to undermine the validity of this clause, and their claims found a ready acceptance among 'revisionist' writers in France, Britain, and the USA. Germany's case against the 'war guilt' thesis grew steadily stronger. The other aspect was the section of the treaty which provided for the trial of the former Kaiser, Wilhelm II, for 'a supreme offence against international morality and the sanctity of treaties', and unnamed persons for 'acts of violation of the laws and customs of war'.[5] Little followed from this. The Kaiser was safe in the Netherlands, whose government would not extradite him; and only a dozen of the lower ranks of alleged war criminals were brought to trial before a German court, which convicted six of them. But again, most Germans did not believe that their own leaders had behaved worse than those of other countries; they were merely being subjected to the spite of the victors.

To all this was added the claim that the Versailles Treaty was a 'dictated peace'. In one sense, this merely stated the obvious. The whole object of winning the war was to impose upon Germany terms which she would never accept voluntarily. Again, the claim referred more to the methods adopted than to the substance of what happened.

At the Paris Peace Conference, the German delegation was simply presented with the Allied terms on a basis of take them or leave them; there was not even a show of negotiation, still less any real chance for Germany to influence the contents of the treaty while it was being prepared. The German complaints about this procedure reached a wide audience and it soon came to be thought (especially in Britain) that terms imposed in this fashion were not morally binding.

The significance of these claims about the harshness of the treaty lay less in their objective fairness (if there be such a standard), or in comparative justice when Versailles is matched against other peace settlements after great wars, but in the widespread and lasting impression which was created. It was natural enough that Germans should resent the fact of defeat, especially when for so much of the war they were sure that they were winning; and it was natural too for this resentment to attach to the peace settlement which registered their defeat. What was less to be expected was the extent to which the same view took hold among the victors. This was especially true of Britain, where it spread rapidly across the whole political spectrum. In France its hold was strongest on the Left – as late as August 1939 some socialist speakers still began their remarks on foreign affairs with a ritual condemnation of the Treaty of Versailles. The stability of the settlement thus came to be undermined by both vanquished and victors alike.

The accusation of harshness was particularly levelled at the reparations section of the treaty; and this may be best considered along with general assertions about the economic errors of the peace settlement. It was not unusual for cash payments, or indemnities, to be imposed upon the losing side in war; and a substantial indemnity was imposed on France as the defeated power at the end of the Franco-Prussian War in 1871. At the end of the First World War the victors renounced the idea of an indemnity, but claimed the right to exact 'compensation for all damage done to the civilian population of the Allied and Associated Powers and to their property'.[6] The treaty itself set no figure for these 'reparations'; but it did establish the headings under which claims could be made, including not only material destruction (under which both France and Belgium had important claims), but also payment of war pensions, an almost unlimited demand which was inserted at the request of Great Britain. The task of producing a figure for reparations, and of deciding how they were to be paid, was delegated to the Reparations Commission, a body established by the victorious allies. In May 1921 this Commission arrived at a figure of 132,000 million gold marks; though at the same time the debt was divided into three sections, represented by A, B, and C class bonds, and the C class bonds were to be held by the Commission until Germany's capacity to pay had been established – which amounted to indefinite postponement of about 80,000 millions, or rather under two-thirds of the total.

In 1919 the young John Maynard Keynes, then at the outset of his career as the oustanding economic theorist of the twentieth century, resigned from the British delegation at the peace conference and wrote at high speed a brilliant book, *The Economic Consequences of the Peace.* With a clarity, vigour, and skill which commanded attention and induced assent, Keynes attacked the principles on which reparations were being imposed. He argued that the figures put forward by the victorious powers were too high in relation to the actual damage they had suffered; that Germany would not have the capacity to pay the amounts envisaged, especially when she was losing territory, resources, and population under other sections of the treaty; and that the problems of transfer (the actual means of payment, whether in kind, in gold, in German securities held abroad, or in foreign exchange earned by Germany), would prove to be insuperable. Keynes maintained that reparations, on anything like the scale being considered, could not work. They would place an impossible strain on the German economy; and involve Germany in permanent balance of payments difficulties, because she would be furnishing exports for which she was not paid, or earning foreign exchange which was not for her own use but for the purpose of making reparations payments.

In such circumstances, Keynes argued, the reconstruction of the European economy and financial system, which before 1914 had functioned as a smoothly working unit, would be impossible. The system could not be restored if one of its vital parts (and Germany remained the foremost industrial power in Europe) was permanently dislocated. This situation was made worse by the entanglement of the reparations questions with the problem of war debts. During the war, the European belligerents borrowed very large sums to sustain their war efforts. Russia borrowed from France and Britain; all the European belligerents borrowed from Britain; and everyone borrowed from the USA, which in the course of the war had been transformed from a debtor to a creditor country. The position at the end of the war may be represented in a diagram.[7]

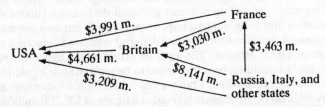

$3,991 m.   France

USA $4,661 m.   Britain $3,030 m. $3,463 m.

$3,209 m. $8,141 m.   Russia, Italy, and other states

In a strict sense, these debts had nothing to do with the peace settlement or with reparations. But not unnaturally the victorious west European powers (Britain, France, Italy, and Belgium) wished to link their debts to the USA with their reparation payments from Germany: as Germany paid reparations, so they would pay their war debts; and since the debts had been incurred in the struggle against Germany, this seemed not only convenient but just. But the USA would not agree. Having declined to ratify the Treaty of Versailles, the Americans were not receiving any reparations from Germany; and on straightforward commercial grounds they expected to be repaid their loans by the various Allied states – in the famous phrase of Calvin Coolidge, 'They hired the money, didn't they?' Eventually, the British government, which was owed sums almost as large as those owed to the USA, announced (in the Balfour Note of 1 August 1922) that since the USA insisted on the repayment of war debts, Britain must do the same, but would only insist on payment up to the level of British debts to the USA. (This would mean Britain renouncing over half her debts.) The Americans for their part set about negotiating separately with each of their debtor governments, offering flexible terms which took into account ability to pay.

War debts were also linked with reparations because they involved a transfer problem – the means by which they were to be paid. They made another distorting element in the structure of trade and payments and added to the balance of payments problems of the debtor states. They also added to the anxiety of those who were owed reparations to ensure that they were paid.

Quite apart from its general distorting and complicating effects, the reparations question also brought about a very sharp international crisis, with far-reaching consequences. In 1923 France and Belgium seized upon a German failure to make deliveries of reparations in kind to occupy the industrial area of the Ruhr, with the object (certainly as far as the French were concerned) either of making the Germans pay, or of inflicting serious damage on the German economy – contradictory aims, doubtless, but either of them satisfactory from a French point of view. The occupation of the Ruhr involved the use of force (invasion, the Germans claimed; police action according to the French) and helped to precipitate the catastrophic German hyperinflation of 1923. This inflation had little direct connection with reparations payments themselves, but a great deal to do with the way the German government chose to subsidize industry and to pay the costs of the passive resistance to the occupation by extravagant use of the printing press. Inflation was already running strongly in 1922; in June 1923 the mark stood at 100,000 to the dollar; in November at 4,000 million. A pay-packet was worthless before a worker got home; and anyone with assets tied to the mark (which meant anyone with savings, insurance policies, or a fixed income) saw their value vanish absolutely. The effects of this in terms of individual lives and collective confidence were far-reaching; and they later contributed to the appeal of nazism. The Ruhr occupation and the German hyperinflation were not inevitable consequences of the reparation clauses of Versailles; but as events turned out, they were among the actual results.

21

Going deeper than claims about the harshness of the peace settlement or its economic errors is the judgement that it was inherently and disastrously unstable. This instability was apparent in a number of ways. The war destroyed the pre-1914 European balance, and the peace could put nothing adequate in its place. A profound shift in the pattern of power occurred while the war was in progress. French losses and weariness were such that France became dependent, even by 1916, on the help of the British Empire; and by 1918 both were dependent on the USA, which alone could provide the economic resources and the fresh troops to defeat Germany. It was the steady flow of American doughboys, raw but enthusiastic, and with limitless reserves, which brought home to the Germans with mathematical certainty that they must lose. Before this, Germany had fought four major European enemies to a standstill, and totally defeated one of them, Russia. The lesson was that Germany was so strong in terms of population, industrial resources, organization, and not least will-power, that four other European great powers had barely the capacity to hold her at bay; and an entirely new force from outside Europe was necessary to tip the balance.

This bleak outlook stood revealed by the facts of war. What could the aspirations of peace do to soften its outlines? It was plain by as early as 1920 that the answer was, very little. The USA, having done so much to win the war and shape the peace treaties which followed it, withdrew her strength and activity back across the Atlantic – not into 'isolation', which is altogether too absolute a term, but into an indifference towards the European balance of power which came only too naturally to a people who found the phrase itself distasteful. The British, surveying with a grievous sense of loss the cost in lives of commitment to a Continental war, thought it best to turn back to empire and the more hopeful patterns of former centuries, or to turn away from all power politics into some form of pacifism. Russia stood transformed by revolution, weak in armed or industrial strength, but powerful in menace to ordered bourgeois society.

No country felt this change more than France. In 1914 her position against Germany rested on her long-standing alliance with Russia and her *entente* with Britain. In the crisis of a German invasion, both came to her help, and in 1914 the Russian attack on East Prussia helped to check the German offensive in France. By 1919–20, Russia was gone, powerless and in any case unreliable, and Britain was anxious to diminish her European commitments. It was possible that the newly created League of Nations might be turned into an organization capable of restraining German power; but this was by no means certain. The situation of France in 1919, and the severity of French attitudes towards Germany, can only be properly comprehended by grasping the facts of French weakness in comparison with 1914.

There was no European balance in 1919–20. Indeed, the precarious nature of the new creation was immediately apparent. General Smuts, a member of the South African delegation at the Paris Peace Conference, wrote to Lloyd George, the British Prime Minister, in March 1919 that the peace treaty then being prepared would be utterly unstable. Notably, he held that Poland and Czechoslovakia, new states coming into existence in eastern Europe, would not be viable without German goodwill – and he was right. In the coming storms, he predicted, they would be the first to go under – and (except for Austria) they were. Germany remained in the centre of Europe, with (even after her losses of territory) a population and industrial resources which were bound, if allowed free play, to give her a predominant position on the Continent. The peace settlement had been harsh enough to infuriate the Germans, but not so crushing as to render them powerless. Machiavelli once advised: 'If you see your enemy in the water up to his neck, you will do well to push him under; but if he is only in it up to his knees, you will do well to help him to the shore.' The peace treaty did neither.[8]

All this has concentrated on France and Germany. But there was another area of instability in Europe: the whole of the eastern half of the Continent was in confusion in 1919, with consequences which persisted for the next twenty years or more. From a British point of view, eastern Europe is a long way off and hard to comprehend. Austen Chamberlain, when Foreign Secretary in 1925, remarked that the Polish Corridor was not worth the bones of a British grenadier; and his half-brother Neville, in a famous broadcast on 27 September 1938, described the crisis in Czechoslovakia as 'a quarrel in a far-away country between people of whom we know nothing'.[9] Yet that quarrel brought Europe to the brink of conflict; and in 1939 British grenadiers (and many others) marched off to a war which arose, at least immediately, from the Polish Corridor. It was an area which had a way of forcing itself upon the attention even of the distant and uncomprehending British.

In 1919, the contrast between western and eastern Europe was striking. In the west, there were some minor territorial changes; but the map remained basically as it had been in 1914. In the east all was transformed. North of the Danube, the whole territory had previously been shared between the three empires of Germany, Austria–Hungary, and Russia. Now in their place there appeared no fewer than eight new or revived states: Finland, Estonia, Latvia, Lithuania, Poland, Czechoslovakia, Hungary, and Austria. To the south, in the Balkans, there was only one new state (Yugoslavia); but most of the others were markedly different in shape, whether larger (Rumania, Greece) or smaller (Bulgaria).

It is certain that the problems created in this wholesale transformation were numerous and profound. It is arguable that they were insoluble, and that they led Europe inexorably towards war. In part, these problems were territorial, in the simple sense that there was scarcely a line on the new map which was not disputed to some degree. But in nearly every case territory was primarily important because it had become a national symbol, or because it involved conflicts of nationality. Nations are troublesome creatures. No one can define them with precision or in such a way as to command general consent; yet if a group of people feel themselves to be a nation there tends to be no limit to what some of them will do to assert their nationality. In eastern Europe, the First World War and the settlement which followed it marked the high-water mark of nationalism and separatism. Nationalist movements flourished both spontaneously and with the encouragement of belligerent states seeking to damage their opponents – Germany, for example, encouraged Polish and Ukrainian nationalism against Russia, and Britain and France supported Czech nationalism against Austria–Hungary. But while nationalist aspirations were aroused, they could not all be satisfied: they conflicted with one another, with the interests of existing states, and with the facts of history, geography, and economics, which made it impossible to draw clear and satisfactory dividing lines between the territory of one nationality and that of another.

The consequence was that eastern Europe produced a welter of conflicting aspirations and claims. Sometimes a nation was left without a state of its own, and so with a restless urge to create one. The Ukrainians were in this position (though a nominally independent Ukraine existed for a brief period in 1918–19); and their position was the more complicated because Ukrainians (or Ruthenians, as their western groupings were usually called) were divided between three separate states – Russia, Poland, and Czechoslovakia. Ukrainian nationalism was a threat to all three, and could be used as a weapon by any of their enemies, among whom Germany was the most prominent; and Ukrainian militants often found a sympathetic home in Berlin. The Croats found themselves absorbed into the new state of Yugoslavia, which was in many ways the old Serbia writ large. There was a strong Croat separatist movement, seeking an independent Croat state and finding support from Italy, an enemy of Yugoslavia, where exiled separatists were allowed to set up camps and prepare assassinations. Half-submerged were the Slovaks, theoretically partners in the new state of Czechoslovakia, but finding that in practice the Czechs came out on top; there was again some impulse towards separatism, or at least towards autonomy within a reorganized Czechoslovak state.

In other cases, the problem was different. A nation-state was created, but many people of its particular nationality were separated from it, as was inevitable in the historical scattering of peoples across the map. The numbers involved were large, and the complaints were bitter. In all, it has been estimated that the 1919 settlement left nearly 19 million people as national minorities in nine nation-states, out of a total population of about 98 million. The position of Poland and Czechoslovakia was particularly difficult, with one person in three belonging to a minority nationality – and that counted the Slovaks as being among the majority in Czechoslovakia: the Czechs themselves did not amount to half the total population. The situation as a whole is illustrated by Table 1.[10]

Table 1. Minorities in the new nation-states

Country	Population	Principal Minorities	
Czechoslovakia	14,700,000	German	3,250,000
	(including	Magyar	700,000
	6,500,000	Ruthene	400,000
	Czechs and	Polish	70,000
	3,000,000		
	Slovaks)		
Estonia	1,700,000	Russian	170,000
		German	17,000
Finland	3,600,000	Swedish	300,000
Hungary	8,700,000	German	500,000
Latvia	2,000,000	German	65,000
Lithuania	2,500,000	German	100,000
Poland	32,000,000	Ukrainian and Byelorussian	6,000,000
		German	800,000
Rumania	18,800,000	Magyar	1,500,000
		German	750,000
		Ukrainian	600,000
		Russian	400,000
		Bulgarian	360,000
Yugoslavia	14,000,000	Macedonian	600,000
	(including	German	500,000
	5,500,000	Magyar	500,000
	Serbs	Albanian	500,000
	4,500,000	Muslim/	
	Croats	Turkish	700,000
	1,000,000		
	Slovenes		

All the new states claimed to be nation-states, with nationality as their only principle of legitimacy. The principle of their governments, at any rate at the start, was democratic. In these circumstances, national minorities were bound to remain minorities. If they were oppressed (and most thought they were) their only hope of release lay in the intervention of a 'big brother' (their own nation-state) over the border; or perhaps in rebellion or war. (It is true that the Covenant of the League of Nations included provisions for the protection of minorities, but these usually remained a dead letter.)

25

The result was a set of territorial disputes, rooted in questions of nationality, which festered for some twenty years after the settlement of 1919–20, and gave much force to the thesis of a Thirty Years War. One after another they broke out afresh in 1938, 1939, and 1940, precipitating repeated crises and providing at least the circumstances, and arguably the causes, of European war.

The most obvious of these involved the boundary between Germany and Poland, where resentment was particularly concentrated on the issues of Danzig and the Polish Corridor. Danzig was a city and port which had been German (or Prussian) since 1793; it was overwhelmingly German in population; and yet in 1919 it was proclaimed a 'Free City' in order to give Poland access to the sea through a port which was not in German territory. The Polish Corridor, territory formerly German but now providing Poland's access to the Baltic, and cutting East Prussia off from the rest of Germany, contained a substantial German population; and according to some estimates and forms of measurement it was impossible to create such a corridor through territory with a clear Polish majority. The Poles, on the other hand, were disappointed that their own claims to annex Danzig and almost the whole of Upper Silesia, which had at first been accepted by the Peace Conference's Commission on Polish Affairs, had not finally been upheld. More important, they were convinced that their commerce, security, and independence were all bound up with Danzig and the Corridor.

Poland was also involved in two other major frontier disputes, one with Lithuania over Vilna, the other with Czechoslovakia over Teschen. The city of Vilna had been in the Middle Ages the capital of Lithuania; but it was also the seat of a Polish university, and was considered by the Poles to be a strategic centre vital to their security. The population of the city and its surrounding district was mixed: Polish, Lithuanian, Byelorussian, and Jewish. A Lithuanian state had come into being, under German influence, in 1918, and was established as an independent republic by the end of the year, just as Poland was achieving its own resurrection as a state. In 1919–20 Vilna was the object of sporadic fighting between the two countries; and in October 1920 an armistice left it in Lithuanian occupation. It was then occupied by a local force under a Polish general; led a nominally separate life for a time; and was finally incorporated into Poland in 1922. The League of Nations took up the case, but failed to persuade Poland to give up the territory. In 1923 France and Britain recognized Vilna as part of Poland. Lithuania did not. Until 1927 the Lithuanian government maintained that a state of war with Poland still continued; and even after that no diplomatic relations between the two states existed until 1938.

Before 1918 the Duchy of Teschen, with its capital of the same name, was part of the Austro-Hungarian Empire. On the collapse of

Habsburg authority, the district, which had a mixed population (according to the last Austrian census, 55 per cent Polish, 27 per cent Czech, and 18 per cent German), was disputed between the two new states of Poland and Czechoslovakia. An eventual award by the Allied powers at the conference of Spa (1920) was favourable to Czechoslovakia, leaving Poland with the actual town of Teschen, but allotting the important suburb of Freistadt, along with the whole of the Karvin coalfield, to the Czechs. Both sides felt aggrieved; and the Teschen dispute was one of the issues which divided Poland and Czechoslovakia in the inter-war period, resurfacing during the Munich crisis of 1938.

On the Baltic Sea lay the port of Memel, which was German in population, and up to 1918 had formed the easternmost part of East Prussia. However, it was also the only available port for the newly emerged state of Lithuania; and its position was thus closely akin to that of Danzig in relation to Poland. Under Article 99 of the Treaty of Versailles, Germany ceded Memel and its hinterland to the Allies, and agreed to accept the provisions they made for it; the understanding being that the city would be transferred to Lithuania under some special arrangement. By the beginning of 1923, the Allies had still not determined the status of Memel. Losing patience, the Lithuanians seized the port and its hinterland on 10 January 1923; and in 1924 the Allies accepted the *fait accompli* of Lithuanian control, though the city was administered as an autonomous district, with its own assembly. As with Vilna, action on the spot, not deliberations in Paris or Geneva, settled the matter; and as with all the other disputes, the issue continued to fester, this time in Germany and among the German population of the city.

Far to the south, on the edge of the Balkans, the region of Transylvania was a long-standing bone of contention between Magyars and Rumanians. The territory had been part of the Kingdom of Hungary within the Habsburg Empire; and had been promised to Rumania by the Allies as the price of intervention on their side during the First World War. This promise was fulfilled in the Treaty of Trianon in 1920, and Transylvania, with about 1.5 million Magyars passed to Rumania. Previous roles were reversed: the Magyars, who had been politically and socially predominant, now found themselves the underdogs. The problem was particularly intractable because a large part of the Magyar population lived together in south-east Transylvania, far removed from Hungary; and elsewhere a number of towns were mainly Magyar, forming islands in a Rumanian-populated countryside. No redrawing of boundary lines, therefore, could settle the issue to anything like the satisfaction of both sides. Relations between Hungary and Rumania were poisoned for the next twenty years, until Hitler produced a new territorial award in 1940, more favourable to Hungary, but still basically unsatisfactory to both sides.

These were the principal specific disputes. But the fact was that almost every frontier drawn in eastern Europe between 1919 and 1921 was unsatisfactory to one state or another, and sometimes to more than one at once. Poland was in particularly difficult straits. Not just Danzig and the Corridor, but the whole of the German–Polish boundary was unacceptable to Germany; while in the east the frontier with Russia laid down by the Treaty of Riga in 1921 was thought in Moscow to be far too favourable to the Poles. It was drawn at the end of a long and swaying struggle, in which Russia finally accepted defeat, and Poland secured territories which contained large numbers of Ukrainians and Byelorussians.

Even those states which did well out of the settlement in eastern Europe were not united in defending it. In this lay the importance of the disputes between Poland and Lithuania, and even more between Poland and Czechoslovakia. By any rational calculation, these states should have made common cause to protect their gains against their enemies in Germany and Russia; but they did not. Instead, relations between them were so bad that they were willing to make common cause *with* their greater enemies against one another. Relations between Poland and Czechoslovakia were particularly embittered and irritable. The Teschen dispute was only part of the story. The two countries differed sharply in their views of the Soviet Union: the Poles were deeply hostile, on both historical and ideological grounds; while the Czechs were anxious for Soviet friendship, out of historic sympathy, and because they sought support against Germany. Many Poles took the view that the whole state of Czechoslovakia was an artificial creation, and both Poland and Europe would be better off without it – a view which influenced policy in 1938 and early 1939.

To all except those involved, the Polish–Czech feud was obviously suicidal. The whole of the east European settlement only came about because, in freakish circumstances, Russia and Germany had both been defeated within a year, one after the other. These two great powers had long dominated eastern Europe; indeed, they had ruled most of it. As the giants regained their strength, which was as certain as anything can be in human affairs, their dominance would be restored. If this process was to be resisted, its potential victims would have to stand together; which they were in no mind to do. Even if they had, success would not have been assured; and it is here that there lay the final and most important element of instability in the east European settlement. It was founded upon the sand; and as the tides of German and Soviet power rose from the low ebb of 1918–19, the sand would be washed away.

It is clear enough that the European order as it stood before 1914 had disintegrated, and that its replacement rested on unstable foundations. From this premise, it is easy, and to some degree convincing, to argue that the whole rickety edifice was likely to collapse in ruin at any time. It held out the prospect of war in a number of different guises: a war launched by Germany to re-establish her dominance in Europe (eastern or western, or both); a preventive war by France or Poland to forestall such action; or war in eastern Europe over one or more of the many points of conflict in that calamitous region. Why look further for the origins of another war in Europe?

The case appears all the stronger if, as many people believed, there was a fundamental continuity in German policy over the whole period between 1914 and 1941. Many Frenchmen never thought otherwise: if the Germans got another chance, they would try again; the only safe course was to sap their economy, keep them disarmed, and surround them with France's allies. Churchill obviously thought the same when he telegraphed to President Roosevelt during the night of 4/5 August 1941: 'It is twenty-seven years ago today that the Huns began the last war. We must make a good job of it this time. Twice ought to be enough.'[11] More strikingly, in the 1960s a similar view began to gain ground in Germany itself, when the writings of Fritz Fischer emphasized the elements of continuity between the war aims of Germany in the First and Second World Wars.[12] This raises the whole question of whether, or how far, German policy in fact embodied such continuity; or whether the advent of Hitler marked a break with the past and the start of a new era, even if it borrowed something from the old. If the continuity of German policy from one war to the next is accepted, this seems to slot the final piece into place in the thesis of a Thirty Years War. The stable, orderly Europe of 1914, with its roughly equal balance of strength between opposing alliances, had not prevented the dynamism and the expansionism of Germany from breaking loose. It took four years of war, and the powerful advent of the USA, to defeat Germany. If Germany still had the same dynamism, the same will to expand, and was set on the same course, but was faced with a Europe in decay, with no balance of strength, and no Americans to restore the balance – if this was so, surely the die was cast, and another European war was a certainty. Only the details of time and occasion remained to be decided.

It is a powerful thesis, resting on much solid evidence and strong internal logic. Yet, in the debate on the origins of the Second World War in Europe, it is confronted by another thesis, of apparently equal cogency and consistency.

REFERENCES AND NOTES

1.   Nancy Mitford, *The Pursuit of Love* (London: Penguin 1980), p. 206.

The book was first published in 1945.

2. W. S. Churchill, *The Second World War*, vol. I (London 1948), p. vii.

3. Gordon Brook-Shepherd, *November 1918: the last act of the Great War* (London 1981), pp. 67–9.

4. H. W. V. Temperley (ed.), *A History of the Peace Conference of Paris*, vol. III, pp. 187, 214. The text of the treaty is printed in this volume, pp. 105–336.

5. Temperley (ed.), *Peace Conference of Paris*, vol. III, pp. 212–13.

6. Ibid., p. 214.

7. Reproduced from A. Sauvy, *Histoire économique de la France, 1919–1939*, vol. I (Paris 1965), p. 169. The figure by each arrow shows the approximate war debt owed by one state (or group of states) to another, in millions of dollars.

8. Quoted in W. K. Hancock, *Smuts: the sanguine years, 1870–1919* (Cambridge 1962), p. 533; cf. pp. 510–11, 524.

9. C. Petrie, *Life and Letters of Sir Austen Chamberlain*, vol. II (London 1940), pp. 258–9; Keith Feiling, *Neville Chamberlain* (London 1946), p. 372.

10. Table from Elizabeth Wiskemann, *Europe of the Dictators* (London 1966), pp. 267–8. Figures for Jews have been omitted, because they were not among those minorities with a nation-state elsewhere; but there were approximately 3 million Jews in Poland and 700,000 in Rumania. The figures are mostly taken from census returns of about 1930.

11. Churchill, *Second World War*, vol. III (London 1950), p. 381.

12. Fritz Fischer, *Griff nach der Weltmacht* (Duesseldorf 1961); English trans., *Germany's Aims in the First World War* (London 1967).

Chapter 3

THE CASE AGAINST A THIRTY YEARS WAR: THE RESTORATION OF EUROPE

The arguments summarized in the previous chapter, if accepted in their entirety, lead to the conclusion that the instability of Europe after 1919 rendered the outbreak of another war almost inevitable. But, however powerful they appear, they have been widely questioned, qualified, or indeed rejected outright. It is impossible to squeeze out of our history the men and events 'between the wars', as though they were nothing more than the ghostly inhabitants of an extended half-time interval. Not even the most fatalistic observer would claim to trace a wholly predestined line from the situation of 1919 to that of 1939–41, leaving no liberty of choice whatsoever to the statesmen and peoples of the inter-war years. At the very least, it remains to be explained how it was that a war of some sort, inherently probable from 1919 onwards, became the specific conflicts which overtook Europe between 1939 and 1941. But it is possible to take the challenge to the 'Thirty Years War' thesis further than that.

In the late 1920s it appeared to contemporaries in western Europe that peace was at length returning to the troubled Continent. The errors which were by that time widely perceived in the 1919 settlement were thought to be not beyond remedy, and steps were taken to put some of them right, notably by changes in the method and extent of reparations payments, and by admitting Germany to a place in the normal working of European relations. It was also hoped that the instability of the Continent could be remedied, on the one hand by the resurrection of something like the nineteenth-century 'Concert of Europe', an informal grouping of the great powers to provide a guiding influence in international affairs, and on the other by the development of the League of Nations. In practice these two devices often over-lapped, because the great European powers were also the most influential members of the League. Finally, it appeared also that the economic and social disruption left by the war had been overcome: currencies were stabilized, industrial production reached and passed the levels of 1913, threats of revolution diminished, and the new states settled down. It was not outrageously optimistic to think that things were looking up.

The symbol of this change in European affairs was the Treaty of Locarno, and the group of political and economic agreements which preceded and followed it. Austen Chamberlain, the British Foreign Secretary, who played a considerable part in the achievement of the Locarno agreements, said afterwards that they marked 'the real dividing-line between the years of war and the years of peace'; and this verdict commanded widespread agreement at the time. The Treaty of Locarno itself was rather a limited measure to bear this heavy symbolic weight. Signed in London on 1 December 1925, after being initialled at the Swiss resort of Locarno on 16 October, it embodied the acceptance of the Franco-German and Belgian–German frontiers by the three states concerned, with an outside guarantee of those frontiers by Britain and Italy. The same acceptance and guarantee applied to the demilitarized zone in the Rhineland, which was imposed on Germany by the Treaty of Versailles. Under this extremely important provision, Germany was forbidden to maintain troops or construct fortifications in an area which included the whole of the left bank of the Rhine and a zone 50 kilometres wide on the right bank; and in the Locarno Treaty the German government freely accepted this limitation, which it previously regarded as only a part of the *diktat* of Versailles.

Though limited, these terms were important in themselves, as confirming the territorial settlement in western Europe on a freely negotiated basis. They were also important for what they represented. An important gain from the French point of view was the British guarantee of their frontier with Germany, which was something the British had avoided giving ever since 1919, when the proposed Anglo-American guarantee which was intended to accompany the Treaty of Versailles was allowed to lapse. This reassurance to France, which contributed to a sense of security, was the counterpart of the other main theme of this agreement, which was Franco-German reconciliation. Looking to the future, this seemed the crucial aspect of the whole affair. The formal political treaty did not stand alone. It was buttressed by an association, perhaps amounting to friendship, between the French and German Foreign Ministers, Aristide Briand and Gustav Stresemann. The diplomatic relationship was accompanied by the activities of various private bodies, for example the Franco-German Committee, which originated with a small group of writers, politicians, and businessmen; and the *Action Catholique de la Jeunesse Française*, which threw itself into the work of reconciliation with German Catholics. In economic terms, French and German industrialists (with others from Belgium and Luxemburg) signed in September 1926 an agreement for an iron and steel cartel, regulating annual production and its division between the countries concerned. It was a time of hope in Franco-German relations.

The Treaty of Locarno was accompanied by other agreements. There was a series of arbitration treaties between Germany on the one hand and France, Belgium, Czechoslovakia, and Poland on the other, laying down that certain types of dispute between the signatories should be submitted to outside arbitration. There were also treaties of mutual guarantee between France on the one hand and Poland and Czechoslovakia on the other, which were intended to close, at least partially, the obvious gap left by Locarno, which was that it concerned only western Europe.

Locarno and its accompanying agreements, and the spirit of reconciliation which flourished with them, were only possible because in the previous year a partial settlement of the reparation problem had been reached. In 1923, with the French occupation of the Ruhr to enforce payment upon Germany, this had seemed scarcely feasible – France was firmly embarked on the course of imposing reparations, not negotiating about them. But in October of that year the French government accepted a British proposal to set up a committee of experts to consider the problem. This committee, set up by agreement between the British, French, Belgian, Italian, American, and German governments, was to consider (supposedly from a purely technical standpoint) means of balancing the German budget, stabilizing the German currency, and fixing both an achievable level of reparation payments and means by which they might be made and secured. The chairman of the committee was an American banker, and Director of the US Bureau of the Budget, Charles G. Dawes; and its recommendations, made early in 1924, came to be known as the Dawes Plan. A vital recommendation was for the stabilization of the German currency, at the rate of 20 Reichsmarks to the pound sterling, controlled by the creation of a new bank of issue, independent of the German government and run by a body of which half had to be non-Germans. The committee then went on to deal with reparation payments. It left the total unchanged, but recommended a new scheme of annual payments starting at 1,000 million gold marks in the first year, rising to 2,500 million in the fifth and thereafter. Some variation in the annual payments was provided for in case of sharp movements in the price of gold or severe transfer problems. Payment of reparations was to be ensured by the appropriation of certain indirect taxes and bonds for the state railways for that purpose; and a Reparations Agency, including Allied representatives, was to be set up to control these arrangements. A foreign loan of 800 million marks was to be raised, partly to back the new currency, and partly to help with the payment of the first annual instalment under the new reparations scheme.

The Dawes Plan was accepted by the French government in April 1924, which was a vital first step, because the whole scheme was contingent upon French withdrawal from the Ruhr; and then by an international conference in London in July and August. The loan was raised without difficulty in October, rather more than half in the USA and a quarter in Britain, with the rest in a number of west European countries. Germany then made reparation payments regularly under the terms of the Dawes Plan. In February 1929 a new committee, under the chairmanship of another American banker, Owen D. Young, was set up to work out a definitive settlement of the reparations question. Its report, presented to the governments concerned in June, recommended a reduction of about a quarter in the total of reparations, with a rising scale of annual payments to be completed by 1988 – the first mention of a final date. The Reparations Agency was to be withdrawn, and foreign surveillance of German finances brought to an end. The proposals were accepted by the various governments; and a German payment under the new arrangement was made in May 1930.

These agreements were not in any final sense a settlement of the reparations problem. Paying reparations at all was still unwelcome to Germany; and there was still a strain on the German balance of payments. However, it was shown that in certain circumstances reparations could be paid, and indeed that they were compatible with a general recovery in European commerce and industry. In France, the index of industrial production passed the level of 1913 in 1924; in Germany, in 1926. In both countries, production continued to be high (though with some fluctuations) in the late 1920s, a tendency which was shared by nearly all European countries, eastern as well as western. Trade between France and Germany grew rapidly: French imports from Germany increased by 60 per cent between 1926 and 1930, including large quantities of coal, iron and steel, chemical products, and machine tools. French industrial growth in the period was closely linked to German production – at the time, another sign of Franco–German co-operation.[1]

Economic progress was accompanied by the stabilization of the major west European currencies. In Germany, this was a matter of replacement rather than stabilization. In November 1923, at the height of the hyperinflation, a new currency, the Rentenmark, was introduced, based on the security of land and buildings. For a time it circulated alongside the old mark; then in August 1924, with the backing of the Dawes loan, a new Reichsmark was introduced to replace the old currency, at the rate of one new Reichsmark to 1 million millions of the old. This registered the acceptance of the obliteration of all holdings in the old currency; but it was a fresh start, and in the following years prices held steady. In Britain, the pound sterling was stabilized with the return to the gold standard in 1925, at the pre-war level which placed the pound at an exchange rate of $US 4.86. This decision was later criticized, notably because it overvalued the pound by about 10 per cent in terms of its actual purchasing power compared with the dollar, and so made British exports over-expensive and condemned governments to rigid financial policies in order to maintain sterling at its overvalued rate. At the time, it was regarded as an essential step (psychological as much as anything else) towards the restoration of pre-war stability. Its main object was to restore stability to rates of exchange, and so to promote international trade, on which Britain was heavily dependent. In France, the franc, which had fallen seriously in terms of the pound sterling (touching 243 francs to the pound in July 1926), recovered sharply when Poincaré became Premier, and stabilized by the end of 1926 at 124 to the pound. France returned to the gold standard in 1928, fixing the new value of the franc at 65.5 milligrams of gold, as against 290 milligrams for the pre-war franc.[2] All this, and especially the concern with the gold standard, later came to appear very rigid and old-fashioned; but at the time it represented an attempt to get back to the well-tried mechanism of the pre-1914 system, and even more to the confidence which had sustained it.

One of the agreements reached at Locarno in 1925 was that Germany should be admitted to the League of Nations and become a permanent member of its Council. This focused attention on another great sign of hope in the 1930s: the apparently firm rooting and strong flowering of the League. Founded in 1919 under the combined impulse of Lord Robert Cecil and President Wilson, the League suffered an early blow when it was rejected by the USA in 1920, and it was viewed with suspicion by most practitioners of the old diplomacy, who saw it, at best, as being no more than a fifth wheel on a carriage. But despite set-backs and doubts, the League began to flourish. The annual meetings of the Assembly, at which all member states were represented, allowed the smaller countries an active role in world diplomacy, an opportunity seized with zeal and success by (for example) Benes of Czechoslovakia, Branting of Sweden, and Hymans of Belgium. The Council of the League, with its permanent membership made up of great powers (Britain, France, Italy, and Japan), acted as a successor to the old Concert of Europe. The Covenant bound all member states to submit disputes to the League before resorting to force, and so held out the opportunity of avoiding war.

The League settled well to its work of international administration, supplying High Commissioners for the Saar and Danzig, providing a channel for loans to Austria and Hungary, and furnishing various humanitarian services for the world at large. It began work (though with painful slowness) on the problems of disarmament. In 1926 the Council scored a success in settling a border incident between Bulgaria and Greece which had threatened to develop into war. With Germany's admission to membership in 1926, the League escaped the stigma of being merely a 'League of victors'. By 1928 every European state except the USSR was a member, and nearly every Foreign Minister attended its sessions. Notably, in the post-Locarno period, Briand, Stresemann, and Austen Chamberlain made a point of meeting at Geneva. In the late 1920s the League was at the height of its prestige, and a beacon of hope in international affairs.

All these achievements of the late 1920s had their flaws, some of which were potentially dangerous. The Locarno agreements contained serious faults and contradictions. Some were immediately apparent, certainly to those whom they affected most nearly. The treaties distinguished between Germany's western frontiers, which were voluntarily accepted by Germany and guaranteed by outside powers, and her eastern borders, which were not. The implication, which was not lost on the Poles, was that some frontiers were more firmly established than others. Other faults were temporarily concealed. By the treaties, Britain publicly guaranteed the Franco–German and Belgian–German frontiers, but she took no steps to ensure that this guarantee could be fulfilled: there was no military commitment nor planning for the defence of any of the territories involved. Most serious of all, the agreements merely disguised a profound difference of approach between France and Germany. It was true that both Briand and Stresemann spoke the language of reconciliation; but each hoped to reconcile the other to something different. Briand wanted to reconcile Germany to the acceptance of the Versailles settlement; Stresemann wanted to reconcile France to its revision. It must be doubted whether so fundamental a contradiction could have been glossed over for long.

It also appeared in retrospect that the economic recovery of Europe was excessively dependent on American loans (see Table 2). The Dawes loan of 1924, which was oversubscribed in New York, was the start of a considerable flow of lending by American investors to Germany (especially to the firms of Krupps and Thyssen, and to German municipalities), and later to other European countries. In the Dawes years (1924–29), German borrowing from abroad always far exceeded her reparation payments. Hence a curious cycle of payments developed: Germany borrowed from the USA; which helped her to pay reparations to France, Britain, and Italy; and in turn these countries made payments on their war debts to the USA. When the source of American loans dried up with the stock market crash in 1929, this cycle was broken at its starting point; and with the calling in of short-term American loans, an important element in the German economic recovery was removed.

Table 2. American loans to Europe
(millions of dollars)[3]

1924	527
1925	629
1926	484
1927	577
1928	598
1929	142

The case against a Thirty Years War: the restoration of Europe

The extravagant hopes invested in the League of Nations by Western liberals and socialists, and by aspiring small states, were probably always greater than that organization could be expected to fulfil. It was easy to exaggerate the success over Greece and Bulgaria, and ignore the League's failure to deal with the Polish–Lithuanian conflict over Vilna. The basic problem presented to the League by the absence of the USA and the Soviet Union had not been resolved. There was a dangerous element of euphoria in the atmosphere of Geneva.

All this may be granted. But does it mean that all the hopes which followed the Dawes–Locarno agreements were illusory? Surely not. The case must remain hypothetical; but it is perfectly conceivable that, without the stock market crash in America in 1929, American support for the European financial system would not have been so abruptly removed, and the system might have adjusted itself gradually to a lesser dependence on US loans. It was first the great crash, and then the even greater world depression which it signalled, which cut off the hopes of recovery in their prime. All over Europe, the British Empire, and the USA, the depression had the effect of driving states (or groups of states) in upon themselves, to try to find salvation in some form of self-sufficiency. Similarly, the political contradictions underlying the Locarno agreements were real; but there was a reasonable chance that they could be resolved, as long as Germany moved towards the revision of Versailles with prudence, and with limited objectives. Britain would have accepted such movement readily and France reluctantly; but the result would have been the same. Locarno at least opened the way for Germany to resume her place as a partner in the European Concert; and after that, perhaps, by stages, to her former predominance, without encountering determined – still less armed – opposition.

In this hypothesis, then, it was the great depression which destroyed a situation offering a real chance of evolution towards a stable European peace. The depression wrecked all the gains in terms of economic stabilization, prosperity, and material progress secured since 1924. It provoked over much of Europe a flight towards political extremes which plunged the Continent into ideological strife, and various forms of economic nationalism which generated constant friction. Above all, by destroying German prosperity and rendering 6 million Germans unemployed, it played a crucial part in the rise of Hitler to power. That, in the eyes of many, was the fatal event, the conjuring up of the demon king. In Churchill's words: ' . . . into that void after a pause there strode a maniac of ferocious genius, the repository and expression of the most virulent hatreds that have ever corroded the human breast – Corporal Hitler'.[4] It then requires only one link to complete the chain: the depression brought Hitler, and Hitler brought the war. For many, like the French historian Maurice

Baumont, the link presents no difficulty: 'the origins of the war of 1939 go back essentially to the insatiable appetites of Adolf Hitler'.[5]

A rival hypothesis to that of a Thirty Years War thus takes shape. Instead of the continuation of the First World War, arising almost inevitably out of the effects of that war and the instability of the peace settlement, there appears the outline of a successful European recovery, cut off in its prime by the great depression and its dreadful consequence, the advent of Hitler. These two broad interpretations have bred many variations, advanced with varying degrees of sharpness, and sometimes venom. Before pursuing the discussion, it may be helpful to look at some other aspects of the historical debate on the origins of the Second World War in Europe.

REFERENCES AND NOTES

1. Carlo M. Cipolla (ed.), *Fontana Economic History of Europe*, vol. 6, part 2 (London 1976), tables on pp. 687ff; *La France et L'Allemagne 1932–1936: Communications préséntées au Colloque franco-allemand tenu à Paris . . . du 10 au 12 mars 1977* (Paris 1980), p. 279.

2. Philippe Bernard, *La fin d'un monde, 1914–1929* (Paris 1975), pp. 139–41.

3. Table in Charles P. Kindleberger, *The World in Depression, 1929–1939* (London 1973), p. 56.

4. W. S. Churchill, *The Second World War*, vol. I (London 1948), p. 9.

5. Maurice Baumont, *The Origins of the Second World War* (New Haven 1978), p. 3.

Chapter 4
HISTORY AND HISTORIANS

Two broad and wide-ranging explanations of the origins of the Second World War thus confront one another. Within their extensive span, one or other of these interpretations subsumes many of the other versions of the problem which have been produced; but they do not exhaust them. 'History will judge', chorused the ambassadors in Berlin in 1939; but the judgements of historians have been almost endlessly divergent.

It is often said that for some twenty years after the coming of the Second World War in Europe there was little or no debate about its origins. Hitler planned and caused the war, and that was an end of the matter. Then in 1961 A. J. P. Taylor published his book on *The Origins of the Second World War*, which by its attack on the simple 'Hitler thesis' opened a controversy which raged for several years. Shot and shell flew round Mr Taylor's head, and enough fragments could be gathered up from the battlefield to make more books in the years that followed.[1]

There is some reality in this picture. The attractions of the simple assertion of Hitler's guilt were certainly strong, and its grip was powerful. The judgement of the Nuremberg tribunal on war criminals, victors' justice though it was, rested on an overwhelming mass of evidence. It scarcely needed to be argued that between 1939 and 1941 Germany attacked her neighbours, and not the other way about: the Dutch did not fling themselves at Germany's throat on 10 May 1940. There was a powerful moral certainty, well expressed by Michael Howard, who fought in the war and later became one of its most distinguished historians: 'There can have been few people in the western world (and even fewer in the Soviet Union) who did not believe in 1945 that the war which they had fought and won had been not only necessary but in every sense "just".'[2] At the end of the war, political convenience was added to moral conviction. Americans, British, and Russians had all united to fight Hitler, and they could still unite to condemn him after his death. To look further than the guilt of that appalling man might raise questions about American isolation, or British appeasement, or the Nazi–Soviet Pact, which at that stage were better left, like sleeping dogs, to lie.

Common sense, morality, and expediency thus combined to reinforce the thesis of Hitler's unique war guilt. The position presented a refreshing simplicity and certainty by contrast with the maze of conflicting interpretations which had arisen around the question of the origins of the First World War. The British historian G. P. Gooch, who spent much of his energies for some twenty years on the origins of the earlier war, was categorical about the contrast:

> While the responsibilities of the war of 1914 remain a subject of controversy, the conflict which began with the German attack on Poland on September 1st, 1939, presents few difficulties to the historian. Opinions naturally differ on the use of their victory by the Allies during the 'twenties and on Anglo-French policy in regard to the dissatisfied Powers since 1931; but the revelation of Hitler's Napoleonic ambitions in March 1939, quickly followed by demands incompatible with Polish independence, places the guilt of the new conflagration squarely on his shoulders.[3]

Gooch's point, made in 1940, had much force at that time. But it is a serious exaggeration to say that in the 1940s and 1950s the consensus was unbroken. Even to concentrate upon the role of Hitler was not a simple matter. From the time of Hitler's rise to power onwards, there were fierce disputes as to the nature of the nazi regime and the position of Hitler within it. Was the nazi regime monolithic, moving as one man under the guidance of its Fuehrer; or was it rather made up of warring groups, with Hitler balancing between them, practising the old skills of divide and rule? Was Hitler himself a Machiavellian, an ideologue, or a psychopath – or perhaps all three at once? Was he an independent agent, or merely the tool of finance capital, a new champion conjured up by the bourgeoisie to protect it against communism and revolution? What was the role of the German officer corps under nazism – did it suffer the 'nemesis of power', or rather the nemesis of helplessness? Such questions had a direct bearing on the apparently simple thesis of Hitler's responsibility for the war; and indeed it was plain from an early date that nothing to do with Hitler was at all simple.[4]

Moreover, the wartime alliance against Hitler did not long survive the victory of 1945; and as it broke up, so the unanimous agreement to cast the whole blame for the war on Hitler disintegrated with it. It was as early as January 1948 that the American State Department published a volume of documents on *Nazi–Soviet Relations*, drawn from captured German archives and emphasizing the pre-war co-operation between Germany and the Soviet Union in a way which cast some of the blame for the outbreak of war in 1939 on Stalin as well as on Hitler. The Soviet Union followed in the same year with a volume entitled *The Falsifiers of History*, which blamed American bankers and industrialists for providing the capital to rebuild German war industries in the 1920s and 1930s, and accused Britain and France of encouraging Hitler to turn his aggressive drive towards the east.[5] The breakdown of

Soviet–American relations and the rise of the 'cold war' thus disturbed the consensus on Hitler's sole war guilt at an early date.

The development of historical discussion about the origins of the Second World War in Europe is represented, not so much by a division into a period of consensus followed by a period of controversy, but by sets of contradictory interpretations which have flourished during the whole period since the 1930s. They have not all been continuously and equally prominent: they have come and gone, flared up and faded; but none has been absent from the discussion for very long. They march two by two like the animals into the ark. The idea of an inevitable war confronts that of an unnecessary war. The notion of a planned, pre-meditated war (war by blueprint, even) stands against that of war by accident or improvisation. Was it Hitler's war, brought about by the character and aims of one man, or another German war, in which Hitler was no more than a new representative of long-standing forces and ambitions? Was it at its heart an ideological war, a European civil war cutting across state boundaries and identities, or was it funda-mentally an old-fashioned war between states, a war about power and material interests in which one state made a bid to dominate Europe and others eventually combined to defeat it? Let us look at these contrasting pairs.

The idea of an inevitable war has taken different forms. There was a widespread belief that another war was implicit in the situation which followed that of 1914–18. The long-standing Marxist view that wars are the inevitable result of capitalism has been applied to this war as to others, notably in East German works designed to show that Hitler was the instrument of capitalists and industrialists seeking to maximize their profits by controlling the markets and resources of Europe. Other historians have noted that to contemporaries, 'from a certain time – earlier for some, later for others – war appeared inevitable; there never was a war which caused less surprise when it began'.[6]

Such notions of inevitability have long confronted a different view, which Churchill embodied in his phrase 'the unnecessary war'. 'One day', he wrote, 'President Roosevelt told me he was asking publicly for suggestions about what the war should be called. I said at once "The Unnecessary War". There never was a war more easy to stop. . . .'[7] This sentiment was echoed by Namier:[8]

> The issue of a crisis depends not so much on its magnitude as on the courage and resolution with which it is met. The second German bid for world domination found Europe weak and divided. At several junctures it could have been stopped without excessive effort or sacrifice, but was not: a failure of European statesmanship . . . the rest of Europe had neither the faith, nor the will, nor even sufficient repugnance, to offer timely, effective resistance. . . . Janissaries and appeasers aided Hitler's work: a failure of European morality.

Both Churchill and Namier were advocates of resistance to

Germany from an early date; and their argument was that at certain points the advance of German power could have been checked by the threat, or the comparatively small-scale use, of force. It is a view which is in fact easily reconcilable with some versions of the inevitable war: it is all a matter of date. What was avoidable at one time was inevitable at another. Churchill includes both views in the same book: 'Once Hitler's Germany had been allowed to rearm without active interference by the Allies and former associated powers, a second World War was almost certain. . . . Almost all that remained open to France and Britain was to await the moment of the challenge and do the best they could.'⁹ Churchill here put the transition from unnecessary to inevitable war in 1935, and linked it to German rearmament. Others have put it in 1936, and linked it to the German occupation of the Rhineland, demilitarized under the terms of Versailles and Locarno. The principle is the same. This fusion of the two apparent opposites has, largely through the writings of Churchill himself, become firmly established in the British mind; and to this day it governs many attitudes towards the origins of the war and especially towards the policy summed up as 'appeasement'.

The next pair of opposites is made up of war planned and premeditated, and war by improvisation, or even by accident. For a long time the view was widely held that war was brought about by a carefully planned and timed programme of nazi aggression – blueprint was a favourite word. In part this arose from a striking appearance of regularity in German moves. In March 1935 the Versailles restrictions on armaments were thrown off and conscription introduced; and March 1936 saw the occupation of the Rhineland. After a fallow year, the series was resumed, but to a six-monthly instead of an annual rhythm: March 1938, the occupation of Austria; September 1938, the Munich crisis and the annexation of the Sudetenland; March 1939, the Prague coup and the destruction of the remainder of Czechoslovakia; September 1939, the war with Poland; April 1940, the invasion of Denmark and Norway, followed at once by the assault in the west. Once again, such an interpretation gained impetus and authority from Churchill. 'Europe is confronted with a programme of aggression, nicely calculated and timed, unfolding stage by stage', he declared in the House of Commons on 14 March 1938; and events seemed to prove him right.¹⁰ In the early stages of the war, the British public formed a strong impression of Hitler's infallibility: he knew everything and foresaw everything, and events moved at his bidding. After the war, the tale was taken up at the Nuremberg trials, where a principal charge was one of *planning* aggressive war. The point was emphasized in the title of a book by a Swiss historian, Walther Hofer, *War Premeditated* (1954); though in fact this book dealt only with the events of August 1939. In 1960 William Shirer, an American journalist and broadcaster turned historian, published his *Rise and Fall of the Third Reich* (a best-seller in Britain and the USA, and much translated), which embodied the 'blueprint' idea in its massive and powerful narrative.

It was this view which was so severely handled in A. J. P. Taylor's book in 1961. Taylor presented Hitler as a Micawber-like figure, always waiting for something to turn up, taking advantage of opportunities presented to him by others; not a planner but a coffee-house talker and dreamer; at best an opportunist and improviser. The war between Germany and Poland assumed almost the appearance of a mere accident, arising because Hitler made a slight error of timing in launching one of his diplomatic manoeuvres, putting off until 29 August a move which he should have made on the 28th.[11] The extreme forms of this argument have found little support; but the theme of opportunism and improvisation is another matter. Years before, in a book which was an uncompromising indictment of Hitler, Alan Bullock had noted the opportunist nature of the Fuehrer's diplomacy in August 1939. Even in a chapter firmly entitled 'Hitler's war', Bullock described how the dictator hesitated between three courses; another Munich; a war against Poland alone; or a war against Poland which might involve France and Britain. He did not make up his mind until the British government made it up for him by declaring war.[12] Three years before the publication of Taylor's book, readers of the *Revue d'Histoire de la deuxième guerre mondiale* had their attention drawn to evidence of hesitation and indecision in Berlin after the Prague coup, indicating that there was no firmly established plan, with a next stage ready to be executed.[13] In 1963, Gordon Brook-Shepherd's book on the German occupation of Austria confirmed with ample proofs that the date and method of the *Anschluss* were forced upon Hitler by circumstances, and were not part of a pre-arranged plan.[14] Since then, the 'blueprint' theory of Hitler's foreign policy, the programme nicely calculated and timed, has been largely abandoned.

This has not meant, however, that the whole notion of a plan has been abandoned. Rather, it has been taken up by German historians and linked to a view of Hitler as a man with a systematic framework of thought, within which he adapted his approach to some of the demands and opportunities presented by events.[15] Andreas Hillgrueber and Klaus Hildebrand have argued a strong case that Hitler had an outline scheme in two phases, the first to establish German control of Europe, and the second (which might well come only after his lifetime) to wrest control of the seas and world domination from Britain and the USA.[16] The European stage of such a programme also forms the basis of K. D. Bracher's view that 'Hitler from the very outset fixed his sights on one unchanging goal: to round off the territory of the national state, and to expand Germany's *Lebensraum* far beyond the "racial core" of the German people'; a goal which involved moving externally against the Slavs, and internally against the Jews.[17] While not every aspect of these positions commands universal assent, they have produced widespread

43

agreement that Hitler's undoubted improvisations must be seen within the framework of a seriously worked out system of thought.[18] In this way, what appeared to be diametrically opposed interpretations have been very largely synthesized into what has emerged as a new orthodoxy.

This leads directly to the third pair of contradictory explanations: was this Hitler's war, or (as the advocates of the idea of a Thirty Years War asserted) simply another German war, the prolongation of that of 1914–18? It is not difficult to discern the similarities between the objectives of the Kaiser's Germany, and especially the war aims pursued by Germany in both east and west during the First World War, and the aims of Hitler's Germany. In eastern Europe, the Treaty of Brest-Litovsk in 1918 placed Germany in effective control of the Baltic provinces, Poland, the Ukraine, and the Caucasus. Among the ideas considered by General Ludendorff was the planting of a German colony in the Crimea. Hitler's Germany in 1941–42 aimed at control of much the same area, though by outright domination rather than indirect means; and a German colony was actually established in the Crimea. In central and western Europe, the zone of German political and economic control sketched out in Bethmann-Hollweg's memorandum of war aims in September 1914 was actually established after the German conquests of 1940. The Kaiser's Germany also embarked on a 'world policy', with a great navy and colonial ambitions, which corresponded to Hitler's distant aims of a large fleet and world domination.

Against this strong evidence of continuity is the view that Hitler's personality, the nature and methods of his new regime, and the overriding demands of nazi ideology constituted a sharp break in German policy, dated either in 1933, when Hitler came to office, or in 1938, when he finally broke the power of the conservative establishment in the Foreign Office and the General Staff. Even though some continuity with the past was maintained, the new elements were more important than the old. In particular, there is a strong case that by the 1930s the old-established German political and military leaders had grown cautious, and were by no means eager for a war of conquest. Hitler introduced a new way of thought, new men from far outside the old élites, and revolutionary new methods.

This contradiction, still unresolved, is closely linked with the last pair of opposite interpretations: was the Second World War in Europe a distinctively ideological war, or a war between states over issues of power, material interests, or simply survival? The ideological element in the Europe of the 1930s was unavoidable. No one could travel in Germany and Italy without observing the ostentatious display of the fascist and nazi regimes. Few travelled in the USSR, but those who did were very vocal. The Soviet regime attracted some and repelled others with tremendous force, and added much to the ideological vibrancy of

Europe. The contrast with the condition of Europe before 1914 was marked. 'Before 1914 the foreign policies of the European states all belonged to a single species. The chancelleries of the parliamentary democracies conformed to the same philosophy of civilized Machiavellianism as that of the dynastic states. . . .' Raymond Aron, who wrote these words, had no doubt of the importance of the change. It was exemplified, before the Second World War and even more after it began, by the number and significance of the 'ideological traitors' – Germans who preferred the defeat of their own country to a victory by Hitler; Frenchmen who supported a German victory out of disillusion with the Third Republic or active sympathy with nazism; Russians who fought with their country's enemies against Stalinism. The same phenomenon was exemplified in the resistance movements against German occupation which took shape in Europe in 1939–41. Resisters were not numerous; and they were usually patriots above all; but often they were also ideologically committed. Aron, as both a Frenchman and a Jew, wrote from the heart: 'man, without being in uniform, was defending his soul. The victory of either side signified, or seemed to signify, a conversion of souls by force.'[19]

The result was a situation in which there was ideological conflict between states – between the nazi and fascist regimes and Bolshevik Russia, and between both of these and the parliamentary, capitalist democracies of Britain and France. There were also frequent cases of rebellion by individuals against the ideological character of their own country. When war came, the battle-lines often ran between fellow-citizens of the same country, as well as between one country and another. Moreover, the ideological conflicts involved ideals, values, and the whole working of political and social systems, so that the stakes of war were very high.

Against this is set the view that, despite the undoubted presence of ideological elements, the war was primarily one between states, fought for issues of national security or material gain. John Lukacs, for example, though well aware of the ideological aspects of the war, insisted that 'Hitler, Mussolini, Churchill, de Gaulle were statesmen first of all. They subordinated their philosophical and political preferences to what they thought were the interests of their states.'[20] Churchill and de Gaulle above all, the men who refused absolutely to come to terms with Germany in 1940, drew their convictions from a simple, old-fashioned patriotism, rooted in the past and in their view of history; and Lukacs believed that their motives were less complicated and their resistance more steadfast than in those who were impelled by ideology. Stalin too seems to have fought above all for the security and survival of his Russian empire, appealing in 1941 to Russian patriotism and the heroes of the past rather than to communism, even though millions in other countries saw him as the leader of the Workers' Fatherland. In other versions of events, the war appears primarily as a struggle for economic advantage. Germany, with a booming domestic economy and a vast programme of armaments, went to war to secure its imports of raw materials and food. The war was launched by those who were convinced it could be made to pay, and forced upon those whose economic interests were attached to the status quo, and who foresaw only economic ruin resulting from another great conflict.[21]

The arguments continue. They are not likely to be stilled unless some complete lack of interest or innovation supervenes, leaving the issues to congeal into some inert and uninspiring immobility. So far, there is no sign of this. 'History will judge' was the cry in 1939. Its judgements have been, and still are, multifarious and often contradictory. Two wide-ranging and conflicting interpretations still stand, in the Thirty Years War thesis on the one hand, and the explanation from the depression plus Hitler on the other. More detailed examination brings out a wide range of differing views, here marshalled into four sets of contrasting pairs. Some of these views lend support to the Thirty Years War thesis: others – notably those which stress the role of Hitler and of ideology – oppose it. Many years of ardent and industrious historical work have brought us into something of a maze. Can we find a thread which will lead us through it?

There are certainly clues which may be followed. First, it helps to remember that even widely differing interpretations are not necessarily incompatible with one another, but sometimes explain different aspects of the same events. Second, several apparent contradictions are less difficult to comprehend when we grasp firmly that we are dealing with a lengthy process, covering some five or six years, as well as with particular events. It is natural that different explanations applied, and in varying degrees, to different elements in this complex development. Third, we must examine both the underlying forces behind the process by which Europe moved from civil strife and undeclared war to local and eventually Continental war, and also the various points along that road when particular states decided, or were compelled, to go to war. The next part of the book is therefore devoted to a consideration of the underlying forces of ideology, economics, and strategy; and the final part moves to a narrative of events from the mid-1930s to 1941. In this way, while we cannot resolve all the problems and conflicts of evidence and interpretation, we can nevertheless follow a thread which offers a way through the labyrinth.

REFERENCES AND NOTES

1. See: E. M. Robertson (ed.), *The Origins of the Second World War: historical interpretations* (London 1971); Joachim Remak, *The Origins of the Second World War* (Englewood Cliffs 1976); W. Roger Louis

(ed.), *The Origins of the Second World War: A. J. P. Taylor and his Critics* (New York 1972).

2. Michael Howard, *War and the Liberal Conscience* (London 1978), p. 115.
3. G. P. Gooch, 'The coming of the war', *Contemporary Review*, July 1940, p. 9.
4. The whole problem is reviewed in Pierre Ayçoberry, *The Nazi Question. An essay on the interpretations of National Socialism 1922–1975* (London 1981). For some of the questions under discussion, see e. g. R. Palme Dutte, *Fascism and Social Revolution* (London 1934); Franz Neumann, *Behemoth: The Structure and Practice of National-Socialism* (London 1942), emphasizing the role of conflicting groups; J. W. Wheeler-Bennett, *The Nemesis of Power* (London 1953), on the officer corps.
5. US Department of State, *Nazi–Soviet Relations, 1939–1941. Documents from the archives of the German Foreign Office*, R. J. Sontag and J. S. Beddie (eds.), (Washington 1948). Soviet Information Bureau, *The Falsifiers of History* (Moscow and London 1948).
6. Marlis G. Steinert, *Les Origines de la Seconde Guerre Mondiale* (Paris 1974), p. 15; cf. John Lukacs, *The Last European War* (London 1977), p. 25.
7. W. S. Churchill, *The Second World War*, vol. I (London 1948), p. viii.
8. L. B. Namier, *Diplomatic Prelude* (London 1950), p. ix.
9. Churchill, *Second World War*, vol. I, p. 148.
10. *House of Commons Debates*, 5th series, vol. 333, col. 95.
11. A.J.P. Taylor, *The Origins of the Second World War* (London 1961), p. 278.
12. Alan Bullock, *Hitler: a study in tyranny* (London 1952), ch. 9.
13. O. Desbrosses, in *Revue d'Histoire de la deuxième guerre mondiale*, no. 29, Jan. 1958, pp. 84–5.
14. Gordon Brook-Shepherd, *Anschluss* (London 1963).
15. Eberhard Jaeckel, *Hitler's Weltanschauung* (Middletown, Conn. 1972).
16. A Hillgrueuber, *Hitler's Strategie* (Frankfurt 1965); Klaus Hildebrand, *The Foreign Policy of the Third Reich* (London 1973).
17. K. D. Bracher, *The German Dictatorship* (London: Penguin Books 1973), p. 37.
18. See William Carr, 'National Socialism: foreign policy and Wehrmacht', in Walter Laqueur (ed.), *Fascism: a reader's guide* (London: Penguin Books 1979), p. 121.
19. Raymond Aron, *Peace and War* (London 1966), pp. 298, 173.
20. Lukacs, *Last European War*, p. 327.
21. A. S. Milward, *War, Economy and Society, 1939–1945* (London 1977).

Part Two

THE UNDERLYING FORCES

THE ROLE OF IDEOLOGY

Carlo Rosselli, the leader of the Italian Action Party, in exile in Paris, wrote in 1936: 'Beware! A European conflict is developing. We have reached the moment when the two opposed worlds, the world of freedom and the world of authoritarianism, are about to find themselves face to face.'[1] He was expecting a war of ideologies, and was conscious that, as a political refugee from his own land, he was already engaged in such a war. In retrospect, these views seem largely justified. Nazi Germany, and to a lesser extent fascist Italy, professed ideologies which, if put into practice, would produce dynamic, expansionist foreign policies which were certain at some stage to be opposed. The war, when it came, was to an important degree a conflict of values and ideas, in which the victors imposed a form of government, an ideology, and a culture on the vanquished. This was usually (though not always) the case with nazi conquests; and it was also true in occupied Germany at the end of the war, when the East became a communist state and the West a liberal democracy, and the Germans themselves were re-educated to fit into the new order.

The line-up of forces was not as simple as that presented by Rosselli, with freedom facing authoritarianism. Fascism/nazism stood opposed to parliamentary democracy; but there was also another brand of authoritarianism in communism, and the result was the emergence of a triangle of forces, each opposed to the other two, though willing from time to time to make tactical alliances with one enemy against the other. It is also clear that the role of ideology was not unique or all-embracing. States continued to pursue material interests, economic advantage, and military security. The continuities of policy imposed by history and geography could not be, and were not, simply discarded. Hitler inherited much from the Germany of Kaiser Wilhelm; Stalin from the Russia of the Tsars; and one of the most determined and courageous opponents of nazi Germany, Winston Churchill, embodied a deeply rooted traditional patriotism rather than any contemporary ideology. Moreover, it is given to no man to achieve an undeviating consistency in thought and action; even the most devoted zealot will change his mind or make mistakes.

Despite such reservations and complications, the role of ideology in the coming of the Second World War in Europe was significant, and any analysis which ignored it would be well wide of the mark. At the least, ideology was a complicating element in international affairs. It produced lines of division which ran within states as well as between them, so that in almost every state in Europe there were individuals and groups whose first loyalty was to an idea rather than to their country – and often to another country which embodied the idea. Ideological links and antagonisms sometimes made it difficult for governments to act solely on the basis of power politics and material interest. At the most, if Hitler and the nazis meant even half of what they said, then war of some kind was surely inevitable: their claims for living space for a master race could never be placidly accepted by all their neighbours.

Our main concern is with the role of ideology in foreign policy and the origins of the war. But to establish this, it is necessary to examine the nature of the ideologies involved, and their roles within the various European states. Much of what follows in the next four chapters bears only indirectly on the Second World War itself; but in so far as it was an ideological war, we must examine the ideologies in order to assess their significance in its origins.

REFERENCES AND NOTES

1.   Quoted in Federico Chabod, *Italian Fascism* (London 1963), p. 80.

Chapter 5

ITALIAN FASCISM

Fascism, which with its close relative nazism was to play a crucial role in European affairs in the 1930s, first came to power and prominence with the rise of Mussolini in Italy in the 1920s. Italy was not in material terms a power of the first rank, and Mussolini is sometimes presented as being little more than a desperado or a mountebank. But the success of Italian fascism encouraged many imitators. It was the start of what proved to be a disruptive movement in European politics, and it deserves serious attention.

THE RISE OF ITALIAN FASCISM

The unification of Italy achieved by 1870 was forced, hasty, and superficial. There was little in common between the primitive agrarian communities of the south and the modern industrial societies of Milan and Turin in the north. The Vatican maintained its opposition to the new state, and forbade Italian Catholics to take any part in national politics; which, even if often disregarded, put a severe strain on a largely Catholic population. The electorate was for a long time tightly restricted by a property franchise; and when this changed with the introduction of manhood suffrage in 1912 the political system could scarcely cope with the results. Nationalists were dissatisfied by the failure to complete the territorial unification of the country, in that Italian populations in the South Tyrol, Trieste, and Fiume still lay outside the frontiers.

These long-standing problems of the Italian state were compounded by the effects of the First World War, in which Italy took part from 1915 to 1918. The end of the war brought an industrial depression, a fall in the value of the lira, and a sharp rise in prices. At the same time, nationalists were disappointed with the results of the war. The Allied powers meeting in Paris in 1919 denied Italy some of the gains she had been promised on her entry into the war in 1915; and the issue came to a head over the question of Fiume. Fiume was a divided city, with an Italian centre and Slovene outskirts. It was not in fact one of the territories promised to Italy in 1915, but it was seen as a part of 'unredeemed Italy', and claimed as such. There was deep resentment among Italians when President Wilson, in a somewhat arbitrary exercise of his lofty principles regarding self-determination, proposed that Fiume should become a free city. In response, Gabriele d'Annunzio, the flamboyant nationalist, poet, and airman, occupied the city in September 1919 with a force of volunteers. He proceeded to run Fiume in an increasingly spectacular, even outrageous, fashion for over a year; and the government in Rome dared not dislodge him until December 1920.

D'Annunzio's coup in Fiume was only one sign of government weakness in the face of a widespread political crisis. In the Chamber of Deputies, two mass parties, the socialists and the new Catholic Party, deprived the older political groups of a majority, but no firm coalition emerged, and there were five different governments between 1919 and 1921. The old politicians, of whom the most prominent and experienced was Giolitti, seemed unable to manage the new situation. In northern Italy there was a series of strikes, culminating in the occupation of factories in Milan and Turin in August–September 1920. It is far from clear how serious these strikes were; but the impression was given that the government was unable to cope with industrial disorder, just as it was unable to cope with d'Annunzio in Fiume.

It was these circumstances that presented Mussolini with an opportunity. Born in 1883, the son of a blacksmith, Mussolini made his early political career as a militant socialist journalist, with a strong line in anti-militarism. He went to Switzerland in 1904 to avoid call-up for the army (though he later completed his military service); and he agitated against the Tripoli War of 1911–12. He became a leading figure in Italian socialism, but in 1914 he broke with his anti-militarist past, and threw himself instead into the movement for Italian intervention in the First World War, in which he served as a soldier from 1915 to 1917. When the war was over, he founded the fascist movement at a hall in Milan on 23 March 1919. He had pursued an erratic career, showing a strong taste for violence, boundless ambition, and a marked talent for journalism and propaganda; but he had yet to achieve any solid success.

The crisis of the parliamentary regime thus came opportunely for Mussolini and his so far hesitant fascist movement. D'Annunzio had aroused the militant nationalists, but his adventure in Fiume petered out, leaving his followers ready to turn elsewhere. Industrialists, property-owners, and the middle classes generally were alarmed by strikes and fear of revolution, and looked for more drastic preventive action than that being taken by the government. The opening was there. Mussolini moved to exploit it. He dropped the left-wing and republican aspects of the fascist programme. The fascists showed their strength by beating up socialists and burning their headquarters, and by marching through the streets wearing black shirts and singing 'Giovinezza', the song of youth which had become popular in Fiume. Mussolini's ploy was to combine violence and displays of strength with a legal approach, using the constitutional organs of parliament, Cabinet, and the monarchy. After a prolonged period of political confusion during 1921 and most of the next year, a turning point was reached at the end of October 1922. During the night of 27/28 October, the fascist militia mobilized and seized control of several provincial towns. The government responded by proclaiming martial law and preparing to use the army to defend Rome and restore order elsewhere. The King, Victor Emmanuel III, then changed his mind and drew back from the use of force. The Prime Minister resigned, and his successor, Salandra, offered to take Mussolini into his Cabinet. He refused, and Salandra advised the King to call on Mussolini himself to form a government. Mussolini took office on 29 October, and on the 30th the Blackshirts entered the capital – the so-called 'March on Rome', though most travelled by train.

Superficially, therefore, all was done in due constitutional form. Mussolini formed his administration at the King's request; the new Cabinet included representatives of various Liberal groups and of the Catholic Party; and Mussolini presented his new government to the Chamber and Senate, and was voted full powers to make financial and administrative reforms, with only the socialists and communists voting against. The 'March on Rome' took place after Mussolini had become Prime Minister. But despite all this, it remained true that the atmosphere of violence and the danger of a rebellion played a crucial part in the events of 28–29 October. When Mussolini asked for parliament's co-operation, he held out the scarcely veiled threat of his Blackshirt squads if he did not receive it. Mussolini came to power through a mixture of force and constitutionality. He liked to boast about the force, but he also made full use of his proper constitutional position. He was a fascist leader, but also the Prime Minister in a parliamentary monarchical state.

FASCIST DOCTRINES AND INSTITUTIONS

What was this fascism which came to power in Italy in 1922, and how did it develop? It was only one (though one of the earliest) of a number of European dictatorships which appeared in the 1920s and 1930s. At the end of the First World War the victory of the democratic and parliamentary powers, and a widespread desire to impress President

Wilson (which was not wholly unconnected with hopes of American largesse) resulted in the creation of a number of new republics on ostentatiously democratic lines in central and eastern Europe, to add to the democratic states which already existed in the west and in Scandinavia. In the following years the swing away from this position was rapid and far-reaching. A list of European countries adopting various kinds of dictatorial forms of government in the 1920s and 1930s comprised the following. (The list is arbitrary, and not everyone will agree with its contents or shorthand descriptions. Some would regard Russia as the only true democracy; or Portugal as an outright fascist state. But at the very least none of these states was a parliamentary democracy.)

Russia	(1917: Dictatorship of Lenin and the Communist Party)
Hungary	(1919: Bela Kun, communist; replaced 1920 by Admiral Horthy, conservative, claiming to be Regent for the Habsburgs)
Italy	(1922–25: Mussolini, fascist)
Turkey	(1923: Mustapha Kemal, secularizing and modernizing)
Spain	(1923: Primo de Rivera, conservative)
Poland	(1926: Marshal Pilsudski, military and conservative)
Yugoslavia	(1929: King Alexander I, monarchical-conservative)
Rumania	(1930–31: King Carol, monarchical-conservative)
Portugal	(1932: Salazar, conservative with some fascist trappings)
Germany	(1933: Hitler, national socialist)
Greece	(1936: Metaxas, conservative with some fascist trappings)

This amounts to eleven states in all. What reason was there to distinguish fascist Italy from the ruck of authoritarian states which emerged in the 1920s?

Many thought there was very little reason. British conservatives, for example, tended to regard Mussolini as a man who had saved Italy from revolution, established order, and encouraged a degree of prosperity. Lord Rothermere, Winston Churchill, and *The Times* all thought of him, in their different ways, as a sensible, dependable, and perhaps even a distinguished figure. While Austen Chamberlain was Foreign Secretary between November 1924 and 1929, he met Mussolini five times. These men did not think his methods suitable for Britain; but compared to the intrigues and instability of earlier Italian politics his regime seemed sound enough for his own country, with no indication that it was particularly evil or dangerous for the rest of Europe. Others who took a much less favourable view of Mussolini and his regime still did not take him unduly seriously. The French socialist politician, Joseph Paul-Boncour (later to be Foreign Minister) called Mussolini in 1925 'César de Carnaval': a mock-up Caesar – a label which has stuck.

There has been a strong tendency to represent Mussolini and Italian fascism as lacking in consistency, depth, and seriousness. In this view Mussolini was a shrewd political operator, with, in his early career, an instinctive sense for an opportunity, and a journalist's flair for publicity and propaganda. He was full of contradictions: socialist and anti-socialist at different times; once an anti-militarist and then an almost lyrical champion of war; an anti-Catholic who reconciled the Italian state with the Vatican. He was unstable in purpose, and often more concerned with appearance than reality. He was brutal, and cultivated an image of ruthlessness, but his violence was unsystematic and on nothing like the scale of that practised by Hitler and Stalin. The crime most often held against him was the murder of a single man, the socialist politician, Matteotti, in 1924, rather than the mass slaughter perpetrated by Hitler and Stalin. His secret police, the OVRA, was less efficient and less cruel than the Gestapo or the NKVD.

Mussolini thus appears as a man who was wilful rather than resolute, a dictator whose tyranny was tempered by inefficiency and vacillation. Fascism is presented as mainly a matter of display and propaganda. Its doctrine is seen as incoherent and full of contradictions, scarcely worth taking seriously, and serving mainly to obscure the compromises with the monarchy, the generals, the Church, and the industrialists, by which the regime survived.

In such an interpretation, fascism ceases to have serious characteristics of its own, and becomes an emanation of Mussolini's unstable personality, with the addition of some spectacular conjuring tricks. But against this should be put the picture which the regime tried to project of itself, which was to a considerable degree shared by some of its most determined opponents, and which deserves serious consideration. In this picture, fascism had important characteristics which separated it from other authoritarian regimes of the day. The role of Mussolini remains crucial – it is scarcely possible to conceive of Italian fascism without him – but this does not mean that everything can be reduced to the impact of one man's personality. Let us examine the main characteristics of fascist doctrine: the cult of dynamism and its totalitarian claims.

Dynamism was a word much in vogue among fascists, who claimed to embody youth, energy, action, violence, revolution. This was particularly important in Italy, where there was little point in a new movement claiming to represent conservatism or tradition, because the Catholic Church, the House of Savoy, and the ancient cities and provinces already played that role with more conviction than any upstart was likely to muster. Fascism made novel claims. When Mussolini presented his first government to the Chamber of Deputies in November 1922, he asserted that he stood for the revolution of the Blackshirts. Fascism proclaimed the primacy of action, the ability to cut through discussion with a command or a blow. D'Annunzio wrote in his *Letter to the Dalmatians* (January 1919): 'Of what value are the secrets of laborious treaties – expedients bred from weakened faith and untimely fear – compared to an upright heroic will?' Ten years before, in 1909, the Manifesto of Futurism, which contributed much to fascist ideas and sentiments, opened with the words: 'We want to sing the love of danger, the habit of energy and rashness'; and went on to assert that 'Beauty exists only in struggle. There is no masterpiece that has not an aggressive character . . . . We want to glorify war – the only cure for the world. . . .' Mussolini, in his article on 'The doctrine of fascism' in the *Enciclopedia Italiana* (1932) wrote that up to 1919 'My doctrine . . . had been a doctrine of action.' Before the March on Rome there had been discussions, 'but – and this is more sacred and important – there were deaths'. 'Above all', he wrote,

> Fascism believes neither in the possibility nor in the utility of perpetual peace. It thus repudiates the doctrine of Pacifism – born of a renunciation of the struggle and an act of cowardice in the face of sacrifice. War alone brings up to their highest tension all human energies and puts the stamp of nobility upon the peoples who have the courage to meet it. All other trials are substitutes, which never really put a man in front of himself in the alternative of life and death.[1]

Words are cheap; but sometimes men mean what they say. D'Annunzio followed words with action at Fiume. The author of the Futurist Manifesto, the poet Filippo Marinetti, volunteered for military service in the Second World War, when he was over sixty. There is evidence that Mussolini seriously intended to harden the Italian people in the fires of war. Adrian Lyttleton has summed up the heart of the matter: 'Fascism, reduced to its essentials, is the ideology of permanent conflict.'[2] Those who chose to ignore this, or to dismiss it as mere braggadocio, did so at their peril.

The totalitarian claims of fascism arose from its conception of the state. Mussolini wrote that 'The keystone of Fascist doctrine is the conception of the State, of its essence, of its task, of its ends. For Fascism the State is an absolute before which individuals and groups are relative.' Giovanni Gentile, one of the regime's most prominent philosophers, defined the point more sharply: ' . . . for the Fascist, everything is in the State, and nothing human or spiritual exists, much less has value, outside the State. In this sense Fascism is totalitarian, and the Fascist State, the synthesis and unity of all values, interprets, develops and gives strength to the whole life of the people.'[3] Totalitarianism meant that the state claimed to control the totality of life, and all aspects of the activities of its citizens. Individuals, families, organized groups of all kinds (including the Church) must be subordinated to the state; and Gentile opposed the Lateran agreements of 1929 with the Vatican because they fell short of this principle.

How far, indeed, such sweeping claims could be made good in Italian conditions was very doubtful; but they were made, and influenced the nature of fascism. Its emphasis was on authority and unity. The *fasces* which were adopted as the Party symbol, and in 1926 became insignia of the state, were taken over from the symbols of authority carried by the Roman *lictors*. Parliamentary democracy was rejected because it meant legitimizing conflict within the state, with political parties as the accepted embodiment of conflicting interests. Socialism, communism, or any sort of Marxist doctrine proclaimed the class struggle, which was equally impermissible in a state aiming at unity. The solution was the corporate state, in which all groups recognized their common interests, whether political or economic, and the institutions of the state were designed to impose unity, not to encourage conflict.

The political institutions of fascist Italy were designed to impose the totalitarian claim and the demand for unity. The parliamentary system was first transformed and then abolished. An electoral law of July 1923 laid down that the majority party in a general election should automatically secure two-thirds of all seats in the Chamber of Deputies; though this provision was not needed in the election of 1924, when fascist candidates won 374 out of 535 seats. A more far-reaching law of 1928 provided that in future elections would be settled by the Fascist Grand Council choosing 400 candidates, who would be put to the voters for election to the 400 seats in a new Chamber. Later still, in January 1939, the Chamber of Deputies was abolished altogether, and replaced by a new Chamber of Fasces and Corporations, made up from members of the Fascist Grand Council and the National Council of Corporations.

This last change emphasized the fascist claim to be evolving a new form of organization, the corporative state, whose ostensible objectives were twofold: to eliminate conflicts of economic interests, notably between employers and workers, by creating a new system of corporations; and then to use the corporative system to replace the old political forms. A law of April 1926 effectively refused state recognition to any but fascist trade unions, and forbade strikes and lockouts. A decree of July 1926 laid down that only twelve 'confederations' would be recognized, six for workers and six for employers in, respectively, industry, agriculture, commerce, sea and air transport, land and inland water transport, banking and insurance. (A thirteenth was added for the liberal and artistic professions.) The twelve confederations, grouped two by two, were to form the first six corporations, with heads nominated by the government. A Ministry of Corporations was set up, and recruited an extensive bureaucracy. A Labour Charter of 1927 declared that work was a social duty, and that all production formed a single whole from the point of view of the state. In 1934 a fresh law on corporations was promulgated; and the number of corporations was increased to twenty-two.

Much of this system remained on paper rather than being translated into practice. Notably, government control was tight over the workers' side of the corporations, but was largely evaded by the employers' side. However, for some time in the early 1930s the system attracted much interest within Italy (where it attracted the left-wing, anti-capitalist elements within fascism), and also in other countries.

While this formal structure of the new state was being set up, the rougher work of crushing opposition to the regime went ahead. Mussolini allowed indiviuals from other parties to remain in his government for a year or two – from the Catholic Party until 1923, Liberals until 1924. In 1924 the murder of Matteotti after a speech in the Chamber attacking fascist electoral malpractices signified that open opposition would be ruthlessly suppressed; and opposition deputies decided to take no further part in the work of the Chamber until the rule of law was re-established – the so-called 'Aventine Secession'. Anti-fascist newspapers were closed down or taken over; political parties opposed to the regime were dissolved; freedom of movement for individuals was curtailed by the cancellation of all passports; and severe penalties were imposed on opponents of fascism who succeeded in going abroad to continue their resistance. One of the most significant moves was also one of the earliest. In December 1922, at the first meeting of the Fascist Grand Council, the Voluntary Militia for National Safety was set up, incorporating the Blackshirt squads into a permanent organization, whose members were paid by the state but owed allegiance only to Mussolini – a political armed force separate from the regular army. Those who, like the old Liberal statesman, Giolitti, had hoped to make use of the fascists and draw them into the parliamentary system found that they were dealing with a political force of a different kind; and when they tried to oppose it (as Giolitti did when at the age of eighty-six he spoke and voted against the electoral law of 1928) it was too late.

In outward appearance, Italy was provided with much of the structure of a totalitarian state. The Fascist Party dispensed patronage and became the way to advancement. Children from the age of eight onwards were compulsorily enrolled in fascist organizations, increasingly military in form as the child grew older. Education, and particularly the teaching of history, was directed towards the propagation of fascism and a fascist view of the past. A Fascist Institute of Culture published books and organized cultural life. Even leisure was supposed to be organized by the state. Yet behind this façade the system was not fully totalitarian, and the state did not control the totality of life. The monarchy remained a focus of loyalty and authority separate from the Party. The law of December 1925 which laid down that the head of the government was not responsible to parliament retained the power of the King to dismiss him – a provision which, to Mussolini's surprise, was invoked in 1943. The army was allowed considerable freedom in its internal affairs and promotions. The Italian Confederation of Industry struck a bargain with the regime rather than being subjected to it. Above all, the Church retained its independent position. The Lateran Treaty of February 1929 gave many advantages to the regime through its recognition by the Vatican; but it also accepted that the Church was a separate, and to some degree a privileged, body within the state – for example, it ran its own youth movement, Catholic Action, and Catholic newspapers were the only legal source of news not controlled by the Fascist Party.

These were important limitations to Mussolini's power; and the regime ran by means of a series of compromises with what were essentially conservative elements. This meant that the dynamism of the fascist movement tended to get lost in domestic affairs, and was redirected outside Italy, into attempts to promote international fascism and into an adventurous foreign policy. If various groups were left alone in important respects, the price they paid was to let Mussolini have his own way in questions of foreign affairs and war. Notably, the army accepted, however reluctantly, Mussolini's decisions as to when and where it should fight. Fascist dynamism was real; and if it could not find expression in a totalitarian revolution at home, its energies were released abroad.

FASCISM AND FOREIGN POLICY

For opponents of fascism in the 1930s it became a truism that fascism meant war. It was a view which received much support from what fascists themselves wrote and said. Mussolini asserted the nobility of war, and its necessity as the final test of character. In a more down-to-earth way, Starace (secretary of the Fascist Party in the 1930s) used to say that war was 'like eating a plate of macaroni' – a simple, straightforward pleasure.[4] Mussolini's public statements were peppered with remarks about an air force which would blot out the sun, or an army of 8 million bayonets. The whole style of the regime was one of belligerence, bullying, and swagger, which at some stage, was likely to find an outlet in foreign war. The Abyssinian War (1935–36), intervention in the Spanish Civil War (1936–39), the invasion of Albania (1939), and the attacks on France and Greece (1940) owed much to this motive, as well as to other calculations.

These are generalizations. How far did fascist ideas affect particular foreign policy decisions? On one point there is no doubt: foreign affairs was the aspect of policy in which the fascist regime came nearest to having complete control. The professional officials and diplomats of the Foreign Ministry, even when they were not replaced by fascist nominees, exercised little influence; and the General Staff raised no serious opposition even to moves of which it disapproved. Foreign policy was that of the fascist regime; and by the 1930s that usually meant Mussolini himself.

The early years of Mussolini's foreign policy were not spectacular; nor did foreign affairs at that time hold the centre of his attention. Mussolini took the post of Foreign Minister (as well as Prime Minister and Minister of the Interior) in 1922; and among his first acts was attendance at international conferences at Lausanne and London. In 1926 the Permanent Under-Secretary at the Foreign Ministry, Contarini, resigned; pressure was put on officials to join the Fascist Party; and members of the fascist militia were forced upon Italian embassies, despite their lack of experience, qualifications, or even good manners. But apart from such changes in personnel, continuity appeared to be the order of the day. Mussolini wanted to emphasize that Italy was a great European power; but so did his predecessors. He shared a widespread dislike of the Versailles settlement, and wanted to change it, notably at the expense of Yugoslavia. He re-established Italian authority in Libya, which had been allowed to slide during the First World War; but Libya had been conquered by the Liberal regime, which would certainly have done the same thing when it could. Only the bombardment and occupation of the Greek island of Corfu in 1923, to force Greece to make apology and reparation for the killing of an Italian member of a boundary commission on Greek soil (by unknown assailants) stood out as an exceptional and brutal act, perhaps the forerunner of a policy of action and violence. Even that was in part a failure: Mussolini wanted to maintain the Italian occupation of the island, but Britain insisted on withdrawal. As for doctrine, fascism was declared not to be for export; though this was not strictly adhered to, with the creation of a press office to promote fascism abroad, and much activity to win support among Italians living in other countries. For the most part, Mussolini chose to cut the figure of a respectable European statesman, with the frock coat as much in evidence as the uniform.

A change began in the early 1930s, when the regime was firmly established at home (the tenth anniversary of Mussolini's coming to power was a landmark); and also when some fascists began to feel that the movement was losing its dynamism and settling into middle age. Fascism had begun by making a cult of youth – fine-sounding, but in the nature of things a fading asset unless perpetually renewed. Between 1930 and 1934 there was an attempt to restore the appeal to youth, and to revive the dynamism of fascism by extending it outside Italy. A number of prominent individuals lent their influence to this attempt: Guiseppe Bottai; Mussolini's younger brother Arnaldo, the editor of the newspaper *Popolo d'Italia*; and Asvero Gravelli, who in 1932 published a book entitled *Toward the Fascist International*. Galeazzo Ciano, Mussolini's son-in-law and the coming man of the regime, also gave his support. The only specific result was the holding of an International Fascist Congress at Montreux in December 1934, at which parties from fifteen countries (but not Germany) were represented. The Congress showed more diversity than unity and the Permanent Committee which was set up to continue its work met only twice, in January and April 1935; after which Ciano cut off Italian government support.

It was a feeble and short-lived attempt to create a Fascist International; but various links with foreign Fascist Parties survived it. Considerable sums of money went to the *Heimwehr* in Austria, the Rexists in Belgium, and the British Union of Fascists. In France, support was given to Déat, Marquet, and their group of dissident socialists who moved rapidly towards fascism, and to the *Francistes*; and in Spain to José Antonio Primo de Rivera, son of the former dictator and head of the Falange. It pleased Mussolini to appear as the leader of European fascism; and there was political advantage in having a prop for Italian policy in Austria, or a means of launching agitation in France.

The practical effect of these activities was limited; but the psychological influence was considerable. International fascism was seen to exist, in both open and covert forms. It was confronted by anti-fascism, in the shape of Italian exiles, notably in Paris and Spain, posing a nagging problem of which Mussolini was always aware. A conflict existed which crossed frontiers and set groups in various countries against their own governments – the outline sketch of an ideological war. It remained to be seen whether the outline would be filled in.

Between 1935 and 1939 there were more substantial steps in Italian foreign policy which appeared to show fascist dynamism at work: the invasion of Abyssinia (Ethiopia), intervention in the Spanish Civil War, and the making of the Rome–Berlin Axis. What was the role of fascism in these events?

The Abyssinian War was in many ways a nineteenth-century colonial campaign waged out of due time. Mussolini's main motive appears to have been political and personal – a demonstration of Italian power to the glory of the regime, which would revenge the defeat inflicted on the old Italy at the battle of Adowa in 1896. He added to this some wildly optimistic economic speculation about raw materials and prospects for emigration; and talk of a native army to help conquer the Sudan. How much of this was fascist? By this time, it was impossible to distinguish. The expedition might well have been contemplated by another kind of Italian government; but without Mussolini's particular brand of drive and self-confidence it is unlikely that it would have been launched. Italian prestige and the prestige of the Duce had become one and the same. Victory was a triumph for the regime; and League of Nations sanctions, imposed by 'fifty nations led by one' (Britain), became the occasion for a marked rallying of support for the war even among opponents of the regime. The war was a personal triumph for Mussolini: he pressed reluctant generals into it; replaced the first unsuccessful commander; and kept his nerve when international opposition proved more extensive than he expected. A success for Mussolini was a success for fascism. The regime imposed on the conquered areas of Abyssinia was ostentatiously fascist, with the imposition of symbols like the fascist salute, and the more substantive refusal to adopt methods of indirect rule through local chiefs.

Much of this success proved ill-founded and short-lived. The areas beyond the main towns and roads were never pacified, and the Italian Army lived as a garrison in a hostile population. The use of mustard gas and evidence of atrocities reinforced external opposition to Italy and to fascism. The cost of the war was high, and the burden of occupation heavy. But the immediate effects of victory were exhilarating. Mussolini had succeeded where the old Italy had failed. He had defeated not only the Abyssinians but the League of Nations. He abandoned his former cautious approach to foreign affairs, and looked for new worlds to conquer.

There followed, almost as soon as the Abyssinian campaign ended, Italian intervention in the Spanish Civil War. This was accident, not design. Despite an agreement with Spanish monarchists in March 1934, there appear to have been no Italian contacts with the officers who launched the revolt of July 1936; and two requests for assistance were turned down before it was decided to provide help, in the shape of twelve bombers, to be paid for in cash before delivery. The hard-headed ring of these terms indicated an important strand in Italian motivation. The most authoritative survey of the subject concludes that 'Italian intervention in Spain was motivated largely by traditional foreign policy considerations relating to Italy's political and military position in Europe and the Mediterranean, particularly her relations with France.'[5] A secret agreement secured with Franco's government on 28 November 1936 provided for refusal of permission to a third power (i.e. France) to use Spanish bases, or to pass troops across Spanish territory; and for benevolent neutrality in case of war with a third power, or the imposition of international sanctions. Equally, there was little sign of Italian interest in the internal politics of the nationalist side of Spain. The most important Italian decision, dictated by a combination of chance and geography, was to aid Franco rather than other military leaders; which meant support for a reactionary rather than a fascist Spain. The Italians did nothing to promote the Falange, the most genuinely fascist movement in Spain; and merely stood by in 1937 when Franco absorbed the Falange with other political parties and brought it under his own control.

This was not to say that fascism went for nothing in Italian intervention in Spain. Mussolini often presented intervention as being ideological in character. In Majorca, the Italian forces were led by the dashing figure of Bonaccorsi ('Conte Rossi'), one of the early fascist squad leaders and a spectacular figure, who led his men on horseback and drove a fast sports car round the roads of the island. He supported the Falange, and carried out large-scale killings, variously estimated at between 1,750 and 3,000. His activities were ostentatiously fascist – unorthodox, flamboyant, brutal; and the tales about them lost nothing in the telling. Anti-fascist sources often put the number of Italians in Majorca at 12,000 or 15,000, when the actual figure was 1,200.[6] The impact of this episode on outside opinion was greater than that of the cautious Italian policy on the mainland, which by its nature went unobserved.

The motives of Italian intervention were also linked to fascism. Fear that a left-wing government (perhaps even revolution) in Spain would stimulate opposition to fascism in Italy was a serious consideration; and anti-fascist exiles made precisely the same calculation in reverse, hoping that victory for the republic in Spain would be a blow to Mussolini in Italy. Moreover, once intervention had begun, in support of what was expected to be a rapid *coup d'état* or a military promenade, not a three year's war, Mussolini's own prestige and that of fascism were engaged. This was particularly the case after the Battle of Guadalajara (March 1937), where Italian troops, including three divisions of Blackshirts, suffered a defeat. This had to be avenged, and fascist prestige restored. When, in 1937–38, the British tried to secure the withdrawal of Italian troops from Spain, they were wasting their time. The fascist regime could not accept defeat or compromise, and had to see the war through. Péguy's maxim, 'Tout commence en mystique, et tout finit en politique', was reversed: what started with politics was caught up in the mystique of fascism.

Before the Spanish Civil War was over, Mussolini addressed the Fascist Grand Council (30 November 1938) on the subject of what he called the 'immediate goals of Fascist dynamism'. These were Albania, Tunisia, Corsica, French territory east of the River Var (to include Nice, but not Savoy), and the Ticino canton of Switzerland.[7] External expansion was by this time the principal remaining object of fascist dynamism. The aims set out by Mussolini were part of a wide-ranging view of Italy's position in the Mediterranean, which he had held for several years, and which he expressed with increasing frequency and emphasis in 1939 and 1940: that Italy was a prisoner in the Mediterranean, shut in between Gibraltar and Suez, with Corsica, Tunis, Malta, and Cyprus as bars of the prison. In a document of February 1939 he declared that the aim of Italian policy was to break the bars of the prison, and then march either to the Indian Ocean through the Sudan and Abyssinia, or to the Atlantic by way of French North Africa. In either case, Britain and France were the enemies; and in a conflict with them, Germany would cover Italy's rear in Europe.

This calculation leads to what appeared at the time to be the crowning influence of fascism on Italian foreign policy: the alliance with nazi

Germany, the obvious ideological partner. Mussolini referred to the Rome–Berlin Axis ('around which can revolve all those European states with a will to collaboration and peace') on 1 November 1936.[8] The relations between the two countries became closer, until they became formal allies in the so-called Pact of Steel, signed in Berlin on 22 May 1939 – in the seventeenth year of the fascist era, as was recorded at the end of the text.[9]

How far did this alliance arise from the ideology of fascism and its affinities with nazism? The two regimes had much in common, in the leadership principle (Duce and Fuehrer both mean 'leader') anti-communism, and hostility to parliamentary democracy. Hitler made a favourable reference to fascist Italy (though not to Mussolini personally) in *Mein Kampf*. In 1931–32, Hitler asked several times to see Mussolini, though without success; and as Chancellor he sent the Duce flattering messages. There was the making of an ideological personal alliance. Yet this was not altogether how events worked out. The first meeting between Mussolini and Hitler at Venice in June 1934 was only a partial success: Mussolini described Hitler as a buffoon, and as a gramophone with only seven tunes. But he changed his own tune by the time of his first visit to Germany in September 1937: Hitler set out to flatter and impress, and Mussolini returned intoxicated. (It was after this visit that he determined to introduce the goose-step into the Italian Army, calling it the *passo romano*.) Thereafter he never escaped from Hitler's influence – he reacted against it from time to time, as he increasingly had to take second place, but he was always drawn back by personal contact.

On the other hand, there were ideological differences, notably on the question of race and anti-Semitism. Fascist journals in the early 1930s attacked the racial theories of nazi Germany. The Italians, after all, were obviously not a Nordic race. On one occasion an article in the *Popolo d'Italia*, unsigned but obviously by Mussolini himself, poked heavy fun at such ideas, arguing that the Lapps, because they lived further north than other peoples, must be the purest of all races. Jews were admitted to the Fascist Party, and over 8,000 were members in 1933. In 1926 Mussolini received Chaim Weizmann, the Zionist leader, and expressed sympathy for his cause; and in April 1933 the Italian press gave much publicity to an interview between the Duce and the Chief Rabbi of Rome, who came to draw attention to the persecution of his co-religionists in Germany. After the reconciliation with the Papacy, the pagan elements in nazi Germany were also unwelcome to the regime, as well as to Catholic Italians.

This hostility was serious. Admiration for nazi Germany was not widespread among Italian fascists – Farinacci was one exception, as was Ciano, who later changed his mind; and anti-Semitism was rare. (The census of 1938 showed only 47,000 Jews in Italy, so there was in any case little to be anti-Semitic about.) When Mussolini took up the racial issue it marked a breach with a section of his party, and with Italian opinion as a whole. In July 1938 he published a manifesto on race, declaring that there was a pure Italian race, a branch of the Aryan race, and that the Jews were separate from it. This was followed by legislation against foreign Jews; naturalizations since 1919 were annulled, and those who were thus made aliens had to leave the country. The Italian Jews were excluded from the teaching profession, from academic, cultural, and scientific associations, and from the civil service, banks, and insurance firms. Their right to hold property or control businesses was tightly restricted. Jewish children were excluded from ordinary elementary schools, and had to attend special schools with Jewish teachers. In practice, there were many exceptions allowed, both openly (e.g. for the families of Jewish soldiers killed in the Italian Army, 1915–18, or for adherents to fascism before the March on Rome) and secretly, by the turning of a blind eye. The policy was not popular. There were protests from the Vatican and the Italian bishops; and it seems to have marked a turning of opinion against the regime – not so much on grounds of principle about anti-Semitism, but because it was rightly seen as a symbol of subservience to Germany. Mussolini chose to demonstrate his unity with Germany by adopting the cardinal point of nazi ideology.

Thus ideology was called in at a late date to consolidate an alliance which began with political and economic matters: German support for Italy during the Abyssinian conflict; the supply of German coal, on which Italy became increasingly dependent; and co-operation in the Spanish Civil War. Above all, the objectives which Mussolini set for his foreign policy – amounting to Italian domination in the Mediterranean – could only be attained in opposition to France and Britain, and therefore only in alliance with Germany. This alliance was consolidated by the developing personal relationship between the two dictators; assisted by the similarity in style and approach of the two regimes; and hindered by the lack of a serious racial and anti-Semitic element in Italian fascism, until Mussolini, for the sake of the alliance, decided to make good this lack.

How should the influence of fascism on Italian foreign policy, and on the movement of Europe towards war, be assessed? This question is complicated by another, to which neither contemporaries nor historians have agreed on an answer: how far did Mussolini follow a consistent foreign policy with defined objectives, and how far were his activities a matter of improvisation, uncertainty, posturing, and propaganda – more a means of raising the blood pressure than of pursuing an aim.[10] In both pictures, fascism plays a part. In the first picture, the part is of fundamental importance: the fascist regime developed existing Italian policies in the Mediterranean and Africa to such an extent that they could only be achieved by a major war against Britain and France, not just by minor wars against small states. It was to this that 'fascist dynamism' in foreign affairs led; and Mussolini's use of these words on 30 November 1938 was not accidental. In the second interpretation, fascism is of lesser significance, and more a matter of display and rhetoric than of stern reality.

If there had to be a straightforward choice between these two interpretations, the balance of probability lies with the first. It has been too easy to turn Mussolini into a figure of fun, a 'sawdust Caesar'. Of course there were improvisations and changes of mind. But the concern to extend Italian territory and influence in the Adriatic and eastern Mediterranean (Yugoslavia, Albania, Greece); to consolidate and increase the African empire (Libya, Abyssinia, with the Sudan in view for later); and to transform the Mediterranean from an Italian prison into an Italian sea, with access to the oceans – all this appears with too great a regularity to be disregarded. When the German alliance and German successes in Europe provided the opportunity in 1939 and 1940, it was towards these objectives that Mussolini moved. Compared with earlier Italian governments, Mussolini both inflated the objectives and changed the methods of Italian policy. Others before him tried to make Italy a great power, with a position in the Mediterranean and Africa; but it was a position to be shared with the other Mediterranean powers, Britain and France, and to be achieved by clever diplomacy, shifting alliances, and small wars against the Turks and Africans. Mussolini repeatedly declared that his policy must be honest; he despised the shifts of diplomacy; and he would not allow Ciano to ease him out of the Axis and resume freedom of action during the phoney war. And the end result of his policy, if it was pursued to its conclusion, was a military show-down with France and Britain.

Italian foreign policy under fascism passed through two main phases. The first, up to 1934–35, was a period of modest activity, in which Italy acted for the most part as a normal and responsible state. In 1925 she was a guarantor of the Locarno agreements, and in April 1935 she was still a welcome partner of Britain and France at the Stresa conference, devoted to maintaining the status quo in Europe. During this period, the rest of Europe became accustomed to the presence of a fascist regime, and found that in most practical matters it made little difference. Even Stalin remarked in 1934 that the existence of the fascist regime had not prevented the establishment of good Italian–Soviet relations.

The second period was very different. From 1935 to 1940, Italy followed a policy of almost ceaseless activity and aggression – the invasion of Abyssinia, intervention in Spain, the occupation of Albania, the declaration of war on France and Britain, and the attack on Greece. Some of these actions – notably Abyssinia, Albania, and the extension of war to the Mediterranean in 1940, had serious and far-reaching consequences, so that the influence of Italy on European affairs was disproportionate to her material strength. In this active, forward policy, fascist objectives played an important part. Mussolini and his enemies both proclaimed that fascism meant war. It certainly brought European war nearer.

REFERENCES AND NOTES

1. Mussolini's speech in the Chamber quoted in Ivone Kirkpatrick, *Mussolini* (London 1964) pp. 196–7. The quotations from d'Annunzio, 'The Manifesto of Futurism', and Mussolini's 'Doctrine of Fascism', from Adrian Lyttleton (ed.), *Italian Fascisms, from Pareto to Gentile* (London 1973), pp. 182, 211–13, 44, 46–7.
2. Lyttleton, *Italian Fascisms*, Introduction, p. 12.
3. Quotations from ibid., pp. 53, 42.
4. Denis Mack Smith, *Mussolini's Roman Empire* (London: Peregrine Books 1979), pp. 124–5.
5. John F. Coverdale, *Italian Intervention in the Spanish Civil War* (Princeton 1975), pp. 388–9.
6. Coverdale, *Italian Intervention*, pp. 127–50, for a description and the various figures.
7. MacGregor Knox, *Mussolini Unleashed, 1939–1941* (Cambridge 1982), pp. 38–9.
8. Kirkpatrick, *Mussolini*, p. 328.
9. Text of the treaty in Mario Toscano, *The Origins of the Pact of Steel* (Baltimore 1967), Appendix, pp. 405–8.
10. Denis Mack Smith's approach in *Mussolini's Roman Empire* and his biography, *Mussolini* (London 1981), stresses the elements of improvisation, the wish to dazzle, and propaganda. MacGregor Knox, *Mussolini Unleashed, 1939–1941* is a careful statement of the opposite point of view.

Chapter 6

GERMAN NAZISM

There has always been a strong and natural tendency to conflate Italian fascism and German nazism under the general label of 'fascism'. The partners in the Rome–Berlin Axis proclaimed their unity. They displayed very similar outward appearances, in their uniforms, marching columns, and propaganda. At a deeper level too they had a good deal in common, especially in what they were against: communism, liberalism, capitalism; and to a lesser extent in what they were for: the vague but potent 'leadership principle'. For many of their friends, and even more of their enemies, the identity between the two movements appeared obvious. In a study of the origins of the war they form a natural pair. They were dynamic forces, glorifying violence and war, and breaking the mould of the European order of 1919. Italian fascism was first in the field; German nazism had greater power at its disposal. Coming together in an alliance, they provided the impulse which drove Europe towards war – thus contemporaries declared, and many have continued to believe.

In all this there is much truth; and yet it is a mistake to compound the two phenomena under the one name 'fascism'. Their sources were different, with nazism deeply rooted in the racial theories and social Darwinism of the nineteenth century, while fascism was more recent in its origins and unconcerned with race. In the long run too their fruits were different, as was shown in their dealings with that other powerful organization with far-reaching claims, the Catholic Church. Italian fascism came to terms with the Church and coexisted with it; but nazism was deeply anti-Catholic, and its totalitarian claims were pressed to the point of fundamental conflict. With nazism one is dealing with a phenomenon more profound and far-reaching, as well as infinitely more brutal, than Italian fascism.

ORIGINS AND NATURE OF NAZISM

There is no agreement about the origins of national socialism in

Germany. Some (mostly non-Germans) have found its roots in almost the whole of German history, stretching back through the militarism and aggressive drive of Kaiser Wilhelm's Germany, Bismarck's slogan of blood and iron, the tradition of Brandenburg-Prussia, where the army was the core of the state, Luther and his anti-Semitism, to the Teutonic Knights and their struggle against the Slavs, and even to the Germanic tribes who fought with ferocity and success against the Romans. All have been pressed into service to explain nazism and the Third Reich; and it is fair to add that nazism itself laid claim to the inheritance of most of them. It is also possible to see nazism as part of a wider movement, whose roots were European rather than specifically German, notably the reaction against industrialization and the anonymity of the production line and the great city; the crisis of confidence and identity brought about by the First World War; and the disintegrating effects of inflation in the 1920s and depression in the early 1930s. Nazism gave an individual a place in a hierarchy, an identity as one of a group; restored confidence after defeat; and promised (more, delivered) economic recovery and a stable currency. In all these ways it provided a German solution to a European problem, in a way which was attractive to many outside Germany.

Whatever stand is taken in this debate, there can be no doubt that in Germany the response to the twentieth-century crisis was greatly reinforced by the appeal to tradition and history. Nazism was able to appear both revolutionary and traditional. The ideas of a national form of socialism, appealing to national unity against the Marxist doctrine of class struggle, and of a revolutionary dynamism under a charismatic leader, were grafted on to ideas of racial superiority, territorial expansion, and martial spirit which went far back into the German past. The graft was not wholly successful; the different parts were not completely absorbed into one another; but still the result was a stronger and more tenacious growth than could have been the case with something which was solely contemporary or only traditional.

It was through an alliance between the revolutionary and the conservative that Hitler and the nazis came into power in Germany. It is true that the original programme of the National Socialist German Workers' Party (*Nationalsozialistische Deutsche Arbeiterpartei*, NSDAP), adopted in 1920, was socially radical; it demanded action against big industries and department stores, the expropriation of land needed for national purposes, the abolition of unearned income and ground rents. It is true too that the Nazi Party made progress at the end of the 1920s at the expense of its rivals on the right, the German National Party; and that Hitler fought the Presidential elections of 1932 in opposition to Field Marshal Hindenburg, the embodiment of conservative values. But despite this, Hitler knew after the failure of his Munich *putsch* in 1923 that he must come to power legally, with the consent of the existing authorities, and above all of the army. This he did. In the Reichstag elections of July 1932, the Nazi Party polled 13.74 million votes, and won 230 seats – not a majority in the country or the Reichstag, but a victory which made it the largest single party. They lost ground in the elections of the following November, which they themselves provoked, dropping 2 million votes and winning 196 seats (though in a smaller Chamber).[1] But they were still the largest single party; and nazis and communists between them held a majority in the Reichstag. Finally, it was by negotiation with the conservative Catholic cavalryman, Franz von Papen, and the nationalist industrialist and newspaper-owner, Alfred Hugenberg, that Hitler became Chancellor on 30 January 1933.

In the Cabinet, Hitler was one of only three nazi ministers. Papen was Vice-Chancellor, and Hindenburg was still President. The conservatives were confident that they could control Hitler. As one of Papen's friends remarked, 'We have him framed in' – which Gordon Craig rightly thought 'should be included in any anthology of famous last words'.[2] The conservatives thought they were using Hitler; in fact he was using them. But he still needed them, as he recognized in the splendidly staged ceremony in the Potsdam Garrison Church on 21 March 1933, when the high officers of the old imperial regime, including the former Crown Prince, gathered to mark the opening of the new Reichstag, and to see Hindenburg give his blessing to the new Chancellor amid all the panoply of the old regime.

The striking visual images of the Potsdam ceremony, caught in photographs and newsreel films, stressed the juxtaposition of the old and the new. The black, white, and red colours of the old German Empire hung alongside the swastika banners of the new Nazi Party; while the army and the SA (*Sturm Abteilung* – the nazi storm-troopers) formed the guard of honour together. Here were the symbols of a dramatic change: the emergence of a new élite, taking its place alongside the existing élites of Germany – predominantly military as represented at Potsdam, but extending to all those who played influential roles in the political, administrative, legal, economic, and cultural life of the country. For some time, the old and the new coexisted; but in the next few years the new élite effectively displaced the old, sometimes by the most dramatic means – only fifteen months after the ceremony at Potsdam, General von Schleicher, a former Chancellor of Germany, was murdered in his own home by nazi gunmen. On 2 August 1934, the officers and men of the German army took an oath of unconditional obedience to the Fuehrer, Adolf Hitler. By 1938 the army high command and the Foreign Ministry, formerly the preserves of the old aristocracy and ruling groups, were brought under nazi control. Other long-standing centres of influence – universities, the legal profession, the organizations of German industrialists – raised no opposition.

Among the new men, the one who was nearest to the old pattern was Hermann Goering, whose father was a Prussian officer and Governor of German South West Africa, and who was himself an air force officer of distinction in the First World War. The others were, from any previous point of view, outsiders. Hitler himself was the most obvious case. In the days of the German Empire, Hitler rose to the rank of corporal. (It is said that Hindenburg referred to him as 'the Bohemian corporal', in the belief that he came from Braunau in Bohemia rather than Braunau-am-Inn in Austria.)[3] In the new, fluid, and uncertain Germany of the 1920s and early 1930s Hitler, who to conservatives was 'neither a gentleman nor a German',[4] became Chancellor and drew with him a whole new élite whose main characteristics were comparative youth and personal instability. In 1934, the average age of Nazi Party members was seven years lower than that of the population as a whole; and the average age of its leaders was eight years lower than that of non-nazi élite groups. Those who held leading positions in the Party tended to marry late; few had had regular jobs except in the Party; of those who went to university, few completed their courses.[5] The drop-outs and the misfits had come to power, with no traditions, no restraints, no code of conduct except that learned in the struggle for power and fighting in the streets. Hitler's closest circle, made up of those who were with him before 1933, and often before 1923, were referred to as 'old fighters'. They owed their rise to the Party and its leader. There is every sign that most of them believed in its causes; but even if they did not there was no future for them outside it. With success there came an influx of new men, some genuine fanatics (Heydrich was a late-comer to the Party), others opportunists and carpet-baggers, moving in to seek advantage in the new regime. But the old core – Goering, Himmler, Hess, Goebbels, Frick – remained.

The new élite exercised power without institutional restraints. Existing constitutional procedures were suspended rather than abolished, and no new constitution was created to replace that of Weimar. The so-called enabling law of 23 March 1933, passed in the Reichstag by 441 votes to 94 in circumstances of heavy nazi pressure, gave the government power to impose laws without the Reichstag, and to depart from the constitution. (Technically, these dispensations were for four years.) All political parties other than the Nazi Party were suppressed. All trade unions were absorbed into the Nazi Labour Front. Other opposition was crushed by drastic methods. Ernst Roehm, head of the SA and leader of a radical faction within the Nazi Party, was murdered along with many of his associates (and others who had little or nothing to do with him) in the Night of the Long Knives, 30 June 1934. Already the camps existed to which enemies of the regime were despatched. Hitler remarked in *Mein Kampf* that authority was founded on popularity, force, and tradition; when all three were combined, it was unshakeable. Hitler and his movement were short on tradition (though he tried to make up by the ceremony at Potsdam and appeals to the Germanic past); but for much of the time strong on popularity and very strong on force.[6]

This did not mean that the state was monolithic and firmly structured. Various entities within the state retained some cohesion and freedom of action: the Party, the SS, the army officer corps, heavy industry, the chemical industry. Individuals set up their own bases of power and patronage. Ribbentrop first created his own private Foreign Service, and then when he became Foreign Minister tried to restore the position of the official Service which he had previously undermined. Goering accumulated offices like a demented Pooh-Bah – he was ruler of Prussia, commander of the *Luftwaffe* (1935), head of the Four-Year Plan (1936), and designated as Hitler's successor. He tried in 1938 to secure control of the army, but Hitler prevented it – such a concentration of authority would have been too great. Groups and individuals were engaged in ceaseless, though usually concealed, struggles – the *Luftwaffe* against the army, chemical industry against steel industry, Himmler against the army high command. This played into the hands of Hitler, as the only man at the top who could resolve disputes. In that way it worked to the advantage of his personal dictatorship, but at the expense of long-term efficiency. The nazi system was extremely good at doing certain things – it revived the economy, built aeroplanes, cars, and roads, and generated a tremendous drive. But the government of a modern state, and even more the preparation of a state for war, demands effective administration and the setting of priorities in the use of resources. Despite its real achievements, and its terrifying reputation for ruthless efficiency, Hitler's Germany failed to devise a regular system for setting priorities and was subject to damaging administrative rivalries. To change this would have meant changing the very nature of the state, which was impossible.

In the 1930s, the new Germany was best described as a 'dual state', in which elements of the old and new ruling groups coexisted side by side, sometimes co-operating, sometimes in conflict.[7] In matters of foreign and military policy, however, it was Hitler and the new élite who called the tune. Whenever the men of the old order – usually the generals, sometimes the diplomats – counselled caution, or tried to obstruct Hitler's moves, they were brushed aside, and sometimes removed from office. The new élite brought new methods, and they brought success. What did they want to do?

HITLER AND NAZI DOCTRINE

German nazism was identified with Hitler. At the end of his biography, Alan Bullock concluded that 'the evidence seems to me to leave no doubt that no other man played a role in the Nazi revolution or in the history of the Third Reich remotely comparable with that of Adolf Hitler'.[8] His success was certainly remarkable. In 1939 he had taken Germany in six years from being a country with millions of unemployed, disarmed and subject to restrictions by various international treaties, supervised by powerful neighbours, to being the dominant military power in Europe, with the treaties torn up and the economy thriving. As one of his opponents remarked, 'It is not an achievement anyone can belittle.'[9]

The scale of this achievement often seemed out of key with his personality and intellect. Despite his immense powers of oratory and his ability to hold a mass audience in thrall, one of his German biographers has written that 'he coined not a single memorable phrase'.[10] His one published book, *Mein Kampf*, is commonly dismissed as confused and absurd. He is sometimes depicted as a madman, perhaps in a technical sense a psychopath, an abnormal personality, given to abnormal concepts and reactions. Lord Halifax, on the other hand, in his aristocratic way, claimed to have mistaken Hitler for a footman.

The danger of all such comments is that of underrating the man. A nonentity or a psychopath cut adrift from reality could scarcely have done what Hitler did. It is more realistic to agree with John Lukacs: 'The mind of Adolf Hitler was a very powerful instrument. To deduce from his awesome defects of the heart that he was wanting insight or intelligence is the commonest mistake most people make about him. Nor was he mad.'[11] George Orwell, unfashionable as always, wrote a review of a translation of *Mein Kampf* in March 1940, arguing that it was too easy to say that Hitler succeeded because he was backed by industrialists – 'They would not have backed him . . . if he had not talked a great movement into existence already.' It was necessary to accept the attractive power of Hitler's outlook: 'he has grasped the falsity of the hedonistic attitude to life. . . . Hitler, because in his own joyless mind he feels it with exceptional strength, knows that human beings *don't* only want comfort, safety, short working-hours, hygiene, birth-control and, in general, commonsense; they also, at least intermittently, want struggle and self-sacrifice, not to mention drums, flags and loyalty-parades.'[12]

In Hitler's lifetime it was safer to take him seriously than to underestimate him; and those who failed to do so paid the price. It is better not to fall into that trap, but rather to see what Hitler had to say.

It is possible to take Hitler's thought entirely seriously, and yet to see in it only a kind of nihilism. This was the belief of one of the most striking contemporary commentators on Hitler's ideas, Hermann Rauschning. Rauschning was a conservative German nationalist, a landowner from near Danzig, who joined the Nazi Party in 1931, became Burgomaster of Danzig in 1933–34, and then broke with

Hitler, tried to oppose him, and went into exile. His books, *Germany's Revolution of Destruction* and *Hitler Speaks*[13] made a lucid and passionate attempt to persuade his readers that Hitler and the nazis were the revolutionaries they proclaimed themselves to be; and that the error of both their accomplices and their victims was to fail to take them at their word. But their revolution had no programme and no fixed aims. Rauschning writes that he asked Hitler in 1934 what was the aim of the revolutionary will. Hitler replied: 'It has no fixed aim. Do you find that difficult to understand? . . . We are a movement . . . Nothing could express our nature better.' Rauschning comments: 'The movement has no fixed aims, either economic or political, either in home or foreign affairs.' Its only policy was action: 'National Socialism is action pure and simple, dynamics *in vacuo*, revolution at a variable tempo, ready to be changed at any moment.' It was 'the St Vitus's dance of the twentieth century', well symbolized in the nazi habit of marching. 'Marching kills thought. Marching makes an end of individuality. . . . The nation is marching aimlessly, just for the sake of marching.'[14]

The only aim behind all this was power, both for its own sake and to keep up the dynamism and the movement. 'The aim of National Socialism is the complete revolutionizing of the technique of government, and complete dominance over the country by the leaders of the movement.' This might lead anywhere – German revolution, world revolution, or eternal war. Rauschning believed that the dynamism of nazism was bound to turn outwards, but wherever it turned it must make a *tabula rasa*: 'National Socialism is at issue with every independent activity or ordering of life. . . . Whatever it cannot dominate it must destroy.'[15]

In this process, doctrine provided not an aim but an instrument. 'The doctrine is meant for the masses. It is *not* a part of the real motive forces of the revolution. It is an instrument for the control of the masses. The elite, the leaders, stand above the doctrine. They make use of it in furtherance of their purposes.'[16] Rauschning thought this applied to anti-Semitism, the function of which was to unsettle the nation and to destroy the existing categories of thought and morality; though he accepted that for Hitler it was more – 'it is also part of his mental make-up. To him the Jew represents the very principle of evil.' To most nazi leaders, however, racialism was 'Adolf's bunkum'. And Rauschning presents Hitler as telling him: 'I know perfectly well . . . that in the scientific sense there is no such thing as race.' But just as Rauschning, who was a cattle-breeder, could not get his breeding right without the concept of race, so he, Hitler, needed a concept which would enable the existing order and its historic bases to be abolished and a new order imposed. France had carried the revolution of 1789 beyond her boundaries with the concept of the nation. 'With the concept of race National Socialism will carry its revolution abroad and recast the world.'[17]

This interpretation denied nazism a programme and it demoted doctrine to the status of a means rather than an end; though it was sufficiently terrifying in itself, and carried with it the assumption of expansion and foreign war. It has been confronted, in the years since 1939, with variations on a completely different theme: that Hitler took his doctrine seriously, and that his writings contained what has been variously described as a programme, a world outlook, or a world picture.[18]

As so often, Churchill set the pattern in the immediate post-war years. He wrote of Hitler's *Mein Kampf:*

> When eventually he [Hitler] came to power there was no book which deserved more careful study from the rulers, political and military, of the Allied Powers. All was there – the programme of German resurrection; the technique of party propaganda; the plan for combating Marxism; the concept of a National-Socialist State; the rightful position of Germany at the summit of the world. Here was the new Koran of faith and war: turgid, verbose, shapeless, but pregnant with its message.[19]

It was frequently said that if only British and French statesmen had read *Mein Kampf* they would have known what Hitler was going to do, and would not have been bamboozled by his professions of moderation in the 1930s. There was little substance in these lamentations and accusations. Western statesmen had *Mein Kampf* summarized for them and the salient elements drawn out by thoroughly competent ambassadors like Sir Horace Rumbold and André François-Poncet. The problem was not to know what Hitler had written, but to know what to make of it.

This has remained the crucial question: what is to be made of Hitler's writings? Some forty years after the start of the war, German historians went back to Hitler's books and their background, and concluded that their substance was of real importance. Werner Maser noted the many defects of *Mein Kampf* as an account of Hitler's early life, but argued that in its pronouncements on politics and race the book was an authentic reflection of Hitler's mind and a guide to what he intended to do. On occasion, he took an almost fundamentalist view: '*Mein Kampf* in fact sets out a clear and detailed programme of the fearful catastrophe which Hitler loosed upon Germany and the world by faithfully following the declarations and forecasts in his book.'[20] Eberhard Jaeckel, in a closely reasoned book on *Hitler's Weltanschauung*, concluded that, even if Hitler did not have in the fullest sense a 'world outlook', he had at least a 'world picture', with a 'systematic and inherent coherence'.[21] He draws attention to Hitler's remark in *Mein Kampf* that 'The enormous difference between the tasks of the theoretician and the politician is also the reason why a union of both in one person is almost never found.' Politics is the art of the possible, but the theoretician must demand the impossible and be content with the fame of posterity. 'In long periods of humanity, it may happen once that the politician is wedded to the theoretician.' Jaeckel observes, surely with justice, that Hitler believed he was such a man.[22]

It may be argued that such considerations should be discounted on the ground that after he became Chancellor in 1933 Hitler showed signs of finding *Mein Kampf* something of an embarrassment. He told Hans Frank in 1938 that if he had known he was going to become Chancellor he would not have written *Mein Kampf*. In 1940 he refused to allow pages from the original typescript of the book to be exhibited during that year's Nuremberg rally. But actions speak louder than words. In 1934 the Prussian Ministry of Education ordered that extracts from *Mein Kampf* should be included in all school-books dealing with racial questions, genetics, or demographic policy. In 1936 the Ministry of the Interior recommended that a copy of *Mein Kampf* should be given to every couple married in a registry office in Germany, or a consulate abroad. In 1939 the Nazi Party stated it was the Party's duty to ensure that every German family should one day possess a copy of 'the Fuehrer's fundamental work'. In 1940 a special rice-paper edition was published for issue to the troops.[23] If *Mein Kampf* had become an embarrassment, these were strange measures; what they in fact indicate is the official standing of the work with the nazi regime.

What are the main outlines of the world picture which may be discerned in Hitler's writings? They may be summed up as anti-Semitism, race, living-space, and the idea of life as perpetual struggle; all of which overlapped and merged with one another.

In a letter of September 1919, and in Hitler's earliest fully reported speech in August 1920, he referred to the need for a rational anti-Semitism, and to the ultimate aim of the elimination of the Jews – which at that stage was left vague, but appeared to mean emigration or the deportation of Jews from Germany. In *Mein Kampf*, anti-Semitism was one of the main centres of attention, and the tone of the discussion was fierce and radical. 'There is no making pacts with Jews; there can only be the hard: either–or.'[24] The *Protocols of the Elders of Zion* (forged documents purporting to reveal a Jewish conspiracy to control the world) were treated as genuine. 'Elimination' began to have a ring of physical extinction about it. The *Secret Book*, which was mostly about foreign policy, ended with a few pages, largely repeated from *Mein Kampf*, about the Jews: the ultimate aim of the Jew was 'the denationalisation, the promiscuous bastardisation of other peoples . . . . The end of the Jewish world struggle . . . will always be a bloody Bolshevisation.'[25] On 30 January 1939 Hitler prophesied that if international Jewry forced the nations into war, the result would be the annihilation of the Jewish race in Europe; a prophecy to which he returned with a strange insistence four times in the course of 1940. On this matter at least Rauschning was mistaken: events proved that anti-Semitism was an end, not just a means. Nazi policy developed from a phase of harassment of the Jews, through deportation and concentration, to the phase of the final solution. From 1942 onwards Jews (along with Slavs and other peoples) were being transported across Europe in tens of thousands in order to be massacred, at a time when by any normal calculation Germany needed all its rolling stock for the war effort, could have used the SS guards from the camps on the battlefield, and might have exploited the victims as forced labour. But against all rational calculations, the extermination went on.

Anti-Semitism was an aspect of the racial theories which were prominent in Hitler's thought. His reflections on race in *Mein Kampf* (notably in Ch. 11) asserted the position of the Aryan race as the founders and transmitters of culture. The Aryan race itself was left undefined; but Hitler claimed it was his mission to preserve certainly the German people, and probably others linked to them, from degeneration. His principal idea of the state was as a means of preserving the race. The opposite to the Aryan, the lowest race, without true culture, merely parasitic, was the Jew – and so we are back to anti-Semitism. But the Slav too was an enemy. Among the cloudy verbiage of much of Hitler's writing, it is startling to encounter a brief, precise assertion in the *Secret Book*:

> The folkish state . . . must under no conditions annex Poles with the intention of wanting to make Germans out of them some day. On the contrary it must muster the determination either to seal off these alien radical elements, so that the blood of its own people will not be corrupted again, or it must without further ado remove them and hand over the vacated territory to its own national comrades.[26]

This is very much what happened in Poland after September 1939. German policies and actions towards both Slavs and Jews during the war bear the mark of Hitler's racial theories.

The preservation of the race was closely bound up with the idea of living space (*Lebensraum*). This is a repeated – not to say repetitious – theme in *Mein Kampf*, the *Secret Book*, and various of Hitler's private talks after he came to power. In *Mein Kampf*, in the course of a critique of German foreign policy before 1914, Hitler argued that the basis of foreign policy must be the question of feeding a growing population. He discussed various options for dealing with this problem, rejecting out of hand the restriction of births, and dismissing the possibility of 'internal colonization' and increasing the productivity of agriculture as inadequate. There remained only two choices: to secure new soil, and settle the superfluous millions on it ('thus keeping the nation on a self-sustaining basis'); or selling industrial products in foreign markets, and paying for imports from the proceeds. Germany had in fact taken the last course; but Hitler argued that it would be healthier to seek new terrain, noting that 'such a territorial policy cannot be fulfilled in the Cameroons, but today almost exclusively in Europe'. He went on: 'If land was desired in Europe, it could be obtained by and large only at the expense of Russia and this means that the new Reich must again set itself on the march along the road of the Teutonic Knights of old, to obtain by the German sword sod for the German plough and daily bread for the nation.'[27]

Much of what followed was repetition of this theme, with or without variations.

> The foreign policy of the folkish state must safeguard the existence on this planet of the race embodied in the state, by creating a healthy, viable natural relation between the nation's population and growth on the one hand and the quantity and quality of its soil on the other hand. . . . Only an adequately large space on this earth assures a nation of freedom of existence.

Space must be judged not only in relation to the yield of the soil, but also in terms of military and political considerations – 'the German nation can defend its future only as a world power'.[28] In the *Secret Book*: ' . . . the bread which a people requires is conditioned by the living-space at its disposal. A healthy people, at least, will always seek to find the satisfaction of its needs on its own soil. Any other condition is pathological and dangerous.'[29] He went again through the options considered in *Mein Kampf*, with the same conclusion. In an almost lapidary chapter on German aims, Hitler rejected completely a policy of having *no* aims, of deciding nothing and being committed to nothing: ' . . . just as in ordinary life a man with a fixed life-goal that he tries to achieve at all events will always be superior to those who live aimlessly, exactly likewise is it in the life of nations'. To be aimless in general was to be planless in particulars, and would turn Germany into another Poland, which was for Hitler the nadir. He rejected any attempt to secure the sustenance of the German people by peaceful economic means; and declared that the simple restoration of the German borders of 1914 was an inadequate aim from every point of view. This left only one choice: Germany must adopt 'a clear, far-seeing territorial policy', abandoning the device of world trade and seeking 'sufficient living space for the next hundred years' – which 'can only be in the East'.[30]

It is necessary to subject the reader to some small part of Hitler's constant reiteration of this theme, to convey something of its for-tissimo quality. It must be added that Hitler expounded the same theme in speech after speech between 1928 (when he composed the *Secret Book*) and January 1933 (when he came to power). After that he fell silent in public, but took up the same tale on several important private occasions. When he first addressed military and naval chiefs on 3 February 1933 he asked how political power should be used, once gained. 'That is impossible to say yet. Perhaps fighting for new export possibilities, perhaps – and probably better – the conquest of new living space in the east and its ruthless Germanisation.'[31] At another meeting of the generals, after war had begun, on 23 November 1939, Hitler told them that the eternal problem was to bring German territory in line with its population; they could not commit themselves against the Soviet Union unless they had free hands in the west, and must therefore attack France and England at the earliest opportunity. Between these two occasions, other examples could be quoted.

The idea of struggle as the basis of life may be briefly dealt with. Hitler absorbed the social Darwinism of the late nineteenth century, according to which the ideas of the life and death of species and the survival of the fittest were translated into terms of states and human societies. In the *Secret Book* he wrote: 'If . . . politics is history in the making and history itself the presentation of the struggle of men and nations for self-preservation and continuance, then politics is in truth the execution of a nation's struggle for existence.'[32] He deduced from this the separate roles of foreign and domestic policy: foreign policy was to pursue the struggle for existence by safeguarding the necessary living space; while domestic policy preserved the force for this task, primarily in terms of the race value and numbers of the population. He believed, therefore, that domestic policy was the servant of foreign policy – a restatement in his own way of the long-standing German view of the primacy of foreign policy in affairs of state.

These main lines of Hitler's world picture were primarily set out in terms of general aims for German policy. There was also, in *Mein Kampf* and the *Secret Book*, a good deal about ways and means of achieving the aims, and specifically about the sort of alliance policy which Germany should pursue. Hitler's scheme of things envisaged two enemies: Russia, as the target for living space in the east; and France, partly as the long-standing hereditary enemy, and partly to cover Germany's rear for an attack on Russia. To deal with these enemies, he proposed to seek two allies: Italy and Britain. His references to an alliance with Italy go back to 1920, before there was any question of an ideological link – Italy was not yet fascist, nor is there any sign that Hitler at that stage knew of Mussolini. *Mein Kampf* included a brief favourable reference to fascism; but the main arguments for an alliance were those of power politics. They were most carefully worked out in the *Secret Book*: Italian expansion in the Mediterranean would bring her into conflict with France, and so into a natural alliance with Germany. For this purpose, Hitler was prepared to give up any claims to the South Tyrol (formerly Austrian, and from 1919 in Italy), where he estimated that there were 200,000 Germans: Italian friendship was worth this sacrifice, just as on her part Italy should give up her opposition to the union of Germany and Austria (the *Anschluss*). As for Britain, Hitler was highly critical of pre-1914

German policy, which had failed to choose between an anti-Russian stance, with British support, and an imperial-cum-naval anti-British stance, with Russian support. Germany had finished up antagonizing both Russia and Britain. In future, it would be necessary to choose Britain as an ally against the Soviet Union, and also against France, for Hitler observed that French hegemony on the Continent in the 1920s was displeasing to Britain.

General ideas about the nature of society and of international affairs; a firm statement of German policy aims; and proposals about methods in terms of alliance policy were all to be found in Hitler's writings. To what extent did they affect the course of nazi foreign policy?

NAZISM AND FOREIGN POLICY

A considerable correspondence between what Hitler wrote and what he did (for example, in terms of anti-Semitism and racial theory) has already appeared. But it is not clear how far German foreign policy under Hitler was actually governed by ideology. The same sort of debate on whether Hitler had a doctrine which should be taken seriously, or merely a commitment to action for its own sake, is carried over into the narrower field of foreign policy. There is a strong consensus in support of Jaeckel's contention that the outline picture which emerged from Hitler's writings formed the guide-lines for his policies as actually pursued, though it had to be adapted to fit circumstances. Opportunism within the framework of a seriously (indeed tenaciously) held set of general ideas is a common way of explaining nazi foreign policy. But this remains a consensus between some fairly wide outer limits, even discounting the more extreme fringes. For example, Hans Mommsen has argued that 'Hitler's foreign policy aims, purely dynamic in nature, knew no bounds: [a] reference to "expansion without object" is entirely justified. For this very reason, to interpret their implementation as in any way consistent or logical is highly problematic.'[33] On the other hand, Werner Maser has written that 'One of the decisive causes of the 1945 catastrophe was the fact that Hitler attempted to adhere rigidly to the doctrine which he had expounded in *Mein Kampf*.' Dietrich Bracher states firmly that 'The foreign policy of the Third Reich derived directly from the ideological principles and long-range goals of National Socialism'; this applied particularly to the 'racist and geopolitical national imperialism of *Mein Kampf*, to which 'Hitler clung . . . with almost manic obsessiveness, up to the eerie end in the bunker of his Chancellery'.[34] Klaus Hildebrand has developed an argument which attributes to Hitler a definite foreign policy programme, in three phases: first the conquest of Europe and the Soviet Union, using an alliance with Britain; next, a conflict with the USA – the struggle of Europe against America for world supremacy; and finally, German mastery of the world, to be held through the racial superiority of the German people. Hitler saw the first of these three phases as his own central task, with the rest left to the future; but in the event, with the British failing to behave according to plan, the stage of European conquest ran directly into the second, Atlantic phase; and in the heady days of 1941 even the aim of world supremacy seemed within immediate reach.[35]

The arguments are not of a kind to be resolved by the available evidence; or, in all likelihood, by the accumulation of evidence in the future. They turn on assessments of Hitler's personality (a dark and murky subject), and on views of the role of planning and consistency as against chance and circumstance in human affairs, as well as on the direct evidence on Hitler's thought and actions.

There are a number of problems in the picture of Hitler adhering (with various degrees of opportunism and adaptation) to the main lines set out in his writings. One is the danger of exaggerating Hitler's control of events, even at the height of his power. Within Germany itself there were obstacles to his will, individuals and pressure groups to be squared or side-tracked; and moreover foreign policy was bound to be affected by the actions and attitudes of other states, and could not be wholly dictated by Hitler. The second is that Hitler was undoubtedly much given to presenting arguments which would be suitable to his readers (or hearers) at any given time, and was increasingly concerned to show in retrospect that he had always been consistent and always been right. Moreover, he was not deeply committed to telling the truth as a matter of principle; so it must be a matter of judgement to know when he was to be believed.

There are also lesser problems relating more to ways and means than to objectives. The policy of an alliance with Britain, much emphasized in *Mein Kampf* and the *Secret Book*, was in practice pursued with a good deal less than single-minded determination. Hitler's attitude to Britain was complex and ambivalent, more of a love–hate relationship than the plain calculation set out in his writings. The English (as Hitler usually called them) were Aryans and successful imperialists, and so commanded admiration; on the other hand he sometimes saw them as hate-filled antagonists. In the early years of the nazi regime, the presentation of Britain in German propaganda was mild and cautious – the press was instructed not to call the Labour Party Marxist, or to enquire whether Sir John Simon, the Foreign Secretary, was a Jew. Hitler was delighted with the Anglo-German Naval Treaty of June 1935, a success in relations with Britain which had eluded the Kaiser's government before 1914. Yet later he made little or no attempt to follow up British offers of negotiations. The British invited the

German Foreign Minister, Neurath, to London in June 1937, and were eager for him to come; the Germans prevaricated, and seized on a thin excuse to decline. In February 1938 the British made proposals for a general agreement, though admittedly starting with some vague suggestions about colonies, where the Germans did not wish to start; no attempt was made to pick up these proposals and see what could be made of them. On this issue, Hitler's actions were hard to square with his words. Similar questions are raised by the Nazi–Soviet Pact of August 1939, which went against the whole direction of his thought, and especially that of the *Secret Book*, where Hitler went out of his way to rule out an alliance with the USSR as making no sense in terms either of ideology or expediency. Yet it is in terms of a short-term expedient, designed to be exploited and then discarded, that the pact can be fitted into the general pattern of Hitler's aims: it is only if the agreement was meant to last that it presents real difficulties.

These problems which arise in regarding Hitler's foreign policy as being fundamentally linked with his world picture must be set against the problems, and indeed the dangers, of seeking to separate the two. To deny all significance to ideology in the conduct of nazi foreign policy must imply that policy was determined either by definable material interests, or by impersonal forces which reduce men to mere puppets, or by sheer opportunism. Any such explanations raise more difficulties than they resolve, leaving unexplained the large and important areas of consistency between Hitler's writings, talk, and actions, and in particular those areas where ideology carried the day against the obvious appeal of opportunism and material interest. We are faced with a balance of probabilities rather than with certainty; but the balance lies on the side of the importance of ideology. One of the advantages which Hitler held in his conduct of foreign policy (exactly as he wrote in the *Secret Book*) was that of a man with a purpose, giving him an advantage over those (whether at home or abroad) whose main object was only to turn the next corner. Equally, one of the handicaps of those who dealt with Hitler was their failure to take him seriously in *all* his aspects. They believed that there must be a distinction between ideology and practical politics, between dream and reality. 'Surely he is a man like unto ourselves' – such seems to have been the thought of Chamberlain and Stalin, and others who dealt with Hitler. (It is true that Chamberlain once described Hitler as 'half-mad', but he did not act on that assumption.) They dealt with him therefore, as a realist, a calculator, an opportunist who could wait for the right moment. So he was. The trouble was that he was more. In Rauschning's striking phrase, he was 'a master tactician with a daemon'.[36]

A further question remains. If it is accepted that nazi ideology played a significant part in foreign policy, and gave that policy a recognizable pattern, how far was that pattern different from that of earlier German policy? What did nazism add to the policy already practised by the German Empire up to 1918? There was much in common between the two. Even before its coming to power in 1933, the Nazi Party attracted support from nationalists of the old Empire, members of the Pan-German League, the Navy League, and colonial societies. Hitler is known to have approved of the Treaty of Brest–Litovsk (March 1918), which brought German predominance over the whole of eastern Europe and the Ukraine. The main aspects of Hitler's policy in central and eastern Europe – union with Austria, living space in the east, and colonization of territory by a German agricultural population, the subordination of the Slav peoples – all were under discussion in Germany before and during the First World War. Hitler picked up the ideas and events of his own time to which he was sympathetic; put them into his writings; and pursued them in action. Similarly, his actions attracted the support of conservative German nationalists – it is notable that in 1938 Carl Goerdeler, the conservative mayor of Leipzig and an important figure in the German resistance to Hitler, took it for granted that the Sudeten areas of Czechoslovakia must be incorporated into Germany. The lines of continuity were important; and Hitler owed much of his success to the support which they brought him. But nazism went further. The restoration of the old German Empire, even at its furthest extent, was not enough; and conservative nationalists found that their country was launched on a war of racial conquest with unlimited objectives and almost certain to end in disaster. At different times from 1937 onwards, and with varying degrees of commitment, numbers of German conservatives parted company with the nazi regime; though they failed to check its growing momentum.

THE METHODS AND TACTICS OF NAZI FOREIGN POLICY

'A master tactician with a daemon' wrote Rauschning of Hitler; and he explained the nature of the tactics involved, which were profoundly different from those of orthodox diplomacy, whether of the old-fashioned nineteenth-century kind or the new style of President Wilson and the League of Nations. The nazis applied to foreign affairs the methods of their struggle for power: 'pressure combined with sudden threats, now at one point, and now at another, in an unending activity that tires out opponents'. They aimed their subversive efforts against individual states and against the whole European order – 'the transfer of the modern technique of the coup d'état . . . to foreign affairs'.[37] These techniques were clearly visible in dealings with Austria in February and March 1938, when the Austrian Chancellor

Schuschnigg was summoned to meet Hitler and subjected to a day of bluff and bullying which was unusual for a conference between the heads of ostensibly friendly and independent states; and then the state of Austria was taken over by a combination of external pressure and internal subversion. At the end, no one could say that the Germans had actually invaded Austria; they had been invited in as the result of the disintegration of the state from within.[38]

The new style was marked institutionally by a downgrading of the role of the Foreign Minister. When the nazis came to power, diplomats and officials almost to a man stayed at their posts. To serve the state was their tradition; to provide continuity, perhaps to steady the new regime, was their function. But Hitler had a low opinion of the Foreign Ministry, and while willing to make use of it he was determined not to be dependent on it. He used parallel organizations for some aspects of foreign policy. The *Auslandsorganisation* (abbreviated to AO – Foreign Countries Organization) of the Nazi Party was used to influence German populations in other countries; and in January 1937 this organization was placed within the Foreign Ministry, with its head actually responsible to Hess, not to the Foreign Minister, Neurath. The AO played an important role in relations with Austria, and in dealings with General Franco at the beginning of the Spanish Civil War. Another organization was the *Dienststelle Ribbentrop*, the 'Ribbentrop Office', which Joachim von Ribbentrop created in 1933 when he set himself up as foreign policy adviser for Hitler. He was appointed Ambassador at large in 1935, and pulled off a spectacular success in the Anglo-German Naval Agreement; and then went as Ambassador to London in 1936, whence he reported directly to Hitler rather than fitting into the normal system of the Foreign Ministry. At the same time, and just as significantly, the Foreign Ministry found itself bypassed or disregarded on vital questions – it was informed only belatedly of the decision to announce conscription in March 1935. It was symbolic of the new approach that during the Czechoslovakian crisis of 1938 Hitler calmly considered producing an 'incident' to justify an invasion of Czechoslovakia by having the German Ambassador in Prague assassinated. The plan was not pursued, but it is worth recalling. To be assassinated by one's own government had not previously been a hazard of ambassadorial life; but this was the new style. Not just the Foreign Ministry, but its members, were expendable.

The new style made itself felt in other ways. The most obvious to the public eye was the surge of self-confidence, indeed arrogance, that came with nazi methods and successes.

No one who did not live in Central or Eastern Europe can understand the force of the impressions of Hitler's year [1938]. The Germans were now the master race. From Podolian villages to the avenues of great cities such as Budapest or Trieste or Prague, Germans, whether tourist visitors or their white-stockinged youth, walked or marched with an arrogance and self-confidence that had never been theirs before. They seemed, moreover, as if they were the incarnations of a new world: strong and contemptuous of the old bourgeois civilization of Europe, or what remained of it. They were feared and admired for this. To new generations come of age across Europe . . . National Socialism had become an object of emulation.[39]

This was the new wave, the wave of the future. Behind the wave, and less publicly, there moved another manifestation of nazi methods in foreign policy. When Austria, the Sudetenland, and Czechoslovakia were occupied, the Gestapo and the security police moved in alongside the army to gather in enemies of the state. On the one hand there was the open, flaunting appeal of vigour and success; on the other, the hidden but pervasive influence of fear.

For a long time, the tactics and methods of nazi foreign policy contributed to its success, and enabled it to advance without war. Its potential opponents were baffled by methods far removed from the orthodox forms of European diplomacy. But eventually a revulsion set in, as much against nazi methods as against their objectives, which were still only dimly perceived. By 1939 and 1940 the representatives of old-fashioned, bourgeois Europe had come to the conclusion that Hitler and his nazis simply could not be trusted. There was no point in negotiating with them: the only thing was to fight them and get rid of them. Thus it was, while the aims of national socialism, if seriously meant, were almost bound to bring about a great war at some time, it was its methods which did much to decide when that war came about.

REFERENCES AND NOTES

1. Election results in Alan Bullock, *Hitler: a study in tyranny* (London 1952), pp. 216–17, 230–1.
2. Gordon A. Craig, *Germany 1866–1954* (Oxford 1978), p. 568.
3. Robert Cecil, *Hitler's Decision to Invade Russia* (London 1975), p. 36.
4. Alastair Hamilton, *The Appeal of Fascism* (London 1971), p. 110.
5. The figures and comments on the national socialist élite are taken from K. D. Bracher, *The German Dictatorship* (London: Penguin Books 1973), pp. 342–4.
6. Paraphrased from Eberhard Jaeckel, *Hitler's Weltanschauung* (Middletown, Conn. 1972), pp. 79–80.
7. The phrase is from Klaus Hildebrand, *The Foreign Policy of the Third Reich* (London 1973), p. 75.
8. Bullock, *Hitler*, p. 805.
9. Hermann Rauschning, *Germany's Revolution of Destruction* (London 1939), p. 284.
10. Joachim Fest, *Hitler* (London: Penguin Books 1977), p. 788.
11. John Lukacs, *The Last European War* (London 1977), p. 17.
12. Review of *Mein Kampf* in *New English Weekly*, 21 March 1940, in Sonia

Orwell and Ian Angus (eds.), *Collected Essays, Journalism and Letters of George Orwell*, vol. II (London: Penguin Books 1970), p. 29.

13. *Germany's Revolution of Destruction* was first published in German in Zurich in 1937, and in London, in English translation, in 1939; *Hitler Speaks* was published in London in 1939.

14. Rauschning, *Hitler Speaks*, pp. 186, 249; *Revolution of Destruction*, pp. 22–3, 25, 51–2.

15. Ibid., pp. 20, 93–4.

16. Ibid., p. 20.

17. Ibid., pp. 23–4; Rauschning, *Hitler Speaks*, pp. 229–31.

18. The writings with which we are concerned are *Mein Kampf* ('My Struggle'), originally published in two volumes, 1925 and 1926; the English translation by Ralph Mannheim, introduction by D. C. Watt (London 1974); and *Hitler's Secret Book* (New York 1962), a translation of *Hitler's Zweites Buch* (Stuttgart 1961), a book composed in 1928 but not published in Hitler's own lifetime.

19. W. S. Churchill, *The Second World War*, vol. I (London 1948), p. 43.

20. Werner Maser, *Hitler's Mein Kampf. An analysis* (London 1970); the quotation is from p. 117.

21. Jaeckel, *Hitler's Weltanschauung*, pp. 23–4.

22. Hitler, *Mein Kampf*, pp. 192–3; Jaeckel, *Hitler's Weltanschauung*, pp. 13–15.

23. Maser, *Hitler's Mein Kampf*, pp. 28–9.

24. Hitler, *Mein Kampf*, p. 187.

25. Hitler, *Secret Book*, p. 213.

26. Ibid., pp. 47–8.

27. Hitler, *Mein Kampf*, pp. 120–9.

28. Ibid., pp. 587–8.

29. Hitler, *Secret Book*, pp. 13–14.

30. Ibid., pp. 142–5.

31. Quoted in Jeremy Noakes and Geoffrey Pridham, (eds.), *Documents on Nazism, 1919–1945* (London 1974), p. 509.

32. Hitler, *Secret Book*, p. 7.

33. Hans Mommsen, 'National Socialism: continuity and change', in Walter Laqueur (ed.), *Fascism: a reader's guide* (London: Penguin Books 1979), p. 177.

34. Maser, *Hitler's Mein Kampf*, p. 138; Bracher, *German Dictatorship*, pp. 359–60.

35. Hildebrand, *Foreign Policy of the Third Reich*; the argument is developed through the whole book, but see especially pp. 21–3.

36. Rauschning, *Revolution of Destruction*, p. 194.

37. Ibid., pp. 148–9.

38. For the *Anschluss*, see below, pp. 226–9.

39. Lukacs, *Last European War*, p. 24.

Chapter 7

PARLIAMENTARY DEMOCRACY: FRANCE AND BRITAIN

France and Britain were not the standard-bearers of an ideology in the same way as Italy and Germany. They were pluralist states, and within their frontiers could be found parties representing all points on the political spectrum, from extreme Left to extreme Right, as well as groups representing all kinds of special interests. Yet all this diversity was founded, if not on an ideology, then on a theory and system of political life: parliamentary democracy, along with the liberties associated with it – freedom of speech, of the press, and of association. The system worked differently in the two countries. France under the Third Republic practised a form of parliamentary government, in which the National Assembly, and especially the Chamber of Deputies, was more powerful than the Cabinet. There were many political parties represented in the Chamber; governments rested on unstable combinations between them; and during the 1930s the average life of a ministry was about six months. The British system was Cabinet government, in which in normal circumstances the Cabinet controlled the House of Commons through a disciplined and stable party majority. In the 1930s there were only two major parties, Conservative and Labour, though Liberals of various kinds retained a foothold. From 1931 to 1940 Britain was ruled by a coalition, the National Government, made up of Conservatives, National Labour, and National Liberals. It was a very stable government (though there were changes of Prime Minister on two occasions); and it was dominated by the Conservatives, who provided the vast majority of its parliamentary support.

Despite these differences, the two countries had much in common, which they felt increasingly as parliamentary democracies became a scarce, and apparently endangered, species. They shared many attitudes and assumptions; and it is necessary to ask how far these contributed to a situation in which European war was likely or even probable. The prevalent attitude on foreign policy in both countries was a combination of a widespread revulsion against war, attachment to the League of Nations, and support for disarmament. This outlook made war almost unthinkable; and it did much to explain why France and Britain acquiesced for so long in the advance of German power, to the point where it probably could not be checked *without* war. So, by an unhappy paradox, devotion to peace and international conciliation helped to create the conditions for war. Later, at a point which cannot be precisely dated because the change came at different times for different individuals and groups, these attitudes were reversed. Other assumptions about the values of parliamentary democracy, or socialism, or political morality, began to prevail, and provided what can properly be called an ideological element in the decision to resist the advance of nazism and fascism – even though that advance had previously been accepted and even assisted.

These developments can be seen in both France and Britain, though in different ways and with varying degrees of intensity.

FRANCE

A profound longing for peace, sometimes emerging as pacifism in the strict sense of the total rejection of war or any use of force, exercised a pervasive influence in France during the 1920s and 1930s. It drew its strength from a range of sources, of which the most important was also the simplest: the experience of the First World War. The total of killed for metropolitan France (excluding overseas territories) amounted to approximately 1.3 million; which constituted 10.5 per cent of the active male population when war began: the figure for Britain was 5.1 per cent.[1] The names of those killed were inscribed on war memorials all over France – no village was without its sombre reminder: 'Morts pour la France'. (The socialist administration of Lille, in a symbolic shift from patriotism to the abstractions of pacifist thought, changed the wording, so that the great memorial in the centre of the city read 'Morts pour la Paix' – died for peace.) The impact was greater in France than elsewhere (particularly in Germany) because the casualties struck a population which was already static and ageing. The effect was heightened by the dramatic fall in the number of births during the war, producing a deficit against 'normal' totals of perhaps 1.4 million births. The years 1915–18 were those with the fewest births, and their consequences moved inexorably through French life; small classes in schools, a drop in those entering employment, and a fall in the numbers available for conscription when this generation reached military age.

The figures and the war memorials spoke for themselves. France could not afford another conflict like that of 1914–18. Less obvious but just as profound were the psychological effects. These were felt particularly deeply in the countryside, where the rural population reacted against war in a way unknown before 1914. They resented both the government which had sent their fellow-peasants to the slaughter, and the industrial workers who had escaped too easily from the trenches to the factories. When Daniel Halévy visited central France in 1920, he reported bitterness at the inequality with which the tax on French lives had been imposed: everyone had had a chance of avoiding it, except the peasant. By 1934 he found that these feelings had sharpened:

> The war assuredly counts for much in this sombre mood which has gripped the peasants. They speak little of its tortures but they forget nothing, and there lies at the bottom of their embittered hearts a desire for vengeance. This is one of the schools of hatred in which the young have been taught. 'They will lead you to the slaughter' the father tells his son. 'I let myself be led, I've been through it. Don't you go.'[2]

Revulsion against war was strong among the peasants who had formed the backbone of the sorely tried French infantry; but it was not confined to them. Before 1914 there was already a significant degree of anti-militarism in the French socialist and syndicalist movements, which affected industrial workers. This continued in the 1920s and 1930s, and also took deep root in other organizations, especially those representing primary school teachers – a respected and influential profession. The effects were cumulative and pervasive. French reservists obeyed the mobilization order in 1938 (at the time of the Munich crisis), as they did again in 1939; but it was in a spirit of grim resignation. They would go through with it; but twice in twenty-five years was too much.

This widespread, instinctive reaction against war, born of personal or family experience, was reinforced by an intellectual and literary current. The decade 1919–29 saw a stream of novels and plays which were in effect overwhelmingly anti-war. They followed the success of what remains the most famous of such books, Henri Barbusse's *Le Feu* (translated into English as *Under Fire*). First serialized in weekly parts in a left-wing journal, then published as a book in 1916 and awarded the Prix Goncourt, *Le Feu* sold 230,000 copies by February 1919. It had many followers – over 150 war novels in the 1920s.[3] They were well received, in terms of both reviews and sales; and as early as the winter season of 1919–20 anti-militarist plays drew great applause in Paris theatres. In the late 1920s the number of books fell away, to revive again in the 1930s under the looming shadow of another war, with an emphasis on the theme of desertion or refusal of service, and on the horrific, catastrophic nature of the next war – air bombardment, chemical warfare, the collapse of civilization. There appeared also, in André Malraux's *L'Espoir* (1937), a novel about the Spanish Civil War, a revival of the theme of heroism, a call to arms in a just cause; but that was about another country, and a different kind of war, and it was against the stream.

The main political home of French pacifism was in the Socialist Party. During the First World War the Party had been divided between supporters of the war and advocates of a compromise peace, with a further small group which proclaimed 'revolutionary defeatism', the acceptance of defeat in war to provoke revolution at home. During the 1920s, these past differences of view were submerged beneath a general programme of disarmament and reduction of military service, which sufficed while there was no serious danger of war. During the 1930s traditional pacifism, represented and led by Paul Faure, revived in strength. Humanitarian and optimistic in nature, its supporters believed that peace could be achieved through disarmament, and by negotiation with Hitler. They argued that it depended on France whether German expansion (inevitable in itself) was peaceful or war-like, because if all his claims were rejected, Hitler would *have* to use the only method left to him, which was war. A more extreme form of pacifism found expression in the writings of Félicien Challaye, a socialist philosopher. One of his books, published in 1933, summed up his position in its title: *Pour la paix désarmée, même en face d'Hitler – For disarmed peace, even in face of Hitler.* He argued that foreign occupation was preferable to war; and that the price of war was always greater than that of remaining at peace. These views were adopted by the so-called 'integral pacifist' wing of the Socialist Party, led by Jacques Pivert; they did not form a majority even among socialist militants, but they were active and influential.

Another important influence working in the same direction was the *Syndicat National des Instituteurs* (National Union of Primary Teachers), which in 1937 had about 100,000 members out of the 130,000 primary teachers in France. These teachers played an important role not only in the schools, but as secretaries in town halls throughout France, and above all as respected representatives of socially acceptable attitudes. In the 1880s and 1890s the primary teachers had been deeply patriotic; before 1914 there was some move towards anti-militarism; and after the war the majority moved towards pacifism, for which the union's weekly journal was increasingly used as a vehicle. In August 1936 the union's annual congress approved a resolution demanding the immediate annulment of the war guilt clause of the Treaty of Versailles; unilateral disarmament, including reduction of military service from two years to twelve months or six; and arrangements with other unions for a general strike as soon as mobilization was proclaimed, for whatever reason. On 26 September 1938, at the height of the Czechoslovakian crisis, the secretary-general of the union, along with a representative of the postal workers, drew up an appeal to the country – 'We do not want war', which received 150,000 signatures in three days, and was specifically noted by the Premier, Daladier, before he went to Munich.

It is impossible to assess the precise weight of these different elements in the revulsion against war; but their combined significance was profound, and coloured all French thought and action in the 1930s. Towards the end of the decade, in 1938 and 1939, there came signs of a change: but until then the momentum of the pacifist movement was unchecked.

This movement was linked, though to a markedly less degree in France than in Britain, with the appeal of the League of Nations and disarmament as means for the promotion of peace. The League of Nations was the central feature of Briand's long years as Foreign Minister from 1926 to January 1932. He was a regular attender at Geneva, and a fervent believer in the promotion of peace through League oratory. The speech in which he welcomed the admission of Germany to the League of Nations became famous. 'Away with rifles, machine-guns, and artillery. Make way for conciliation, arbitration, and peace.'[4] It was Briand who took the initiative for the Kellogg–Briand Pact (signed by the USA and France, February 1928) renouncing war as an instrument of national policy; a pact to which practically every country in the world adhered, and which may stand as a symbol of the attempt to attain peace by wishing for it. The Socialist Party also became a firm supporter of the League, after a period of hesitation and division as to how far the League was merely a cover for the great powers and for bourgeois capitalism. As early as 1921 the socialist leader Léon Blum described the League as the embodiment of the civilized world; and his colleague Marcel Sembat called it the only effective means of preventing war.

One of the main objects of the League of Nations was to promote disarmament. The cause of disarmament lay at the heart of French socialist thought and sentiment on international affairs, especially between 1930 and 1934, a period dominated by the Geneva Disarmament Conference. In the four months from November 1930 to February 1931, Blum published thirty-six articles in the socialist daily *Le Populaire*, which he edited, on the subject of disarmament; and he reprinted them, with only minor changes, in a book, *Les Problèmes de la paix* (1931).[5] For Blum, all the problems of the day would be solved by disarmament – security; the revision of the Versailles settlement; and not least economic problems, for disarmament would create confidence, diminish attempts at self-sufficiency, open the way to freer trade, and liberate for constructive purposes funds which were tied up in military budgets. It was the philosopher's stone which would turn base metal into gold. At that stage, Blum was in opposition, and did not have to cope with translating such aspirations into practice. But those who held office also pursued the theme of disarmament, and hoped that it would contribute to the security of France. Edouard Herriot and Joseph Paul-Boncour (at the time Premier and Foreign Minister respectively) prepared in October 1932 a French plan to put to the Disarmament Conference. Presenting this plan to the *Haut*

Comité Militaire, a joint body of politicians and generals, Herriot argued that the defence of a country did not reside solely in soldiers and guns, but in the strength of its position in law. General Weygand, the head of the French Army, replied that it was his duty to defend the frontiers by force, not with words; on which Paul-Boncour commented afterwards – 'Lack of imagination'.[6] Was it lack of imagination on the part of the soldier, or perhaps too much imagination on the part of the politician? Either way, the comment illuminates the strength of the idea of disarmament among French politicians.

This discussion has so far dealt mainly with parties and organizations of the Left; but the revulsion against war was not a left-wing monopoly. In the mid-1930s, rejection of war came also to be the stock-in-trade of much of the French Right. When the German Army moved into the demilitarized zone of the Rhineland on 7 March 1936, the French press and organized opinion, from Left to Right, was unanimous; there must be no war. The communists accused the Right of wanting war; the socialists accused the government of provocation by manning the Maginot Line; but at the same time the Right proclaimed that peace must prevail and denounced the Left for wanting war. Right-wing newspapers claimed that France was being drawn by its pact with the USSR (signed in 1935) into a German–Soviet quarrel. Charles Maurras, leader of the *Action Française* and formerly the embodiment of right-wing patriotism and anti-German sentiment, wrote: 'And above all, no war. We do not want war.'[7] Similarly, during the Czechoslovakian crisis of 1938, opposition to war was found as much on the Right as on the Left. By that time, there was more division of opinion, but it was not along party lines, or along the old Left–Right divide: there were pacifists and advocates of resistance on both Right and Left. In part, this new pacifism of the Right arose from hatred of the Soviet Union and communism, and fear of being drawn into war on the side of the Soviets; which leads to another aspect of French attitudes towards foreign policy: the complications and confusions introduced by ideology.

The central threat to France was recognized to be Germany, the old enemy, from 1933 under new and dangerous management. One simple reflex action to meet such a threat was to build up French armaments and to seek powerful allies. But a policy of armaments was hard to pursue in a country devoted to peace; and the search for allies was hampered at almost every turn by the ideological sympathies and antipathies of Frenchmen. Hardly ever could French politicians (even if they wanted) devise and carry through policies based solely on grounds of power politics and French interests.

France was divided. This was scarcely new: France had been divided since 1789, between the party of movement and the party of order, the Red and the Black, Left and Right. But each generation lived out the conflict in a new form, and that of the 1930s was particularly virulent.

This was partly because political tensions were heightened by economic distress; partly because of the presence of outside powers (fascist Italy, nazi Germany, communist Soviet Union) with which the extremist parties were identified; and partly because of a natural tendency to make political judgements largely in terms of one's enemies – those who saw the main enemy as fascism were drawn towards the communists, while those who were most fiercely anti-communist were drawn to fascism. There was a strong tendency to simplify the issues, and lump all one's enemies together under one label. To the Left, everyone on the Right was a fascist – even if, like Maurras, he remained a reactionary monarchist, though an admirer of Mussolini. To the Right, everyone on the Left was a Bolshevik, even if, like Blum, he had broken with the communists in 1920 and was completely devoted to the parliamentary system.

The extremists on the Right went out of their way to court publicity and demonstrate their strength. The small fascist groups of the mid-1930s were conspicuous and noisy – the *Francistes* wore blue uniforms and went in for ritual and display, and the *Solidarité Française* had bands of street fighters modelled on nazi storm-troopers and fascist *squadristi*. Jacques Doriot's *Parti Populaire Française* (PPF) was much stronger than either; had a big working-class following in Paris, which Doriot brought with him from his years as communist mayor of St Denis; and could claim its own intellectual and writer in Drieu la Rochelle. Colonel de la Rocque's *Croix de Feu*, strong in numbers and with a basis as an ex-servicemen's organization, was not strictly fascist, but certainly on the Right, and conspicuous through its great gatherings and torch-light parades. The strength and potential danger of the Right were dramatically demonstrated in the great riots of 6 February 1934, one of the traumatic 'days' of French history, when the *Croix de Feu, Action Française*, and fascist leagues came near to storming the Chamber of Deputies.

These groups on the far Right of French politics, whether in any strict sense fascist or not, were easily and often correctly identified as sympathetic to foreign powers. Their admiration for Mussolini was unstinted and unalloyed. He showed the power of leadership (so lacking in the shifting combinations of French politics); he imposed order; he crushed the Left. Sometimes, as in the case of the *Francistes*, this approbation was reinforced by the receipt of funds from Italy, but was none the less real for that. The case of Hitler and the nazis was less clear-cut, because the Right was torn between traditional opposition to Germany and admiration for a vigorous, authoritarian, and anti-Bolshevik regime. The *Action Française* newspaper was at first dismayed by Hitler's hostility towards France in his writings, and published some of the more belligerent passages from *Mein Kampf* as a warning to its readers. On the other hand, Gustave Hervé greeted Hitler's rise to the Chancellorship with acclamation, as saving

Germany from the Red tide. In 1937 Alphonse de Chateaubriant visited Hitler and returned full of praise for the Fuehrer's vibrant personality and high ideals, which he proceeded to pour out for the benefit of his readers for some years to come. Favourable French reactions to the nazi regime were cultivated by Ribbentrop's private office and by other German organizations, working through the *Comité France-Allemagne* and a number of ex-servicemen's organizations and pacifist groups. Here, the appeal was not to ideological sympathies, but simply to the memory of war and the need for reconciliation; but the result was still to promote sympathy with nazi Germany.

On the extreme Left, the most formidable group was the Communist Party. The communists (unlike the right-wing groups) contested elections, so their support in the country could be measured. They did badly in the election of 1932, with only ten deputies elected on some 700,000 votes (in the second round). In 1936, on the wave of support generated by the Popular Front and their conversion to a patriotic stance, the communists polled 1.5 million votes and won 72 seats. At the same time there was a massive increase in membership of the Party, from about 28,000 in 1932 to about 330,000 at the end of 1936.[8] The Party appeared the most anti-fascist in the Popular Front; the most committed to the republican cause in Spain; and the most zealous in attacking capitalism. It also had the support of intellectuals (André Gide, André Malraux, Romain Rolland, and others), which was important among some sections of French society.

The communists were therefore prominent. They were also, despite their new-found patriotism, obviously Soviet-controlled and Stalinist. The Popular Front policy itself (the union of all left-wing parties against fascism) had to wait officially for the word from Moscow, and Doriot, who broke away from the Party to form the PPF, was denounced for advocating a Popular Front only two months before it was formally adopted. The adulation of Stalin began in 1934, with a resolution at the Party Congress praising the genial artisan of success, the watchful pilot, the steely Bolshevik, and the world leader of the revolutionary struggle. Thereafter, such an address became obligatory at each Congress. By a process of assimilation the same treatment was given to Maurice Thorez, who took the title of Secretary-General of the Party (Stalin's position in the USSR). He had a ghosted autobiography published (1937), with all errors and deviations from the Party line written out; and was made the object of a similar cult to that of Stalin – though of course the pedestal was lower. At the very time when the Communist Party opened itself to contacts with socialists and radicals in the Popular Front, it congealed completely in its internal structure and discipline. It was not surprising that its opponents described it as a foreign army encamped on French soil, aiming to make France into Stalin's soldier in western Europe; or that this accusation came with particular force from the PPF, led by Doriot, who had been a leader of the Communist Party and knew how it worked.

The extreme parties of Right and Left were bitterly opposed to one another and to the political system which functioned in the no man's land between them. They were also aligned closely with foreign powers, whether Italy, Germany, or the USSR. The effects of these divisions on French foreign policy were extensive and damaging. In May 1935 the French government, represented by the Foreign Minister of the day, Pierre Laval, signed in Moscow a treaty of alliance with the Soviet Union, negotiations for which had been pursued on and off since 1933. Such an alliance was perfectly designed to bring out the complicated divisions of French opinion. The communists supported it, even though at one time they had claimed to oppose the whole idea of alliances and national security. Equally, a group on the Right, represented in the Chamber by Louis Marin and André Tardieu, and in the press by *Le Matin, Le Journal des Débats*, and other papers, opposed it, both on foreign policy grounds (it would push the states of eastern Europe, especially Poland, into Germany's orbit), and on grounds of domestic politics, because it would strengthen the communists in France. Others on the Right, the *Action Française* and the fascist journal *Je suis partout* also opposed the alliance. But this did not mean that there was a simple split between Left and Right. The 'realist' Right, represented among the press by *Le Figaro* and *L'Echo de Paris*, and a majority of right-wing deputies, supported the alliance, on straightforward anti-German grounds and in the belief that it would have little effect on the communists in France. The socialists were divided. Some supported the pact on grounds of French security or of the defence of the Revolution; others opposed it on grounds of revolutionary defeatism and total pacifism. The socialist leader, Léon Blum, hesitated for some time. In 1934 he was still primarily an advocate of the League of Nations, and opposed to any alliance policy; at the end of that year he said in the Chamber that French security could not be assured by pacts or increased military strength. But in April 1935 (after German rearmament was openly proclaimed in March) he declared that the guarantee of peace lay in unity of action between the Western democracies and the USSR, and came down in favour of the pact – with the rather curious rider that it was an 'open' pact, which the Germans could always join if they wished.

These contorted divisions did not prevent one Foreign Minister, Barthou, carrying on negotiations with the USSR in secret, nor another, Laval, from signing the treaty. But they did mean that the alliance received varying degrees of support from different ministries; that it had an uncertain welcome from the Chamber and Senate, where eventually it would have to be ratified; and that its fulfilment was likely to be half-hearted.

The same was true, for different reasons, of an agreement with Italy, which was another possible anti-German move. Paul-Boncour took up the idea of a *rapprochement* with Italy in January 1933, but encountered difficulties. He was the author of the contemptuous phrase, 'César de Carnaval', to describe Mussolini, which made a bad start. In the Chamber the socialists were almost unanimously opposed to Mussolini (Blum had a particular aversion for him, and as late as 1933 regarded him as a greater danger to peace than Hitler). When Italy was mentioned, some socialist usually raised the name of Matteotti, the Italian socialist murdered in 1924. The communists too were consistently hostile to fascist Italy. The Right and Centre favoured an agreement; so that on this issue, unlike that of a Soviet alliance, the division was on straightforward lines. But the moral issues were not simple, as was seen in the reactions to the Franco–Italian agreement of January 1935 by Blum in *Le Populaire* and Georges Bidault in the Catholic *L'Aube*. Blum approved the settlement of disputes, but cried shame to see a French minister as the guest of the murderer of Matteotti. Bidault saw no shame in an agreement with a dictator when peace was at stake; and observed that France had negotiated with Stalin despite the repression in the Soviet Union. The Italian attack on Abyssinia later in 1935, in defiance of the League of Nations, compounded the difficulties by forcing a split in the Right when France was forced to choose between Italy and Britain. The victory of the Popular Front in the French elections of April–May 1936 confirmed the break with Italy; the socialists and communists were consistently hostile to Mussolini, and he to them. Agreements across such an ideological divide were not impossible, as the Nazi–Soviet Pact was to show; but they needed both a very powerful impulse from circumstances, and more freedom to practise *realpolitik* than was available in the French political system.

Repeatedly French governments found that the requirements of power politics, which pointed towards alliances with the USSR or Italy (or both), were impeded by ideological conflicts which crossed the dividing line between foreign and domestic policy. This would have been less important if France had been ruled by strong, stable governments capable of absorbing or overriding ideological conflicts; but this was not the case. Governments were short-lived; the Chamber of Deputies had to be won over to any policy which was to issue in a treaty; and it was only too easy for foreign policy to be paralysed.

Revulsion against war and the results of ideological divisions weakened the French reaction to the growth of German power in the 1930s, and thus helped to promote the conditions in which war might come. But in themselves they would not produce war – indeed they made it unlikely that a French government could commit the country to another great conflict. For that to happen, at least something in these attitudes had to change: revulsion against war had to be in some measure overcome, and internal disunity patched up to a sufficient extent to allow a declaration of war. To see how this came about, it is useful to trace the evolution of French socialist opinion, and particularly the opinion of Léon Blum. Blum was a figure with an appeal and a significance wider than that of the Party which he led. In 1936 he described himself to a German visitor as a Frenchman, a socialist, and a Jew; and he always regarded himself as the heir to Jaurès, the great French socialist assassinated in 1914, who himself combined socialist beliefs with deep love of his country. Blum's evolution towards a reluctant acceptance of the necessity of war had an importance greater than the simply personal.

At the end of the 1920s Blum stood, with most French socialists, for a policy of commitment to the League of Nations and disarmament; the revision of the unjust parts of the Treaty of Versailles; opposition to all alliances. His sentiment of pacifism did not absolutely exclude self-defence or all use of force, but was overwhelmingly against war in almost any circumstances. Of the various elements in this position, disarmament was that with which Blum was most passionately concerned; and in 1930–31 he argued in favour of unilateral disarmament by France (differing in this from the majority of his party, which advocated simultaneous disarmament). In all his thinking, Blum was much influenced by his diagnosis of the causes of war in 1914, among which he gave first place to the arms race and the alliance system. The rise of Hitler did not immediately disturb him. He thought nazism was merely a more virulent form of nationalism, and thought it less dangerous than Italian fascism. When Germany withdrew from the Disarmament Conference in October 1933, he urged that the Conference should continue its work, and reach a disarmament agreement which would leave Germany in isolation. He continued to believe that if other powers were not building up their armaments, Germany would not increase hers.

From 1934, with the final breakdown of the Disarmament Conference, to 1939, the French Socialist Party was divided into two main tendencies. There developed on the one hand a policy of firmness: both fascist and nazi regimes were by their nature expansionist; peaceful coexistence with them was impossible; and France must seek security by means of alliances which would deter the fascist states from going to war. Others held to the older policies: to join no alliances which were provocative; to avoid clashes with Germany and Italy by making concessions; and, for some individuals, to cling to total pacifism, preferring foreign occupation to war. Of these two positions, Blum came gradually to support the first, though hesitantly and with occasional reversals of view. In April 1935 he supported the Franco-Soviet Pact, after long opposition to it. Later in 1935 he supported sanctions against Italy over the invasion of Abyssinia both on grounds of morality and because to stop Italy would set up a barrier against Germany. When Germany occupied the Rhineland, Blum did not advocate immediate armed action by France, but wanted the issue referred to the League, which he speciously claimed was the line of resistance, not acceptance. Up to 1934, Blum always refused to vote for military credits, and in 1935 he voted against the law extending the period of military service from one year to two. But thereafter he began to vote for the military credits; and as Prime Minister he doubled the sums to be spent on a four-year armaments programme.

The year of Czechoslovakia and Munich, 1938, was decisive for Blum. It saw his last hesitations. He argued that what was at stake in the crisis was not just the fate of the Sudeten Germans or of Czechoslovakia, but the fate of Europe and European liberties. He opposed sacrificing Czechoslovakia to Germany, and going back on France's pledged word. At the end of September, with war imminent, he wavered, and took part in the search for a compromise solution. After Munich, he shared in the outburst of relief, and wrote: 'We can get back to work and sleep soundly again. We can enjoy the beauty of the autumn sun.'[9] On 4 October he and his party voted for the Munich agreement. Thereafter, he went back to a position of firmness, from which he did not again depart. His articles in *Le Populaire* in November 1938 argued the necessity of opposing Hitler by means of armaments and alliances; and at the Socialist Congress at Montrouge on 24–25 December he carried by a comfortable margin a resolution that the Party would take part without reserve in the defence of the country against 'any attack which threatened its integrity, sovereignty and independence'.[10] After the German occupation of Prague in March 1939, Blum urged Daladier, the Prime Minister, to reaffirm French obligations to Poland, and to press on with military conversations with the Soviet Union. On 2 September 1939, Blum, along with the Socialist Party, voted for war credits. It was a far cry from his earlier position.

Frenchman, socialist, and Jew: all three identities for which Blum stood were menaced by the rise of nazi Germany. The triple threat forced itself upon him, overcoming the beliefs of the 1920s, and thrusting the full horror of the twentieth century upon a man who was imbued with the optimism of the nineteenth – Blum was already forty-two in 1914, and had been shaped by an earlier age. Not all socialists, not all Frenchmen, and doubtless not even all Jews, followed this agonized pilgrimage. Pacifism was deeply rooted, on the Right as well as on the Left. France was still divided in 1939. But without such a pilgrimage on the part of Blum and many others, there would not have been sufficient resolution to go to war at all.

BRITAIN

For most of the period between the wars, Britain was of smaller importance in European affairs than France. In political, strategic and above all psychological terms, Britain was not a Continental power. In the mind's eye, the narrow waters of the Straits of Dover became a great divide; isolationism was strong; and there was a widespread feeling that never again should Britain send a great army to fight in Europe. Britain suffered much less than France in the First World War – about 750,000 dead (about 950,000 when Dominion and Empire casualties were added); but the impact on a profoundly unmilitary country was still formidable, and there was a strong disinclination to repeat the experience. If that was the price of a Continental commitment, the British would prefer not to pay it.

Despite all this, Britain could not contract out of Europe. She was one of the victors of 1918; one of the makers of the 1919 settlement; a guarantor of the Locarno agreement; and an important element in the European economy. Moreover, several European states, and especially France, regarded British policy in Europe as of crucial importance. For these reasons, British attitudes and sentiments remained important in European affairs; and for a short time in 1939–40 they were decisive.

As with France, we may begin with general attitudes towards international relations, and the atmosphere of the inter-war period. The picture was broadly similar to that in France, but the shades of emphasis were different. Support for the League of Nations came first, followed by pacifism (absolute for a few, and a general revulsion against war for many). The two combined to feed a widespread belief in disarmament as a means of securing peace. All these sentiments crossed party boundaries. They were more firmly established in the Labour and Liberal Parties than among the Conservatives, but even so, few Conservatives cared to damn the League of Nations out of hand, or openly advocate heavy armaments.

Belief in the League of Nations was the nearest thing to an ideology in Britain between the wars. The League of Nations Union, which existed to promote the League's cause in the country, was under royal patronage, which was the sign of being wholly respectable and above party; its committee was drawn from all three parties; and it had just over 400,000 subscribers in 1931.[11] It was allowed, and indeed encouraged, to propagate its views in schools. On one occasion, in the so-called 'Peace Ballot', it organized a widespread canvass of public opinion in which the immense number of 11.5 million people expressed their support for the League. They voted almost unanimously for continued British membership of the League and for general disarmament; nearly as heavily for the abolition of military aircraft and prohibiting the private manufacture of armaments; and for economic sanctions against a country which insisted on attacking another. Military sanctions (the current euphemism for war) were less readily approved of; but 8 millions were still in favour of them, at least in principle.

In terms of party politics, Labour was by the end of the 1920s the most ardent supporter of the League, after (as in France) a period of hesitation as to whether it was not merely a League of victors and of capitalist states, and therefore to be shunned. The League came to be regarded as an important step towards internationalism, and as a safeguard against any return to the alliance system which (it was believed) had led to war in 1914. As late as June 1936, when the Minister for War, Duff Cooper, made a speech in Paris about Franco-British friendship, the leader of the Labour Party, Clement Attlee, complained that the speech made no reference to the Covenant of the League of Nations – Labour was not prepared to accept, in any form, a military alliance with France. The League was also a natural focus for the remnants of the Liberals, embodying as it did, in new guise, the old Gladstonian ideals of mediation, arbitration, and the Concert of Europe.

What of the supposedly hard-headed realists of the Conservative Party? Whole-hearted League enthusiasts were doubtless few in its ranks. Lord Robert Cecil, a highly individual Tory, did as much as any single man to found the League, and he remained devoted to it; but he was not characteristic of his party. Austen Chamberlain, the sober and respected Foreign Secretary of 1924–29, made a point of going to Geneva, but at least in part this was to keep an eye on Cecil. However, Stanley Baldwin, who had a shrewd eye for popularity, thought it best in 1935 to establish a Minister for League of Nations affairs; and Anthony Eden, who took this post, the brightest rising star in the Conservative Party, saw in the League a passport to public favour as well as sound international thinking. The League made much sense in terms of foreign policy, as a place where influence could be exercised and negotiations pursued; it was also reckoned to be an electoral asset which should on no account be thrown away. A Conservative Party official wrote to Baldwin on 1 August 1935 that they might lose the next election if the bulk of the Liberal vote went to Labour; and no political issue was more likely to influence the Liberal vote than 'the question of peace and war and the future of the League of Nations'.[12] Besides which, there was always the possibility that the vision of collective security might actually materialize. In 1935, at the time of the Abyssinian crisis, Neville Chamberlain, who was far from being a Leagueomaniac, agreed that sanctions against Italy should be tried, in the hope that the League might yet be vindicated; and he believed that Britain should give a lead, and not let the issue go by default.

Here lay an important strand of thought – or rather of belief – which was shared across all parties. Beween the wars it was an article of faith in Britain that the country had a special moral role as a leader in world affairs; and that other countries would naturally follow whatever direction the British chose. It was a remnant of the complete self-confidence of the Victorian era; and it remains mildly astonishing that in the Abyssinian crisis the fifty members of the League of Nations did indeed consent to be led by Britain – until, alas, they all fell into the ditch. The British retained as their heritage from the nineteenth century a rather specialized form of moral conscience and a remarkable faith in their own power of leadership. The two together gave a particular quality and tenacity to faith in the League of Nations. As late as April 1938 the deputy editor of *The Times* could write with confidence that 'the British people is more League-minded than any in the world'; and he was probably right.[13]

In strict logic, support for the League was incompatible with absolute pacifism, because the Covenant of the League included the use of military sanctions against an aggressor. Naturally enough, strict logic was often defied, and pacifists usually supported the League, as offering the best chance of general peace. Pacifists in the absolute sense were in any case a small, though active, minority. The largest pacifist group of the 1930s, Canon Dick Sheppard's Peace Pledge Union, began with 50,000 postcards accepting the uncompromising statement: 'We renounce war and never again, directly or indirectly, will we support or sanction another.' The maximum membership of the Union was reached *after* war had begun – 136,000 in April 1940.[14] These were impressive figures; and presumably the activist core was surrounded by a larger number of sympathizers. In a much more general sense, almost the whole population was united in the desire to promote peace and avoid any repetition of the events of 1914–18 and the as yet unfathomable dangers of aerial bombardment. Revulsion against war was as widespread and profound in Britain as in France, and it was nourished by a stream of war (or anti-war) literature by Sassoon, Graves, Blunden, and others.

Disarmament was the link which bound the League and revulsion against war together. 'I give you my word there will be no great armaments', Baldwin told the British electorate in 1935, even when appealing for a mandate for limited rearmament.[15] Disarmament was one of the major principles of Labour foreign policy; and Arthur Henderson ended his political life as Chairman of the Geneva Disarmament Conference of 1932–34. The National government too, despite many accusations to the contrary, pursued the aim of a disarmament agreement throughout the conference, trying repeatedly to reconcile the positions of France and Germany – which in effect meant allowing German armaments to increase while seeking to diminish those of France. When this failed, the government went ahead with a separate Anglo–German Naval Agreement in 1935, and sought persistently for an agreement to restrict air bombardment. Governments, of course, pursued disamament for a variety of reasons, many of them to do with financial economy and political self-interest; but the degree of commitment to disarmament as a means of securing peace should not be underestimated, nor should the force of public opinion which was concentrated on this issue.

The element of confusion imparted by ideology to the conduct of foreign policy was much less in Britain than in France. There were several political conflicts in Britain, and a good deal of bitterness over questions of unemployment and the means test. There was some overheated language. Even Attlee, who is not usually associated with extremism, wrote in 1937 that 'MacDonaldism is . . . in its philosophy essentially Fascist. MacDonald himself uses the same phrases that may be found in the mouths of Hitler and Mussolini.'[16] But even so Britain was much less seriously divided than was France. All the major parties, and almost every member of the House of Commons, continued to accept the rules of the political game. There were, it is true, groups in the country which wanted some completely different political system. There were the communists, supported by numerous and influential fellow-travellers. There was Sir Oswald Mosley and his British Union of Fascists; and a strange assortment of enthusiasts, eccentrics, and extremists who have been neatly summed up as 'fellow-travellers of the Right'.[17] But in 1935 the British electorate was invited to vote for parties led by Mr Baldwin and Mr Attlee – safe, unexciting, middle-of-the-road men; and they did so in their millions. The votes given to the extreme parties were derisory in number. The British reaction to years of economic depression, high unemployment, and a European crisis which produced one authoritarian regime after another, was to return Stanley Baldwin with a comfortable majority. It was not a step along the road to revolution.

During the 1930s British governments had substantial (indeed up to 1935 overwhelming) majorities in the House of Commons, and firm backing in the country. If they knew their course in foreign policy, and cared to press on with it, then short of a political earthquake they could do so. The kind of paralysis induced in French foreign policy by ideological divisions would not occur at Westminster. Yet the political assumptions which underlay British policy, whether we dignify them with the name of ideology or not, still created problems, which were strikingly revealed during the Abyssinian crisis of 1935–36.

When in October 1935 Italy attacked Abyssinia, a fellow-member of the League of Nations, a number of possible courses were open to the British government. The French, with Laval as Prime Minister, wanted to retain Italy as an ally against Germany, and were willing to pay for this alliance by handing over large areas of Abyssinian territory to Mussolini; and the British went some way down this path in preparing the Hoare–Laval agreement of December 1935. If they had been willing to pursue this course with sufficient determination and ruthlessness, it might have produced results. On the other hand, if they wished to oppose Italy, then bold action – to close the Suez Canal, and risk a battle with the Italian fleet and air force – might well have done the trick. The government went part-way down this path by reinforcing the Mediterranean fleet. But both these courses were essentially nineteenth century in character – the cynical diplomacy of imperialism, or the threat of sea power and the mailed fist. Neither fitted with the attitudes of the League, collective security, and the new morality. Moreover, the crisis occurred just after the declaration of the results of the 'Peace Ballot', and just before a general election. Not surprisingly, neither course was followed to its conclusion. The British government went instead for half-hearted League action – economic sanctions against Italy, but excluding oil; with the result that Italy was infuriated but not stopped, and Abyssinia was encouraged but not saved. It was a clear case of British policy being caught between the old attitudes and the new, and falling with a bump between two stools. If the Abyssinian crisis marked a step towards European war (which it surely did), then British attitudes contributed much to its development.

Less dramatically, and indeed much less decisively, political attitudes did something to obscure, or to blunt the edge of, British reactions to nazi Germany. There was first the question of whether there should be any reaction on ideological grounds at all. Geoffrey Dawson, the editor of *The Times*, wrote in a leading article in August 1937:

> The notion that there can be no dealing with National Socialism (or for that matter with Bolshevism) has found no countenance in these columns. . . . The distinction which it has always drawn is between the internal affairs of Germany (which are her own concern) and those national activities – due to some extent to the character of her rulers – which may threaten the peace and security of other countries or strike at the world-wide freedom of religious belief.[18]

This was the traditional attitude of British governments and the Foreign Office – that the internal affairs of other states were their own concern. It appeared the only safe rule: after all, no one wanted German intervention in, say, the affairs of Northern Ireland. The consequence of these lines of argument was that the coming to power of the nazis should not fundamentally affect British policy towards Germany. But there were those who thought otherwise. Attlee said in the Commons on 13 April 1933 that Britain should not countenance 'the yielding to Hitler and force what was denied to Stresemann and reason'.[19] In February 1938 Ernest Bevin, the trade union leader, put the matter bluntly (as was his wont):

> I have never believed from the first day when Hitler came to office but that he intended at the right moment and when he was strong enough, to wage

war in the world. Neither do I believe, with that kind of philosophy, that there is any possibility to arrive at agreements with Hitler or Mussolini.[20]

On the whole, the government held to the first view, which appeared to be practical as well as traditional – after all, there were so many dictatorships in Europe that one could scarcely take issue with them all. But as early as July 1934 Neville Chamberlain wrote of the murder of Dollfuss, the Austrian Chancellor: 'That those beasts should have got him at last . . . makes me hate Nazi-ism, and all its works, with a greater loathing than ever.'[21] Eventually, such feelings were to gain the upper hand, and contributed to a change in policy.

At the time of the German take-over of Austria in March 1938, the reaction of the Labour and Liberal press was muted because Schuschnigg's regime was regarded as fascist, the heir to that which had crushed the Austrian socialists in 1934. Again, according to one's prejudices, Czechoslovakia was either a model democracy or a random collection of nationalities under Czech domination – 'a medley ruled by a minority'.[22] Poland presented more severe problems from an ideological point of view. In 1939 when the British guarantee was given, Poland was a military dictatorship, frequently anti-Semitic, and oppressive in its treatment of national minorities. As the editor of the *Manchester Guardian* had remarked earlier, 'I don't see why, if we trounce the Germans for their abominable behaviour, the Poles should be allowed to get away with it.'[23]

The most serious ideological problems of all arose in connection with the Soviet Union. Conservative opinion was universally hostile to communism, which was the declared enemy of 'bourgeois democracy' and capitalism. Neville Chamberlain's correspondence was sprinkled with phrases which showed the depth of his distaste for the Soviet regime. The Labour Party included many admirers of the Soviet Union, though the leadership would never countenance communist affiliation to the Party. Of course it was possible to argue for a Soviet alliance on grounds which had nothing to do with ideology. Labour and Liberal leaders did so in 1939; so did Churchill, with his long record of anti-Bolshevism; so, in the Cabinet, did Samuel Hoare and others. But the problem was not easy, as a summing up by a very shrewd journalist demonstrates:

> We ought, I think, to be critical about Russia. We need her and it isn't the time for polemics against her. But we must not, in my opinion, refer to her as a democracy – she is more tyrannically governed than even Germany is. The number of people done to death in Germany runs into thousands – in Russia into tens of thousands. Altogether, the terror in Russia is such that persons living even under the Nazi terror could hardly conceive of such a thing. But we cannot afford to be particular about our allies, though we must, I think, always remain particular about our friends.[24]

As in the case of France, the simple calculations of power politics, which pointed towards a Soviet alliance, were obscured by problems arising from ideology and morality. A somewhat abstract discussion on ideology within the Foreign Office in 1938 was brought to a close by Cadogan, the Permanent Under-Secretary, with the comment that discussing whether fascism or communism was more dangerous to Britain was like determining the relative disagreeableness of mumps and measles; but at that moment fascism was more dangerous, 'because it is the more efficient, and makes more and better guns and aeroplanes'.[25] The point was well made; but not everyone took such a brisk, no-nonsense approach to the problem. It was more common for those of conservative views to take the view that if nazis and fascists were opposed to communism, then there was something to be said for them. Hitler's Germany, until it became an obvious danger to British security, possessed the considerable attraction of being a powerful enemy of Bolshevik Russia.

The effect of these ideological issues on the course of British policy was limited. In the general matter of relations with Germany, the policy which became known as 'appeasement' arose from hard considerations of strategic and economic interests, as well as from the soothing climate of opinion represented by the League, pacifism, and disarmament, or from anti-Bolshevik zeal. Among specific questions, Abyssinia and the problem of a Soviet alliance were those which suffered the most from ideological complications; policy towards Austria and Poland was not seriously affected by the character of their governments. However, the effect should not be discounted. Ideological considerations played some part in Britain's acceptance of the growth of German (and to a lesser degree Italian) power which was so marked a characteristic of the 1930s, and which itself paved the way for the coming of war.

Ideology also played some part in the reversal of British policy, and in the decision that the growth of German power must be resisted. A significant part of this development may be traced through changes in the Labour Party's attitude to war. In the 1920s and early 1930s, Labour was profoundly anti-militarist and in the broad sense pacifist. Attlee, who had volunteered for the army in 1914 and had an outstanding war record, said in the House of Commons in 1923, 'Personally, I think the time has come when we ought to do away with all armies and all wars.'[26] In 1926 the Party Conference accepted without demur a resolution in favour of opposition to war 'including the refusal to bear arms, to produce armaments, or to render any material assistance.'[27] From 1931 to 1935 the Party was led by George Lansbury, an absolute pacifist. A change began in 1935, when the Party Conference agreed to support war if necessary in support of League sanctions against Italy. This marked the end of any commitment to complete pacifism, and Lansbury ceased to lead the Party. But for some time this change of view did not emerge as support for British rearmament. Distrust of the government, arising from the Hoare–Laval Pact and its pusillanimity over the Spanish Civil War, was too strong for that. Up to 1936 Labour continued to vote against the Service estimates in Parliament; and in 1937 they shifted only as far as abstaining. Labour opposed the Munich agreement, but did nothing to provide the military means to resist Germany. It was only at the eleventh hour that Labour awoke fully to the realization that the greatest danger lay not in armaments but in Britain's lack of them.

By September 1939, however, the conversion was complete. When Germany attacked Poland, Attlee was convalescing after illness. Arthur Greenwood, acting as leader in his absence, telephoned him. 'Put all pressure you can on the P.M.', said Attlee. 'We've got to fight.' On 2 September that was what Greenwood did. He asked in the Commons how long the government was going to hesitate about going to war; and then went to see Chamberlain in his room to tell him that unless war was decided on by the next day it would be impossible to hold the House in check.[28] In fact, the government was waiting for the French, not hesitating or hankering after appeasement as Greenwood thought; but that does not matter. The point was that the Labour Party, with hardly a dissentient voice, saw its duty as being to force a reluctant government into war. This remarkable development was in large part due to the conviction that Nazi Germany threatened not only British material interests and the balance of power, but the whole way of life in which Labour believed. Instinctive patriotism, which was still powerful in the Labour Party, combined with ideological conviction to make Labour a force for war.

The same was true for the Conservative Party, and across the country as a whole. At bottom, most Conservatives had never abandoned their traditional concern with the balance of power and British security. 'Appeasement' never meant peace at *any* price. When it was ended, and the decision was taken to resist the further growth of German power, it was not only on traditional grounds, but also on grounds of ideology – indeed of conscience. It was notable that *The Times*, which for so long extended the benefit of every doubt to Germany, proclaimed in its leader columns after the German occupation of Prague in March 1939 that Germany no longer sought the protection of a moral case; the expansion of national socialism meant the expansion of 'political tyranny, cruel police methods, and a new kind of paganism'.[29] Chamberlain too saw the issue in moral as well as power-political terms. He was a loyal and upright man, and in March 1939 he felt that he had been double-crossed. Even more, the growth of nazi power now palpably threatened the whole system in which he had spent his life and to which he was devoted – Parliament, the rule of law, the workings of business, the rules of decent behaviour. For many others, who might not see their lives or values in such terms, it was still true that Hitler was going too far, and would have to be stopped.

Britain entered the war in September 1939 reluctantly, but with a degree of unanimity which would have been inconceivable even a year earlier. Indeed, at the start of the 1930s it must have seemed doubtful whether the British people would go to war at all, unless directly attacked. Such near-unanimity could never have been achieved on the old grounds of power politics and the control of Europe. It was the product of the fusion of these long-standing traditions with a newer but powerful reaction against the excesses of nazi ideology. It mattered little that what was considered evil in 1939 paled into insignificance in comparison with later monstrosities, and that the British people had scarcely begun to understand their adversary. The important point was that they had begun.

What part did the ideological attitudes and divisions in the parliamentary democracies of France and Britain play in the movement towards war? They contributed to this movement in two very different ways. First, for several years the concern of the French and British peoples (and their political leaders) with peace and disarmament left an easy path for the advance of Germany and Italy, beyond any point where it might have been resisted without large-scale war. Ideological divisions, especially in France, and a deep-seated hostility to Bolshevism which encouraged some sympathy for nazism and fascism in both countries, helped in the same direction. The democracies thus gave an opportunity to their enemies, which was fully and ruthlessly exploited in ways which led in the long run towards war.

Second, as the two democracies slowly came to grips with the new situation created by the advance of hostile powers, an element of genuine ideological conflict between democracy and nazism/fascism emerged. We have already noted, at the end of the previous chapter, that the methods of nazi Germany produced a revulsion among the adherents of an older morality. In both France and Britain, opposition to Germany arose out of ideological revulsion as well as from motives of patriotism and calculations about power. In the circumstances of the 1930s, this combination eventually produced a firmer determination to go to war than could have been secured on any narrower ground of national self-interest. France and Britain were eventually impelled into war for reasons which combined power politics with ideology: German expansion and nazi domination both had to be resisted.

REFERENCES AND NOTES

1. Philippe Bernard, *La fin d'un monde, 1914–1929* (Paris 1975), pp. 108–9.
2. L. Mysyrowicz, *Autopsie d'une défaite* (Lausanne 1973), p. 332.

3.　　Ibid., p. 288.
4.　　Georges Suarez, *Briand*, vol. VI (Paris 1952), p. 197.
5.　　R. Gombin, *Les socialistes et la guerre* (The Hague 1970), pp. 142–3.
6.　　Jean-Baptiste Duroselle, *La Décadence, 1932–1939* (Paris 1979), p. 41.
7.　　Ibid., p. 171.
8.　　Henri Dubief, *Le déclin de la Troisième République* (Paris 1976), pp. 173–5, 195.
9.　　*Le Populaire*, 1 October 1938, quoted in Gombin, *Les socialistes*, pp. 234–5.
10.　There were 4,322 votes for Blum's resolution: 2,837 for a resolution restating traditional policy; 60 for a total pacifist motion; and 1,014 abstentions (Gombin, *Les socialistes*, p. 253).
11.　Martin Ceadel, *Pacifism in Britain, 1914–1945* (Oxford 1980), p. 317.
12.　Quoted in Maurice Cowling, *The Impact of Hitler* (Cambridge 1975), p. 93.
13.　Donald McLachlan, *In the Chair: Barrington-Ward of 'The Times'* (London 1971), p. 106.
14.　Ceadel, *Pacifism in Britain*, pp. 177, 318.
15.　Quoted in G. M. Young, *Stanley Baldwin* (London 1952), p. 215 (speech to the Peace Society, 31 October 1935).
16.　Quoted in John F. Naylor, *Labour's International Policy: The Labour Party in the 1930s* (London 1969), p. 21.
17.　Richard Griffiths, *Fellow Travellers of the Right: British enthusiasts for Nazi Germany, 1933–9* (Oxford 1983). The left-wing equivalents are examined in David Caute, *The Fellow Travellers* (London 1973).
18.　Quoted in McLachlan, *In the Chair*, p. 110.
19.　*House of Commons Debates*, 5th series, vol. 276, col. 2742.
20.　Quoted in Alan Bullock, *Ernest Bevin*, vol. I (London 1960), p. 624.
21.　Quoted in Keith Feiling, *Neville Chamberlain*, (London 1946), p. 253.
22.　J. L. Garvin in *Observer*, 6 March 1938, quoted in F. R. Gannon, *The British Press and Germany, 1936–1939* (Oxford 1971), p. 18.
23.　Crozier to Voigt, 16 February 1936, quoted in Gannon, *The British Press*, p. 20.
24.　F. A. Voigt to Crozier, 21 March 1939, quoted in Gannon, *The British Press*, p. 24. Voigt was a foreign correspondent for the *Manchester Guardian*. His figure of tens of thousands done to death in the Soviet Union was itself a substantial understatement.
25.　David Dilks (cd.), *The Diaries of Sir Alexander Cadogan, 1938–1945* (London 1971), p. 132; cf. Donald Lammers, 'Fascism, communism and the Foreign Office, 1937–39', *Journal of Contemporary History*, **6** (3) (1971).
26.　Quoted in Kenneth Harris, *Attlee* (London 1982), p. 64.
27.　Naylor, *Labour's International Policy*, p. 9.
28.　Harris, *Attlee*, p. 166; T. D. Burridge, *British Labour and Hitler's War* (London 1976), p. 20.
29.　Quoted in Gannon, *The British Press*, p. 238.

Chapter 8
SOVIET COMMUNISM

Of all the European states, it was Bolshevik Russia which most obviously conceived of itself in ideological terms, and gave ideological explanations for everything it did. As such, the state set up by Lenin and the Bolsheviks in 1917 was a new and profoundly divisive element in world affairs. The regime called itself a dictatorship of the proletariat, dedicated at home to the building of socialism and abroad to the promotion of revolution.

This revolution was believed to be imminent, for many signs in war-torn and weary Europe pointed to it; and also to be necessary for the salvation of the Bolsheviks, who had boldly embarked on a proletarian revolution in a country which as yet had only a tiny proletariat. The Bolsheviks set out to hasten the advent of revolution by all the means at their command: by propaganda to the European peoples; by organization, through the Third, or Communist, International, which was founded in Moscow in 1919 and took firm shape at its Second Congress in 1920; and, when the opportunity offered, by force. In 1920 the Bolshevik forces, having expelled the Polish Army from the Ukraine, crossed what they recognized to be the ethnic frontier of Poland in the hope of carrying revolution through to Germany on the bayonets of the Red Army. In the rear of their army they set up a Provisional Polish Revolutionary Committee. The invasion failed, and the Committee was heard of no more; but the episode was instructive to all European governments, and alarming to many.

At the same time, and to their surprise, the Bolsheviks found that they also had to conduct an orthodox foreign policy. Trotsky, when he became Commissar for Foreign Affairs, remarked 'I will issue a few revolutionary proclamations to the peoples of the world and then shut up shop.'[1] But this was not to be. Most immediately, Germany was still at war with Russia, and a peace had to be negotiated; and despite Trotsky's revolutionary style of diplomacy, the Treaty of Brest-Litovsk (March 1918) was dictated by the German General Staff, with the weight of the German Army behind it. Later, another war, that with Poland, had to be brought to an end (by the Treaty of Riga, 1921); and in 1920–21 a number of treaties were signed, mainly with neighbouring countries (Turkey, Afghanistan, the Baltic and Scandinavian states) with which some form of normal relations was needed. So Bolshevik foreign policy adopted almost at once a form which it was long to maintain: a dual relationship with the rest of the world, in which the Bolsheviks set out with one hand to subvert other governments, and with the other to maintain normal relations with them.

Meanwhile, the rest of the world reacted to this new phenomenon of a revolutionary state. At first, reactions were mainly influenced by the circumstances of war. The Bolsheviks took Russia out of the war against Germany; and the Allies' first response was to try to restore an eastern front, and to keep certain territories out of German control. This produced intervention in various parts of Russia by forces from Britain, France, Japan, the USA, and Canada. This intervention continued after the war in Europe came to an end, with the Allies supporting anti-Bolshevik forces in their attempts to overthrow the revolutionary regime. These activities came to a ragged and untidy end between 1919 and 1922. They were small in scale and half-hearted in spirit, and had little unity of purpose. The French hoped to restore the old Russian Empire in its unity; the British to maintain the separate states into which the empire had dissolved. The Japanese hoped to secure their own influence in Vladivostok and the Maritime Province; the Americans to prevent them from doing so. This made little difference to the Bolsheviks. Foreign troops operated in Russia. Foreign supplies were provided for anti-Bolshevik forces. The capitalist and imperialist powers acted in the way in which Bolshevik beliefs indicated they would act; and the regime had to survive a period of siege.

Relations between the new regime in Russia and the rest of the world got off to a thoroughly bad start. In part this was due to circumstances; but it was also due to a deep ideological conflict. Bolshevik Russia and other states, especially the homes of advanced bourgeois capitalism, were opposed to one another because they represented opposite philosophies and ways of life. The Bolsheviks were as much opposed to the governments of the Netherlands or Switzerland, which posed no military threat, as to those of Britain or France, whose troops fought in Russia. This hostility was reciprocated, and Bolshevik Russia was the outcast of Europe. This divide could be bridged for powerful reasons of *realpolitik* or economics; and the first country to build such a bridge was Germany, which in the 1920s developed open economic and clandestine military links with Russia. But the divide remained, and introduced into European affairs a source of suspicion, tension, and conflict unknown since the wars of the French Revolution.

STALIN AND STALINISM

In 1922 the new state took the name of the Union of Soviet Socialist Republics, asserting its ideological claims in its very nomenclature. The relations between the USSR and the outside world, and the mixture of repulsion and attraction with which the Bolshevik regime was regarded, cannot be understood without some discussion of the nature of that regime.

During the 1920s, the USSR settled into a new shape. After the death of Lenin in January 1924 there was a prolonged struggle for power, in which Stalin emerged as the victor by December 1927. His great rival Trotsky was exiled in January 1929; and Stalin's fiftieth birthday on 21 December of the same year was marked by a new form of adulation – fulsome tributes in the press, floods of congratulatory telegrams, the display of countless pictures, the renaming of towns. The USSR not only had a new leader, but a new cult.

The century of the common man thus received another recruit. Mussolini was the son of a blacksmith; Hitler of a minor customs official; Stalin of a worker in a shoe factory. Each became dictator of his country – a career open to talent. Stalin probably wielded greater power than did Hitler; he certainly exercised it for longer. His name became synonymous with the whole character of his rule, so that we speak of Stalinism in the same way as we speak of nazism or fascism. As with the other great dictators, there are paradoxes and puzzles about his character, notably the contrast between what is often described as a colourless personality and the scale and monstrosity of his deeds. Colourless he may have been; and it is often remarked that he made no profound contribution to communist theory. He did not need to. Stalin was a practical man, and his political ability left everyone standing. He outmanoeuvred his Bolshevik opponents in the late 1920s, and later destroyed them – even Trotsky, far away in Mexico. During the Second World War, he persuaded a series of foreign statesmen, none of them political simpletons, that he recognized, or even sympathized with, their points of view. He convinced Churchill that they were both realists, who could strike a bargain which would be kept; Roosevelt that he understood the language of international agreement; de Gaulle that he took him seriously as a world statesman.

It is frequently asked – though with no certainty of there being an answer – where the balance lay between Stalin's socialism and his realism. He is often referred to as a 'Red Tsar' but how far was he a tyrant who happened to speak the language of Marxism–Leninism, and how far a Marxist–Leninist who happened to take the form of a tyrant? Khrushchev, in the speech of February 1956 in which he denounced Stalin's cult of personality and some of his misdeeds, still concluded that Stalin believed that all his measures were necessary for the interests of the working class and the victory of socialism. Adam Ulam, in his biography of Stalin, also wrote that he was 'a true believer: to his mind capitalism was doomed'; and its end would come through the military and industrial strength of the Soviet Union.[2] Roy Medvedev, in his powerful indictment of Stalin from the point of view of a Soviet Marxist, repeatedly appealing to Lenin as the source of unquestionable truth, held the opposite view. Stalin's mind was formed in a Marxist mould; and he wrote and spoke the language of Marxism; but he was not truly a Marxist, because he lacked the basis of conviction and moral principle which lies in devotion to the happiness of all working people.[3] The questions remain open. Was Stalin concerned with power for its own sake, or power to transform the Soviet Union into an efficient vehicle for the advancement of socialism? If Stalin wrote and spoke like a Marxist all his adult life, how far was it possible for him not to think like a Marxist, or at least to see the world through Marxist spectacles? With a man who lived so secretive a life, and rarely if ever let down his guard, it is impossible to tell.

The regime created by this grim and enigmatic man had four major characteristics: the concept of 'socialism in one country'; the collectivization of agriculture; rapid industrialization; and repression. All were accompanied by the process, common to the great dictatorships of the 1930s, by which the leader was elevated into a sort of god. The singular aspect of the cult of Stalin was the degree to which he was worshipped outside the USSR, in countries where coercion could play little part and there was ample access to non-Stalinist sources of information. In France, for example, that home of the intellect and rational enquiry, Stalin's death in 1953 was still mourned as that of a hero and superman.

The concept and practice of socialism in one country, taken up by Stalin in 1925–26, recognized that there was likely to be a prolonged wait before revolution spread to the more advanced industrial countries. There would be an extended period of coexistence between the new socialist state and its capitalist opponents; and meanwhile the socialist society must be built. The collectivization of agriculture, forced through with extraordinary rapidity and brutality between 1929 and 1934, was a crucial element in this process. The human cost was enormous – the death-toll certainly ran into millions; and the economic gain was doubtful – there was a great famine in 1932–33, and grain production in 1935 was only marginally above that of 1928, even on Soviet figures.[4] But the political and psychological results were formidable: rural society was shaken to its foundations; the control of the state was forcibly imposed upon the peasant population; and the Soviet Union began to make its name abroad for large-scale economic planning and modernization. Industrialization ran alongside collectivization, with greater economic success. The first Five-Year Plan (1928–32) was followed by two others. The statistics claiming their triumphant fulfilment took the form of percentage increases which cannot be checked; but certainly heavy industry (iron and steel) and fuel production (coal, oil, electricity) developed rapidly, and new industries, notably chemicals, were started from scratch. The Soviet Union became, with exceptional rapidity, a great industrial state. Not least in importance from the point of view of prestige, the process included a number of dramatic projects: the Dnieper dam, the White Sea Canal, the creation of a new city at Magnitogorsk in the Urals.

These changes were accompanied and enforced by a vast system of repression, directed against both individuals and whole categories of the population – kulaks, the intelligentsia, subject nationalities. The great empire of the camps, later made famous under the name of the Gulag Archipelago, grew in numbers and ferocity in the 1930s. Its victims were uncounted, but certainly ran into millions – perhaps 10 millions at any one time, with a constant turnover secured by a high death-rate and an influx of new prisoners.[5]

The most extraordinary manifestation of repression was the great wave of purges which swept the USSR between 1936 and 1938. The purges took several forms. The most spectacular were the public show trials, which have been well likened to great theatrical productions. In August 1936 eight major political figures, including the old Bolsheviks Zinoviev and Kamenev, along with some lesser figures and four junior officers of the NKVD, were put on trial in Moscow. All confessed abjectly to a variety of crimes – the murder of Kirov (a close colleague of Stalin and Communist Party boss in Leningrad, shot on 1 December 1934), conspiring with Trotsky to seize power, plotting to assassinate Stalin. Sentences of death were passed, and it was announced that they were carried out within twenty-four hours of the end of the trial. (The NKVD officers, though only there to make false confessions, were shot with the rest.) The second show trial was in January 1937, with the Deputy Commissar for Heavy Industry, Pyatakov, and sixteen others accused of the systematic wrecking of Soviet industry as part of a plot by Trotsky to restore capitalism in the USSR, with help from Germany and Japan. All were found guilty, but only thirteen condemned to death. Finally in March 1938 another 'old Bolshevik', Bukharin, was put on trial, along with twenty others (including Yagoda, former head of the NKVD). Eighteen were sentenced to death, three to prison.

The second great element was the purge of the army. On 11 June 1937 it was announced in Moscow that eight members of the Soviet high command, including Marshal Tukhachevsky, Deputy Commissar for Defence, had been charged with treason. On 12 June it was further announced that they had been tried and shot. This time there was no public trial, and it is uncertain whether there was a trial at all. This was followed by purges which continued into 1938, and in some cases beyond. The whole existing high command, and something like half of the entire officer corps, were shot or imprisoned – figures, which are necessarily estimates, vary between 30,000 and 40,000 victims, including about 10,000 dead. Roy Medvedev summed up the effects thus: 'The shocking truth can be stated quite simply: never did the officer staff of any army suffer such great losses in any war as the Soviet Army suffered in this time of peace.'[6] The operation was accomplished with astounding ease. While Hitler had to work hard, and exploit folly on the part of a senior officer, to remove two generals and put others on the retired list, Stalin simply swept away half the officer corps of the Red Army. When it came to dealing with the military men, the Fuehrer came some lengths behind the Red Tsar.

These operations were only the tip of the iceberg. In less spectacular fashion, the purge fell heavily on the Communist Party. The NKVD itself was purged, and two of its heads (Yagoda and Yezhov) fell victims. In the Ukraine in 1937 and 1938 the whole government and party were purged twice over. Foreign communists in Moscow were killed; and the NKVD stretched its arm abroad, notably to Spain during the Civil War, and to France. Many were swept in for no particular reason. Estimates of total casualties vary from a low figure of 400,000–500,000 executions and 4–5 million arrests, 1936–39, to figures of about 1 million executions and 7 million arrests. Another figure estimates a total of 10 million deaths, counting 1 million executions and about 1 million deaths per year in the camps for nine years.[7]

The motives behind the great purges remain obscure. Stalin may have been seeking the security of total control over his country, with no vestige of independent initiative or organization surviving. It may be that he genuinely feared political opposition from the army, or the resumption of the old contacts with the German General Staff. Whatever the motives, the effects of the purges on the Soviet position in world affairs were far-reaching. For a period of three years, and perhaps longer, the Soviet Union was so racked internally, and its military organization so disrupted, that it was gravely weakened as a power. It could contemplate war only in the case of absolute necessity, or in very favourable circumstances against a weak opponent.

THE SOVIET UNION AND ITS FOREIGN SUPPORTERS: THE 'GREAT LIGHT IN THE EAST'

Stalinism was a regime of terror. In 1939, by the simple test of casualties caused among the people of its own country, it far outstripped either nazism or fascism. In sheer destructive capacity, Stalin made Hitler look a beginner. Moreover, the main features of Stalinism were essentially inward-looking, making the Soviet Union a fortress of socialism in one country, fighting its own internal battles and building its own industrial base. At the time much of this was concealed, and the rest was easily justified in the eyes of the Soviet Union's supporters who looked to it as the Workers' Fatherland, the beacon light of their existence, for which they would work, go underground, betray their country, and if need be, die. The Communist Parties of Europe embodied the central core of this support, and were controlled through the tightly knit, disciplined organization of the Communist International (Comintern). In 1920 the Second Congress of Comintern laid down the 'Twenty-one Conditions' which had to be accepted by parties affiliating to the International. A powerful form of central control was set up; and it was laid down that it was the overriding duty of all Communist Parties to protect existing socialist states – which meant in practice the Soviet Union, since no others emerged. Foreign Communist Parties followed faithfully the line laid down in Moscow, and in the 1930s became wholly Stalinist. They denounced Trotsky, though in 1918–19 he had been a hero of the Revolution and Civil War. Those who unwarily chose what proved to be the losing side in the power struggles of the 1920s in Russia had to cover their tracks and expunge their error from the record, as Thorez did in France. For a prolonged period in the 1920s and early 1930s the main enemies of communism were proclaimed to be the Social Democratic Parties, often called 'social fascists'; and there was tactical co-operation between communists and nazis in Germany against the social democrats. Then suddenly in 1935 the line was changed to the creation of a Popular Front against fascism, and the social democrats became allies. The French Communist Party, after years of denouncing militarism and conscription, accepted (though in a qualified manner) the two-year conscription law of 1935 after the signature of the Franco-Soviet Pact in the same year. Later, the policy of the Popular Front and anti-fascism was itself overthrown by the Nazi–Soviet Pact of August 1939; and after a period of some confusion and heart-searching on the part of individuals, discipline prevailed and the Communist Parties moved into line behind the new policy.

These turns in policy (sometimes of 180 degrees) were executed like warships responding to a signal; and were accompanied by a crescendo of praise for Stalin, the admiral who sent the signals. There can be no doubt that most of this adulation was voluntary and sincere. The whole point of being a Party member was the belief that communism represented the only way forward for mankind; and Stalin was by common consent the leading communist, a father figure, at once stern and reassuring.

This faith sustained both communists and fellow-travellers through what might have been the disturbing shock of the show trials and the purges. Foreign communists showed complete loyalty to Stalin during the purges. Aragon, the French novelist and poet, wrote in 1937 that 'to claim innocence for these men is to adopt the Hitlerian thesis on all points'; while Bertolt Brecht, the German playwright, remarked

117

enigmatically but ominously of the accused in 1936: 'The more innocent they are, the more they deserve to die.'[8] This loyalty, in Ulam's words, 'was the product of faith rather than of fear'.[9]

The heart of the faith lay in the conviction that the organized working class, animated by Marxist-Leninist theory, was the only force capable of overthrowing capitalism. The Soviet Union was the Workers' Fatherland, and represented the only successful proletarian revolution so far. The Communist Parties and Comintern provided the necessary organization by which that revolution could be spread. The bare essentials of this creed were reinforced in the 1930s by many attendant circumstances. The economic depression, with its decline in trade and industry and masses of unemployed, provided proof that capitalism was both evil and in disastrous decline. Against this spectacle stood the shining example of scientific, socialist planning, displayed for all to see in the great Five-Year Plans and a society where all worked together for the public good. The glistening new constitution of 1936 guaranteed rights to all citizens of the Soviet Union: freedom of speech, of assembly, of the press, of both religious worship and anti-religious propaganda. A formidable list of Western intellectuals enthused over this extraordinary piece of window-dressing, introduced by Stalin in the same year that the great purge was launched. The prestige and gullibility of intellectuals, indeed, was one of the assets of Stalin's regime in its dealings with the outside world. Between 1936 and 1939 there was added the spectacle of the Spanish Civil War, where only the Soviet Union and Comintern were prepared to stand up and fight fascism; and the appeal of the Popular Front against fascism, which acted powerfully upon those who feared Hitler, Mussolini, and all their works, and could see no sign that other governments were willing or able to stop them. If Chamberlain and Daladier, with their policies of appeasement, were the best that the parliamentary states could produce, many turned, in either hope or despair, to Stalin. The more who turned, the greater was the attraction. In France in the summer of 1936 there was a wave of new members entering the Communist Party; marches, demonstrations, and Popular Front rallies created the exhilarating feeling of belonging to a mass, moving and growing with a kind of inevitability. For those caught up in this movement, to stand aside was more difficult than to be carried along.

The Soviet Union thus drew on a substantial element of support from outside its borders. The hard core of this support, in the Communist Parties, was disciplined and organized, and (because in many countries the Party was illegal) well adapted to clandestine activity. The fellow-travellers and sympathizers were less committed, but more important for propaganda purposes simply because they were *not* Party members, and therefore seemed to offer independent endorsement of the regime. The significance of all this for international affairs was considerable. In every country there was an organized body on which the Soviet government could rely to promote its interests, as they were interpreted in Moscow at any given time. Equally, every other government in Europe knew that an organized group of its own citizens owed its primary allegiance to a foreign state, and was working openly or in secret for the overthrow of the existing social order. It was impossible to treat the Soviet Union simply as another state, even though for practical purposes it was necessary to have dealings with it, and on calculations of power politics it might be desirable to form alliances with it. Both practical dealings and diplomatic negotiations were made difficult by the nature of the Soviet state, and by the fact that relations with the Soviet Union were always a contentious issue in domestic politics.

Above all, the existence of the foreign Communist Parties and their sympathizers focused the attention of all governments on the fact that the USSR was both a state and the centre of an international revolutionary movement. Communism and its homeland were in existence before Italy became fascist, and long before Germany turned to nazism. It was natural, and in many ways reasonable, that other European states, and especially the great imperial powers, Britain and France, should continue to regard Soviet communism as a dangerous enemy. From this it was a short step for some to the assumption that the enemies of communism were your friends; and that fascist Italy and nazi Germany were sturdy bulwarks against communism. Once this notion had taken root, it was hard to believe that the nazi regime was itself a threat, nearer and more powerful than the Soviet Union. Even if nazism was perceived as a threat, the background of hostility, rooted in ideological antagonism and fostered by Comintern activity, could not be instantly dispelled or ignored, but remained to clog and hamper all dealings with the Soviet government – as was shown in the British and French negotiations for a Soviet alliance in the summer of 1939.

Ideological conflicts, and the presence of committed adherents of the Soviet system in other countries, therefore affected the foreign policies of various European states. How far did ideology affect the foreign policy of the Soviet Union itself?

IDEOLOGY AND SOVIET FOREIGN POLICY

Every state and regime is subject to the influences of geography and history. The Soviet Union, with all its Marxist–Leninist ideology and its revolutionary claims, occupied roughly the same geographical area as the old Tsarist Russia, and perforce inherited its concerns and constraints. The Dardanelles and Bosporus still linked the Black Sea with the Mediterranean; and the USSR took a leading part in negotiating the Montreux Convention on the straits (1936), which gave her a generally favourable position, especially on the question of the passage of warships through the straits. The Soviet Union still sprawled across two continents, with one extremity in Europe and the other on the Pacific; and when Stalin met Anthony Eden in March 1935 he showed his visitor a map, with Germany on one side, Japan on the other, and the USSR in between.

A purely ideological foreign policy was out of the question for the USSR – any illusions on that score were shed by the time the Treaty of Brest-Litovsk was signed in March 1918. Much of Soviet foreign policy, especially under Stalin, was hard-headed and cautious in the extreme, going for material gain if it was available, and bargaining with great toughness. At another meeting between Stalin and Eden, in December 1941, Stalin remarked that a declaration of principle was algebra, but a treaty was arithmetic – and he preferred arithmetic. This does not mean that ideology was abandoned, or had no influence, especially on attitudes to the world outside the Soviet Union; for the question is above all one of the spectacles through which that outside world was seen. Lenin, at whose name every knee in the communist camp continued (and indeed continues) to bow, left his successors with important assumptions about the nature of international relations.

The most significant was his view of the nature of war. Lenin read Clausewitz, and accepted his view that war was the continuation of policy. Moreover, he believed that the existence of capitalist states meant that they were in a state of war with socialist states; and that capitalism, and its most extreme stage, imperialism, inevitably produced war between capitalist states themselves. It followed that two types of war were virtually inevitable; war between capitalist and socialist powers, as seen in the wars of intervention against the Bolsheviks; and wars between imperialist powers, usually over markets and fields for investment, as in the First World War. The second type of war was bound to weaken the capitalist states and assist the advance of socialism, as in fact it did in 1914–18; and in logic it was therefore in the interest of a socialist state (the Soviet Union, in practice) to keep out of a capitalist and imperialist war as long as possible, allowing the imperialists to destroy one another.

Lenin also believed that, strictly speaking, no lasting alliance was possible between socialist and capitalist states. They were fundamentally opposed to one another, so that socialists must consider all bourgeois capitalists as enemies, just as the capitalists would regard them as enemies. This did not rule out particular arrangements for specific purposes – the Treaty of Brest-Litovsk, the Treaty of Rapallo with Germany in 1922, the scheme under which Germany developed weapons in the USSR; but they could not be expected to be permanent. (There was nothing singular, or even particularly Bolshevik, in this: Palmerston held that Britain had no perpetual allies – only her interests were eternal.) The making of such particular arrangements was a matter of tactics; and Soviet negotiators were naturally expected to drive the hardest possible bargain.

Lenin attached much weight to this kind of ideological analysis, and yet he also behaved in foreign affairs as a hard-headed realist, operating within the limits of the possible and the expedient. Much the same seems to have been true of Stalin. We cannot tell how fully he remained committed to the ideology, but he used the language, and it is probable that he was influenced by its thought-forms. Above all, he was unavoidably cast for the role of leader of world socialism, and as such he had to be seen to lead it. Yet at the same time he was a realist, with a power base to protect; and he had to be cautious, for that base was not yet of great strength. The result was a foreign policy in which ideology and realism were always mixed, and could always be reconciled with one another, because after all the power base and the Workers' Fatherland were one and the same.

Ideological analysis resting on the belief in the hostility of all capitalist states was prominent in 1927–28, when Stalin publicly referred to the threat of a new imperialist war. He claimed that various events in 1927 (the British raid on the Soviet trade mission in London, and subsequent rupture of diplomatic relations; the French request for the recall of the Soviet Ambassador in Paris; the assassination of the Ambassador in Warsaw) were all parts of a single plot, designed to culminate in an attack on the USSR by the imperialist powers. The same assertion followed the first of Stalin's show trials, in 1928, when mining engineers at the town of Shakhty in the Don Basin were accused of sabotaging coal production on the instructions of foreign capitalists. (The only evidence was their confessions; five were shot.) Stalin claimed in a speech of 1929 that such 'bourgeois wrecking' was proof that the capitalists were preparing new attacks on the Soviet Union.

How far such claims were believed, even by Stalin, must be open to doubt. Those were the days of the struggle against Trotsky, and the 'war scare' was used to denounce those who sought to divide the country in the face of an outside threat. Equally, there was little sign of the capitalists keeping the Soviet Union in a state of siege, or blockade. Relations with Germany were good, in political, commercial, and military terms. After the Treaty of Rapallo, over 2,000 German engineers and technicians went to work in Soviet industry. Junkers, the German aircraft firm, had a factory at Fili, near Moscow; and Krupps were making guns in factories in central Asia. Despite the Shakhty trial, in 1929 the USSR still had technical agreements with many German and American firms, and Standard Oil won a contract to build an oil refinery at Batum. As Lenin predicted, the capitalist search for profits caused firms to contribute to building up the Soviet economy; and the Soviet authorities were willing to allow them to do so.

The assumption of capitalist hostility continued to exist; but for practical purposes it seems unlikely that an actual attack was expected, and economic co-operation was the order of the day. The same was true of Italy, the first fascist power,·with which Soviet relations were good in the 1920s. During the first Soviet Five-Year Plan large orders for industrial equipment were placed in Italy; and for its part the Italian government, despite its declared hostility to communism, guaranteed the long-term credit arrangements which firms offered to their Soviet customers. Early in 1934, addressing the Seventeenth Communist Party Congress in Moscow, Stalin remarked that the Soviets were far from enthusiastic about the new fascist regime in Germany, but pointed out that fascism in Italy had not prevented the establishment of excellent relations with that country.

Despite this hopeful comment, the rise of fascism and nazism presented a serious ideological problem to the Soviet regime, and the answer produced had important effects on policy. As early as 1922 Comintern publications identified fascism as a manifestation of monopoly capitalism. It was easy to find in the writings of Marx and Engels the view that the bourgeoisie sometimes protected its interests by renouncing the direct exercise of power in favour of a dictator – Louis Napoleon was Marx's case in point. The parallel with fascist dictatorships seemed simple: fascism corresponded to a phase in the decay of capitalism; the bourgeoisie was trying to prolong its existence and protect its profits by bringing in a dictator; fascist leaders were paid by, and were the instruments of, big business. For a long time in the 1920s and early 1930s this theory was accompanied by the view that the bourgeoisie was also in alliance with the social democrats, who were themselves in league with the fascists. In November 1923, for example, the German Communist Party declared that the true fascists were not in Munich, where Hitler had just attempted his *coup d'état*, but in Berlin, where the social democrats were in alliance with the military fascists of the German Army. In 1928 Thaelmann, the German communist leader, described the German government as a 'social-fascist gang'; which was at the time a conventional term of abuse for the social democrats.

As late as 1930–33, facing the rapid rise of Hitler, the communists accepted that the nazis had revolutionary aims, but refused to regard them as the greatest danger. The nazi movement, which was the symptom of the decay of capitalism, bore within itself the seeds of its own destruction. Even when Hitler came to power, the Comintern line was that he was merely hastening the coming of the proletarian revolution; and the Night of the Long Knives, when Hitler crushed his rivals in the SA, was greeted as a demonstration that the nazi movement was tearing itself apart. If all this was true, then nazi ideology was only so much mumbo-jumbo and mystification to cover the nakedness of the nazi alliance with big business and monopoly capitalism; and so it came about that the communists, looking at nazism through their own ideological spectacles, misunderstood its nature as much as did the bourgeois liberal statesmen of France and Britain. Moreover, if a change of attitude and policy were to be made, and an alliance against nazism/fascism attempted, the communists would have to get themselves out of an ideological box. Social democrats could no longer be social fascists, but would have to become allies *against* the fascists. How could this be done?

The answer was found by redefining fascism, at the Seventh Congress of Comintern, held in Moscow in August 1935 to proclaim the new doctrine of the Popular Front against fascism. The Secretary-General, Dimitrov, described fascism as the open dictatorship of the most reactionary, chauvinist, and imperialist elements of finance capital; which allowed it to be deduced that social democrats and even bourgeois liberals did not fall into this category. The former simple rule that fascism amounted to finance capital, the bourgeoisie, and their accomplices was tacitly abandoned.

These contortions, and in particular the long struggle against the social democrats/social fascists, showed both the real effect of ideology on Soviet and Comintern policy, and the way in which that effect could be reversed for tactical reasons. They were developments which influenced the movement towards war in two different ways. First, the division on the Left of European politics, and notably the long feud between communists and social democrats in Germany, assisted the rise of fascism in general and of Hitler in particular. Defeated and disgruntled German socialists claimed after 1933 that without Stalin there would have been no Hitler: which is doubtless an exaggeration, but not wholly without substance. Second, the swing to the Popular Front against fascism was one of the elements which helped to move left-wing opinion in Europe towards the idea of war. For those who took their line from Moscow, war in defence of one's own country and a bourgeois social order was anathema; but war to protect the Soviet Union was an imperative.

From the point of view of the Soviet government (which in the last resort meant Stalin), ideological influences on foreign policy appear to have diminished during the 1930s. Ideological analysis of the international situation naturally continued. In his speech to the Eighteenth Communist Party Congress in Moscow, on 10 March 1938, Stalin's discussion of the European position was authentically Leninist. He distinguished between the aggressive capitalist powers (Germany, Italy, and Japan) and the non-aggressive capitalist powers (Britain, France, and the USA); but he was conscious that all were capitalist first and foremost. The non-aggressive powers were as great a threat as the aggressive ones, because they were playing a waiting game, hoping that the forces of nazism and communism would become engaged in war and exhaust one another. Indeed, Stalin had more to say about Britain and France than about Germany; he argued that the Western powers had, in the Munich agreement, yielded Czech territory to Germany as an inducement to the Germans to attack the USSR, and that their policy amounted to an encouragement of the aggressor states.

This was both orthodox Leninism and a plausible interpretation of the facts. But, though we cannot see into Stalin's mind, there is every sign that his foreign policy in the late 1930s was dominated by a cautious, and sometimes ruthless, realism. The great purges and the pursuit of industrialization were presumably decisive in this: while they were in progress, foreign war was unthinkable unless it was absolutely forced upon him. (When it was so forced, in the Far East, by the danger of Japanese encroachment on Soviet territory in 1938 and 1939, the Red Army stood and fought, in large-scale and notably successful actions.) Stalin took precautions against a German attack – the Franco–Soviet Pact (signed on 2 May 1935), and the Popular Front policy adopted by Comintern in the same year. But both stopped carefully short of advocating or preparing war against Germany. The alliance with France was not followed up by a military convention, or even serious military conversations, and this was not just the fault of France. The Comintern Congress which adopted the Popular Front stopped short of calling for war against fascism; the object was the limited one of preventing European states from remaining neutral, or even joining Germany in a possible war between Germany and the Soviet Union.

Stalin said in January 1934 that the advent of the nazi regime in Germany, though unwelcome, need not preclude good relations. He tried to keep open a line to Berlin, making approaches through the press attaché at the Soviet embassy in Berlin in 1935, and through David Kandelaki, a trade representative in Berlin (and reputedly a boyhood friend of Stalin), in the same year. Soviet policy in the Spanish Civil War showed no profound commitment. It was not until 4 October 1936, two and a half months after the war began, that Stalin sent a telegram to the Spanish Communist Party expressing his support for the republic. Most Soviet aid to the republic was channelled through Comintern, allowing the government to adopt a position of reserve and to adhere to the non-intervention agreement. Soviet military 'advisers' were sent to Spain, but no regular units as in the case of Germany and Italy. In so far as there was ideological involvement in Spain, it was as much against Trotskyists and anarchists as against fascists; and the NKVD extended the purges from its home ground to Spain, where Spanish and other foreign communists were their targets. The Soviet attitude during the Czechoslovakian crisis of 1938 was similarly cautious. The Nazi–Soviet Pact of August 1939 was a stroke of *realpolitik*, coming to terms with the highest bidder. It is often described as a denial of ideology; but this is not so – it was perfectly compatible with an ideological stance. All capitalist and imperialist states were enemies, and there was no reason to regard the Anglo-French imperialists as more favourable to the Soviet Union than the Germans.

The Nazi–Soviet Pact, despite its horrifying appearance and the shock which it created, was the result of a marriage between Leninist ideology and political opportunism. As such, it was in line with much Soviet foreign policy between the wars, which followed a double line of realism and ideological commitment. When one asks how far the ideological element contributed to the coming of war in Europe, the answer seems to be threefold. First, the very existence of communism and its international organization, Comintern, introduced a degree of permanent discord in Europe. The liberal democracies (France, Britain, and the smaller states) had a declared enemy within their own boundaries as well as in a foreign state; and it was natural for them to seek ideological allies in fascism and nazism, underestimating the threat to themselves inherent in those regimes. It was also difficult to deal with the USSR simply on a basis of power politics: an alliance with her was seen also as an alliance with communism. Second, the excessively simple and blinkered communist interpretation of nazism, and long insistence that the social democrats/social fascists were the greater enemy, helped to open the way to the nazis in Germany, and almost certainly caused Stalin to underrate the danger posed by nazi Germany in international relations. This was almost a mirror-image of Western attitudes, based on ideological misconceptions and hopes of 'appeasement'. Third, the Nazi–Soviet Pact, which was at least compatible with Soviet ideology and well within a Leninist analysis of the European situation, helped to create the circumstances for a war between the capitalist and imperialist states, which should in theory have been favourable to the interests of the Soviet Union and of communism. These influences were of real significance; but it is hard to think that they place Soviet communism high among the ideological forces pressing towards war in Europe.

REFERENCES AND NOTES

1. Quoted in E. H. Carr, *The Bolshevik Revolution, 1917–1923*, vol. III (London 1953), p. 16.
2. Adam B. Ulam, *Stalin: the man and his era* (London 1973), p. 361.
3. Roy Medvedev, *Let History Judge* (London 1971), especially pp. 333,

336.

4.   1928: 73.3 million tons; 1935: 75 million tons. Alec Nove, *An Economic History of the USSR* (London: Pelican 1972), p. 186.

5.   Ronald Hingley, *Joseph Stalin: man and legend* (London 1974), pp. 213–15.

6.   Different figures in Hingley, *Stalin*, pp. 257–65, and Robert Conquest, *The Great Terror: Stalin's purge of the thirties* (London 1968), pp. 484–5. Quotation from Medvedev, *Let History Judge*, p. 213.

7.   The low figures are from Medvedev, *Let History Judge*, p. 239; for the others, see Conquest, *Great Terror*, Appendix A, pp. 525–35, Hingley, *Stalin*, p. 282.

8.   Aragon quoted in David Caute, *The Fellow Travellers* (London 1973), p. 118; Brecht in Conquest, *Great Terror*, p. 501.

9.   Ulam, *Stalin*, p. 471.

ECONOMIC ISSUES AND THE COMING OF WAR

During the Second World War there was a widespread belief that the great depression of the early 1930s had played a crucial part in causing the war, and prescriptions for future peace often concentrated on trying to eliminate economic problems. These views on the economic origins of the war comprised three principal arguments. First, it was held that the depression of 1929–35 destroyed the atmosphere of confidence and *détente* which flourished in Europe after 1925, and created in its place fierce economic nationalism and cut-throat competition for the shrinking amount of world trade. Second, the social and political tensions engendered by the depression brought Hitler to power in Germany at the head of an aggressive and self-confident dictatorship, and at the same time sowed dissension within Germany's likely opponents. France in particular was riven by internal disputes which were exacerbated by the depression; and in Czechoslovakia the Sudeten Germans, in their economic distress, looked across the border to Germany for support. Third, there was a strong feeling, voiced for example by Cordell Hull, the American Secretary of State, that the closed trading systems of the 1930s led towards war. Too many states were trying for self-sufficiency, and saw the raw materials or food supplies which they needed at the mercy of the policies of other governments and the vagaries of foreign exchange. Some countries then sought to break out and secure their own positions by force of arms: Germany and Japan went to war to conquer zones of economic control, in which they could safeguard their own imports and fix their own rates of exchange, free from the uncertainties of foreign trade.

In the lengthening perspective since the end of the war, and with the advent of another great depression which has brought economic difficulties and social strains, yet leaving international stability largely undisturbed, these analyses have not always carried the same conviction. But there remains a powerful school of argument that the Second World War in Europe had significant economic origins.

We must therefore examine the impact of the economic depression in the early 1930s; ask how far it created the preconditions for a European war; and analyse the links between economic issues and the actual coming of war. The issues involved were sometimes technical, concerning currency exchange rates and international clearing agreements; but their effects were practical and down-to-earth, touching the livelihood of millions. These were matters which had a more immediate (though not necessarily in the long run a more profound) influence than ideology on the daily lives of whole peoples.

Chapter 9

THE GREAT DEPRESSION AND INTERNATIONAL RELATIONS

Economic analysis often appears to approximate more to the arts of divination than to the exact sciences; and economists have produced an array of different explanations of the great depression, and why it proved so widespread, deep-seated, and long-lasting. There is, however, common consent that the onset of the depression dated from 1929. In that year, a number of economic indicators in various industrial countries took an ominous turn; notably in Germany, where unemployment rose to 1.9 million in the summer, and the USA, where car production fell sharply between March and September and building slackened off. Moreover, the harvests of 1929 in almost all kinds of agricultural produce were exceptionally good, resulting in a glut on the market which brought a sharp fall in prices, and therefore in the incomes of farming communities. To these signs of economic depression were added the abrupt and far-reaching effects of the collapse of the New York stock market in October 1929 – 'the Great Crash', in which share prices began to move downwards on 3 October and fell with dizzying speed on the 24th. This marked an almost total loss of business confidence in the USA, which from recovery was extremely slow. The immediate results were a sharp drop in American spending (because millions lost their savings and their incomes) and investment (for which there were neither the funds nor the confidence). There was a widespread move to get resources out of company shares and other forms of investment, and into ready cash. Mortgages were foreclosed and loans called in – including overseas loans, which had already diminished markedly during 1928. The consequences of the stock market crash were thus immediately felt abroad, and became rapidly more acute as the USA reduced its imports, and later its exports.

The effects of these events were cumulative and interlocking. Agrarian depression began in 1929 with a fall in agricultural prices, which was particularly sharp for cereals, and especially wheat, of which there was substantial overproduction in relation to demand. In the USA and Canada there was some attempt to meet this problem by stockpiling; but in Australia and Argentina there was neither the storage capacity nor the financial resources to attempt such a policy, and growers simply had to sell as best they could, driving prices down still further. The Soviet Union was just embarking on its policy of financing rapid industrialization by pushing up wheat exports. Caught in the trap of falling world prices, the USSR found that to sustain even a modest value for its exports, their volume had to be greatly increased. In 1931, Soviet exports of wheat were 2.29 million metric tons, at a value of $150 million; in 1932, the amount was more than doubled to 5.22 million metric tons, but the value remained the same.[1] So the Soviet Union too pushed its grain on to the world market, lowering prices still further. The consequences were severe for all wheat-producing countries; and particularly so in eastern Europe.

In the 1920s, most of the new states of eastern Europe had embarked on 'land reform' – the expropriation of large landowners and the distribution of land among small peasant farmers. (This was often a nationalist measure. The peasant farmers were usually of the dominant nationality, the great landowners often aliens – in the Baltic states, for example, Germans.) The consequences in most cases were economically disastrous, notably in terms of the yield and quality of wheat. Rumania (where Magyar landowners were expropriated) never exported more than 270,000 metric tons of wheat in any single year in the 1920s, though its average exports (from a smaller area) in 1909–13 had been 1.33 million metric tons a year.[2] In consequence it was difficult even in favourable circumstances for east European countries to compete on world markets with their exports of wheat. The continuous fall in wheat prices from 1929 to 1932 was catastrophic for those farmers who produced for export; even when they could find a market, their income was slight. They were forced to join those who already practised subsistence farming, or merely local sale or exchange. Large numbers of the agricultural population were reduced to subsistence, barter, and poverty. The consequence was that the rural economy, which was predominant over most of eastern Europe, ceased to provide customers for other goods and services, so that industry, shopkeepers, the professions, and all providers of services suffered severely. Government revenue from taxation declined, forcing reductions in expenditure and even cuts in the civil service, that backbone of the state and fount of patronage for politicians. Moreover, without the foreign currency produced by agricultural exports, the states of eastern Europe could not service the debts they had contracted during the growth years of the 1920s.

Other crucial elements in the depression were the collapse of international trade, and the crisis in credit and banking. The collapse of trade was dramatic. The total imports of seventy-five countries, valued in US dollars, fell as shown in Table 3.[3] Since everyone's import was another man's export, the contraction in the volume of trade was severe. The consequence in industrialized countries, where the recourse to subsistence agriculture available in eastern Europe was not open, was large-scale unemployment, amounting in 1932, in approxi-

Table 3. Value of imports of seventy-five countries, 1929–1933

January 1929	2,997.7 million
January 1930	2,738.9 million
January 1931	1,838.9 million
January 1932	1,206.0 million
January 1933	992.4 million

figures, to 3 million in Britain, 6 million in Germany, and 13 million in the USA. Industrial recession brought a sharp fall in demand for raw materials for industry: the the same was true for a wide range of primary products – timber, for example, suffered from the decline in building.

As prices of all commodities (foodstuffs, raw materials, and industrial goods) fell, business profits declined or vanished, share prices collapsed, and demand for services dwindled. Pressure grew on the banking system and all arrangements for credit. Banks and other creditors found it impossible to secure repayment of loans, or even sometimes the payment of interest. Some banks had lent very heavily; and some had themselves borrowed in order to conduct their business, and were being pressed for payment. There were occasional bank failures towards the end of 1930; and the crisis came in May 1931 with the failure of the Credit-Anstalt Bank in Austria, when for the first time an important and well-established bank could not meet its obligations because its own debtors could not meet theirs. After this, confidence was shaken, and there were runs on banks all over central and eastern Europe. Pressure was particularly severe in Germany, where memories of the great inflation of 1923 were vivid – the terms of the problem were different in 1931, but what mattered was that people had seen their savings and assets wiped out once, and had no wish to see it happen again. There were heavy withdrawals of gold from the Reichsbank in June, and in July the Darmstaedter National Bank had to close its doors. Several countries tried to check runs on banks by declaring 'bank holidays', and to prevent the movement of capital abroad by freezing deposits, imposing exchange controls, and delaying payments to foreign creditors. Such suspensions of payments were usually followed by the negotiation of agreements to resume them only out of a favourable balance of trade, i.e. by reducing imports from and increasing exports to the country concerned. Since every country was trying to do this at the same time, the result was to reduce international trade still further, and to channel much of what there was through a system of bilateral clearing arrangements, negotiated between states determined to control their external payments.

In many ways, the collapse of credit had the greatest impact of all the elements in the depression, because everything in the economic system – farming, industry, commerce, government activity – depended on credit. It also had profound effects on international currency exchanges. In 1931 and 1932, under the pressure of runs on the banks and the demand for gold, one government after another took its currency off the gold standard. The former monetary unity of most of the world, based on the gold standard, broke down.

The world rapidly divided into three main currency groups. First there were the countries which took their currency off the gold standard, devaluing considerably to try to assist their exports, and to reduce the pressure on the banking system and their gold reserves. Britain took this course (though out of necessity rather than choice) in 1931, and was soon followed by the Dominions (except Canada), Japan, several South American states, and a number of countries in central Europe. The USA left the gold standard and devalued in 1933, accompanied by Canada. Second, there was the Gold Bloc – countries which held their currencies on the gold standard, and maintained free exchange of currency. This group began to take shape in 1931, and came formally into existence in 1933. It was made up of France, Belgium, the Netherlands, Switzerland, and Luxemburg, with Italy as a partial member. (The Italian government kept to the gold standard, but did not operate free exchange of currency.) The Bloc began to split up with Belgian devaluation in 1935, and came to an abrupt end when the French, Swiss, Dutch, and Italians all devalued their currencies in rapid succession in September and October 1936.

Third, there were the countries which practised various forms of exchange control and blocked-currency regulations. These included the USSR (which had always operated such measures), Germany, and eventually some twenty other countries. The German arrangements were both remarkably complicated (there were at least thirteen different varieties of 'blocked marks' in 1936) and particularly important, because of Germany's economic and commercial significance; and they will be examined later in this chapter. But in practically all cases the principles of the clearing arrangements and blocked-currency accounts were the same. A firm in country A exporting its products to country B was obliged to spend its earnings in that country, whether there was anything it wanted to buy or not; if it made no such purchase, then its earnings remained, in country B's currency, in a blocked account. In these circumstances it mattered little whether a currency remained formally attached to gold (as some did) or not; its exchange was not free. and its export was forbidden except with government permission.

Naturally, these practices invited retaliation from firms which were losing their export earnings, and countries which were losing foreign exchange. Retaliation took different forms, notably blocking foreign earnings in one's own country, and the imposition of quotas on foreign trade. Such measures were widespread. Countries in the Gold Bloc took their own protective action against cheap imports from states which had devalued – for example, France imposed quotas on goods from Britain, which after the devaluation of sterling were cheap in terms of French francs. The whole complicated and fragmented set of devices caused constant friction, and imposed a series of restrictions on international trade.

The last chance (at best a slim one) of finding a way out of these difficulties by means of a general agreement on exchange rates and terms of trade was the World Economic Conference which met in London in June–July 1933. Such hopes as there were for the success of this conference were ended by President Roosevelt's rejection of even a temporary stabilization of the dollar against sterling for the duration of the conference. If such a temporary arrangement could not be reached, it was plain that a permanent agreement on exchange rates was out of the question. The conference broke up, and the USA devalued shortly afterwards. Nothing was left but an economic free-for-all, dominated by the search for self-sufficiency, sometimes within a single country, sometimes within an area or group of countries.

THE DEPRESSION: REACTIONS IN PARTICULAR COUNTRIES

Britain, as a major industrial and commercial country, was rapidly affected by the collapse in world trade; and in 1931 the country faced both a financial and a political crisis. Ramsay MacDonald's Labour government, without an overall majority in the House of Commons, clung to the economic and fiscal orthodoxies of free trade and a balanced budget, and found itself squeezed between falling revenue from taxation and rising expenditure, not least in unemployment payments. Sterling was on the gold standard, and British gold reserves came under heavy pressure as the European banks began to collapse from May 1931. Turning to American bankers for a loan, the government found itself unable to accept the terms which they insisted on, involving an assurance of a balanced budget through reduction of government expenditure, including unemployment benefit. The Labour government fell in August, and was replaced by a coalition, or National government, dominated by the Conservatives, though including some Liberal and Labour members, and retaining MacDonald as Prime Minister. The Labour Party split, with the great majority rejecting the coalition and going into opposition. The National government, under various Prime Ministers (MacDonald, Baldwin, and Neville Chamberlain) remained in existence for the rest of the decade, becoming steadily less National and more Conservative with the passing years.

The new government began with the declared intention of defending the exchange rate of sterling and staying on the gold standard. Within a month of taking office it was compelled to devalue by continuing pressure on the gold reserves, culminating when news of the refusal of duty by a number of crews in the fleet at Invergordon (after a reduction in pay clumsily introduced among the economy measures) shook the remaining foreign confidence in sterling. If the Royal Navy was not safe, what was? Britain went off the gold standard on 21 September 1931. Within a few days the pound fell against the dollar by 25 per cent, and by the end of the month by 30 per cent (from $4.86 to $3.25). Since sterling was at the time still the most important international currency, this was a severe blow to international financial dealings, and of course to all those who were holding their assets in sterling. It was a long step towards economic nationalism and international confusion; but from a purely British point of view it allowed sterling to reach a realistic level on the foreign exchanges. Early in 1932 the pound began to rise again, and by the end of March reached $3.80. At that point the government began to use the device of an Exchange Equalization Account to hold the pound roughly at that level; but made no attempt to return to gold. The effects were somewhat favourable to British exports, notably to countries which stayed on the gold standard. At the same time, in February 1932, the bank rate was reduced from 6 per cent to 2 per cent, encouraging domestic borrowing, which had a stimulating effect, especially on house-building; and the resulting semi-detached houses, in their avenues and crescents, are still to be seen up and down the land.

The other element in government policy, deliberately adopted in this case, was one of protective tariffs and imperial preference. In February 1932 the British government introduced a duty of 10 per cent on all imports except most raw materials and food, and a number of items imported from the Empire. In April the duty on manufactured goods was increased to 20 per cent, and in some cases more; and the trend in the following years was upwards. At the Ottawa Conference in July–August 1932 Britain agreed to give preference to foodstuffs imported from the Dominions, in return for preference for British manufactured goods in Dominion markets. The preferences were usually secured by raising the rates on foreign goods rather than by lowering them on Dominion goods; and they extended to some foodstuffs, notably wheat, butter, eggs, and cheese. Britain also imposed import quotas on foreign meat and bacon. The results were slender in terms of the volume of British trade but considerable in terms of its direction. Britain moved towards greater self-sufficiency within the Empire and Commonwealth, at the expense of trade outside it.

In economic terms, some substantial recovery followed these measures. The effects of devaluation on exports were real though short-lived, being overtaken by retaliatory measures by the countries of the Gold Bloc, and by devaluations by the Americans and others. Protection of the home market and low interest rates assisted domestic recovery; and by the end of 1934 Britain became the first major industrial country to surpass 1929 figures for industrial production. The recovery was patchy, with the old industries (textiles, coal, and ship building) remaining stagnant, and other areas (cars, chemicals, light engineering, consumer durables, and house-building) making progress. Unemployment, which reached a high point of approximately 3 million at the end of 1932, declined to 1.7 million by the beginning of 1937; this was still just over 11 per cent of the insured population.[4]

Despite these substantial unemployment figures and the other strains of the depression, the normal processes of British political life continued to work. There was some movement towards political extremes. Small fascist groups sprang up, of which the most prominent was Sir Oswald Mosley's British Union of Fascists; but there was never the slightest chance of them winning a seat in Parliament, still less posing a serious threat to the government of the country. The Communist Party won two seats in the general election of 1935; and the widespread admiration for the Soviet Union which found expression in fellow-travelling was stimulated by the depression. The apparent breakdown of capitalism and the dreary waste of unemployment made the great light in the east shine ever more brightly. But the movement for a Popular Front made little progress, and the Labour Party resolutely rejected affiliation by the Communist Party. The general election of 1935 returned a solid Conservative majority, despite a substantial Labour recovery. But this basic political steadiness went along with some profound and bitter divisions. The Labour Party and trade unions found the government's economic policies wholly inadequate; and resentment against its administration of unemployment relief was deep and long-lasting. (The term 'means test' retained its bitter flavour long after the 1930s were past.) There was little chance of a bipartisan approach on any aspect of policy, whether economic or foreign; and there were those on the Left who thought that Baldwin and Chamberlain were enemies as dangerous as Hitler – and much nearer.

Government policies to cope with the depression had direct consequences on foreign policy. A Foreign Office memorandum put to the Cabinet in December 1931 warned that a high protective tariff along with imperial preference would separate Britain from European affairs and diminish British influence on the Continent. Such effects, however, were not unwelcome: isolation from Europe was by no means an unpopular prospect, and in any case considerations of foreign policy were firmly subordinated to those of economics. The consequences for foreign policy followed their predicted course. In 1933 and 1934 the Foreign Office urged the importance of Britain providing a market for bacon, eggs, butter, and timber from the Baltic states and Poland, which might otherwise come into the economic orbit of either Berlin or Moscow. Similarly, it was argued that Britain should buy cereals and other farm produce from Hungary and Yugo-slavia, to prevent them from becoming over-dependent on the German market. In both cases the government refused, partly because it was tied by the Ottawa agreements, and partly because it disliked allowing political considerations to interfere with economic policy. In 1934, Vansittart, the permanent head of the Foreign Office, advocated competing with German influence in Austria by allowing tariff pre-ferences for various Austrian exports, but his proposals were rejected by the Board of Trade and the Treasury. This attitude persisted for some years, and helped to open the way for German economic influence in central and eastern Europe.

The position of France differed considerably from that of Britain. France was much less dependent on foreign trade, and was therefore largely sheltered from the immediate effects of the depression, and able to operate from a position of strength, taking the lead in the Gold Bloc. As it developed, French economic policy had three main strands. First, France kept its currency on the gold standard, giving it a very high exchange rate when Britain and the USA devalued in 1931 and 1933 respectively. This created serious difficulties for French exports, which had to contend with a severe price disadvantage in many markets, as well as the tariffs with which most countries protected their own producers. Failure of exports led to problems in paying for imports; though this was not so grave for France as for some other countries because of the balance of the French economy – the country remained, for example, largely self-sufficient in food. The problem of imports was met by the second element in French policy: the imposition of quotas on imports, and a system of imperial preference more far-reaching and effective than the British equivalent. In July and August 1931 import quotas were introduced arbitrarily on nearly all agricultural products; followed later by quotas on industrial products which were usually negotiated with the countries concerned. French colonies were exempt from these quotas, and also had con-siderable tariff advantages over foreign countries. The third aspect of economic policy was deflation at home – the attempts to meet the problem of the price of French exports by reducing domestic costs. In fact, the wholesale price index fell by about a quarter between 1931 and 1935 (from 462 to 347: 1914 = 100); though this was more the result of low commodity prices throughout the world than of direct government policy. At the same time wages were reduced by about 12 per cent; and government expenditure was also cut.[5]

The worst effects of the depression struck France later than other countries. Agricultural production kept up, but income fell, with serious results for the domestic market. Industrial output showed two low points, in 1932 and 1935, with only a modest upturn in between. Foreign trade suffered drastically, with both exports and imports down by more than half in 1935 from the levels of 1930.[6] The number of registered unemployed never reached substantial figures compared with Britain or Germany – the maximum was about 500,000 in February 1935. The official figures were misleadingly low, partly because large numbers of foreign workers were dispensed with, and partly because many townsmen who were out of work did not register, but simply went to live with relatives in the countryside. Conscription for the army also kept the figures lower than those in Britain. But even when all allowances were made, unemployment did not appear to be at crisis level.

The internal political effects of the depression, however, were more severe in France than in Britain. Under the Third Republic, governments had never been stable or long-lived – before 1914, their average life had been about a year. In the 1930s, this span shortened drastically, and a period of chronic ministerial instability set in, as a direct result of France's economic problems. Government revenue fell with the decline in foreign trade and domestic prices; yet governments were committed to balancing their budgets. They were therefore compelled to reduce expenditure, which meant holding down the service estimates, and also attacking civil service pay, pensions, and payments to ex-servicemen. In practice, measured against the movement of prices, these reductions did not damage spending power; but in psychological terms this made no difference. Payments made, for example, to the severely disabled from the First World War were reduced in cash terms; and the outcry may easily be imagined. The result was that successive Ministers of Finance proposed reductions in government expenditure, only to have them rejected in the National Assembly; and governments were repeatedly brought down on their financial measures. There were three changes of government in 1932, four in 1933, two in 1934, and two in 1935 – a total of eleven in four years. It appeared that the political system of the Third Republic, which had passed the stern test of war with flying colours, was breaking down under the less dramatic but more divisive strains of economic difficulty.

The combination of economic stagnation and political paralysis produced in France a marked movement towards political extremes. The fascist and conservative Right flourished in the middle 1930s. Their numbers were uncertain, but they thrust themselves into the public eye and showed their strength on the streets in the riots of 6 February 1934. On the Left, the Communist Party revived in 1935 and 1936, partly through the effects of the depression, and partly through the attraction of Popular Front slogans. On both Right and Left, opposition grew against the existing regime, which seemed unable to grapple with the country's problems.

The worst point in France's difficulties – the lowest level of foreign trade, the highest in unemployment, the resort to economic government by decree – came in 1935, at the time when the British economy was beginning to recover, and in Germany the nazis were well established and producing a striking improvement in the German economy. At that stage, France made her own bid for change and improvement – the Popular Front. The Popular Front's programme was more social than economic in content – the forty-hour week without reductions in wages and holidays with pay were two important items. The government intended to end deflation, keep up expenditure on pensions and payments to ex-servicemen, and increase revenue by tackling tax evasion; they also hoped that extra purchasing power from higher wages would stimulate demand. They were pledged not to devalue the franc. In economic terms this programme failed entirely. Industrial production remained stagnant. Wages rose in money terms, but fell in purchasing power: in the two years from April 1936 to April 1938, the retail price index rose by 46 per cent.[7] The wave of left-wing euphoria which accompanied the Popular Front victory – strikes, occupation of factories, demonstrations – alarmed investors and produced a flight of capital abroad, which in turn put pressure on the franc. This compelled the government to devalue on 26 September 1936. The devaluation was accompanied by a joint statement by the French, British, and United States governments, expressing their desire to minimize the disturbance to exchange rates caused by the French action – in less veiled language, Britain and the USA agreed not to retaliate by devaluations of their own. In general, the stagnation of the French economy continued, and no recovery was visible until the end of 1938. At the same time, the extreme fear of the Left aroused by the Popular Front victory embittered still further the political divisions within France.

These economic conditions and policies had various consequences for foreign policy. As with Britain, there was a conflict between economic and foreign policy in central and eastern Europe. France had a network of alliances with Poland, Czechoslovakia, Yugoslavia, and Rumania; and it was in her interests to strengthen these alliances by economic links. From 1934 onwards, the French Foreign Office was aware of the growth of German economic influence, and urged commercial concessions to combat it. But the preference given to imports from the French colonies (especially cereals) allowed little room for manoeuvre; and in any case the tendency of French commercial policy was to reduce imports. In December 1936 France agreed to make a purchase of wheat from Yugoslavia at a lower tariff rate than usual; but the Ministry of Agriculture insisted that this must not become a precedent. Another important influence of economics on foreign policy lay in the dependence on Britain and the USA which was marked, in however veiled a manner, by the three-power statement on French devaluation. The independence of the early 1930s, when France was leader of the Gold Bloc and in a stronger economic position than Britain, was over. Devaluation would offer no advantages if the British and Americans retaliated by lowering their own exchange rates; and two further devaluations in 1937 and 1938 emphasized the degree of French dependence on Anglo-American co-operation.

In Italy, the fascist state was put to the test by the depression. Parts of Italian agriculture remained very close to subsistence farming and so felt little effect; but the modern industry of the north and the banking system were seriously damaged – the more so since the Italian economy was already in difficulties in the late 1920s. There was a severe fall in foreign trade. Imports were valued at 21,303 million lire in 1929, and only 7,432 million in 1933; and exports fell in the same period from 14,767 million lire to 5,991 million. Industrial production also declined by one-third between 1929 and 1932.[8] At the same time, earnings from Italian shipping and remittances home from Italian emigrants (notably in the USA) diminished, as did income from tourism; all of which contributed to a serious balance of payments problem. Unemployment was high, with 1,132,000 registered unemployed in December 1933. This figure was almost certainly too low, and in the winter of 1933–34 1.75 million families were registered for the free state distributions of flour, rice, and milk. The state took action to reduce the figures in 1934, when the working week was reduced from forty-eight hours to forty, with an accompanying drop in earnings.[9] Under these pressures, a number of firms went into bankruptcy and banks failed. Government revenue fell, and expenditure rose; and budget deficits were serious between 1931 and 1934. The fascist economy was in as much difficulty as others; and the Italian people were subjected to unemployment, a lowering of wages, and rising prices.

In face of these difficulties, Mussolini rejected for a long time the devaluation of the lira. In 1926–27 he had declared 'the battle of the lira', fixed its value at 92.46 to the pound sterling, and held to the gold standard. His own prestige and that of the regime were committed to maintaining this very high rate of exchange, which as other currencies were devalued put up the price of exports and made life difficult for foreign visitors. This policy was accompanied from 1934 onwards by high customs duties, which severely restricted imports other than of vital raw materials (which were subsidized) and some foodstuffs. For some commodities, a system of import licences was introduced. In 1934 also strict exchange controls were imposed. These measures were presented as an attempt at self-sufficiency, for which the Italian economy was almost wholly unsuited. Mussolini made great play with 'the battle for grain' (he liked to present economic questions in military terms); and indeed Italy became self-sufficient in wheat, though at the expense of other crops, and only by using imported fertilizers. Other measures included a search for oil in the valley of the River Po, and for bauxite in the south. Eventually, when the Gold Bloc disintegrated and its other members devalued, Italy followed suit with a drastic 41 per cent devaluation on 5 October 1936, which had a stimulating effect on exports and thus eased the purchase of imports.

In 1935 the Italian economic position was further complicated by the attack on Abyssinia, and the League of Nations sanctions which followed. The war was not primarily waged for economic reasons (despite talk of Abyssinia's potential resources of raw materials); but it had a number of economic consequences. The war provided a stimulus for industry, and production increased; and mobilization for the army brought down the unemployment figures. On the other hand, the budget deficit was pushed up sharply in 1936, having been almost eliminated in 1935. League sanctions, often dismissed as totally ineffectual because they were half-hearted and failed to halt the Italian conquest of Abyssinia, had serious adverse effects on the Italian economy. The cost of imports went up, because they often had to be obtained from unusual suppliers or through states which did not apply sanctions; many foreign banks ceased to extend credit to the Italian government or firms; and governments blocked Italian accounts in their countries. One result was to give an added impulse to the idea of self-sufficiency; another was to push Italy into greater dependence on imports from Germany, which did not apply sanctions.

In 1934 Italy and Germany concluded an agreement by which all payments for trade between the two countries were to go through a single clearing account, in which export and import payments were to be kept in balance. The exchange rate between the two currencies was fixed at a rate favourable to Germany; and also 7.5 per cent of German exports to Italy were to be paid for in currency freely usable in international exchange – sterling, dollars, or Swiss francs. These terms were favourable to Germany; and in a further economic agreement of December 1937 Italy undertook to import industrial goods from Germany, and to pay for them in part by sending 30,000 agricultural workers to Germany in 1938, an arrangement which emphasized Italy's subordinate role as a mere provider of labour. Italy became particularly dependent on imports of coal from Germany. In 1932 over half Italian coal imports came from Britain; in 1936 the figure was reduced to 1 per cent, and the bulk of supplies (over 7 million tons) came from Germany. In 1938 the Germans agreed to increase this to 9 million tons. In that year, Italy drew 42.4 per cent of its European imports from Germany (including Austria), against only 3.6 per cent from France and 10.2 per cent from Britain. This was a marked change from the position ten years earlier, when the British and French shares together considerably exceeded the German and Austrian.[10] This was no small element in the making of the Rome–Berlin Axis, and in the subordination of Italian policy to Germany.

Germany suffered particularly badly under the effects of the depression. The economic prosperity of the late 1920s was supported by short-term American loans, and the recall of this capital after the crash of 1929 had disastrous results. There was a rapid and continuous fall in industrial production from 1929 to 1932. A banking crisis of 1931 saw one big bank fail completely, and the government had to declare a number of 'bank holidays'. Unemployment, which averaged about 11 per cent even in the years of prosperity, rose from 2.4 million in March 1930 to a peak of 6 million (30 per cent) in May 1932.[11] The severity of these effects was made worse by the policy of strict deflation applied by the government headed by Chancellor Heinrich Bruening, who refused any devaluation of the mark, insisted on balanced budgets, and tried to reduce prices.

Bruening fell from office in May 1932, to be succeeded in rapid succession by Papen and Schleicher, and in January 1933 by Hitler. In a simple yet accurate sense it is permissible to see the advent to power of Hitler as the most far-reaching political consequence of the depression. There was a close psychological link between the great inflation and the great depression: the large numbers of Germans with savings, insurance policies, or fixed incomes, who had seen all such assets wiped out once, cast round desperately for someone who could save them from a repetition of such events. They needed someone to offer them confidence; and Hitler at that stage was a most tremendous generator of confidence. Moreover, a number of German industrialists and bankers, who until 1929 showed no interest in the Nazi Party, began to offer it financial support during the years 1929–32, though usually hedging their bets by contributing also to the funds of other parties. The Nazi Party, which enjoyed only modest success in the late 1920s, flourished in the depression, at the same time as the trade unions which might have been its most serious opponents were weakened and demoralized by mass unemployment. Without the particular circumstances of the depression in Germany, it is at least likely that Hitler would have remained a fringe figure in German politics.

In the few months before Hitler came to power, the Papen and Schleicher governments reversed Bruening's policies, and began to encourage credit, increase government spending, and undertake public works. These were policies advocated by a number of critics of Bruening's government, including the trade unions as well as the nazis. In the first instance, Hitler did nothing to change these policies. He did not put nazis in charge of economic affairs. The Economics Minister was Hugenberg, the leader of the Nationalist Party, with an economic expert from the same party as the State Secretary; and Hjalmar Schacht, with his reputation as 'the man who saved the mark' after the collapse of 1923, was recalled as President of the Reichsbank in March 1933 as a guarantee, by his very name, that the government would maintain the value of the currency.

Hitler's own economic ideas, as developed in the 1920s, were fairly simple. It was the business of government to ensure for its people the best conditions for their life and development; and one vital condition was a secure food supply. To import large quantities of food meant putting the state and its people at the mercy of the world economy, the terms of trade, and the sale of exports. Hitler rejected this as a long-term policy, arguing that Germany must produce her own food on her own soil; since that was inadequate for a growing population, the solution was to conquer new territory in eastern Europe and above all in the USSR. The events of the depression bore out at least part of these ideas, demonstrating the unreliability of the world economy and the difficulty of paying for imports with exports. In a speech to the Industrial Club of Duesseldorf in January 1932, carefully designed to appeal to the audience of industrialists and businessmen gathered to hear him, Hitler argued that exporting countries, faced with declining markets, could only compete with one another by cutting prices; but in the long run they must protect themselves by aiming at self-sufficiency, which would itself be precarious if their area was insufficient. Germany, therefore, before organizing a vast internal market, must gain more territory.

The idea of self-sufficiency was far from being peculiar to Hitler. It was practised within the British and French empires; and to a considerable degree it was also the policy of President Roosevelt, seeking to base recovery on the vast internal market of the USA. In Germany in the late nineteenth and early twentieth centuries extremely rapid industrialization put the country in the position of being dependent on foreign trade, with a fear in many hearts that Germany could be strangled through this dependence, unable to feed its population or to keep its factories turning. The Allied blockade in 1914–18 brought such fears to life; and Germany was forced to rely on her own sphere of control in eastern and central Europe. By 1932–33, even those industrialists and entrepreneurs who were most committed to international trade and the world market were compelled to acknowledge that markets were being closed everywhere, and to turn to a German sphere which seemed marked out for her by history and geography. The idea of world trade was everywhere giving way to that of self-sufficiency and closed economic systems.

Hitler thus shared economic ideas which had a currency far outside the Nazi Party. The same was true of his simplest notion about economics. He told Rauschning in 1932 that 'You get inflation if you want inflation. . . Inflation is lack of discipline – lack of discipline in the buyers, and lack of discipline in the sellers.' His storm-troopers would control prices when he came to power – if they 'cleaned up' an offending shop, it would not put up prices again. He had no objection to disguised devaluation, but he would not have it in the open – no devaluation, and no ration cards.[12] As these comments indicate, Hitler believed that economic phenomena would bend to his will – economics were to be at the service of politics, not the other way about. Goering put it thus in 1936: 'We do not recognise the sanctity of some of these so-called economic laws. It must be pointed out that trade and industry are servants of the people, while capital also has a role to play as the servant of the economy.' There is a story that once, in an argument with Schacht, Goering banged the table and shouted: 'if the Fuehrer wishes it, then two times two is five'.[13] In the long run, such doctrine proved difficult to sustain; but in the short run it produced some surprising results.

At the end of 1932 and in the first part of 1933 the German economy began to pick up; industrial production rose, and the total of unemployed fell. By the autumn of 1933, this very recovery was creating difficulties for German foreign trade and the balance of payments. As the domestic economy improved, imports rose; but exports did not keep pace, because of the increase in domestic demand, the high exchange value of the mark, and the imposition of trade barriers by other countries. It became increasingly difficult to pay for imports and service the country's foreign debts. In October 1933 the new State Secretary at the Economics Ministry, Hans Posse, put forward proposals for a changed trade policy, of importing mainly from countries which were prepared to purchase equivalent amounts of German exports. If the USA and the British and French empires obstructed German exports, the answer was to concentrate on markets close at hand where German economic influence could be predominant; which meant primarily the countries of south-east, central, and northern Europe. These proposals were adopted by the German Cabinet on 4 October 1933; and there followed trade treaties and clearing agreements with Hungary (February 1934) and Yugoslavia (May 1934). These followed a common pattern. Germany undertook to import agricultural produce, and the other countries lowered their tariffs on German industrial goods, which they paid for from the proceeds of their exports. The terms were favourable to Germany, because in the circumstances of the time the Hungarians and Yugoslavs were happy to be assured of any market for their farm produce. Germany also hoped for political advantage, by weaning Hungary away from Italian influence and Yugoslavia away from France. A similar agreement was signed with Rumania in March 1935. There followed a marked increase in German trade with all three countries, and the junior partners became more dependent on it; though this was less true for Rumania than for the others.

The consequences for Germany's total foreign trade, however, were limited. During 1934 the balance of trade deteriorated sharply, showing an excess of imports over exports of 284 million marks against an export surplus of 667 million in 1933.[14] Schacht became Economics Minister in July 1934 (retaining his position as President of the Reichsbank); and in September he introduced his 'New Plan' for German foreign trade, based on the principles of buying nothing which could not be paid for by foreign exchange earned by German exports, and of making imports conform to national needs as decided by the government. All imports were subject to licences, which were used to differentiate between essential and non-essential items, with raw materials and food classified as essential. Whenever possible, imports were to be bought only from the countries which were willing to accept German goods in return; and any foreign exchange involved was to be paid into a clearing account, and not used freely by the exporting country.

This policy was not wholly welcome to German industrialists, who mostly believed that in the long run their future lay in trade with other industrial economies, and who wished to work out ways of re-entering the markets of the British Empire and the USA. Schacht himself regarded the New Plan as a temporary expedient, to be abandoned when world economic conditions improved. He was willing to seek raw materials and food in south-east Europe; but recognized that this policy could not create a self-sufficient system. As regards food, the Danubian states could provide cereals, meat, and dairy products which would go far to meet German needs. Of raw materials, Germany produced only coal and potash in sufficient quantities within her own borders. South-east Europe could provide oil (Rumania), bauxite (Yugoslavia and Hungary), nickel (Greece), chromium (Yugoslavia, Greece, and Turkey), and antimony (Czechoslovakia), in which Germany was entirely lacking; and make up a sufficient balance of timber, pyrites, and graphite. But this was far from enough to meet all Germany's needs – it was calculated that German industry needed in all thirty-five raw materials, of which thirty-three had to be imported.[15]

In these circumstances, the New Plan and links with south-east Europe could offer only partial advantages; but these were still worth while. In 1934 and 1935 German rearmament began to get under way. The import controls of the New Plan were used to give priority to items needed for armaments; and for some commodities the Danubian states formed a good source of supply. German imports of bauxite (the raw material for aluminium) rose from almost nil in 1933 to 981,000 tons in 1936, largely to feed the new aircraft production programmes; and rather over half these imports came from Hungary and Yugoslavia.[16] In the long term, too, south-eastern Europe offered sources of supply which were close to Germany and immune from naval blockade in time of war.

In the short term, the New Plan was successful in shifting the balance of trade in favour of exports. From an import surplus of 284 million marks in 1934, Germany developed an export surplus of 111 million in 1935 and 550 million in 1936.[17] This success was only temporary. Germany's need for imports was increasing rapidly. Domestic recovery pushed up demand, and armaments production required increasing quantities of raw materials. Germany began to be faced with the question of whether the rearmament drive could be continued at its existing (or indeed increased) momentum, or whether it would be better to pause, consolidate, and find some long-term solution to the problem of paying for imports and finding foreign exchange. At that point Hitler himself intervened seriously in economic questions for the first time. A new Four-Year Plan was launched, under the direction of Goering; there was a struggle for the control of the German economy between Goering and Schacht, with various groups in support of each; and the economy was set on a course which was more dominated by questions of armaments than hitherto. It was also a course which led to steadily deepening difficulties, which will be examined in the next chapter.

Recovery from the depression was uneven and slow, beginning in some countries in 1933, while the countries of the Gold Bloc were beginning their decline. In 1934 and 1935, industrial production, exports, and prices in several European countries were moving upwards, and by the end of 1936 and early 1937 raw material prices were demonstrating the extent of the recovery in demand – the price of tin rose by 50 per cent in six months, while copper, lead, and zinc doubled in price.[18] What had been a world surplus of raw materials was replaced quite suddenly by an excess of demand over supply; and with several European countries in the process of rearmament, questions arose about access to raw materials, especially on the part of Germany and Italy in Europe, and Japan in the Far East. In the new circumstances created by economic nationalism and self-sufficiency, the revival of world trade lagged behind that of industrial activity; the League of Nations index of industrial activity (1929 = 100) stood at 111.3 in 1936, but that for world trade only at 85.9.[19] Recovery took place in semi-insulated compartments, which were in some ways restrictive; but their advantages were shown in 1937, when the USA suffered a further very serious depression (with unemployment back to 13 million). This American relapse had serious effects in the primary producing countries, but much less so in Europe, which had to a considerable extent protected herself.

The great depression itself clearly did not lead directly to war – war came after recovery was well under way. But its effects were far-reaching, and no analysis of the origins of the war would be complete without taking them into account. The social unrest which often accompanied the depression was particularly marked in eastern Europe, where it affected many different groups – industrial workers, farmers, unemployed civil servants, young graduates who could find no work. Usually governments were the natural targets for the discontent; but so were alien minorities, particularly when they showed signs of prosperity among the general adversity. In parts of eastern Europe some Jews were in this position; and in Czechoslovakia the

German-speaking population of the Sudeten areas were a focus for Czech resentment, creating tensions which played their part in the origins of the Munich crisis of 1938. The approaches of different countries to the question of armaments were closely bound up with their economic circumstances. Some, like Britain, tended to allow economic and financial conditions to predominate over the strictly military and strategic; others, like Germany, tried to assert the predominance of political will over economic constraints. All found that in practice such lines were hard to hold – economic and strategic policies were too closely linked to be kept separate from one another.

The part played by the great depression in the origins of the war was indirect, and to a large degree intangible, though no less real for that. It destroyed the positive and encouraging economic and political developments of the years between 1924 and 1930. Franco–German co-operation and 'the spirit of Locarno' fizzled out. No more was heard of economic collaboration, and the World Economic Conference of 1933 broke up in disorder and recrimination. Self-preservation through some form of economic nationalism became the order of the day, and a climate of opinion was created in which conflict was both more likely and more acceptable by 1934 or 1935 than it had been in 1929 or 1930. Above all, the depression generated fear: fear that the mechanism of international trade would not deliver the necessary raw materials or foodstuffs, fear about jobs and livelihoods, fear of other states' policies – sometimes fear of one's own government's policies. If wars begin in the minds of men, it is fair to say that men's minds were shaken and disturbed by the effects of the depression.

REFERENCES AND NOTES

1. Charles P. Kindleberger, *The World in Depression, 1929–1939* (London 1973), pp. 93–4.
2. David E. Kaiser, *Economic Diplomacy and the Origins of the Second World War* (Princeton 1980), pp. 17–18.
3. Kindleberger, *World in Depression*, p. 171.
4. G. C. Peden, *British Rearmament and the Treasury, 1932–1939* (Edinburgh 1979); B. R. Mitchell, Statistical Appendix to Carlo M. Cipolla (ed.), *Fontana Economic History of Europe*, vol. 6, part 2 (London 1976), p. 667.
5. Kindleberger, *World in Depression*, pp. 248–9; Derek H. Aldcroft, *The European Economy, 1914–1970* (London 1978), p. 102.
6. Kindleberger, *World in Depression*, pp. 248–9; Henri Dubief, *Le déclin de la IIIe République* (Paris 1976), pp. 20–3.
7. Alfred Sauvy, 'L'évolution économique', in René Rémond and Janine Bourdin (eds.), *Edouard Daladier, chef de gouvernement, avril 1938–*

septembre 1939 (Paris 1977) p. 87.

8. John F. Coverdale, *Italian Intervention in the Spanish Civil War* (Princeton, N.J. 1975), p. 23; Shepard B. Clough, *The Economic History of Modern Italy* (New York 1964), pp. 246–7.

9. P. Milza and S. Berstein, *Le Fascisme italien, 1919–1945* (Paris 1980), pp. 240–1; Coverdale, *Italian Intervention*, pp. 20–1.

10. Clough, *Economic History*, pp. 273–4; Denis Mack Smith, *Mussolini's Roman Empire* (London: Peregrine Books 1979), p. 160.

11. *Fontana Economic History of Europe*, vol. 6, part 2, Statistical Appendix, p. 690; Karl Hardach, 'Germany 1914–1970', ibid., vol. 6, part 1, pp. 196–9.

12. Hermann Rauschning, *Hitler Speaks* (London 1939), pp. 29, 207.

13. Amos E. Simpson, *Hjalmar Schacht in Perspective* (The Hague 1969), pp. 124, 146.

14. Table in Kaiser, *Economic Diplomacy*, p. 319.

15. *Bulletin of International News*, vol. XIII, pp. 3–8.

16. Kaiser, *Economic Diplomacy*, pp. 137–8.

17. Simpson, *Schacht*, p. 98; cf. table in Kaiser, *Economic Diplomacy*, p. 319.

18. *Bulletin of International News*, vol. XIII, pp. 839–41.

19. Ibid., XIV, pp. 3–4.

Chapter 10

ECONOMIC PROBLEMS AND THE COMING OF WAR

War came to Europe when the depression was passing; indeed, preparation for war gave a stimulus to the economy of a number of countries. Economic recovery brought its own problems; and we must now ask how far the new economic pressures of the late 1930s provided motives for states to go to war.

In the case of Britain, all the major economic influences were against war, and especially against war with Germany. The First World War had done irreparable damage to Britain's economic position, and there was every reason to believe that another major conflict would repeat the dose, probably with fatal results. Britain lived by imports of food and raw materials, which had to be paid for, mostly by exports or the provision of services. War meant that the import bill would go up, to sustain the war economy, while the ability to pay that bill would go down, because industry and services were directed to military purposes. It was correctly foreseen that within about a year of sustained war effort, Britain would no longer be able to pay for her imports. In the previous war, this crisis had been staved off by borrowing in the USA; but in the late 1930s this option appeared to be firmly closed. American neutrality legislation, put into permanent form in 1937, forbade altogether the export of implements of war to belligerent powers, and the export of other materials could not be financed by loans or credits. In addition, the Johnson Act (1934) forbade any government which had defaulted on its debts to the USA (which included Great Britain) to raise loans in that country. The door was not merely shut; it was locked and bolted.

To make military preparations for war also presented economic difficulties. There were budgetary restrictions on the amount of money allocated to the armed services; limited physical resources, in terms of factory space, equipment, and skilled manpower; and difficulties in meeting the bills for imports, because between 25 and 30 per cent of the cost of armaments lay in the price of imported raw materials. In addition to these constraints there was the wider question of the nature of the economy and how it was to be run. The British government wished to preserve a market economy, and to avoid forms of compulsion which would arouse the opposition of industrialists and dislocate normal business activity. Rapid rearmament, on the other hand, would be best achieved through a command economy, in which the government set priorities and gave orders. In Britain in the late 1930s, such a course was ruled out as both economically and politically unacceptable.

All this applied to war, and preparations for war, in general. When the question turned to war with Germany in particular, there were further economic reasons against it. Germany was an important market for British exports – the fifth in terms of value in 1938, just ahead of the USA.[1] As a result of the Anglo-German Payments Agreement of 1934, revised after the *Anschluss* with Austria in 1938 on favourable terms for Britain, this market was fairly stable; and Germany also took considerable amounts of British coal and textiles, offering an outlet for sectors of the economy which remained in depression. In late 1938 and early 1939, negotiations were in progress for a coal cartel, by which German and British producers would agree on a division of markets between them. The British government continued to believe, right up to 1939, in the importance of restoring Germany to her central place in the European trading system.

They believed, too, that German economic anxieties could and should be assuaged by offering guaranteed access to raw materials outside Europe. In 1937 and early in 1938, the British were willing to explore the possibilities of returning to Germany some of the colonies lost in 1919. They put this suggestion to France in April 1937, with the slightly embarrassing condition that the French would have to provide the major share of territory to be restored, because the Dominions would not budge from their mandates, and there were insuperable (though unexplained) reasons against the return of Tanganyika. The French were naturally sceptical about such proposals. In March 1938, Britain put to Germany a complicated proposal by which territory over a large part of central Africa (most of which did not belong to Britain) might be brought into a form of joint trusteeship, in which Germany could share – thus resuming her place as a colonial power without actually having any colonies. Such proposals were too thin to be taken seriously. Access to colonies could not meet German problems about raw materials, because the most important raw materials (coal, iron, petroleum, cotton) were hardly produced in colonies at all; the great exception was rubber, with 96 per cent of world production coming from colonial sources in 1936.[2] No one, however, proposed to cede Malaya to Germany. The proposals did not offer Germany very much. If in return she gave serious undertakings of good behaviour in central and eastern Europe, and accepted a limitation of armaments, these would be disproportionate concessions. However, it was significant that the British were willing to make even token economic moves to assure Germany of their goodwill; and they expected to get a response from the 'sensible men' in Berlin, notably Schacht, who himself took the question of colonies far more seriously than Hitler did.

In other respects, economic relations between the British and German governments during the 1930s were mainly good. The British recognized that the Anglo-German Payments Agreements of 1934 and 1938 provided Germany with foreign exchange which was used to finance rearmament, but still believed that the balance of advantage lay with Britain. In November 1937 an Austrian proposal for the abolition of exchange control by the Danubian states, aimed at diminishing German influence in the area, received a hostile reception from Chamberlain, who thought it would imperil the general settlement with Germany which was his ultimate goal. Only in May 1938 did the government begin to examine possible economic actions against Germany, setting up an Inter-Departmental Committee on South-East Europe for this purpose. The results were not great, though they did mark a change of emphasis in British policy: a loan to Turkey, credits to Greece and Rumania, and the purchase of 200,000 tons of Rumanian grain in October 1938. After the Munich agreement, British influence in much of south-eastern Europe inevitably collapsed, though in Rumania Britain and France kept up a successful economic defence against Germany for a prolonged period.

Despite these late changes, the general British position was that the economic interest of the country benefited from good relations with Germany, from restraint in rearmament, and from the avoidance of war. Only the threat of total German economic control over Europe was likely to change that assessment. Much the same was true of France. The stagnation of the French economy which was evident from April 1936 to April 1938 persisted for the next six months. Two further devaluations of the franc (July 1937 and May 1938) failed to have more than a fleeting effect on industrial production, which was held back by internal constraints, and mainly by trade union insistence on the forty-hour week. In November 1938, Daladier appointed Paul Reynaud as Minister of Finance, and embarked on a new economic policy. Credit was eased; and the forty-hour week was relaxed by means of exceptions for armaments industries and their suppliers, so that from October 1938 to June 1939 the average working week rose from 39.2 hours to 41.9, and in armaments factories it reached 50 or even 60 hours. In the same period, industrial production rose by 20 per cent, and unemployment fell by 10 per cent (to about 380,000). An attempted general strike against these measures in November 1938 was a failure. The upturn came belatedly, leaving France acutely conscious of industrial weakness in face of Germany – by the end of 1938 German steel production was almost four times greater than that of France.[3] There was every reason in economic terms for France to avoid a confrontation with Germany, and to seek at least a breathing-space to allow economic recovery to develop.

France, like Britain, showed a growing tendency to dispute German economic predominance in eastern Europe, though only after the basis of French influence there had vanished almost beyond recall. In September 1936 there had been a Franco-Polish agreement for a French loan of 2,000 million francs, of which 800 millions were to be spent on French armaments; but by January 1938 practically none of these had been delivered, and the French government admitted to the Poles that it could not meet its commitments. The Czechoslovakian crisis brought French influence to a very low ebb; and it seemed reasonable to think that France had chosen to abandon eastern Europe to Germany. However, in 1939 this movement was checked, and France took up the cudgels in Rumania, with considerable success; though without changing its central premiss that on economic grounds it preferred to avoid, or at least postpone, a war with Germany.

France and Britain were both on the defensive, in economic as well as other terms. The position of Italy was in many ways different. Italian policy was expansionist, as its moves into Abyssinia (1935–36) and Albania (1939) showed; but only a part of the impulse behind this expansion was economic in nature, and even then more in theory than in practice. From 1935 onwards Mussolini talked a good deal about self-sufficiency, which would be based on an economic zone in Africa and the Balkans. But in fact little progress was made. There was little time or opportunity to explore the resources of Abyssinia; Libyan oil remained untapped; Albania offered limited possibilities; and Italian aspirations in Yugoslavia were kept firmly in check by Germany, which had taken control of much of Yugoslavian trade, and had no wish to see it disturbed. Italy made herself self-sufficient in wheat; and developed enough bauxite mining to secure an adequate supply of aluminium. Otherwise, she remained heavily dependent on imports, not least of oil and raw materials for the armaments industry.

There was some possibility of conquering or controlling sources of raw materials – there were minerals in the Balkans, and oil in the Middle East if Italy were to replace Britain as the predominant power there; and such ideas formed part of Mussolini's aspirations to become the principal Mediterranean power. But though the aspirations were there, the economic power to make them good was not. Steel production in 1938 was only 2.3 million tons, and coal a mere 1.5 million tons. Most imports were sea-borne, with (in 1939) about 80 per cent coming from outside the Mediterranean, and therefore subject to naval blockade. Imports of coal came mostly from Germany, by sea; though it was found in 1940 that some 12 million tons of coal could be moved in the year by rail, using lines through Austria and Switzerland.[4] From a strictly economic point of view, Italy had some motive for expansion by war and conquest, but insufficient capacity to carry it out. In terms of profit, neutrality in the war which actually began in 1939 offered substantial advantages, with Italy being able to benefit from transit trade to Germany to avoid the Allied blockade, and with the belligerents seeking to buy Italian exports. Such simple calculations of profit and loss, however, did not come high on Mussolini's order of priorities; and when he went to war, it was not primarily for economic reasons.

The Soviet Union was in the paradoxical position of devoting a large part of its economic efforts to armaments, yet having the strongest economic reasons for remaining at peace. According to official Soviet figures, armament expenditure increased from 5.4 per cent of expenditure under the first Five-Year Plan to 26.4 per cent during the first three years of the third Plan.[5] Soviet production of weapons (tanks, guns, and aircraft) reached high figures in the late 1930s, though the development of new types was held back by the purges and by Stalin's arbitrary decisions. At the same time, heavy industry had developed very rapidly, at the expense of agriculture and consumer goods, and it was in the process of being dispersed so that a proportion was beyond the Urals, far distant from any European attack. But this did not mean that the Soviet economy was prepared for war. Growth in the crucial iron and steel industry was painfully slow (only 3 per cent, 1938–41)[6]; and the processes of change were still under way. The immense economic and social dislocation wrought by collectivization, industrialization, and the purges had not yet been overcome. The Soviet Union needed a long period of peace to recuperate, and in economic terms there was no better indication of this than the price which Stalin was willing to pay for an agreement with Germany. The economic agreement signed with Germany late in 1939 was favourable to the Germans, and was executed more faithfully on the Soviet side than the German (see below, p. 290). Economic considerations combined with others to confirm the Soviet desire to keep out of war, except when Soviet territory was at stake (as in the Far East), or when a walk-over was expected (as with Finland).

THE GERMAN PROBLEM

The exception to this catalogue of states which for economic reasons would prefer to avoid war lay in Germany, less because the German economy was fully prepared for war (certainly general and prolonged war) than because Germany was going through a severe economic crisis, of which one possible solution was a war of conquest. The process was circular. The economic crisis itself was largely caused by the extreme pace of German rearmament. One way out would have been to slacken that pace; when that was rejected, Germany was in a position where she was arming in order to expand, and then had to expand in order to continue to arm. One belief was crucial, and totally at variance with all assumptions made in the liberal democracies: that war could be made to pay.

In the course of 1936, difficulties accumulated in the German economy. There was a problem of food supply, partly because restrictions on the import of animal fodder had resulted in the widespread slaughter of pigs and cattle in the winter of 1935–36. (This was the background to one of Goebbels's most famous remarks, on 17 January 1936, about guns and butter. His actual words may need to be recalled: 'We can do well without butter, but we must have guns, because butter could not help us if we were to be attacked one day.')[7] The Germans had, in fact, gone short of butter and other dairy and pork products during that winter; and it was Hitler's intention to make good these shortages without cutting back on armaments – not to choose between the two. There was pressure on raw materials which were important for the rearmament drive; and an increasing problem of securing foreign exchange to pay for imports whose cost could not be met by exports. At home, there was a shortage of labour in some sectors of the economy. All this, in the normal workings of supply and demand, meant pressure for prices to rise.

In these circumstances, Schacht (who since 1935 had combined the posts of Economic Minister and President of the Reichsbank, and been effectively in control of the German economy) recommended that the time had come for consolidation: to slow down the pace of rearmament and increase exports, allowing freer multilateral trade by relaxing the tight restrictions of his own New Plan. He received support in this from Colonel Georg Thomas, the head of the Economics and Armaments Section of the War Ministry, who favoured a slower, long-term programme of armaments in preparation for a long war; from the banks; and from the steel and coal industries, which wanted to get back to a wider trade system. Hitler would not accept such proposals, refusing to allow any pause in rearmament, and indeed seeking to accelerate it. In this he was supported by Goering and the *Luftwaffe* high command; important elements in the Nazi Party; industrialists in the sectors concerned with aircraft, motor cars, machine tools, and chemicals; and some members of the army high command.

In August 1936 Hitler intervened with a memorandum on the Four-Year Plan.[8] He restated his basic aims and principles. Germany was overpopulated, with neither the food nor the raw materials necessary for her needs. 'The definitive solution lies in an extension of our living space, that is, an extension of the raw materials and food basis of our nation.' But in the meantime various steps were necessary to tide Germany over until this definitive solution could be attained. At present, Germany could not afford enough imports to meet all her needs. It was impossible to increase exports to pay for more imports; and equally impossible to reduce imports, because to do so would hamper rearmament. It was therefore necessary to produce in Germany, at whatever cost, synthetic rubber and oil, and to mine German iron ore, even of poor quality, in order to release foreign exchange to pay for food and for raw materials which could not be produced at home or in substitute form. Nearly four years of nazi rule had gone by without making progress with such a programme. (The first synthetic oil contract had in fact been signed in December 1933, but Schacht had held it back, because he regarded the necessary investment as uneconomic.) Hitler concluded: 'There has been time enough in four years to find out what we cannot do. Now we have to carry out what we can do. I thus set the following tasks: I. The German armed forces must be operational within four years. II. The German economy must be fit for war within four years'.

This was not in strict terms a plan for self-sufficiency. When Hitler announced the Four-Year Plan publicly at the Party Congress in September 1936, he carefully said that Germany must be independent of foreign countries for those materials which she could produce herself, either by chemical means or by mining; this would reserve foreign exchange for food and materials which could *not* be so produced. It was rather a policy of preparing for war, which alone could bring about the definitive solution set out in his memorandum, though not in his public speech. Goering was appointed as Commissioner for the Four-Year Plan by a decree of 18 October 1936; and he defined the objects of the plan as being to increase self-sufficiency while continuing rearmament at a rapid pace. The production of synthetics was to be pursued, with the aim of meeting by 1939 all the oil needs of the mobilization plan, 50 per cent of the rubber needs, 30 per cent of the textiles, and 33 per cent of the animal fats. Domestic production of iron ore in the Salzgitter area was to be increased, to meet 50 per cent of mobilization needs by 1939.[9] Food production was to be further improved; and controls over the movement of labour were tightened.

No fixed organization was set up to carry out the plan. Goering declared that his tasks, and those of agencies which he set up, were to provide leadership, initiative, and drive, not administration; and the organizations created under the plan were typical of the Third Reich in their fluidity, improvisation, and overlapping. Schacht remained as Economics Minister until November 1937, and continued to oppose the self-sufficiency aspects of the Four-Year Plan, with the support of business circles, the banks, and large parts of the steel industry. In particular he objected to the development of the Hermann Goering Iron and Steel Works, set up to exploit German iron ore, which he thought to be a wasteful and inefficient organization. His struggle was unavailing, for Goering had Hitler's backing, as well as that of the industries which did well out of the plan, notably I. G. Farben in chemicals, which was heavily involved in the synthetics programme, and the aircraft firms. Schacht's value to the regime lay mainly in his reputation as an opponent of inflation at home, and his contacts abroad – as long as some co-operation was sought from foreign industries and banking, Schacht was useful. After he resigned from the Economics Ministry, Germany declined to take part in a world raw materials conference at Geneva, which Schacht had wished his government to attend: a co-operative approach to the problem of raw materials was thus openly ruled out. Schacht remained as President of the Reichsbank; but his successor as Minister of Economics, Walther Funk, was Goering's nominee. The struggle for control of the German economy, which had been going against Schacht from 1936, was finally decided.

Goering might say that, if the Fuehrer wished it, two times two made five: but they did not. The proclamation of a plan and victory over its opponents did not mean that the facts of Germany's economic situation disappeared. The facts came home, even for the *Luftwaffe*, which Goering favoured, and for the synthetics programme which was the centre-piece of the new policy. In 1937 and 1938 Germany was short of aluminium, steel, and labour to meet the various demands which were being made on the economy. At the end of 1936, the requirement of aluminium by aircraft manufacturers to meet the *Luftwaffe*'s programmes was 4,500 tons per month, of which only half was available. In 1937 the three armed services together asked for 750,000 tons of steel per month, but received only 300,000. Steel production remained at the same level as 1936 (about 19.8 million tons a year), while demand went up, and no systematic order of priorities for its use was worked out. The same problem hit the synthetic oil programme, which in 1938 required 120,000 tons of steel per month for construction purposes; the actual allocation was 42,000 tons, though in February 1939 Goering undertook to bring the deliveries up to the level required. Synthetic oil also depended on coal, which was the basis of the process. In July 1938 it was estimated that 20,000–30,000 extra miners would be needed in the next three years, but in fact there was a shortage of labour in the coal-fields. This was part of a wider problem of manpower: in October 1938 the Economic and Armaments Office of the War Ministry estimated that by March 1939 Germany would be short of 600,000 workers in industry and 1 million in agriculture.[10]

Even for the *Luftwaffe*, production of aircraft fell back, though not by much; and monthly output did not reach the level of March 1937 again until May 1939. As for synthetic oil, it was recognized in July 1938 that production would meet only 20 per cent of needs by 1939, as against the original target of 100 per cent.[11] When, in October 1938, Hitler set out a new armaments programme which involved a fivefold increase in the size of the *Luftwaffe*, which would require the building of 47,500 aircraft by spring 1942, the resources to carry it out were simply not available – neither raw materials, steel, fuel, nor manpower. The fuel supply for the force envisaged would have used up 85 per cent of the total world production of aviation fuel. It was to that sort of directive that the divorce between the nazi regime and economic reality led.

Even well short of this type of fantasy, however, Germany faced a grave economic problem, which may be summed up in terms of food, raw materials, and foreign exchange. Hitler's exposition of Germany's situation at the so-called Hossbach conference on 5 November 1937 was largely about economics. Food consumption in Germany was increasing, which meant reliance on imports, often from overseas. There was a danger that any year might bring a food crisis which could not be met by the available foreign exchange. In the event of war, overseas sources of supply would be subject to British blockade. The only remedy, Hitler went on, lay in the acquisition of greater living space, starting with Czechoslovakia and Austria, which would provide food for between 5 and 6 million people, if the compulsory emigration of 2 million from Czechoslovakia and 1 million from Austria could be accomplished.

This was only a partial statement of the problem, omitting the question of raw materials and the strains imposed by rearmament. The proposed remedy was dubious, because neither Austria nor Czechoslovakia was a major food producer. Even in 1939, after absorbing Austria and Czechoslovakia, Germany remained dependent on imports for 20 per cent of its foodstuffs; and supplies from south-east Europe, under Germany's influence, could not meet all her needs. The raw material situation was worse. In 1939 Germany depended on imports for 33 per cent of her raw materials; and the proportion was much higher in particular cases – 66 per cent for oil, 70 per cent for copper, 85–90 per cent for rubber, and 99 per cent for aluminium. Roughly half of Germany's normal supplies of raw materials would be subject to Anglo-French naval blockade.

The foreign exchange position was getting steadily worse. In 1938 Germany's trade balance was unfavourable (imports totalled 6,051.7 million RM, against exports of 5,619.1 million). This was reversed in 1939 (exports 5,222.2 million; imports 4,796.5 million) but this still left many imports which had to be paid for in foreign exchange, which was running short. By September 1939, reserves of gold and foreign exchange amounted to only 500 million RM. The annexation of Austria and Czechoslovakia had brought some temporary easing of the problem (Austria had 305 million RM in reserves of gold and foreign exchange), but in the longer term they were a liability, because both needed imports from outside Germany, and both cut down their exports after the occupation in order to meet German demands.[12]

Under the terms of the Four-Year Plan, the production of synthetic materials and domestic German iron ore was meant to cope with such problems. The synthetics programme proved in the long run a remarkable success; but in the short term it failed to achieve the over-optimistic targets set for it in 1936. Self-sufficiency in oil within eighteen months was Hitler's aim in 1936; by 1937 the date was put off until 1940; and then it vanished into the future. Production reached 2.3 million metric tons in 1939, or approximately a quarter of estimated mobilization needs; and 5.7 million tons in 1943, or about half Germany's supplies for that year. The programme was extremely expensive, demanding heavy capital investment, a big construction programme, and the use of 4 tons of coal and 8–10 tons of lignite to produce 1 ton of oil.[13] As for iron ore, German domestic production increased after 1936, but it was expensive and of poor quality, unsuitable for high-quality steel products. These two commodities, oil and iron ore, exemplified Germany's problems. In 1937 Germany imported oil from the sources given in Table 4,[14] which shows that 65 per cent of Germany's oil imports came from the American hemisphere, a pattern which had also prevailed for the previous three years.

Table 4. German oil imports, 1937

Country	Amount (Tons)	Percentage
Mexico and Neth.		
West Indies	1,796,000	42
USA	1,000,000	23
Rumania	520,000	12
USSR	301,000	7
Others	690,000	16
Total	4,307,000	

These sources would be immediately cut off in time of war by naval blockade. Middle East oil was under British control; the Soviet Union seemed likely to be among Germany's enemies. This left Rumania as the only significant source of oil not subject to blockade or enemy control. With synthetic production lagging, and demand rising, the importance of Rumanian oil was increased. Total Rumanian production in 1937 was 7.1 million tons; but most of this went to other markets.

The Germans therefore set themselves to increase their purchases of oil from Rumania, and to secure their source of supply by tightening their hold on the Rumanian economy. Their starting-point was unfavourable. German investment in Rumania in 1938 amounted to about 1 per cent of the total share capital; British and French to about 16 per cent. In the oil industry, British, French, Belgian, and Dutch capital totalled 45 per cent of investment; German a mere 0.2 per cent. Germany's only advantage was as a market for Rumanian exports; in 1938 Germany took 26.5 per cent of Rumanian exports, against 22.4 per cent going to Britain and France together. On the other hand, only

15 per cent of Rumanian oil exports went to Germany, against 25 per cent to Britain and France together. Moreover, the possession of oil, a highly saleable commodity, put Rumania in a stronger position than other countries of south-eastern Europe, which were much more dependent on the export of agricultural produce.[15]

In November 1938 Germany opened an economic offensive against Rumania, designed to secure a new trade agreement which would adapt the Rumanian economy to German needs, and secure a large increase in oil exports to Germany. The Rumanian government resisted, with encouragement from Britain, which set out in autumn 1938 to use economic weapons to obstruct German influence. In September 1938 an Anglo-Rumanian clearing agreement was signed, involving a devaluation of the Rumanian currency against sterling, leading to a sharp rise in Rumanian exports to Britain. In October, the British government agreed to buy 200,000 tons of Rumanian grain, despite opposition from the Treasury and Board of Trade: the first occasion that Britain allowed political considerations to predominate in a deal of this kind. During the winter of 1938–39, the British were generally successful in blocking German efforts to increase imports of Rumanian oil. In March 1939, however, the situation changed. Germany occupied Czechoslovakia, and was able to apply heavy pressure on Rumania, leading to a trade agreement on 23 March which met nearly all their demands. From April to August 1939 Rumanian exports to Germany increased sharply, including a rise in the supply of oil.[16]

The British did not give up. They gave a political guarantee to Rumania in April 1939 (see below, p. 256) and made a new economic agreement in July, extending a credit of £5 million, and undertaking to buy another 200,000 tons of grain at the next harvest. When war broke out between Britain and Germany in September 1939, the British sucessfully bought up oil on the Rumanian market, to the detriment of Germany. In March 1940 Germany imported only 45,000 tons of oil from Rumania, while Britain took 130,000 tons, or nearly 44 per cent of Rumanian exports, to which France added a further 6 per cent. Germany responded with economic and political pressure, and a new German–Rumanian agreement in March 1940 put imports of oil up to 104,000 tons in April. Then on 27 May 1940 a further oil agreement, signed in the full flood of German military victory in western Europe, was highly favourable to Germany. By August, German imports of oil were up to 187,000 tons, and British down to 6,000 tons.[17]

The story is instructive. When the weapons used were economic, the conflict between Germany and Britain for Rumanian exports, and especially for oil, was evenly balanced. The definitive German success was brought about by military action, not in Rumania itself, which the Germans did not want to invade for fear of damage to the oil installations, but in the Low Countries and France. When Germany controlled almost the whole Continent, Rumania was in no position to hold out, and British purchasing power lost all effect. The Germans wanted secure access to a large share of Rumanian oil exports: the lesson of these events was that the only certain way to attain it was by force.

German imports of iron ore posed rather different problems, with a much lower proportion of the sources being subject to naval blockade or likely enemy control. In 1938 German imports were as shown in Table 5[18] (amounts in 1,000 tons of iron content).

Table 5. German iron-ore imports, 1938

Country	Amount	Percentage
Sweden	5,395	52.1
France	1,517	14.6
Norway	671	6.5
Newfoundland	561	5.4
Luxemburg	553	5.1
Spain	542	5.0
Spanish North Africa	398	3.8
French North Africa	340	3.3
Others	408	3.9

In the event of war with Britain and France, Newfoundland, France, and French North Africa would become enemy territory, and their supplies cut off. During the Spanish Civil War, Germany put much effort into establishing a share in the control of mining companies in Spain; but this proved something of a blind alley. When the Civil War was over, General Franco proved resistant to German economic domination. A German trade delegation went to Spain in June 1939, but did not secure an economic agreement until December; and even this was immediately followed by economic agreements between Spain and France (January 1940) and Britain (March 1940). Beween September 1939 and June 1940 the Anglo-French blockade curtailed all German trade with Spain, and in 1940 German imports of iron ore from Spain totalled only 1,000 tons. By the time a land route to Spain was opened up by the fall of France, Germany had other sources of iron ore at her disposal, and even at their maximum in 1942 German imports of Spanish ore did not attain pre-war levels.[19]

The key to German imports of iron ore lay not in Spain but in Sweden. Here, from August 1939, Germany held many advantages. After the Nazi–Soviet Pact of August 1939, German influence was predominant in the Baltic. When war began, the Swedish government undertook to maintain normal pre-war deliveries of iron ore to Germany, which would keep supplies at a high level, though not necessarily high enough to meet wartime demands. The British meanwhile disputed the German position by trying to buy up Swedish iron ore and by using their control over the oceanic trade routes to put pressure on the Swedish government. In terms of economic pressure, the balance as between Germany and Britain was only marginally in favour of Germany. The decisive push was given by German military action, not directly against Sweden, but by the German occupation of Norway in April–May 1940, which largely cut Sweden off from the outside world. Invasion of Sweden was unnecessary to give German effective control of Swedish exports. Finally, military victory in western Europe in May–June 1940 brought Germany physical control of the ore-fields of Lorraine and Luxemburg.

In both these cases, of oil and iron ore, Germany's shortage of raw materials and lack of foreign exchange with which to pay for imports was dealt with by conquest – not of the countries most involved (Rumania and Sweden), but of most of the rest of Europe, so that German predominance was firmly established.

In 1939, however, there was another solution available for problems of raw materials and food: a deal with the Soviet Union. The USSR possessed more of the commodities Germany needed than did the countries of south-east Europe; and communications with it could not be affected by naval blockade. In December 1938 the German government approached the Soviet government with a request for 300 million RM worth of raw materials and agricultural produce over the next two years, to be supplied in return for manufactured goods. In February 1939 the Soviets offered 200 million RM worth, and the talks were still going on when, on 20 May, Molotov stated that there would have to be a new political basis before they could go any further – the nature of the negotiation was changed, and the road opened to the Nazi–Soviet Pact of August. The point here is that, quite apart from political issues, there was an economic impulse for Germany to come to an agreement with the Soviet Union in 1939.

How long such agreement would last was another matter. In all these calculations of Germany's needs and supplies, the basic assumption was that Germany intended to go to war. This was why dependence on imports from across the oceans was so dangerous: they were vulnerable to naval blockade in the event of war with Britain and France. A form of self-sufficiency in food and raw materials which could only be secured by the direct control of large parts of eastern Europe and the Soviet Union meant at some stage fighting to establish that control. German policy created a vicious circle. Hitler embarked on rapid rearmament, with the intention of gaining territory either by threat of force or by actual conquest. The rapid rearmament itself created a crisis of raw materials and foreign exchange, which made the acquisition of territory necessary to keep rearmament going. Unless this circle was broken, either by accepting a pause in rearmament, or by acquiescing in restrictions on expansion, there seemed no way out except a major war.

When the Germans went to war, they found that the successful use of force dealt with their immediate economic problems. They secured access to Rumanian oil and Swedish iron ore. They conquered the ore-fields of Lorraine. They captured stocks of all kinds of materials, including large quantities of oil. They gained control of a vast pool of manpower – already by August 1940 about a million foreigners were working in Germany. They dealt with their foreign exchange problem either by straightforward plunder or by compelling occupied countries to accept an overvaluation of the Reichsmark and by fixing their own prices for commodities. In France, for example, Germany levied occupation costs of 20 million RM per day, with the mark overvalued against the French franc by some 50 per cent in terms of the dollar exchange rate of each currency in June 1940; and the Germans were then able to pay for their imports from France without difficulty. At least in the short run, war was made to pay.

The great depression unsettled Europe, and set the great powers in pursuit of self-sufficiency. Recovery in the late 1930s did not restore harmony, and indeed produced its own difficulties in the form of widespread balance of payments problems. In most states, however, economic difficulties did not lead towards war. In France and Britain in particular, economic factors held back the pace of rearmament, and both these countries believed that war would be economically damaging. Much the same was true of Italy, where neutrality was likely to be more profitable than war. Only for Germany did it seem likely that war would pay in an economic sense; and then only on the assumption that the nazi rearmament programme was to be pursued unchecked, and the balance of payments problems which it created should be resolved by force. The decisions which lay behind these assumptions were matters of politics rather than economics.

REFERENCES AND NOTES

1. Central Statistical Office, *Annual Abstract of Statistics, No. 88, 1938–1950* (London 1952), p. 213. Value of exports (produce and manufactures of Britain), 1938: To S. Africa, 39.5; Australia, 38.2; India, 33.8; Canada, 23.5; Germany, 20.6; Eire, 20.6; USA, 20.5 (figures in millions of pounds).
2. *Bulletin of International News, vol. XIII*, p. 846.
3. Alfred Sauvy, 'L'évolution économique', in René Rémond and Janine Bourdin, (eds.), *Edouard Daladier, chef de gouvernement, avril 1938 – septembre 1939* (Paris 1977), pp. 91–6.
4. Shepard B. Clough, *The Economic History of Modern Italy* (New York 1964), p. 261; MacGregor Knox, *Mussolini Unleashed, 1939–1941* (Cambridge 1982), pp. 30–1.

5. M. Heller and A. Nekrich, *L'Utopie au pouvoir: Histoire de l'URSS de 1917 à nos jours* (Paris 1982), pp. 266–7.
6. Ibid., p. 266.
7. Quoted in David E. Kaiser, *Economic Diplomacy and the Origins of the Second World War* (Princeton 1980), p. 151.
8. Text, *Documents on German Foreign Policy*, series C, vol. V, No. 390; it was presented to Goering on 26 August 1936. Cf. Jeremy Noakes and Geoffrey Pridham (eds.), *Documents on Nazism, 1919–1945* (London 1974), pp. 401–10.
9. Edward L. Homze, *Arming the Luftwaffe: the Reich Air Ministry and the German aircraft industry, 1919–39* (Lincoln, Nebraska 1976), p. 143.
10. Matthew Cooper, *The German Air Force, 1933–1945* (London 1981), pp. 62–3; Philippe Marguerat, *Le IIIe Reich et le pétrole roumain, 1938–1940* (Geneva 1977), pp. 96–8; Kaiser, *Economic Diplomacy*, p. 268.
11. Cooper, *German Air Force*, p. 76; Marguerat, *Le IIIe Reich*, pp. 18–19. The synthetic oil projections were prepared by Carl Krauch, formerly a director of I. G. Farben.
12. Marguerat, *Le IIIe Reich*, p. 157; Kaiser, *Economic Diplomacy*, pp. 268, 319; Cooper, *German Air Force*, p. 75.
13. Marguerat, *Le IIIe Reich*, pp. 18–19; Alan Milward, *War, Economy and Society, 1939–1945* (London 1977), p. 178.
14. Marguerat, *Le IIIe Reich*, p. 19.
15. Ibid., pp. 29–61, 73, 84.
16. Ibid., pp. 150–1.
17. Ibid., pp. 168–77, 192–3, 200.
18. Martin Fritz, *German Steel and Swedish Iron Ore, 1939–1945* (Göteborg 1974), p. 34.
19. K. J. Ruehl, 'L'alliance à distance: les relations économiques germano-espagnoles de 1939 à 1945', *Revue d'histoire de la Deuxième Guerre Mondiale*, **118** (April 1980), 86–7; Fritz, *German Steel*, pp. 51–2.

THE ROLE OF STRATEGY AND ARMED FORCE

There is a close relationship between foreign policy and strategy. In principle, the two should be kept in line with one another, so that it is certain that an important interest in foreign policy can be sustained by force if necessary, and that the armed services are able to perform the tasks which foreign policy may impose upon them. If this alignment is not maintained, so that for example foreign policy commitments far exceed the military capacity to sustain them, or foreign policy demands offensive action of an army capable only of defence, then trouble follows.

In the case of states considering going to war, these matters assume a sharper and more crucial form. A state may be encouraged to resort to force by confidence in its armed strength and expectation of victory. Equally, the fear of defeat and destruction may often deter a country from risking war. In most circumstances, a precondition for war is that each side believes that it can win, or at least avoid defeat; though in desperate straits governments may decide that on certain issues their country must fight, and the armed forces must simply conform, whatever they think of the chances of success.

These questions had a powerful effect on international relations during the 1930s. The actions of states were frequently influenced by the condition of their armed forces and by calculations of the likely outcome of a conflict. The next two chapters examine the armed forces of the principal European powers, and the influence of strategic issues on foreign policy.

Chapter 11

ARMED FORCES, STRATEGY, AND FOREIGN POLICY (1): FRANCE AND BRITAIN

War has long been regarded as an instrument of policy. If certain aims are considered vital and cannot be attained by diplomatic, economic, or other means, then at some stage force must be used to secure them. It is a less familiar idea that peace, as well as war, is linked with power and the presence of force. Raymond Aron has described peace as

> the more or less lasting suspension of violent modes of rivalry between political units. Peace is said to prevail when the relations between nations do not involve the military forms of struggle. But since these peaceful relations occur within the shadow of past battles and in the fear or the expectation of future ones, the principle of peace . . . is not different in nature from that of wars: peace is based upon power. . . .[1]

These concepts were still soundly based in the 1920s and 1930s and were indeed particularly relevant in the period between 1938 and 1940, when the borderline between peace and war was blurred and the two merged into one another. But in many minds they had ceased to carry conviction. Men were indeed in the shadow of past battles; and it was reasonable to ask whether warfare of the 1914–18 kind was entirely serviceable as an instrument of policy. Were the costs and potential dangers of war – the mobilization of manpower and the economy, the casualties both military and civilian, the possibility of total disruption in politics and society – commensurate with the aims of policy? Frequently, it did not seem so. If the interest at stake was not immediately crucial, then the price likely to be demanded by war was hard to equate with the objects of policy. What was the use, for example, of fighting another war like that of 1914–18 to prevent the frontier between Czechoslovakia and Germany being moved from one line to another? The idea of war as an instrument of policy was in such circumstances unconvincing.

At the same time, the idea of war and peace as a continuum, and that peace as much as war was dependent on military power, was repugnant to many minds. The First World War appeared as a gigantic aberration, the nemesis which followed the granting of too much power and too many resources to military men. Peace was seen as entirely different from war, in legal, practical, political, and perhaps above all in moral terms. There was a strong belief that peace, far from being based on power, could only be secured by the limitation or even elimination of military force.

Such views were at their strongest in France and Britain, the principal European victors of 1918. In both countries, the predominant weight of both opinion and sentiment was opposed to the sterner views of the relation between war and policy, and the dependence of peace upon power. Peace was assumed to be the natural relationship between states; there was a strong hope that it could somehow be made self-sustaining; and the idea of war as a means of policy was rejected as both irrational and repugnant. Professional military men had lost much of their prestige and influence. The two great civilian leaders of the First World War, Clemenceau and Lloyd George, had little respect for generals, as Lloyd George made clear in his widely read war memoirs. It was true that the French and British armies had emerged victorious, and their leaders enjoyed a moment of glory at the victory parades of 1919; but the conviction grew that they had not waged the war efficiently, imaginatively, or with sufficient regard for the lives of their men. They had been surprised by the problems of modern warfare, and had failed to master them. Even when they had won, there was no agreement as to how victory had been achieved. Was it a victory for attrition, wearing down the German Army, as the orthodox western-front generals advocated? Was it the result of the naval blockade and economic warfare? Was it a success for new weapons and techniques, notably the tank? Was it simply a victory for the Americans? If there really was an art of war (and after 1914–18 that seemed doubtful), it was by no means clear that generals knew how to practise it.

In the post-war period, generals and admirals were uneasily aware that they were in an era of new machines and new techniques, whose full significance had not emerged. The German submarine campaign of 1917 had inflicted devastating losses on merchant shipping. But had the submarine then been mastered by the convoy system? It was not fully clear. The tank had made its appearance, with sometimes startling effects; yet it was a primitive weapon, slow, cumbersome, and much subject to mechanical failure. Some theorists were willing to make great claims for it as the weapon of the future, round which armies should be built; but others were sceptical, and thought in terms of infantry, guns, and a balanced force. As for air power, the most dramatic new development of the First World War, sweeping prophecies were made by its advocates. The Italian writer Giulio Douhet, in a book published in 1921, claimed that aircraft would decide the next war in a few days, by bombing attacks on both civilian and military targets. Governments would be compelled by their peoples to sue for peace.[2] In Britain, Hugh Trenchard, founder of the Royal Air Force and Chief of the Air Staff 1919–29, made equally strong claims, both out of genuine belief and out of the need to promote his new service. Yet the evidence on which these vast claims were based was limited and fragile. The British Independent Air Force, set up in 1918 as a bomber force, dropped only 550 tons of bombs in 239 raids between June and November 1918, with results which could be described as no more than a nuisance to the enemy. In German raids on London by Zeppelins and aircraft, only 1,127 people were killed, though the psychological and political effects were far greater than such numbers might imply.[3] Projections made from such evidence were of dubious value. Uncertainty prevailed, and fear of the new weapon often had free rein.

Technical uncertainty was accompanied by a new political and economic climate. Disarmament was the watchword of the day. Even the Royal Navy, the embodiment of British power and the focus of national pride, was subjected to international disarmament agreements, the Treaty of Washington (1922) for capital ships, and the Treaty of London (1930) for cruisers. While the Geneva Disarmament Conference of 1932–34 was in session, neither the British nor the French government felt that it could increase any of its service estimates. The whole position of the armed forces in a political climate dominated by the idea of disarmament was one of considerable difficulty. The same was true of the economic climate. Even in the comparative prosperity of the late 1920s the services, in both France and Britain, were subjected to strict budgetary limitations; and in the period of the depression controls were very tight. The service departments were well accustomed to the struggle between themselves, as spenders of public funds, and the Ministry of Finance and the Treasury, as the keepers of the purse. At no time had the services been accustomed to a free hand in financial terms; but in the 1920s and most of the 1930s they were subjected to far tighter restrictions than before 1914, when their prestige was higher and views of their role and value were firmer and clearer.

Yet among all these uncertainties and difficulties, the armed forces were still expected by their governments to fulfil traditional roles. They had to ensure the safety of the national territory; protect and keep order in the empire; and secure the sea-lanes which linked the two and carried sea-borne trade. These tasks assumed different proportions for France and Britain. For the French, the defence of the homeland was by far the greatest demand on resources, and the French Army had to plan for a Continental war before all else. The empire, important as it was, came second, and sea-borne trade third. For the British, the homeland had to be defended, which was the task of the navy and air defence. The sea-lanes were equally crucial, because without them industry would run down and the population starve. The army's major task was the imperial commitment, notably in India and the Middle East. (It is a striking fact that in 1938 there were more British troops deployed in Palestine to cope with an Arab revolt than were available to be despatched to France if war arose out of the Czechoslovakian crisis.) No government proposed that these tasks should be abandoned; only that they should be performed with limited resources and in an atmosphere of scepticism about the effectiveness and morality of the use of force.

All these considerations affected the development of the French and British armed forces, their strategic doctrines, and their influence on foreign policy. The services (with the exception of the new air arm) were much shaken in their self-confidence by the experience of 1914–18. Their strategic doctrines had to cope with changes in weaponry and techniques of war whose effects were uncertain and little understood, in political circumstances which demanded simultaneous obeisance to the new concepts of disarmament and to the old demands of domestic and imperial security. In these circumstances, it is not surprising, or even remarkable, that the advice given by French and British service chiefs to their governments tended to err on the side of caution.

FRANCE

These problems were much in evidence in the development of the French armed forces between the wars. The basis of French military power remained the army, which was mainly raised by a system of compulsory service, with contingents of conscripts passing through a period of training with the army and then going into the reserve, to be mobilized in case of need. There was also a force of regular soldiers, including the officer corps and most of the non-commissioned officers. Like nearly all armies based on conscription, the French Army was therefore made up of three elements: the regulars, conscripts serving their time with the colours, and reservists, back in civilian life but liable to recall.

During the 1920s, the period of military service in France was progressively reduced. Immediately after the victory of 1918 it stood at three years; in 1921 it was reduced to two years; in 1923 to eighteen months; and in 1928 to one year. At that time, the annual contingent of conscripts was 240,000; and the regular element was fixed at 106,000. Because of the short fall in the birth-rate during the First World War, it was easily predictable that in 1936 and for four years to come, the annual contingent would amount on average to only 120,000 – half the number provided for by the military law of 1928.[4] In March 1935 the Chamber of Deputies therefore amended the law to extend the period of service to two years, starting with the class to be called up in

October. By October 1937, the conscript contingent would again reach 240,000.

To bring the army up to its full strength required the mobilization of the reserves, which took millions of men out of their civilian employment, with all the economic and social disruption which that entailed. This process did not at once produce a fully effective fighting force, for many of the reservists required a prolonged period of training, and the whole army had to undergo a difficult adjustment. All this must be remembered when we consider the crises of 1936, 1938, and 1939, when the French either contemplated or carried out general mobilization. It was a process which on the one hand disrupted the social and economic life of the country, and on the other produced for a time an army which was in the throes of reorganization and retraining. It was not an easy course to take; and in some circumstances it might not prove effective.

The total mobilized strength of the French Army in September 1939 was eighty-four divisions, of several kinds – infantry, Alpine, fortress, cavalry, light mechanized, armoured, North African and colonial. This army was in the process of being re-equipped. In September 1936, the Popular Front government, despite its strong anti-militarist tendencies, judged the position of the country to be so serious as to demand a substantial armaments programme. A scheme was accepted for the ordering of 6,600 anti-tank guns (mostly the small 25 millimetre gun, but some 600 larger); and 3,200 tanks, mostly light, but including over 400 heavy tanks (Type B), and over 300 mediums (Somua), which were both very good, well-armed vehicles. There was at this stage little problem with finance – some 31 billion francs were spent on rearmament between September 1936 and September 1939; but there were problems in French industry, which could not immediately cope with a flood of orders. There were also many difficulties within the army itself; for example, it took four years to move from a first proposal to modify the Somua medium tank to the actual placing of an order. But both army and industry made great efforts, and in September 1939, after three years of the 1936 programme, about 4,500 anti-tank guns and 2,200 tanks had been produced, though there were still serious shortages.[5]

What was this force intended to do, and what strategic doctrines did it profess? From the end of the First World War, it was the working assumption of the French high command that they would at some time have to fight another war with Germany. They recognized that in such a war France would be at a disadvantage in terms of numbers and industrial capacity. France therefore would need allies, and must think in terms of a long war, in which the German economy could be undermined by blockade and outmatched in production as it had been in 1914–18. At the start of a war, France would have to stand on the defensive, with no repetition of the disastrous assault of 1914 in

Alsace–Lorraine. Offensive operations could be considered only in the long term, when Germany would be overcome by the forces of a great coalition.

The necessity for a prolonged defensive found physical expression in the Maginot Line, a great system of fortifications on the Franco–German border, which was discussed from 1925 onwards and decided upon in 1929. It was not strictly speaking a continuous line, but a system of fortified zones, the strongest of which faced northwards from the Rhine to Luxemburg and the southernmost corner of Belgium. A series of forts and blockhouses ran along the Rhine, south to the Swiss border. The fortifications were not extended along the Franco-Belgian border to the sea, partly because the terrain was difficult and the cost would have been very great, but also because until 1936 France was allied to Belgium, and could scarcely fortify their common frontier, with the clear implication that in the event of war the Belgians would be left to their fate.

After the disaster of 1940, the Maginot Line was much criticized; but at the time its main purposes were entirely sensible. It defended the newly recovered provinces of Alsace and Lorraine, including their valuable iron-ore deposits. It formed a barrier behind which the unwieldy army which the French system of military service produced could be organized and trained in the event of war. It would save lives for a country which was acutely conscious of its demographic stagnation. Unless the Germans chose to make a frontal assault on the Maginot Line, it would force them to invade France (as in 1914) through Belgium, where French forces would advance to meet them. The problems lay, not in the Maginot Line itself, but in the passive and defensive mentality which it came to represent.

In principle, the need for mobility and a concept of offensive warfare was appreciated in the French Army in the 1930s. In 1930 General Weygand, the Chief of Staff, began to mechanize a number of divisions, and set out to form a light armoured division. In 1933 he insisted that the army must have forces which could manoeuvre, as well as fortress troops. In 1936 a new set of strategic instructions for the army emphasized the importance of taking the offensive, and laid down that tanks should be used in independent units as well as in conjunction with the infantry. The creation of armoured divisions was under discussion in 1937, though only one such formation was in existence by September 1939. The ideas of attack and manoeuvre were alive in the manuals and in terms of theory. In practice, they were heavily outweighed by commitment to the defensive. The investment made in the Maginot Line, and the public attention which was focused upon it, created a weight of assumptions from which the army could not escape. The whole force of French emotions, more powerful than theory, was concentrated upon defence. Moreover, the sort of army produced by the one-year service of the early 1930s was inadequately trained for rapid offensive operations. Despite the theories and the manuals, the French Army was in practice committed to the defensive. The consequences for French foreign policy were far-reaching.

What of the new air arm? An Air Ministry was created in 1928 to administer the air forces, but for operational purposes they remained under the control of the army and navy; and an independent air force was set up only in 1933. At that stage, it possessed just over 1,000 first-line aircraft, with a similar number in reserve, but its planes dated from the 1920s. Efforts at re-equipment began in 1933 with a scheme (Plan I) to produce just over 1,000 new aircraft. From 1936 onwards, other schemes followed with bewildering rapidity. Plan II (November 1936) aimed at the delivery of 2,400 aircraft by June 1940. By January 1938 the Air Ministry had already reached Plan V, which set a target of 2,600 first-line aircraft, plus reserves, by April 1941.

Targets were one thing, production quite another. Official figures for annual deliveries of aircraft to the French Air Force oscillated round the 500 mark between 1935 and 1938, before attaining over 2,000 in 1939. The air force came low in the government's order of priorities, receiving only a small proportion of the defence budget up to 1938.[6] The aircraft industry was still in many ways craft-based, with a multiplicity of small firms (there were twenty separate firms making cockpits, for example). The Popular Front nationalized the industry, with improvements which were marginal at best. A change to mass production was begun in 1938, but was slow to get under way.

The Air Ministry programmes, therefore, produced only small results up to 1939. In September 1939 the French Air Force had about 700 fighters in squadron service, with another 450 in reserve; but only just over 300 were of modern type, and these were of poorer quality than their German or British counterparts. The bomber force was in even worse condition: 125 in squadron service, with another 50 in reserve, all slow and obsolescent. No modern bomber was in sight, and effectively the French had no bombing capacity.[7]

No clear doctrine had been developed on whether the main role of the air force was to act as an auxiliary to the army and navy, or whether it was to operate independently. A bomber manual of 1939 referred both to intervention in a land battle and to attacks behind the enemy lines; but since the aircraft necessary for either sort of operation did not yet exist this was of slight significance.

The late 1930s thus saw the French Air Force at its lowest ebb. It was in the first years of existence as an independent service, and without a coherent strategic doctrine. Its programmes of re-equipment had yet to produce results. For a few years, which could scarcely have come at a worse time, French air power virtually ceased to exist.

The navy, on the other hand, was strong and of high quality. Its five battleships were elderly, but most of the other ships were modern and powerful, including two new battle-cruisers, an aircraft-carrier, 18 cruisers, over 50 destroyers, and over 70 submarines. The main fleet was designed to match Italy in the Mediterranean; and in the 1930s the French battle-cruisers were also designed to be crushingly superior to the German 'pocket battleships'. The navy was the best of the three French armed services. Assuming co-operation with the Royal Navy, the prospect of war at sea presented France with the least of its problems in the 1930s; though it was far from certain that there would be enough strength to cope with a simultaneous threat from Japan in the Far East, Italy in the Mediterranean, and Germany in the North Sea and Atlantic.

In the late 1930s, then, the French had a strong navy, a very weak air force, and an army which was strong in numbers but was essentially limited to a defensive role. The consequences which followed from this situation for French foreign policy were profound, though they were not always faced with honesty or clarity. Much of French foreign policy between the wars was in principle based on a network of alliances with east European states – Poland, Czechoslovakia, Yugoslavia, and Rumania. The hope was that these allies would help to protect France against Germany; but in practice it was more likely that France would have to protect them. To help Poland or Czechoslovakia against a German attack, France's only move would be an offensive across the German border in the west – yet how could this be done with an army which was defensive in its nature, and how did it fit in with a concept of war based on a long conflict, not a sharp attack? In fact, it could not be done unless the French Army was completely reorganized, and strategy were completely out of step, as was painfully clear in the crises over Czechoslovakia in 1938 and Poland in 1939. The problem of bringing them into step was beyond the capacity of French governments to solve. To reorganize the army to provide a force capable of rapid offensive action was impossible on social and political grounds. (De Gaulle's suggestion for a professional élite armoured force would have put too much power into the hands of the officer corps and was politically unacceptable.) To scrap the east European alliances, once made, and resign all influence in that area, was almost impossible in terms of French prestige and self-respect, though they came very close to this drastic step in autumn 1938. This problem was fundamental, insoluble, and fatal.

The French tried to improve their parlous strategic position by seeking new allies against Germany. An Italian alliance appeared to offer advantages. Italy's military strength and geographical position were of great importance to France: General Gamelin said repeatedly during 1935 that it depended on the attitude of Italy whether or not fifteen French divisions could be stationed on the German rather than the Italian border. There were also common frontiers between the two countries' colonies in Africa, where Italian friendship or hostility could affect French interests. The Franco–Italian military agreement of June

1935 was thus seen as a great coup. The three French Chiefs of Staff went to Rome to conclude this agreement, which provided for a mutual guarantee of common frontiers in the Alps and Africa, and in the event of war with Germany the despatch by Italy of nine divisions to France, and by France of a corps to the Italian–Yugoslav border. There was also a separate agreement between the air staffs, made in May and supplemented by further conversations in Paris in September, providing for co-operation in the event of German air attack on either country.

The satisfaction with which the French staffs greeted these agreements was matched by their chagrin when the Abyssinian crisis of 1935–36, and in particular the British insistence on sanctions against Italy, virtually destroyed them. For some time the French hoped that something might be salvaged, and some part of the agreements revived (Mussolini at least referred to them as being still in existence); but this proved vain. In 1936 Gamelin reflected grimly that fifteen French divisions which might have faced Germany must now be deployed in the Alps: would the British, he wondered, make up the difference?

French views of the importance of Italy were to some extent based on overestimates of the strength of the Italian services, and especially the air force; but even so, considerable strategic advantages had been lost as the price of maintaining good relations with Britain. A British alliance was the crucial element in the French scenario of a long war to be won by an economically superior coalition. In these expectations, British sea power and economic potential played vital roles, outweighing the paucity and uncertainty of a British military intervention on the Continent. In April 1936 the French Deputy Chief of Staff, General Schweisguth, on a visit to London, reported that, if the British decided to intervene in a Continental war at all, which was not certain, they might be able to send two divisions to the Continent, without air support. There would be a two-week delay between the decision to send them and their actual departure; and then another week or two before they could be operational.

The British Army was therefore a very doubtful asset. But in 1938 and 1939, as the French became acutely conscious of their weakness in the air, they began to place increasing reliance on the support of the RAF. In Air Staff talks from November 1938 onwards, the French sought promises of the rapid despatch of British aircraft to France in the event of war. The British, through their own weakness, had less to offer than the French wanted; but the French need was so great that they were thankful for small mercies.

Strategic considerations played less part than might have been expected in French relations with other allies or potential allies. Military contacts with Poland languished from 1934 until the eve of war in spring 1939; and the French Air Staff did not speak to their Polish opposite numbers between September 1937 and May 1939, when the

French made a hollow promise to base five bomber groups in Poland in the event of war. Military contacts with the Soviet Union were inhibited by ideological considerations, by service reluctance to give the Soviets any information, and by the purges that the doubt they cast on the effectiveness of the Red Army. The French Army had conflicting reports on the fighting capacity of the Red Army after the purges; the air staff retained a good opinion of the Soviet Air Force; but in any case close co-operation was not pursued.

In all these matters, the dominant feature was France's need for allies, and the considerations forced upon her by the concept of a long war starting with a defensive phase. Britain was the key ally, because of her economic strength, sea power, and long-term military potential. In French eyes, the British were exasperatingly short-sighted about European affairs; they had to be cajoled, threatened, or deceived into a Continental commitment; but as long as Germany was the enemy, they could not be dispensed with. When it appeared (as it often did) that in the late 1930s France yielded too much of the initiative to Britain, and appeared to follow the British even though it was a case of the blind leading the sighted, we must remember this fundamental strategic background.

All this presupposed that Germany was the enemy; and the other great influence of strategic thinking upon French policy came from French estimates of German power. In the late 1930s, these tended to be pessimistic, exaggerating German strength. This was particularly the case in March 1936, at the time of the German occupation of the demilitarized zone in the Rhineland. The *Deuxième Bureau* (French military intelligence) produced what proved to be generally accurate information on the German Army as a whole, and on the forces which entered the Rhineland – seven divisions and a total of about 60,000 men, including some armed police units. But when the Army General Staff reported to the government, it added to these figures about 235,000 from paramilitary formations (SA, SS, Labour Front), saying that these constituted another fifteen divisions, though the *Deuxième Bureau* had specifically mentioned these men and considered their military value practically nil. It is not clear why this was done – it may well have been simply a 'worst case' appreciation to be on the safe side; or it may have been designed to discourage any pressure for an attack on the Rhineland, for which the army had no plans ready. In any case, it produced an extremely pessimistic estimate of German strength.

By 1939 an even gloomier picture had been built up. Most of it was accurate, though there were still elements of exaggeration. French military intelligence reported that when the Germans occupied Czechoslovakia in March 1939 they made a great haul of military equipment, including 600 very good tanks and 4,000 guns.[8] (In the campaign of 1940, when France was defeated, three of the ten German Panzer divisions were mainly equipped with Czech-built tanks.)

Another report of March 1939 assessed that Germany could concentrate 30 divisions in the west in three to four days, and could overrun Holland and Belgium in a day or two. The events of 1940 were to show such estimates to be a shade pessimistic, but not too wide of the mark. In July 1939 the French General Staff put the number of German divisions on general mobilization at 120 to 130. The actual figure was 103. The French could muster 86 divisions, so the estimate made the disproportion of strength rather greater than it actually was.[9]

As to the air, there was from 1937 onwards a tendency for French air intelligence to overestimate the strength of the *Luftwaffe*. In January 1938 they attributed to the *Luftwaffe* a total of 207 squadrons (including 36 fighter, 15 dive-bomber, and 93 medium bomber), and a total of 2,800 aircraft to set against 1,450 French, which were also of poorer quality. In September 1939 the same source put German strength at 75 fighter squadrons, 36 dive-bomber, and 102 medium bomber squadrons.[10] These figures were too high, and contributed to the process by which the French contrived to frighten themselves about the extent of German air strength. In August 1938 the Chief of the French Air Staff, General Vuillemin, visited Germany and fell victim to the ruse of aircraft being flown from one airfield to another, to be displayed to the visitor as separate parts of a great air fleet. But however much the French exaggerated the strength of the *Luftwaffe*, they were only too right in believing their own air force to be far inferior.

It might have been expected from all this that the French military leaders would advise their government against a war with Germany, on the grounds that it would invite disaster. But in 1939 this was not the case. The main lines of French military opinion, as put to the Prime Minister, Daladier, in 1939, were that the French Army was prepared for a successful defence of the country, sustained by its fortifications, by the recent effort in rearmament, and by British assistance, which became steadily more certain as the year went on. The German Army was technically excellent, but there was reason to doubt its morale. (Much was made of the lack of popular enthusiasm for war at the time of Munich, in 1938.) The Poles were expected to hold out for some months; and if Italy came in on Germany's side, France could take the offensive against her. When ministers met military leaders for a review of the situation on 23 August 1939, with the Polish crisis boiling up, the Air Minister estimated that French and British fighter strength was roughly equal to that of Germany and Italy (which, surprisingly enough, was correct); though the commander of Home Air Defence said bluntly that he was not ready for war. Gamelin estimated that Polish resistance would keep Germany occupied until spring 1940, by which time British forces would begin to arrive in strength. On the whole, it was a confident review, and there was no hesitation on military grounds in supporting a declaration of war on behalf of Poland.

There was considerable inconsistency between these views and the earlier pessimistic trend of French estimates of German strength. When put on the spot, the French military leaders were naturally reluctant to say that they had failed in their duty and the country could not be defended. But the key element in the advice tendered by the French soldiers was that they were ready for *defence*. This was what they had been preparing for, and they believed that their preparations were adequate. They recognized that they were open to air attack; but with British help, and if the process of mobilization could be safely completed, German bombing was not likely to prove fatal. At the end of August 1939 therefore, French military opinion was sufficiently confident to accept war, though it was by no means eager for it. It was a somewhat surprising conclusion to a decade of weakness and self-doubt; but when it came to the point the soldiers believed they could do the defensive part of their job. To take the offensive would be another matter; but they did not intend to do that for a long time.

GREAT BRITAIN

Britain was, by long tradition and in accordance with her interests as an island state, primarily a maritime power. During the 1920s and 1930s, the Royal Navy remained one of the strongest fleets in the world, roughly comparable with that of the USA. It had serious problems: financial restrictions; the terms of various naval agreements, which affected the numbers, tonnage, and design of warships; the unresolved question of the role of air power in maritime war; and world-wide commitments to protect trade and empire, which had grown beyond the unaided strength of the navy even in its palmiest days. New construction of warships was limited, and the fleet was impressive in size but ageing in composition.

In September 1939, the Royal Navy consisted of 12 battleships and 3 battle-cruisers, the newest of which dated from 1927, and most from the First World War. There were 6 aircraft-carriers, only one of them new; 68 cruisers and 201 destroyers and sloops included a larger proportion of newer ships; and there were 69 submarines. Substantial programmes for the expansion of the fleet were adopted in 1936 and following years; so that at the outbreak of war 5 battleships, 6 carriers, 21 cruisers, and 50 destroyers were being built.[11]

The British Army was the only European army made up entirely of regular soldiers, with no conscripted element (conscription had been introduced in 1916, but abandoned in 1920). This produced a force 197,000 strong in January 1938, including the British component of the Indian Army; to which should be added another 190,000 Indian troops. The total strength was thus 387,000, which at first sight compared favourably with the size of the French Army actually with the colours. But there were none of the reserves which were automatically produced by a system of conscription (some were provided by the Territorial Army); and the army was widely dispersed, its major tasks being imperial defence and policing. In January 1938 its distribution was as in Table 6.[12]

Table 6. Distribution of the British Army, 1938

Station	Approx. total	Infantry battalions
Home	107,000	64
India and Burma	55,000	47
plus Indian Army	190,000	
Middle East and Mediterranean	21,000	18
Far East	12,000	8
West Indies	2,000	1

In the crisis of September 1938 Britain was in a position to send only two divisions to France in the event of war. When war came in 1939, four divisions were sent as the basis of the new British Expeditionary Force, fewer in numbers and less well trained than its predecessor of 1914. The French put 84 divisions into the field, and the Germans 103; which puts the British military contribution into perspective.

In February 1939, under the pressure of events in Europe, the British government decided in principle to create a field force of thirty-two divisions twelve months after the outbreak of a war in Europe. This was, of course, a decision which would take a very long time to implement, in terms both of manpower and equipment; and it had little immediate effect on British armed strength. The same was true of the decision, announced in April 1939 and put into legislation in May, to introduce conscription in peacetime, for the first time in British history. It was a very limited measure: full-time service was to be for six months only, and 80,000 out of the 200,000 conscripts expected each year were to go into anti-aircraft units; conscripts were not to serve abroad unless war broke out. The first contingent was not called up until August 1939, so the measure had no effect on the numerical strength of the army before war broke out.

The Royal Air Force was the newest of the three services, but in the 1930s, with the acute fear of bombing which prevailed in both civilian and military circles, it attained a position of priority, so that in 1938 and 1939 expenditure by the Air Ministry was greater than that by either the Admiralty or the War Office.[13] The size of the RAF was kept down in the 1920s, and no increase was embarked on until 1934, when it became clear that the Geneva Disarmament Conference had failed.

There then followed, in rapid succession, a series of plans for expansion, each setting a new and higher target. The actual growth in numbers was less than that aspired to, but still considerable. In March 1934 the first-line strength of the RAF at home was 605 aircraft. At the end of September 1938, at the time of the Munich crisis, it had reached 1,102; and at the beginning of September 1939, 1,377. (Aircraft stationed overseas, and with the Fleet Air Arm, raised these totals to 977, 1,642, and 1,996 respectively.)[14] This increase in numbers was accompanied by an improvement in quality, so that by September 1939 most of the fighters were new Hurricanes and Spitfires, though the bomber force was still largely made up of older types.

The considerations governing the strength of the British armed forces were partly the tasks they were expected to perform and the strategic doctrines professed by the different services; but still more decisive were the constraints of finance and economics. The first question was one of budgeting: how much of the government's resources were to go to the armed forces, and how were those sums to be divided between them? In August 1919, the Cabinet laid down that the service departments, in preparing their estimates of expenditure, should assume that there would be no major war for ten years – the 'Ten-Year Rule'. In 1928, while Churchill was Chancellor of the Exchequer, it was agreed that, subject to review once a year, the ten-year period should be extended on a day-to-day basis. In March 1932 the Chiefs of Staff recommended that, as a result of the Japanese occupation of Manchuria in 1931–32, the ten-year assumption should be abandoned. The Cabinet accepted this in principle, but there was no actual increase in expenditure until the Disarmament Conference broke down in 1934. A five-year rearmament programme was agreed on in February 1936; and in 1937 the Treasury imposed a system of financial 'rationing' to settle priorities between the three services. In April 1938 the Royal Air Force was allowed to order as many aircraft as industry would build, without financial rationing; and after the Munich crisis of September 1938 rationing went into abeyance for the other two services as well.

Budgetary restrictions were only part of the constraints on rearmament. Small armaments industries faced problems of manpower, factory space, and machine tools if they were to expand rapidly. Such problems might have been dealt with more effectively if the government had been willing to impose its political will and transfer to a command economy, but this it would not do. Both in accordance with its own economic ideas and in deference to the wishes of industrialists, the British government tried to avoid controls and direction, even when civilian demand impeded the process of rearmament. The government also moved very carefully in relation to the trade unions, whose restrictive practices obstructed change, particularly in the aircraft industry. Above all, the government believed that the demands of rearmament had to be kept in balance with the normal needs of the economy. It was necessary to avoid inflation, and so to limit borrowings; to maintain a satisfactory balance of trade, and so to keep up exports; and to be prepared to sustain the effort of rearmament for a long period. Even in the event of war, the accepted wisdom was that victory would go to the country with the strongest economy and the greatest staying power. A stable economy was therefore seen as the fourth arm in warfare, which might actually be weakened by over-hasty rearmament.

In all these calculations, the position of the USA loomed ominously in the background. In the previous war, only heavy borrowing had enabled the British to sustain their imports from America, but this was now excluded under the American neutrality legislation. To sustain a great war without imports from the USA was impossible; but in the late 1930s it was equally impossible to borrow dollars to pay for those imports. The British faced an impasse.

Economic restraints did much to decide the size of the armed forces Britain possessed. What were these forces intended to do, and what strategic doctrines informed their development? Long tradition laid three tasks upon the navy: to bring the enemy's fleet to battle; to protect the country's sea-borne trade; and to strangle the enemy's economy by means of blockade. In a war against Germany, the enemy's surface fleet was not expected in the late 1930s to pose a serious problem. Sea-borne trade was crucial, and it was hoped that convoys would succeed in protecting it. Blockade (recently given the more elevated name of economic warfare) was expected to be a crippling, if slow-acting, offensive weapon, cutting off German supplies of vital raw materials, and so opening the way to victory. The problem with all these tasks was that there might be two or three enemies – Germany, Italy, and Japan were likely opponents; and the fleet's strength would then be stretched far too thinly over the globe.

The role of the army was mainly imperial, as its dispositions bore witness. If Britain were to be involved in a European war, there was a powerful school of thought that she should proceed on a policy of 'limited liability', and engage only small land forces on the Continent, putting her main effort into sea and air warfare and into the economic sustenance of a coalition. This was seen as a return to traditional British strategy after the costly and largely fruitless aberration of the First World War. A classic statement of this view was put to the Cabinet by Neville Chamberlain on 5 May 1937, just before he became Prime Minister: 'He did not believe that we could, or ought, or, in the event, would be allowed by the country, to enter a Continental war with the intention of fighting on the same lines as in the last.'[15] A paper by Thomas Inskip, Minister for the Co-ordination of Defence, accepted by the Cabinet in December 1937, placed British strategic objectives in order of priority: (1) the protection of the home country against air attack; (2) the safety of the trade routes; (3) the defence of British territories overseas; and (4) co-operation in the defence of the territories of any allies we may have in war'.[16]

The attraction of such a strategy from a British point of view is clear enough. For the French, however, who were to be assisted on a basis of limited liability, the prospect was far from attractive. They would be expected to sustain the battle on land, and to pay the price in blood. In December 1938, an officer on General Gamelin's staff told the British military attaché in Paris that France needed from Britain 'un effort du sang', an effort of blood – an ominous phrase, which grated unhappily on British ears.[17]

The doctrine of limited liability undermined French confidence in Britain, and helps to explain their sense of grievance against the British at this time. But it was also highly questionable whether it had any true advantage for the British themselves. In a reappraisal of the strategic position on 20 February 1939, when the threat posed by German power had become more immediate, the Chiefs of Staff pointed out that it was hard to say how the security of the British Isles could be maintained if France was forced to surrender, and therefore even self-defence 'may have to include a share in the land defence of French territory'.[18] It was at this point that the Cabinet decided in principle to create a large army of thirty-two divisions in the event of war on the Continent. They recognized, doubtless belatedly, that even in terms of British security and self-interest there was no alternative. A Continental commitment, not limited liability, was the only realistic military policy.

The Royal Air Force, like the army, had an important imperial role, as a cheap and effective method of imposing order and conducting frontier warfare. In European affairs in the 1930s, its main function was linked to a theory of deterrence: that the existence of a bomber force would deter another country (i.e. Germany) from attacking Britain. This theory was not backed by the possession of adequate aircraft, or reliable means of bombing accurately; but it was clung to for want of anything better to replace it. The expansion schemes of 1934–38 provided for a greater proportion of bombers than fighters, and this began to be changed in 1938 mainly because fighters were cheaper to produce than bombers. The government was also able to claim that, by building up a fighter force, it was doing something to protect the civilian population against air attack; though it could not mention the development of radar, which for the first time held out the possibility of intercepting the enemy bomber in flight.

The Air Staff's emphasis on the power of the bomber coincided with and reinforced a widespread popular fear of bombing attack. In October 1936 the Joint Planning Committee of the Chiefs of Staff (on which the RAF representative was Group Captain Arthur Harris, later the head of Bomber Command during the war) submitted a report which argued that by 1939 Germany would be able to deliver a series of knock-out air attacks on Britain from the first day of a war. It estimated that there might be 20,000 casualties in London in the first 24 hours, rising to 150,000 within a week. (In the event civilian casualties in Britain during the whole of the Second World War, from bombing and other bombardment, amounted to just under 147,000.) This was a 'worst case' scenario, and of course the Chiefs of Staff were not averse to giving the government a jolt which might produce more funds; but even so they broadly accepted the picture of danger from the air.[19] Naturally enough, politicians who saw the report were much impressed. Earlier, in 1934, Stanley Baldwin had said in the House of Commons that 'the bomber will always get through' – a simple phrase which was never forgotten. The impression on the public mind was reinforced by popular literature and films, and by the newsreels of the Spanish Civil War. The result was that both the government and large sections of the public were thoroughly alarmed at the prospect of air attack.

The effects on foreign policy of the state of British armaments and strategic thinking were far-reaching. The fundamental problem was the disparity between Britain's commitments and her resources. The commitments were almost literally world-wide. The British Empire was at its greatest extent. The Dominions, though asserting their independence of the mother country, still relied on her for protection. Australia and New Zealand, Malaya and Singapore, the Middle East and Mediterranean, western Europe and the British Isles were all under some kind of threat as the 1930s went on. In 1937 the Chiefs of Staff produced a gloomy review of Britain's enemies: Japan in the Pacific, Italy in the Mediterranean; and Germany in western Europe. Their conclusion was that until rearmament was further advanced, it should be the first task of foreign policy to diminish the number of Britain's enemies. The policy of 'appeasement' should never be appraised without recalling this sternly realistic recommendation. To reach an accommodation with Italy in the Mediterranean; to avoid confrontation with the Axis powers over the Spanish Civil War; to find the basis of a settlement with Germany; to make only the most cautious response to Japanese aggression in China – all this followed in large part from the need to diminish the number of one's enemies.

What of Britain's friends? The almost inevitable result of the concept of 'limited liability' was at best an ambiguous attitude to France. On the one hand, the British took the link with France almost for granted – if there was to be another war, Britain and France would be allies. But, on the other, for a long time the British refused to translate this assumption into any form of specific commitment. There were no staff talks between the two countries until the end of 1935, when the British suddenly pressed for conversations in the crisis over Italy and Abyssinia; and these were dropped by January 1936. There were staff meetings after the German occupation of the Rhineland, but they could make little headway when British strategic priorities put help to allies last in the line. As late as November 1938 the Chiefs of Staff were opposed to pursuing talks with the French in too much detail, for fear of being committed to a French war plan over which they had no control. A note from the Air Staff for RAF representatives in talks with French officers (15 June 1938) laid down that the words 'ally' or 'allies' should never be used, either verbally or in writing. It was a fair summing up of the British attitude: and if the British would not treat the French as allies, they had no reason to expect anything better in return.

Next, what were British views of their most dangerous enemy? Estimates of German strength moved rapidly in the 1930s from complacency to excessive pessimism. In the early stages of open German rearmament, from 1935 onwards, the War Office tended to be sceptical of reports of the rate of growth of the German Army, largely on the ground that it could not envisage the British Army growing at such speed. By 1939, however, partly under the influence of high French estimates of German strength, the War Office came to take too gloomy a view. In July 1939, military intelligence put the number of German divisions available for immediate mobilization at 99; in deference to French information this was raised to 120–130; the actual figure was 103. The number of German tanks was put in September 1939 at 5,000, including 1,400 medium tanks; the actual figure was 3,000 including only 300 mediums, the rest being light tanks.[20]

Land warfare was not seen as primarily a British problem; and estimates of the German Air Force were of more immediate significance. Early estimates tended to be low. In 1934, when the German Air Force had a total of 550 aircraft, the Air Ministry put the figure at 350, and thought it would reach 480 in 1935. The Air Staff could not believe that the Germans, notoriously efficient by their very nature, would accept anything less than the highest standards of training, support services, and reserves; and therefore their progress was bound to be slow. Hitler's public announcement in March 1935 of the existence of the *Luftwaffe* came as no surprise; but his claim in April 1935 that Germany had already achieved parity with Britain in air strength was regarded with scepticism.[21]

At that time, the Air Staff was right about current German strength, but wrong about future expansion. At the end of 1936 and the beginning of 1937, this complacency came to a sudden end, and estimates of German strength rose rapidly, until they became substantially exaggerated. It is possible to compare actual German strength in August 1938 with RAF estimates in September, the month of the Munich crisis (Table 7).[22] The overestimate of the combat-ready bomber force was almost twofold, and fed the fear of air bombardment which profoundly affected British policy at the time of Munich. At the time this fear was almost entirely misplaced. In September 1938 the commander of *Luft-waffe* Fleet 2, General Felmy, reported to the German Air Staff that bombing operations against England without advanced airfields in the Low Countries were impossible. The *Luftwaffe* had no aircraft with sufficient range, nor crews with adequate training, for the purpose. But, as is often the case, beliefs were more important than facts.

Table 7. German air strength and British estimates, 1938

	German air strength August 1938		British estimates September 1938	
	Total	Combat ready	Total	Combat ready
Fighters	643	453	810	717
Bombers	1,157	582	1,235	1,019
Dive-bombers	207	159	247	227

It is easy to see why the British government preferred to avoid war in 1938. It faced too many enemies; its resources were overstretched; it shrank from a Continental commitment on land; and it was afraid of sudden bombing attack from the air. What is less easy to see is why the same government, only the next year, went to war, not with a light heart, certainly, but with a modest confidence that they could win.

The answer appears to lie in two estimates which were current in 1939. The first was a belief that Britain was near to turning the corner in the matter of air power. Desmond Morton, who ran the Industrial Intelligence Committee, predicted in February 1939 that British aircraft production would overtake German by the autumn – which proved to be correct; and the air attaché in Berlin reported in the same month that he thought Germany had reached the peak of its re-armament – which proved incorrect. At the same time, radar was coming into service, with its promise for the first time that the bomber might *not* always get through. The second was the estimate by British economic intelligence that the German economy could not sustain a long war. Reports made by the British embassy in Berlin, from 1936 to 1939, all indicated an economy under strain, with the iron and steel industry working at full capacity and a shortage of skilled labour. Reports from German opposition sources in September 1938 and January 1939 pointed in the same direction: the financial position was desperate, manpower and transport were under strain, and Schacht knew that chaos lay ahead. This information led to two conclusions. First, it was likely to mean further adventures in foreign policy. As the Berlin embassy put it in May 1939: 'Sooner or later further teritorial expansion will be necessary', because Hitler would have either to accept limitations on self-sufficiency or go to war. But second, if Germany went to war she would do so with her economy already fully stretched; and unless she made great gains in resources in the first twelve or eighteen months, she must run into serious difficulties. A Chiefs of Staff strategic assessment of 20 February 1939 held, on the economic side, that 'Germany, if favoured by fortune, might maintain her industrial resistance for about a year'.[23] This optimism was not universal. The Industrial Intelligence Committee indicated that Germany had substantial stocks of raw materials; and a Treasury paper in July 1939 pointed out that Germany had established power over neighbouring countries, so that payment for her imports in case of war was unlikely to pose serious problems. The Chancellor of the Exchequer (Simon) told the Cabinet on 5 July that Germany was *better* prepared for a long war than Britain.

None the less, the favourable reports were strong enough to encourage those who were ready to believe them. Intelligence reports, like other sources of information, tend to be believed when they tell the listener what he wants to hear. Up to February and March 1939, intelligence about German strength gave ample support to a policy of seeking a settlement with that country. At that time, for reasons which were only partially related to the military balance, British policy changed; and there were enough indications in the intelligence material to give the change of policy some backing. In part the indicators proved correct – the corner had been turned in the air, though only just; in part they were quite wrong – the German economy, with the help of all the loot of 1940, had plenty of life in it, and was to show more staying power than anyone predicted. At the time, there seemed to be enough good news to sustain the spirits of those who, however reluctantly, decided that they had taken enough from the Germans.

REFERENCES AND NOTES

1. Raymond Aron, *Peace and War* (London 1966), p. 151.
2. Guilio Douhet, *Il Dominio dell'aria*; English trans., *The Command of the Air* (London 1943).
3. H. Montgomery Hyde, *British Air Policy between the Wars, 1918–1939* (London 1976), p. 46; E. L. Woodward, *Great Britain and the War of 1914–1918* (London 1967), pp. 370–3.
4. John Gooch, *Armies in Europe* (London 1980), pp. 191–5; Guy Chapman, *Why France Collapsed* (London 1968), p. 21.
5. The figures for French armaments in the late 1930s bristle with difficulties, and these must be taken as approximations. See Robert J. Young, *In Command of France: French foreign policy and military planning, 1933–1940* (Harvard 1979), pp. 166–73, 185–90; J. A. Gunsburg, *Divided and Conquered: the French High Command and the defeat of the West, 1940* (London 1980), pp. 39–40; Chapman, *Why France Collapsed*, pp. 66–8 and Appendix A.

6. Deliveries of aircraft to French Air Force:
   1934 – 197;   1935 – 494;   1936 – 570;   1937 – 422;   1938 – 533;   1939 – 2227.
   Air force expenditure as a percentage of the defence budget:
   1934 – 12.3;   1935 – 18.8;   1936 – 18.0;   1937 – 18.0;   1938 – 23.0.
   Patrick Fridenson and Jean Lecuir, *La France et la Grande-Bretagne face aux problèmes aériens, 1935–mai 1940* (Vincennes 1976), pp. 31, 43.
7. The assessment of the size of the French Air Force in 1939–40 is a notorious statistical, historical, and political quagmire – Robert Young has rightly remarked that counting aeroplanes is an art form rather than an exact science. See the summary in Henri Michel, *La Seconde Guerre Mondiale*, vol. I (Paris 1968), p. 11; cf. Gunsberg, *Divided and Conquered*, p. 75; Fridenson et Lecuir, *La France et la Grande-Bretagne*, *passim*; Young, *In Command of France*, p. 163.
8. Ibid., p. 228.
9. F. H. Hinsley, *British Intelligence in the Second World War*, vol. I (London 1979), pp. 75–6.
10. Gunsburg, *Divided and Conquered*, pp. 53, 76. For actual German strength, see below, pp. 190–1.
11. S. W. Roskill, *The War at Sea 1939–1945*, vol. I (London 1954), p. 50 and Appendix E; the building programmes are detailed in S. W. Roskill, *Naval Policy between the Wars*, vol. I (London 1968), Appendix C. The figures include the Dominion navies.
12. Brian Bond, *British Military Policy between Two World Wars* (Oxford 1980), p. 98, map and table, pp. 118–19.
13.

	Admiralty	Air Ministry	War Office
	(Actual expenditure; in thousands of £)		
1938	127,295	133,800	121,361
1939	149,339	248,561	243,638

   G.C. Peden, *British Rearmament and the Treasury 1932–1939* (Edinburgh 1979), appendix III.
14. Sir Peter Masefield, 'The Royal Air Force and British military aircraft production, 1934–1940', published in French translation in Comité d'Histoire de la 2e Guerre Mondiale, *Français et Britanniques dans la Drôle de Guerre* (Paris 1979), pp. 411–56, table on p. 426. Note that the definition used is the strictest definition of first-line aircraft; serviceable aircraft in operational squadrons with trained crews. It is an excellent definition, but it makes comparison with other statistics and other countries difficult.
15. Quoted in P. J. Dennis, *Decision by Default: peacetime conscription and British defence, 1919–1939* (London 1972), p. 98.
16. Quoted in Peden, *British Rearmament and the Treasury*, pp. 134–5.
17. Quoted in Michael Howard, *The Continental Commitment* (London: Pelican Books 1974), p. 128.
18. Quoted in Howard, *Continental Commitment*, p. 129.
19. Uri Bialer, *The Shadow of the Bomber* (London 1980), pp. 128–32.
20. Hinsley, *British Intelligence*, vol. I, pp. 62, 76.
21. Wesley K. Wark, 'British Intelligence on the German Air Force and aircraft industry, 1933–1939', *Historical Journal*, **25** (3) (Sept. 1982), 627–48.

22. Edward L. Homze, *Arming the Luftwaffe: the Reich Air Ministry and the German aircraft industry, 1919–39* (Lincoln, Nebraska 1976), p. 241.
23. Hinsley, *British Intelligence*, vol. I, pp. 67–8, 70–1.

Chapter 12

ARMED FORCES, STRATEGY, AND FOREIGN POLICY (2): ITALY, GERMANY, AND THE SOVIET UNION

In Britain and France, there were grave doubts as to whether war was still an instrument of policy, and little understanding that war and peace were part of a single process. In Italy, Germany, and the USSR a very different view prevailed. It is true that they dressed up their attitudes to war in different ways. The Soviets created a Red Army, with people's commissars alongside the officers, and spoke of peoples' wars. The fascist and nazi regimes talked in exalted and cloudy terms of the purifying and ennobling nature of war. But for all of them, force was something to be used without inhibitions as an instrument of policy. It might be the service of ideology, to carry revolution across Poland on the bayonets of the Red Army. It might be a straightforward border conflict: Stalin had no hesitation in fighting a serious battle with the Japanese in the summer of 1939 on the frontiers of Outer Mongolia. It might be a war of colonial conquest, such as the Italians waged in Abyssinia; or of conquest nearer home, like the German invasion of Poland. Moreover, Hitler was a master of the fluid tactics of subversion and undeclared war, blurring the line between peace and war.

In all three states, force was simply regarded as part of life, and was used whenever it was thought necessary or advantageous. This had an important effect on their foreign policies.

ITALY

There was a striking contrast between some of Mussolini's claims for the Italian forces and the reality. In 1927 Mussolini claimed that he could mobilize an army of 5 million men, and by 1936 his slogan was 'eight million bayonets'. In practice, when Italy went to war in June 1940, the mobilized strength of the army was 1.6 million. Similarly, Mussolini asserted in 1927 that he would build an air force whose planes would blot out the sun. In 1939 he claimed to have 8,500 aircraft; the Air Ministry figure was 3,000; and an enquiry carried out by the sceptical Naval Staff could not find even 1,000.[1] The disparities were bizarre, but the consequences of both the inflated claims and the exiguous reality were very serious.

The Italian Army was based on conscription with a cadre of regular soldiers. The period of military service was fixed in 1923 at eighteen months; but in 1926 this was amended to six months for those with family commitments or for men with a brother already serving in the army. Up to 1937, the main body of the army was made up of thirty-eight infantry divisions, each comprising three regiments. In that year, General Pariani proposed to reduce this complement to two regiments, aiming at greater manoeuvrability in the expectation of further campaigns in Africa. Reorganization began in December 1938, and by 1940 the army included seventy-three of the smaller infantry divisions instead of the thirty-eight larger ones. The change disrupted the army at what proved to be a crucial period.

In 1940 the Italian Army also included three armoured divisions, but these were more formidable in name than in fact. Their main equipment was a light tank, thinly armoured and armed only with machine-guns. A new medium tank was in production, but only a few were in service. A programme to modernize the artillery was begun in 1937, but made only slow progress. Production of heavy guns in 1939 was only seventy per month, and much of the artillery remained of the 1914–18 vintage. The supply and transport services were weak.[2]

The air force was always the pride of the fascist regime, and projected a suitable image of modernity and dynamism. Its aircraft competed successfully for records in speed and altitude. It produced spectacular displays, such as a formation flight across the Atlantic. However, during the Abyssinian crisis of 1935–36 it appeared that the air force was unready for a European war, and a programme of expansion was begun. Between 1935 and 1939, 8,700 combat aircraft were ordered, but actual production fell far short of these figures. The Spanish Civil War proved a drain on resources, with over 700 aircraft being sent to Spain and some losses being incurred. Accurate figures are hard to arrive at, but it appears that the air force had less than 1,000 aircraft in service in 1939.[3] Effort was dispersed among too many types of aircraft; and the planes themselves were often unsatisfactory. As late as June 1940, when Italy went to war, 150 out of the 400 fighters in service were biplanes, and the other 250 were inferior in performance to the British Hurricane and Spitfire. The main strike aircraft was a three-engined medium bomber, the Savoia-Marchetti S79, which was to prove more successful as a torpedo-bomber than against land targets.

The best equipped of the Italian services was the navy. In June 1940 the Italian fleet had available for action 4 battleships, 6 cruisers, 16 destroyers, 26 torpedo-boats, and 64 submarines. Other vessels were in the course of refitting. Numerically, the fleet compared well with British and French naval forces in the Mediterranean, and had the geographical advantage of a central position.[4]

Some of the defects in the equipment of the army and air force arose from weaknesses in Italian industry, but some arose from lack of proper direction. The motor-car industry, for example, was perfectly capable of producing a good medium tank if specifications and orders had been provided in good time. There was a lack of direction and consistency in Italian strategic policy, despite the fascist regime's claims to provide drive and decisiveness. In theory, there was ample machinery for central direction. Mussolini himself held the three posts of Minister for the Army, Navy, and Air Force from 1925 to 1929, and again from 1933 onwards. General Badoglio, as Chief of the General Staff, gave advice to Mussolini on the affairs of all three services. In practice, this apparent centralization produced little co-ordination. For Mussolini to hold all three service ministries as well as being head of the government simply meant that he did none of the work properly, and no inter-service staff was developed to give substance to Badoglio's position.

None of the three Italian services had a clear set of strategic principles to guide its development. From 1925 onwards the main task of the army was conceived as a defensive war in northern Italy against France and Yugoslavia. In 1937 General Pariani, the new Army Chief of Staff, took up a proposal made by his predecessor in 1936 to create motorized divisions and assault brigades, but by 1940 this change had not gone far, and the attempt to graft an offensive element on to a basically defensive system does not appear to have succeeded. The air force hesitated between ideas of strategic bombing and co-operation with the army. The navy had a large number of submarines, but no plan for making use of them. For a long time it had regarded the French fleet as its main rival, and it developed no plans for a war against France and Britain together.

There was in fact a wide gap between foreign and strategic policy. The Rome–Berlin Axis was likely to lead to a war alongside Germany against Britain and France, but no strategy for such a war was developed. If, on the other hand, foreign policy was to be adapted to the actual state of Italy's armed forces, then the intervention in Spain, especially the despatch of over 700 aircraft from an inadequate air force, was ill-judged. The Italian forces were ill-prepared for serious war in Europe and the Mediterranean in 1940. Badoglio was cautious and pessimistic, and he advised Mussolini against going to war in 1940, but was overruled. Mussolini did not anticipate a serious war, but a military promenade, for which Italian preparation was doubtless adequate.

Yet it is dangerous to be too preoccupied with the faintly absurd air which envelops Italian military policy and preparations. The Italian forces scored real successes during the 1930s. They conquered Abyssinia more rapidly than most observers expected. In Spain, they sustained a defeat at Guadalajara; but this was less serious than republican propaganda made out, and afterwards they fought with some success, notably round Bilbao. Moreover, for a long time the appearance of Italian strength was more important than reality. The French set great store by their military agreements with Italy in 1935. The British Mediterranean fleet withdrew from Malta to Alexandria in 1935, during the Abyssinian crisis, for fear of Italian air attack. In 1937–38 Italy was courted by both Britain and Germany, partly because of the valuation put upon her armed forces. As long as Mussolini kept up a balancing act, and allowed himself to be courted by all and sundry, all was well; the error was to come down on one side and commit himself to war. Looking back, it is easy to see the gap between image and reality in the Italian armed forces, and perhaps to smile at Mussolini's self-deception. But he was not the only one to be deceived, and the fact that others took Italian strength at Mussolini's valuation played some part in the coming of the war.

GERMANY

No one smiled at the German armed forces. The German Army and the *Luftwaffe* swept all before them and conquered almost the whole of Europe between 1939 and 1941. The German Navy, the weakest of the services, launched an astonishing sea-borne invasion of Norway, and then fought a long and often successful submarine campaign in the Atlantic. Indeed, there was for a long time a tendency to exaggerate the quality and degree of preparedness of the German war machine. It was more than a match for its opponents, failing only in the air over Britain in autumn 1940 and then at the last stretch in Russia in the winter of 1941–42. Despite this remarkable record, the German forces had more weaknesses than appeared on the surface; which explained the profound ambiguities in German attitudes towards the prospect of war in the late 1930s. On the one hand, Hitler and the nazi leadership were full of confidence and daring; on the other, many of the professionals in the Army General Staff were doubtful and cautious. Both had sound reasons for their views, though it was Hitler who emerged triumphant, to the extent of making the more cautious among the generals appear hidebound, if not actually cowardly.

The German Army expanded with extraordinary rapidity between 1933 and 1939. The restrictions imposed by the Treaty of Versailles had been secretly evaded under the Weimar Republic, which prepared outline plans for trebling the size of the army from 100,000 to 300,000.

In December 1932 these plans were set in motion, and by 1935 Germany's seven infantry divisions had been translated into twenty-one. On 16 March 1935 the nazi government announced the reintroduction of conscription, with the term of service set at one year. (It was extended to two years in August 1936.) At the same time, the army was reorganized into thirty-six infantry divisions, involving serious problems of administration and training. In October 1935 the first three armoured (Panzer) divisions were created, in rudimentary form and equipped only with light tanks.[5]

Expansion and reorganization were pressed forward at a great pace. By the middle of 1939 the army consisted of a total of 103 divisions, 52 active and 51 reserve, including 86 infantry and 6 armoured divisions. There were 730,000 men under arms in the peacetime army, and mobilization brought the total to 3.7 million.[6] The sheer speed of the expansion brought its difficulties. The army's equipment fell short of its commanders' requirement. The armoured divisions in September 1939 were mainly equipped with light tanks, and only about 300 of the 3,200 armoured vehicles were the new and well-armed medium tanks. Even by the time of the German invasion of France and the Low Countries in May 1940, only about a quarter of their tanks were medium tanks.[7] There were also problems of personnel, notably in the officer corps, which grew headlong in six years from 4,000 to over 100,000 with inevitable defects in training and integration. The German Army of 1939–40 fell short in equipment, training, and cohesion of the standards of its predecessor in 1914. That despite these limitations it won such extraordinary victories was a tribute to the way in which it was handled and to its fighting powers – the armoured divisions in particular rose far above the deficiencies of their equipment. It was also a reflection upon its opponents.

The pace of the German Army's expansion remains astonishing, and its defects and deficiencies were of secondary importance. When Germany's neighbours often exaggerated the size of the German Army in their intelligence reports, this was not unnatural, because the rate of change was such that the exaggeration of one year tended to become the truth of the next. The central fact stood out with stark clarity: Germany moved in six years from being one of the weakest land powers in Europe to being the strongest.

The same was true, with very similar qualifications, of the German Air Force. Under the terms of the Versailles Treaty, Germany was forbidden all military aircraft, but this restriction was clandestinely evaded on a small scale throughout the Weimar period. Notably, there was a useful scheme of collaboration with the USSR, where the Germans operated an aircraft factory and a training base. The results were valuable without being substantial. In February 1932 the German Army possessed 228 aircraft, 36 military and 192 converted civilian planes. The aircraft industry was tiny, employing only 3,200 workers at its lowest point in 1932, with firms going out of business in the depression.[8]

This situation was transformed by the nazi regime. The *Luftwaffe* was the nazi service *par excellence*. The nazi leaders included airmen, Goering and Hess; and Hitler grasped both the popular appeal and the potential power of the air arm. The new government determined at once to set up an independent air force and a separate Air Ministry. Through government orders and finance (mainly disguised at the start – out of 30 million RM for air-frames, 26.6 million appeared under the unemployment relief programme), the aircraft industry grew at a prodigious speed, and by mid-1936 it employed nearly 125,000 workers.[9]

In 1933 the new Air Ministry embarked on a programme to build 1,000 aircraft. This was rapidly superseded, and the 'Rhineland Programme' of July 1934 aimed to produce 4,021 aircraft by the end of September 1935, with an emphasis on bombers – 822, as against 245 fighters. By the time the existence of the *Luftwaffe* was publicly announced on 10 March 1935, nearly 2,500 aircraft had been delivered. Of these, a large proportion were trainers, and many of the combat planes were obsolescent models. But it was a remarkable start, and the basis had been laid for mass production.[10]

Thereafter, new production programmes succeeded one another with bewildering speed. During 1936 there were as many as three in the year. After a very steep rise between 1933 and 1935, actual production levelled off at an average of between 5,000 and 5,500 aircraft per year in 1936–38. During this period, there were problems in production with the introduction of new types, and shortages of raw materials. In 1938, government pressure to increase production was stepped up. On 8 July Goering held a conference of aircraft manufacturers at his country estate at Karinhall, telling them that they must get on to a war footing and concentrate on producing fewer types of aircraft in longer runs. In August the Air Ministry introduced yet another new programme (Plan 8), aiming at the production of over 3,700 fighters and over 3,000 bombers in the next eighteen months. Within two months this was superseded. On 14 October Goering announced Hitler's new armaments programme, including a fivefold increase in the size of the *Luftwaffe*, requiring the production of 45,700 aircraft by spring 1942. (This programme, an interesting sequel to the Munich agreement, referred specifically to building long-range bombers to operate against England.) The resources for such a prodigious expansion were simply not available, and in practice the plan was quietly set aside in favour of more modest, though still considerable, objectives.[11]

On 5 August 1939, with war with Poland very close, Goering held a conference with his principal *Luftwaffe* officers, and worked out with them a plan to prepare the air force for a general European war in 1942, notably to achieve higher production by concentrating on only four types of combat aircraft, two bombers and two fighters. Orders to this effect were given in September, development projects were sharply reduced, and the *Luftwaffe* staked its future on four types, of which two (the He177 and Me210) were untried and proved to be failures.

As events turned out, the *Luftwaffe* had to face general European war before 1942. In September 1939, to wage real war on Poland and phoney war with Britain and France, the Germans had a first-line strength of 3,374 combat aircraft, of which 75 per cent were service-able. Transports and seaplanes raised the total to just over 4,000.[12] The quality of the force was at this stage good. The principal fighter was the excellent Me109.[13] The medium bombers were the Do17 and He111, the latter being a particularly adaptable and successful aircraft; and the Ju87 dive-bomber had been effective in Spain and was to be so again in Poland and France. As events turned out, the German Air Force found 1939 and 1940 a relatively advantageous time to go to war, before the problem of being committed to so small a number of aircraft types came home to roost.

The German Navy received the lowest priority among the three services in the allocation of resources. Moreover, Hitler assured Admiral Raeder, the commander of the navy, in 1935 that war was not to be expected until 1944, and construction planning proceeded accordingly. At the outbreak of war in September 1939, the strength of the navy stood at 2 battle-cruisers, 3 pocket battleships, 6 cruisers, 17 destroyers, 17 torpedo-boats, and 56 submarines. Of these last, only 26 were ocean-going vessels, capable of operating in the Atlantic; and only 46 out of the total were actually operational. On the other hand, Hitler's armaments proposals of October 1938 included large-scale naval building, and early in 1939 a plan (Plan Z) was adopted which was to provide Germany, over a period of years, with a powerful battle-fleet, 4 aircraft-carriers, and about 250 U-boats. Most of this was abandoned when war came, to concentrate on what could be completed quickly. However, two formidable battleships, the *Bismarck* and *Tirpitz*, had been laid down in 1936 and were nearing completion.[14] It was a fleet which was not yet ready either for surface operations in the North Sea or for effective U-boat warfare against commerce in the Atlantic.

The doctrines of war professed and practised by the German armed forces have been the centre of keen interest ever since the striking victories of 1939–41 attracted both admiration and the desire to explain how they came about. For a long time the explanation was that the German Army had whole-heartedly put into practice ideas of mobile armoured warfare, including the tactical use of the dive-bomber as flying artillery. Such ideas were widely current between the wars, starting in Britain with J. F. C. Fuller and Liddell Hart; pro-pounded rather vaguely by de Gaulle in France; taken up by the Red

Army in the forming of mechanized brigades; and brought to fruition in Germany through the advocacy of General Guderian. The Germans concentrated their tanks in Panzer divisions, capable of rapid movement and deep penetration into enemy territory; and in the campaign of 1940 their armoured divisions outnumbered the French by ten to four – of which the fourth was only being formed in the course of the battle.

In substance this remains the key to the German success, though it appears that the victory of the 'armoured idea' within the army was much less complete than was once thought. A more traditional strategy, emphasizing manoeuvre but retaining the key role of the infantry, persisted alongside the new ideas. The German Army of 1940 was mainly modelled on that of 1914. Even the campaign in France in 1940, which was a great triumph of armoured-cum-aerial warfare, was affected by this conflict of views, and the Panzers were sometimes held up to wait for the infantry.[15]

Luftwaffe doctrine was also less clear-cut than has often been assumed. The nazi government decided at once in favour of a separate air force; but what was to be its role? An early answer was put forward by Robert Knauss, a pilot in the First World War and later a *Lufthansa* official, who prepared a memorandum in May 1933 for Erhard Milch, State Secretary at the Air Ministry, and a key figure in the new *Luftwaffe*. Knauss saw the immediate problem as that of deterring France and Poland from attacking Germany during the early stages of her rearmament, and he proposed the rapid building of 400 heavy bombers to act as a deterrent. Milch agreed in principle, but the scheme posed too many practical difficulties, not least that the creation of a heavy bomber force could only be a slow process.

The result was a compromise. The Germans sought the deterrent effect of a bomber fleet, but tried to secure it with the types of aircraft which were to hand. The idea of a heavy bomber force was not entirely abandoned. General Walther Wever, the first head of the Air Staff, had read *Mein Kampf* and prepared seriously for a war with Russia by putting in hand in 1934 a project for a 'Ural-bomber', capable of reaching the furthest points of European Russia. Two prototype four-engined bombers were produced, but their development was suspended in 1937 after Wever's death, and the project never achieved significant priority. The *Luftwaffe*'s thinking on the conduct of air war, set out in a manual of 1936 prepared under Wever's supervision, was based on the concept of a balanced air force equipped for a number of roles. The *Luftwaffe* would secure air supremacy by destroying an enemy air force and aircraft industry; bomb centres of war production and communications; and give direct support to the army and navy in battle. During the next few years, an emphasis on direct support for the army developed more by chance and experience than as a matter of theory. The *Luftwaffe*'s first officers mostly came from the army. The experience of the Spanish Civil War showed the value of close air support for ground troops. (The bombing of cities was spectacular, but of no great military importance.) Existing types of aircraft were well adapted to support the land forces. It therefore came about that, though the first intention was to create a balanced air force with a strategic bombing component, what actually developed was a force directed mainly towards co-operation with the army, though with functions much wider than that of providing 'flying artillery' which caught so many eyes in 1940.

German military and air doctrines were thus less clear-cut and coherent than was widely believed at the time of their greatest successes, when everything seemed to point to a highly developed system of armoured attack with close air support. There was a good deal of compromise and much difference of opinion. None the less, it was still the case that Germany possessed, in the period 1938–41, an army and air force which were far better adapted to offensive warfare than those of any other European country; and this had significant effects on German foreign policy.

The *Luftwaffe* in particular played a vital role in foreign policy by providing Germany with the power to threaten. For some time, the very existence of the *Luftwaffe* was as far as possible concealed, so as not to provoke intervention from foreign powers; but from the moment of the open announcement of its existence in March 1935, this caution was replaced by the diametrically opposite policy of exaggerating German air strength. Hitler started this with his claim to have already reached parity with the RAF in March 1935, and thereafter everything possible was done to display the *Luftwaffe*. Its planes appeared at international air shows; they flew past at party rallies and at the Berlin Olympics; they were written up, with official encouragement, in foreign aviation journals; they were shown off to foreign visitors – Balbo, Lindbergh, Vuillemin. Goering told his officers in 1936 that the important thing was 'to impress Hitler and enable Hitler, in turn, to impress the world.'[16]

The world was only too ready to be impressed. Lindbergh was overwhelmed by what he saw, and with the prestige of his Atlantic flights behind him, he proceeded to overwhelm others. The British were already afraid of the bomber, and their fears were easily exploited. During the Spanish Civil War, the bombing of Guernica on 26 April 1937 was not publicized by the Germans, but by the opponents of General Franco, whose propaganda seized on the episode as a symbol of German brutality and the power of the bomber. The Germans thus reaped the benefits of terror spread by their enemies.

The greatest triumph of the menace of the *Luftwaffe* came in the Czechoslovakian crisis of 1938. At the time, the British Air Staff believed the combat-ready German bomber force to be twice its actual strength. Neville Chamberlain, flying back from one of his meetings with Hitler, looked down on London and its defenceless inhabitants, whom he sought to preserve from the horrors of air attack. In large part, Munich was a victory for the terror which the Germans inspired by displaying the *Luftwaffe* with panache, and letting their opponents' nerves do the rest. The method was highly successful, and it may in the long run have tempted Hitler to overreach himself. He appears to have relied heavily on air power in deciding to go to war in 1939 and to extend that war in 1940; and it may well be that he did not grasp the deficiencies which lay behind the *Luftwaffe*'s fearsome appearance. He got most of his information and impressions from Goering, who was certainly not given to underestimating the force which he commanded. An interesting symptom of this was the order, on 24 May 1940, to leave the closing of Dunkirk and the destruction of the British Expeditionary Force to the *Luftwaffe*. This order was the result of a direct intervention by Goering on the 23rd, when he telephoned Hitler to insist that his air force would destroy the BEF. Goering told Milch, when he had secured agreement to this plan: 'The *Luftwaffe* is to wipe out the British on the beaches. . . . The Fuehrer wants them taught a lesson they will never forget.'[17] There was no question of Hitler wanting to allow the British to get away – he wanted them destroyed, but agreed to let the *Luftwaffe* do it. In doing so, he overrated its power: it failed to do the job, with far-reaching consequences. Similarly, and on a larger scale, it seems at least likely that an overestimate of German air power predisposed Hitler to take risks in 1939 and 1940, and so played a part in bringing about the war.

In relation to the army, the evidence is that Hitler did not proceed from calculations of military preparedness, still less from the advice of the General Staff, but from his own convictions as to what the army should be made ready to do. Shortly after becoming Chancellor, in February 1933, he addressed a meeting of high-ranking army and navy officers, and outlined his general ideas with surprising frankness: to get rid of the Versailles settlement, and then to go for the conquest of living space in the east, which would be ruthlessly Germanized. For all this, large-scale rearmament would be necessary. The service chiefs welcomed rearmament, but appear to have thought that war in the east was a long way off, and that they could impose a cautious approach on Hitler.

In this they were mistaken. During the next few years, Hitler pushed his generals into a series of rapid moves, brushing aside their caution. The high command thought the occupation of the Rhineland in March 1936 was too risky. When the Spanish Civil War began, Generals Blomberg and Fritsch opposed German intervention, on the ground that it would risk a European war for which Germany was not ready. During the Czechoslovakian crisis, General Beck was strongly opposed to Hitler's policy, which he again believed was courting general war when Germany was unprepared; and he urged General

Brauchitsch, the Commander-in-Chief, to organize collective opposition by senior officers. (This was when Hitler exclaimed 'What kind of generals are these which I as head of state may have to propel into war? By rights I should be the one seeking to ward off the generals' eagerness for war.')[18] There was one exception to this rule – the *Anschluss* with Austria in March 1938. On 10 March Hitler asked for an operational plan for an occupation of Austria. None had been prepared, but the army staff set to work to produce one in short order. There were no objections, even from Beck. The *Anschluss* was part of German sentiment, and was welcome even to otherwise cautious generals.

By the time the attack on Poland came round, the opposition of the generals was over. Nothing succeeds like success. Hitler had delivered the goods so often when the generals had warned of failure and danger that they could no longer sustain the role of Cassandra. Moreover, Hitler had by 1939 established complete control over the German high command. The process started on the Night of the Long Knives on 30 June 1934, when amid the purge of the SA two army generals (von Schleicher and von Bredow) were murdered, without investigation and without protest from their fellows. There followed in August 1934 the oath of unconditional obedience to Hitler in person, taken by all members of the army, after which the officer corps in particular was bound to Hitler by its own old-fashioned code of honour.

Much later, in February 1938, Hitler exploited the indiscretion of General Blomberg in marrying a former prostitute, and a false charge of homosexuality brought against General Fritsch, to get rid of both these officers. They had both been at the so-called Hossbach conference on 5 November 1937, at which Hitler had set out his ideas for expansion, and both had expressed doubts. Fritsch was replaced as Commander-in-Chief by Brauchitsch, who has been neatly described as 'an anatomical marvel, a man totally without backbone'.[19] Hitler also took the opportunity of these changes to reorganize the command structure. The Ministry of War was abolished, and the *Oberkommando der Wehrmacht* (OKW – High Command of the Armed Forces) put in its place. Hitler became Supreme Commander of the Armed Forces, with authority to issue orders to all three, and the wholly pliable General Keitel became his Chief of Staff. Keitel's younger brother became head of the Army Personnel Office, which gave Hitler a means of influence over appointments within the army. In all these ways, an institutional control over the army was added to the psychological effects of repeated success. By 1939 there was no question of caution on the part of the high command having any restraining effect on German policy.

Where was this policy leading, and what was the object of the headlong increase in the German armed forces which has been described? It was possible to want rearmament simply to restore

Germany's prestige and security, and to re-establish the status of the armed forces in German society. If this was all that Hitler wanted, he did not need to part company with Schacht by pushing rearmament to the point of economic catastrophe, or to force his own ideas upon a cautious General Staff. Hitler wrote and said repeatedly that he needed rearmament in order to go to war, and his actions were suited to his words. The only question worth asking is what *sort* of war was intended as the object of the forced march of German rearmament. On this, there have been divided opinions.

There is a powerful case that Hitler sought a series of short wars, waged by rapid movement and speedily concluded. As early as January 1937 the British military attaché in Berlin reported that the development of the German military machine suggested just such an intention – short wars with limited objectives, most likely in eastern Europe but possibly in the west as well. Historians have elaborated such views into a general interpretation of the concept of blitzkrieg.[20] Blitzkrieg was more than a theory of swift-moving armoured warfare. It involved all aspects of Germany's life and preparations for war, military, political, and economic. Short wars suited the nature of the German economy, which was heavily dependent on imports, because they could be waged on existing stocks of oil and raw materials, and could be made to pay by capturing further stocks and sources of supply. They fitted in with the political and administrative methods of the regime, which were divisive and ill-coordinated, but were well adapted to improvisation and speed of execution. Germany was prepared for the sprint, but not for the marathon. They were consonant with the domestic policy which, for as long as possible, sought to give the Germans both guns and butter: that is, to rearm while preserving the civilian standard of living. Short wars would avoid the economic strain and heavy casualties of the First World War, and because Germany was surrounded by weaker powers which could be isolated by skilful diplomacy and picked off one by one, they would be amply effective.

Against this there stands the view that most of Hitler's statements before the war indicated that he was thinking in terms of a large-scale and lengthy war, perhaps a war of continents. In May 1939, for example, he told service chiefs that Germany must prepare for a war of ten to fifteen years' duration. Many of the preparations being made, notably the programmes for synthetic oil and rubber, were long term in their nature. The naval programme of 1939 aiming for both a battle-fleet and a large force of submarines, was geared to a naval war in 1943 or 1944. As late as 1939, Goering produced schemes to get the *Luftwaffe* ready for large-scale war in 1942.[21] In this view, Hitler was preparing both the economy and the armed services for a long war at a date later than 1939, but in fact got himself into a general war at a time and place which he did not expect.

Of these interpretations, the first, or 'blitzkrieg' view, concentrates primarily on what Hitler did. The second looks more seriously at what he said, which should certainly never be disregarded. The present analysis is concerned primarily with what happened between 1938 and 1941, and in that context it is important that Hitler always expected quick results even from his long-term projects. The synthetic oil programme, for example, was at first intended to make Germany self-sufficient by 1939. The evidence is strong that Hitler anticipated rapid results from the campaigns which he undertook between 1939 and 1941. The plan for the invasion of France, which owed much to Hitler's intervention, was designed to produce quick victory, though even Hitler was surprised when the French surrendered in a mere six weeks. In planning for the attack on the Soviet Union, the time allowed to secure victory grew shorter and shorter, until the final estimate envisaged only a campaign of ten weeks. There still lay ahead the sweeping vistas of Hitler's remarkable visions: a war of continents against the USA, and expansion into Africa. From the point of view of what happened in Europe between 1938 and 1941, the short-war concept corresponds with Hitler's expectations, and also (with the exception of the Russian campaign) with what he achieved. It is true that Germany had produced rearmament in width rather than in depth, and in some cases rearmament mainly for display. But her armaments were remarkably effective. They gave Germany, for a brief but vital period, the ability to terrify her opponents, to take the offensive, and to strike down one country after another. In the possession of that power, and the will to use it, lies a major explanation of the coming of war in Europe.

THE USSR

During the 1930s, the Soviet Union maintained very large armed forces. In 1935 the Red Army had a peacetime strength of some 940,000 men. It included 90 infantry (or rifle) divisions, and 16 cavalry divisions. (These latter were almost entirely horsed cavalry, and were actually increased to 30 divisions by 1941 – the Red Army was the only European army to retain so large a cavalry force.) Its armour included at least 3,000 tanks (some estimates went as high as 10,000), organized into heavy tank brigades and mechanized brigades, some of which were grouped into mechanized corps. These very large numbers of tanks were sustained by factory production which, according to Soviet figures, ran at over 3,000 per year between 1935 and 1937. The tanks themselves were mostly light, and many were obsolescent. The medium tanks of the period, designed with several gun-turrets, proved unwieldy and unsatisfactory. The highly successful T-34 medium tank only came into production in 1940, and about 1,000 were with the armoured units in June 1941.[22]

The Soviet Air Force was not a separate service like the RAF or the *Luftwaffe*, but an extension of the army under military command. Its numbers were very large, outstripping any other European air force in the late 1930s: in 1938 it comprised about 5,000 aircraft, with production figures of about 4,000 – 5,000 per year in support. Most of its aircraft, however, were obsolescent. Many of the fighters were biplanes; a four-engined bomber whose prototype flew in 1936 encountered serious problems, and began to come into service only in 1940. The same was true of modern types of fighters and ground attack aircraft, which were delivered to units only in small numbers during 1940.[23]

The doctrine professed by the Soviet armed forces was widely separated from their actual organization and capabilities. Strategic theory stressed the importance of the offensive, which it was assumed would be assisted by risings of the proletariat in whatever country was at war with the Soviet Union. When the USSR was attacked, the Red Army would move at once to the offensive, and win a decisive victory at a low cost in casualties. In 1934, the needs of this strategy were partly met by the division of the Red Army into two parts: a partly mechanized shock army, combining tanks and aircraft with other arms, and the mass infantry army. By 1939 there were seven mechanized corps, but in 1939, applying what were taken to be the lessons of the Spanish Civil War, these were broken up and the tanks distributed with the role of supporting the infantry. The German victories of 1940 brought a rather laggardly reconsideration of this policy, and during 1941 mechanized corps were reconstituted, this time on the model of the German Panzer divisions, with a motorized infantry element. This change was actually in progress when the German blow fell in June 1941.

The capacity of the Red Army to take the offensive to which it was theoretically dedicated was also limited by the effects of the great purges, which swept away the high command and much of the officer corps, leaving a shaken staff structure manned by inexperienced officers. Moreover, the standard of training of the army was poor, a fault recognized after the disasters of the Finnish campaign of 1939–40, when the Soviet infantry suffered heavy losses in mass attacks. The results were seen in new training directives and a new code of discipline in the summer of 1940.

Soviet foreign policy was only partially inhibited by considerations of strategy. The Red Army remained an instrument of policy, even in the direst period of the purges. Soviet territory, even in far distant parts of the empire, was defended with tenacity and success. In July–August 1938 a serious battle was fought against the Japanese round Lake Khasan, about 110 kilometres south-west of Vladivostok, even though the Soviet commander in the Far East, Marshal Blyukher, was actually removed from his post in the course of the action; he was sent to Moscow and later shot. Between May and September 1939 an even bigger battle, involving up to 35 Soviet infantry battalions, 500 tanks, and 500 aircraft, was fought at Khalkin-Gol, near the border with Manchuria and Outer Mongolia.[24] After some reverses and heavy casualties, the Soviet forces won an important victory, and drove the Japanese back across the frontier. In September 1939 the Red Army occupied eastern Poland, against minimal opposition. At the end of November, it attacked Finland, to secure territorial gains, this time with disastrous results in the short run, though victory was eventually secured by weight of numbers and reorganization.

The army, therefore, though weakened by the purges and ill-judged changes in its mechanized forces, was used with success to defend, and sometimes to extend, Soviet territory. Despite these successes, the army was of dubious value for large-scale offensive purposes outside the frontiers of the Soviet Union, and for participation in a general European war except in self-defence. In 1939 the prospect of a war on two fronts, against Japan in the Far East (where battle was already joined) and Germany in Europe, was certainly unwelcome; and the influence of this simple calculation on the making of the Nazi–Soviet Pact should not be underrated. The state of the Soviet armed forces, and the strategic problems of the USSR, made it much more desirable to stay out of a European war than to enter one.

REFERENCES AND NOTES

1. Denis Mack Smith, *Mussolini's Roman Empire* (London: Peregrine Books 1979), pp. 177–8; MacGregor Knox, *Mussolini Unleashed, 1939–1941* (Cambridge 1982), p. 32.
2. Knox, *Mussolini Unleashed*, pp. 25–6; P. Milza and S. Berstein, *Le Fascisme italien*, p. 396; Shepard B. Clough, *The Economic History of Modern Italy* (New York 1964), p. 261.
3. Knox, *Mussolini Unleashed*, p. 22–3.
4. F. Minniti, 'Il problema degli armamenti nella preparazione militar italiana del 1935 al 1943', *Storia contemporanea*, **10** (1978), p. 50. I am grateful to Dr John Gooch for supplying this reference.
5. J. Defrasne, 'L'événement du 7 mars 1936', in Centre National de la Recherche Scientifique, *Les Relations franco-allemandes, 1933–1939* (Paris 1976), pp. 250–1; Wilhelm Deist, *The Wehrmacht and German Rearmament* (London 1981), p. 41.
6. Matthew Cooper, *The German Army 1933–1945* (London 1978), pp. 131, 164–5, Appendix.
7. Ibid., pp. 154–5, 209.

8.   Edward L. Homze, *Arming the Luftwaffe: the Reich Air Ministry and the German aircraft industry, 1919–39* (Lincoln, Nebraska, 1976), pp. 33–4, 46–7.

9.   Ibid., pp. 109–10.

10.   Ibid., pp. 79, 93; Matthew Cooper, *The German Air Force, 1933–1945* (London 1981), pp. 35–6.

11.   For figures in this paragraph, see Homze, *Arming the Luftwaffe*, pp. 157–8, 222–6; Cooper, *German Air Force*, pp. 76–80.

12.   Ibid., pp. 92–3. This total included 1,179 fighters, 1,176 bombers, and 366 dive-bombers.

13.   Strictly, this aircraft should be referred to as the Bf109 (Bayerische Flugzeugwerke); but popular usage in Britain has long referred to it as the Me109, and it seems best to keep to this.

14.   S. W. Roskill, *The War at Sea 1939–1945*, vol. I (London 1954), pp. 56–9, Appendix G.

15.   For cogent expositions of this recent view, see Cooper, *German Army*, part 2, pp. 113–66; Williamson Murray, *The Change in the European Balance of Power, 1938–1939* (Princeton 1984), pp. 30–8.

16.   Quoted in Homze, *Arming the Luftwaffe*, p. 106.

17.   Quoted in Cooper, *German Air Force*, p. 118; see the account of the whole episode, pp. 116–18.

18.   Quoted in K. D. Bracher, *The German Dictatorship* (London: Penguin Books, 1973), p. 489.

19.   Gerhard Weinberg, 'The German generals and the outbreak of war, 1938–1939', in Adrian Preston (ed.), *General Staffs and Diplomacy before the Second World War (London 1978), p. 34*.

20.   The classical statements of this interpretation are to be found in A. S. Milward, *The German Economy at War* (London 1965), and the same author's *War, Economy and Society, 1939–1945* (London 1977), especially the summary at pp. 26–30.

21.   For a succinct and lucid statement of this view, see R. J. Overy, 'Hitler's war and the German economy: a reinterpretation', *Economic History Review*, 2nd series, **35** (2) (May 1982), 272–91.

22.   John Erickson, *The Soviet High Command: a military-political history, 1918–1941* (London 1962), pp. 389–90, 766, 304; John Erickson, *The Road to Stalingrad* (London 1975), p. 93; Albert Seaton, *The Russo-German War 1941–45* (London 1971), pp. 93–4.

23.   Erickson, *Road to Stalingrad*, pp. 34–5; Seaton, *Russo-German War*, pp. 86–7.

24.   Erickson, *Soviet High Command*, pp. 518–37.

Part Three

THE COMING OF WAR
1932–1941

INTRODUCTION

The underlying forces at work in Europe in the 1930s explain much of the instability and violence of the period. They produced a form of 'continental drift' towards war, and lay behind the growth of conflict which characterized the years 1936–41. Competing ideologies created confusion within states and brought a dangerous turbulence into international affairs. In particular, nazi Germany professed – and very largely practised – an ideology which exalted war and set objectives which could only be achieved by war. The same was true, though to a lesser degree, of fascist Italy. Nazi Germany, in pursuit of rapid rearmament to achieve expansionist aims, ran itself into an economic impasse from which war offered (at least in the short term) an escape. Germany also possessed at the end of the 1930s the only army and air force in Europe capable of taking the offensive, and the confidence and ruthlessness to use them – which was another result of its ideological drive.

In all this there was much that was leading towards war, and ample reason for the sense of fatality and inevitability which hung over Europe by 1939. But this is far from being the whole story. No one behaved as though everything was decided by underlying forces. Men took decisions, often in agonized uncertainty, and only rarely did they believe that they had no choice before them. Events occurred which were unexpected and accidental. It is time to change our point of view, and turn to the course of events during Europe's long drawn out descent into war.

Chapter 13

FROM PEACE TO THE EVE OF WAR, 1932–1937

At the opening of the 1930s there was no doubt that Europe was at peace. The economic depression was severe, but the friction which it generated fell far short of any impulse towards war. In the Far East, the Japanese Army occupied Manchuria at the end of 1931; but Manchuria was far away, China had never settled down to an orderly existence, and there seemed no good reason to expect this episode to have more than local consequences. After 1941 and the great war in the Pacific, it was often argued that such a view was complacent and mistaken, and that the road to the Second World War, even in Europe, started with the Japanese occupation of Manchuria, which set off a chain reaction of aggression. There seems little substance in this argument. It was several years before Japan moved again to attack China in 1937, and any effect on Mussolini over Abyssinia or Hitler over the Rhineland can only have amounted to marginal encouragement to do what they intended to do anyway. The Manchurian episode did not endanger the peace of Europe.

European peace rested upon two foundations. The first was the international co-operation which marked the late 1920s, as demonstrated in the Locarno treaties and the heyday of the League of Nations. Even those who wished to change the status quo thought in this period in terms of negotiation, not force. The second was the harsher reality that the preponderance of power and prestige lay with the states which wished to maintain the settlement of 1919, and principally with France. In this situation, prestige was as important as power: as long as the reputation of the French Army and faith in French will-power remained intact, the European system set up in 1919 could be sustained.

Between 1932 and 1937 both these foundations were progressively undermined. The Locarno treaties were broken, the League of Nations discredited, and French influence in Europe was replaced by that of Germany. How this came about may be illustrated by examining a number of significant events: the Disarmament Conference of 1932–34, the Abyssinian crisis of 1935–36, the German occupation of the Rhineland in March 1936, and the first stages of the Spanish Civil

War in 1936–37. Through all these events ran the theme of the revival of German power and growth of German armaments, and the reaction of France and Britain to these developments.

In retrospect, the Geneva Disarmament Conference of 1932–34 wears an air of slightly farcical unreality, heavily tinged with cynicism. Its oratory was interminable and empty. Its attempts to distinguish between offensive and defensive weapons were absurd – as a British delegate observed with some asperity, it largely depended which end of the weapon one was standing at. Participants attempted, with transparent ingenuity, to restrict armaments of which they possessed none or for which they had no use. Yet despite all this, the conference was the focus of widespread hope and aspiration, and it had important effects on international affairs.

The British government was the prisoner of the Disarmament Conference and the disarmament idea. In 1932 the government agreed in principle to abandon the assumption that no major war was expected for ten years, but it also decided that while the Disarmament Conference was in session no action would be taken to rearm. It was politically impossible to begin rearmament during the conference. Instead, the British laboured tirelessly to find the basis for an agreement on arms limitation, which meant primarily in their view reconciling the positions of France and Germany, by bringing French armaments down and allowing German armaments to rise. When Germany first left the conference, at the end of 1932, Britain played the leading part in wooing her back with a formula that accepted German equality of rights in armaments in a system which would provide security for all nations, an important step towards acknowledging German claims. The British later proposed an increase in the German Army from 100,000 to 200,000, while the French Army would be reduced, and then agreed that Germany should have an air force half the size of the French. Public respectability was thus conferred on the idea of German rearmament, which was already secretly under way, as the British government well knew. By the time it was openly proclaimed in March 1935, it had already been discounted in advance.

The French government too, under pressure from domestic opinion and reluctant to isolate itself from Britain, made considerable concessions during the conference. Following Britain's lead, the French abandoned their long-standing insistence on security as the precondition for disarmament, putting in its place the idea of verification to ensure that an agreement was being observed. It is true that by this means they hoped to ascertain the extent of existing German rearmament, but it also meant an implicit acceptance that rearmament could not be prevented. Only as late as April 1934 did the French government declare that the latest German budget showed a clear intention to rearm, and therefore France would not discuss the recent German proposals for a 'disarmament' agreement.

This brought the Disarmament Conference to an end, but by that time a good deal of damage had been done. The first fifteen months of the nazi regime coincided with the last phase of the conference, which offered excellent cover for the first risky stages of German rearmament. Neither Britain nor for a long time France would risk the opprobrium of torpedoing the conference by denouncing Germany. Even when the Germans finally left the conference in October 1933, the British spent another six months trying to tempt them back. The cover was perfect, and the first steps in the restoration of German power were taken while all eyes were fixed firmly on the illusory hopes of the Disarmament Conference.

Even when disarmament failed, the League of Nations still represented the other great hope of the 1920s: peace through collective security. This hope foundered in the Abyssinian crisis of 1935–36, which ironically might not have been a serious issue at all without the existence of the League. Before 1914 it was customary for European states to occupy parts of Africa, and under pre-1914 rules, if Italy secured the consent of Britain and France as the major colonial powers, there was no reason why she should not conquer Abyssinia. But since 1920 new rules were supposed to apply. Abyssinia was a member of the League of Nations, and so a crisis arose.

Ever since the defeat of an Italian Army at Adowa in 1896, revenge for this humiliation had been in Italian minds. Mussolini began to consider an invasion of Abyssinia in 1925; plans took definite shape in 1932, with autumn 1935 as a likely date; and at the end of December 1934 the Duce laid down that the Italian objective must be nothing less than the total conquest of the country. The year 1935 appeared to offer favourable circumstances for the Italian enterprise. In 1934 there had been an attempted nazi coup in Austria, but it had been defeated, and the country had settled down (see below, p. 220). Laval visited Mussolini in January 1935 and signed the Rome accords, which settled a number of African questions which had long been at issue between France and Italy. It remains an open question whether in his conversations Laval offered Mussolini a free hand in Abyssinia, or whether, as he always claimed, he referred only to a free hand in economic affairs. At any rate, Mussolini drew encouragement from Laval's visit, which was followed by the Franco–Italian military agreements of May and June 1935. The links between the two countries became close.

On 11–14 April 1935 there was a conference between Italy, France, and Britain at Stresa, to discuss the recent announcement of German rearmament and the position of Austria. By this time, the build-up of Italian forces in East Africa was obvious. Abyssinia was discussed by officials outside the formal sessions, and a British representative gave a diplomatically phrased warning that the consequences of an invasion could not be foreseen. However, the Italians secured a copy of an assessment by an inter-departmental committee in June 1935, concluding that no vital British interests in Abyssinia or neighbouring countries obliged Britain to resist an Italian conquest. With this document in his hands, Mussolini might reasonably assume that the British government would not oppose him. He had no grasp of the significance of League sentiment in Britain, or of the range of influences which could be brought to bear upon a British Cabinet. His information was correct, but its context was inadequate.

On 3 October 1935 the Italian invasion of Abyssinia began. Britain and France met it with a two-sided (not to say two-faced) policy. First, on British initiative, and not least because a general election was impending in Britain, the League was mobilized to condemn Italian aggression. On 18 November a limited range of economic sanctions was imposed on Italy. These were sufficient to cause considerable difficulties for the Italian economy, and no small damage to the countries which applied them, but they did not include an oil embargo. This was partly because the USA was an important supplier of oil to Italy, and also because an oil sanction might lead to war, which was not a risk the British wanted to take; though they took the precaution of moving naval reinforcements to the Mediterranean. In these measures, France was a reluctant participant, delaying sanctions for as long as possible, and temporizing over British requests to use French naval bases in the event of hostilities.

The second line of policy was in practice preferred by both countries. This was to negotiate a settlement with Italy at the expense of Abyssinia. Talks on such a project were pursued by officials in Paris, culminating in an agreement between Sir Samuel Hoare, the British Foreign Secretary, and Laval on 8 December 1935. In broad terms, the proposal was that Abyssinia should cede a large area to Italy outright, with another area reserved for Italian economic influence and exploitation. A rump Abyssinian state would survive, receiving as compensation a strip of British Somaliland giving access to the sea. These terms were to be put to Mussolini, Haile Selassie (Emperor of Abyssinia), and to the League. In fact, they were rapidly leaked to the French press, and when news of them reached Britain they were denounced by the League of Nations Union, by MPs, and by some Conservative stalwarts in the constituencies, a combination of pressure group and parliamentary opinion which was sufficient to persuade the government to draw back. Hoare resigned as Foreign Secretary, and the proposals were abandoned.

The Italians pursued their invasion of Abyssinia, using aircraft and mustard gas to secure a quicker victory than was generally expected. The capital, Addis Ababa, was occupied in May 1936, and Mussolini proclaimed King Victor Emmanuel as Emperor of Abyssinia.

The reasons why Britain and France followed their ambiguous policy were clear. The British wanted a League policy, to please the electorate and Parliament, and also, in the case of some individuals, out of genuine attachment to the League. But they also wanted to avoid a breach with Italy, and had no wish to court a naval war in the Mediterranean when they were nervously conscious of weakness in the Far East. The French had every reason to maintain the military agreements which they had only just reached with Italy, and yet they dared not break with Britain. The reasoning seemed sound, but the results were disastrous. There was enough *realpolitik* to undermine the League, and enough League sentiment to nullify the *realpolitik*. Neither line was pursued to a successful conclusion. The British felt that the French had let them down, and the leaking of the Hoare–Laval plan was not easily forgotten. The French felt that the British, in a fit of morality and Leagueomania, had lost them a valuable Italian alliance. Anglo-French relations collapsed at a time when their solidity was sorely needed.

Mussolini, on the other hand, won a great success. He defeated not only Abyssinia but the League, and above all the British. He was at the peak of his popularity at home; he was convinced of the strength of his army; and he looked round for new worlds to conquer. In the face of League sanctions, Italy developed new economic links with Germany. From being a member of an anti-German coalition, Italy began to cultivate German friendship. It was a turning-point in European affairs, and the turn was towards war.

With the Abyssinian crisis persisting, and dissension rife between Britain, France, and Italy, Germany was presented with an opportunity to move into the demilitarized zone of the Rhineland. This zone was set up under the Treaty of Versailles, and reaffirmed by the Treaty of Locarno, with Britain and Italy acting as its guarantors. What exactly their guarantee entailed was not precisely defined, but in any case it was inoperative by early 1936. As early as January 1935 the British Cabinet had concluded that the demilitarized zone was not a vital British interest; and in February 1936 Mussolini assured Hitler that he would not join in any action under the Locarno Treaty. The opening for Germany was there for the taking. A pretext of sorts was presented in February 1936 when the French Chamber of Deputies ratified the Franco-Soviet Treaty signed in May 1935. Germany claimed that the terms of this treaty were incompatible with those of Locarno, which had thus been rendered null and void.

It had been the fixed intention of all German governments to do away with the demilitarized zone when it became possible to do so, partly because it was an affront to German sovereignty and self-respect, and partly because it left the Rhineland exposed to attack. For some time, France and Britain had been expecting Germany to open negotiations to bring the zone to an end. Hitler chose instead to act, and on 7 March 1936 troops moved into the Rhineland. But at the same time he offered negotiation, in the shape of a set of new proposals:

non-aggression pacts with France and Belgium, the limitation of air forces, new demilitarized zones on both sides of the Franco–German border (which if accepted would have meant the French dismantling large parts of the Maginot Line). The mixture of military *fait accompli* with diplomatic smoke-screen was masterly, and the temptation for nervous and peace-loving governments to examine the offers was overwhelming.

All turned on the response of the French and British governments to the German move. Much later comment on the crisis has assumed that an immediate military response was simple, and would have been rapidly successful, perhaps even leading to the fall of Hitler. 'Police action' was a favourite phrase, implying the brushing away of a screen of German forces, ready to retreat at the sight of French uniforms. Hitler later remarked that if the French had marched, the Germans would have had to withdraw, their tails between their legs. Closer examination, however, reveals a different picture.

The German forces which moved into the former demilitarized zones consisted of about 10,000 men, organized into 12 infantry battalions and 8 groups of artillery. There were also 22,700 armed police, who on 8 March were incorporated into the army as 21 further infantry battalions. These units were formed into 4 new infantry divisions, and after the end of March further forces moved in to form 2 more divisions in the zone. Behind these forces lay the rest of the German Army, made up of 24 infantry and 3 Panzer divisions, not as yet fully trained or equipped since the great expansion of 1935.[1] The *Luftwaffe* was strong in numbers but not yet supplied with modern aircraft.

The German forces in the Rhineland were not large, but it is rash to assume that they would simply have retreated before a French advance. In principle, such conduct was scarcely to be expected of German troops who had just reoccupied their own territory with much flourish and display. More specifically, orders prepared when a similar operation was considered in 1935 provided that, in the event of a French reaction, units were to retreat to the line of the Rhine and then stand and fight. In 1936 Hitler laid down that the troops should resist step by step in case of enemy attack. Generals Blomberg and Fritsch proposed instead to order the retreat of the advanced battalions. This difference of opinion never had to be resolved, but it is at the very least unlikely that Hitler would have abandoned the line of the Rhine, or the Ruhr on the west bank, without a fight.

In all realism, therefore, the French had to be prepared for serious action, not a military promenade, if they moved to expel the German forces. The French General Staff, however, proceeded to exaggerate the problem by producing a grossly inflated estimate of the German forces in the Rhineland zone. They gave an accurate figure for the army units, but added 235,000 auxiliaries, supposedly organized into 15 further divisions (see above, p. 172). The General Staff then insisted, on the basis of these figures, that it could not take even limited action to occupy part of the Rhineland without a partial mobilization of the reserves, involving calling up a million men in seven days.

The French high command thus added its own self-induced difficulties to a perfectly real military problem. To mobilize a million reservists would have the temporary effect of decreasing the fighting power of the army, by producing a mass of men who would have to be organized and equipped. Moreover, mobilization would have serious social and economic effects on the country when a general election was due to be held in two months' time. The existing government, under Albert Sarraut, was acknowledged to be only a stop-gap until the elections, which the Popular Front coalition was expected to win. In such circumstances, it would have needed a bold and determined government, confident of parliamentary and popular support, to call up a million men and launch a serious military operation – in effect, go to war.

The government was neither bold nor determined. Sarraut was no Poincaré or Clemenceau, but a run-of-the-mill politician of the later Third Republic. In the country, the almost unanimous view of the press on 8 March and the following days was to renounce the idea of war, or action of any kind, except (in the socialist papers) an appeal to the League. The same message came from trade unions, ex-servicemen's organizations, and the political parties. Left and Right each accused the other of wanting war. In fact, neither did: there must be no war over the Rhineland.

The government turned to Britain. The Foreign Minister, Flandin, went to London on 11 March to ask for British support for actions which he speciously claimed to be planning against Germany. He met no encouragement from either the Foreign Secretary, Anthony Eden, or the Prime Minister, Baldwin. The almost unanimous view of the British press and the political parties was that the Germans had only moved into their own territory – 'their own back garden' was a phrase with much homely appeal. The government had long expected the remilitarization of the Rhineland, and in a sense discounted it in advance. To the British, the best course seemed to be to examine Hitler's various diplomatic offers, and to mollify the French by agreeing to staff talks. This response allowed Flandin to return to Paris and add one more reason for inaction to all the rest: the British would not move.

So the crisis passed. The French Army limited its actions to cancelling leave and moving some units to the frontier to man the Maginot defences. On the diplomatic side, the British government, in consultation with France, put various questions to Germany to elucidate the meaning of Hitler's offers of new agreements. There was no reply. Meanwhile, the Germans pressed on with the fortification of their frontier with France.

The Rhineland occupation has been rightly seen as a crucial point in the move towards war. It is usually presented as the great 'might have been': the last chance to stop Hitler without war. This puts the issue wrongly. The opportunity open to France was to stop Hitler *by war*, not without war. It would have been necessary to invade German territory, and to fight the German forces if, as seems probable, they resisted. It is true that this war would have been fought in more ' favourable military circumstances than the later one; and if the French had shown boldness and determination it could surely have been won. But the political circumstances rendered such a course almost impossible. The 'might have been' on which so many regrets and recriminations have been lavished was not seriously considered by anyone, and if attempted would have been universally condemned by politicians and public in both France and Britain. Only the Pope told the French Ambassador to the Holy See, on 16 March, that if the French had moved 200,000 troops into the Rhineland they would have done everyone a great service. It was stern advice from His Holiness, but there was no chance that it would be followed.

The real weight of the event lay not in any 'might have been', but in its actual consequences. The demilitarized zone was the last safeguard left to France from the 1919 settlement. On 30 April 1936, General Gamelin told his government that if (he really meant when) the Germans fortified the Rhineland, the French Army would be unable to invade Germany. The Germans could hold the frontier with comparatively few troops, while in the east they attacked Czechoslovakia or Poland. The defensive organization of the French Army had already undermined the basis of French alliances in eastern Europe, and now that basis was vanishing completely. There was an even more fundamental result: France's complete lack of will to maintain the 1919 settlement had been openly exposed. If France would not fight over the Rhineland, the immediate guarantee of her own security, would she go to war at all?

The Rhineland coup also had consequences for other countries, and most ominously for Belgium. On 6 March, the day before the German occupation, the Belgian government renounced its alliance with France, and in October it declared a policy of 'independence', claiming neutral status without going back to the full juridical neutrality of pre-1914 years. France was now faced with a hopeless dilemma. To fortify the Belgian frontier was extremely expensive, and would abandon Belgium to a German invasion; yet to leave it unfortified meant laying open the north-eastern frontier of France. The Belgians, for their part, had apparently decided that they were better off without any alliance with France; yet the tacit assumption behind their 'independence' was still that the French would come to their help in the event of a German attack. It was an illogical position. The danger of a German invasion was not diminished, but if the French came in as rescuers they would do so without preparation. The new position of Belgium added to the instability of western Europe, and played into the hands of Germany.

Less than five months after the German occupation of the Rhineland, civil war broke out in Spain. The causes of this conflict were deeply rooted in Spanish history; the issues at stake were complicated; and each side in the war was divided within itself. The right-wing (or nationalist side) was largely made up of monarchists, the officer corps, and the Catholic hierarchy; but the monarchists were split between Alfonsists and Carlists, and the small Fascist Party, the Falange, claimed to be revolutionary and modernizing rather than reactionary. On the Left, supporting the republican government of Spain, were socialists, anarchists, and a small Communist Party, all opposed to one another in various ways. There were also strong separatist movements in Catalonia and the Basque country, which in general supported the Left and the republic.

The war began with a military rising to overthrow the republic and its Popular Front government, brought to power by a general election in February 1936. The revolt began in Spanish Morocco on 17 July 1936, and spread to Spain the next day. Its object was a rapid seizure of power, but the republican government put up a determined resistance, holding on to Madrid, Barcelona, and large parts of central and western Spain. The result was that an attempted *coup d'état* became a civil war which lasted nearly three years, until the end of March 1939. It was a bloody struggle, in which both sides committed atrocities, and whose deep-rooted complexities tended to be hidden by a smokescreen of slogans and propaganda. Supporters of the republic claimed to be fighting against a fascist dictatorship in defence of democracy or socialism (or both). Nationalists presented themselves as the champions of order and Christian civilization, at grips with red revolution and a communist plot.

Such views were at best gross simplifications, but they met with ready support outside Spain, where there was a strong inclination for men to project their own fears and hopes upon the Spanish Civil War. Outsiders created the war in their own image, and saw it as an extension of their own struggles. The conflict drew in individuals by a magnetism of idealism and commitment which can exert its attractive power even now. But of itself this did not mean that the Spanish Civil War was bound to become a European crisis. Indeed, in many circumstances the governments of Europe would doubtless have been content to allow the Spaniards to pursue their internecine feuds alone. In the event, a number of foreign governments took a very different line, and outside intervention in the war began at an early date.

It began in the first instance because Spaniards asked for it. On 20 July 1936 General Franco, anxious to get his rebel forces across the straits from Morocco to Spain and finding the sea controlled by republican warships, asked Mussolini for aircraft, and was refused. On the same day, the Spanish government asked France for the sale of aircraft, arms, and ammunition – a perfectly proper request, which the French accepted in principle. The nationalists tried again. On 22 July General Mola sent emissaries to both Italy and Germany, this time successfully. In Rome on 25 July the Italian Foreign Minister, Ciano, agreed to provide twelvè aircraft; and the same day at Bayreuth Hitler (who was attending the Wagner festival) decided to send some Ju52 transport planes to Morocco. They arrived on the 27th, and played a vital part in ferrying troops to Spain. Foreign intervention had begun.

The Italian contribution to the nationalist camp was at first in terms of equipment – by 1 December 1936, 118 aircraft, 35 light tanks, some artillery and machine-guns, and 16.5 million rounds of small-arms ammunition had been sent. In December, the Italians offered to send troops, and by February 1937 there were nearly 49,000 Italian soldiers in Spain. During the whole war, a total of nearly 73,000 Italian troops served in Spain; and Italy provided 759 aircraft, 157 tanks, 1,800 guns, and 320 million rounds of small-arms ammunition.[2] In a war fought at a fairly low level of technology and supply, this was a considerable contribution.

The motives behind it were mixed. There appear to have been no previous contacts with the officers who led the rising of July 1936, though in 1934 Mussolini had promised aid to monarchist emissaries who visited him in Rome. Intervention was seen as a move against France, and as strengthening Italy's strategic position in the Mediterranean, but nothing systematic was done to follow up this idea. Italian troops landed on Majorca in 1936, but the island was not turned into an Italian base. In terms of ideology, intervention was seen more as defending fascism at home in Italy rather than promoting it in Spain. A Popular Front victory in Spain, with Italian anti-fascists prominent, would be a dangerous precedent. Within Spain, the Italians understood clearly that they were giving aid to conservative generals, not to Spanish fascists, and they did little to further the cause of the Falange. Above all, intervention became a matter of prestige. What began as small-scale help for a supposedly rapid coup became a commitment to a long and dreary war; but Mussolini's reputation and that of Italian fascism were at stake, and retreat was impossible. The Italians made little attempt to press economic demands, except in the simplest sense of trying to secure payment for their aid – not always with success. The whole Italian operation in Spain was carried out with surprisingly little precise result being sought. What was attained was simply the aim of victory for the side which Mussolini had backed.

German intervention began with the provision of transport aircraft in July 1936. At the end of October, the Germans offered to send a combat force to Spain, on condition that it should be under a German commander, responsible directly to Franco. The Condor Legion began to arrive in Spain in November 1936. Its main contribution was in the air, and a total of some 600 aircraft were sent to Spain. At its greatest strength, in autumn 1938, the Legion's air component consisted of 105 aircraft, including 45 modern fighters, 45 medium bombers, and 3 dive-bombers. The Legion also had a small force of light tanks, of which 200 were sent in all, anti-aircraft guns, and support units.[3] The contribution of this compact and efficient body was out of all proportion to its size.

Hitler's first quick decision at Bayreuth, which began the intervention, seems to have been motivated by a desire to prevent what he saw as a Bolshevik regime controlling Spain. The despatch of the Condor Legion seems to have owed something to sheer pique. Ciano, the Italian Foreign Minister, visited Berlin in October 1936, and showed Hitler British documents obtained by Italian intelligence in which Eden described Germany as being ruled by a band of adventurers. Hitler at once suggested that Germany and Italy should go over to the offensive against the democracies, and they agreed forthwith to increase their help to Franco. But pique was very much accompanied by calculation. The Condor Legion's operations gave the German Air Force combat experience and an opportunity for self-advertisement. In terms of foreign policy, Hitler was happy to see the war kept going. It provided an opportunity to consolidate the alliance with Italy, and it appeared to open wide possibilities of war between France and Italy, or of civil strife in France. Moreover, the Germans insisted that they should receive precise economic concessions in return for their aid, notably in the shape of a measure of control over the Spanish iron-ore mines. The last deliveries of German aid, at the end of 1938, were made in return for specific concessions on German holdings in Spanish mining companies.

The other great power to intervene on a substantial scale was the Soviet Union, which provided assistance to the republican government. The first delivery, comprising about 100 aircraft and 100 tanks, arrived in October 1936, along with perhaps 500 specialist troops who were ordered to keep out of the combat zone. Shipments of equipment were frequent up to March 1937, diminished after that date, and ended in the middle of 1938. The total aid sent is uncertain, but probably amounted to about 1,000 aircraft, 900 tanks, 1,500 guns, and large quantities of small arms and ammunition. Soviet personnel in Spain, mainly tank and aircraft specialists, probably did not number more than 1,000 at any one time. Soviet military advisers were very important in the republican armies. Most republican generals had a Soviet officer on their staffs, and General Pavlov, the Soviet tank commander in Spain, sometimes led his units in action. The advisers themselves were watched by the NKVD, whose operations in Spain were controlled by Alexander Orlov.[4]

Soviet assistance to the republic also took the indirect form of the

International Brigades, units of volunteers recruited and organized through the machinery of the Comintern and individual Communist Parties. Most passed through France, where a barracks was set up at Perpignan, and the French Communist Party formed a shipping company, *France-Navigation*, to provide sea transport from Marseilles. Numbers serving in the Brigades probably reached a total of between 25,000 and 35,000 with perhaps 15,000–18,000 in Spain at any one time. This was not a large force, but its psychological impact was considerable. The Brigades went into action in defence of Madrid in November 1936, and by the time they were withdrawn from Spain in November 1938 they had played a substantial military role as well as creating one of the legends of the twentieth century.[5]

Soviet motivation, as so often, was enigmatic. The ideological dimension was surely important: this was the era of the Popular Front movement, and it was presumably impossible for the Soviet Union and the Communist Parties to stand idly by in the Spanish struggle. Stalin was the acknowledged leader of the international proletariat, and he had to act as such. That the Soviet Union was the only great power to help the republic became, in fact, a crucial propaganda asset for the communists. In strategic terms, Spain was too far distant to matter much to the Soviet Union. It may be that after the Franco–Soviet Treaty of 1935 Stalin preferred France not to face the enemy on the Pyrenees; but since neither the French nor the Soviets chose to make much of their alliance this motive appears no more than tenuous. It may well be that, like Hitler, Stalin was content to see the Spanish Civil War continue, absorbing some of the attention of the capitalist states in a far-distant corner of Europe. The great purges in the Soviet Union presumably occupied most of Stalin's attention from 1936 to 1938, and Spain was probably only of peripheral interest to him. At any rate, he provided enough help to keep the republic going, but not enough to enable it to win. He pulled out in the autumn of 1938, and at an early stage he secured payment by getting most of the Spanish gold reserves (worth about $US 500 million) sent to the Soviet Union at the end of October 1936.[6] Meanwhile, as a by-product of intervention, he used the presence of the NKVD in Spain to eliminate Trotskyists, anarchists, and other enemies.

All this intervention in the Civil War went on while the powers concerned were parties to a non-intervention Agreement, and members of a non-intervention Committee were meeting regularly in London. This macabre piece of play-acting may be explained by looking at the policies of France and Britain.[7]

France was closely concerned with events in Spain, both as a geographical neighbour and because in 1936 both countries had Popular Front governments. When approached for help by the Spanish government on 20 July 1936, the French Premier, Léon Blum, at once agreed in principle and asked for a list of what was needed. During the next few days, the French government changed its mind no less than three times, ending during the night of 8/9 August by forbidding the despatch of war material or even civil aircraft to Spain. On 1 August the government decided to propose to other states a general policy of non-intervention, and by 15 August this emerged as a formal Franco-British proposal for a Non-intervention Agreement. Other governments accepted, and the Non-intervention Committee held its first meeting in London on 9 September. During this period of vacillation, aid of various kinds in fact passed through France to Spain: 38 aircraft were sent during the week of 2–9 August, and a further 56 afterwards.[8] The border was opened occasionally during 1937 and 1938, and the government turned a blind eye to the transit camps of the International Brigades. In general, however, the policy of non-intervention, once begun, was adhered to.

It was a policy which ran counter to Blum's personal sentiments and his first reaction. It was not a decision reached primarily on strategic grounds, though the strategic arguments were marginally in favour of it. In support of intervention was the likelihood that a nationalist victory might produce a hostile government in Spain, which might allow the use of Spanish territory by the enemies of France. On the other hand, intervention would use up military resources needed by the French armed forces, risked spreading the war, and might force the nationalists into a hostility which was by no means inevitable. The French General Staff believed that the nationalists would win, but that after victory they would get rid of all foreign forces and follow their own policy. The main impulse for non-intervention, however, came from French internal politics. Blum rapidly found that his Cabinet was split on the issue, and the stability of his government was in jeopardy when it had barely been in existence for three months. Blum was also afraid that intervention might bring France itself to the brink of civil war, which in view of the country's internal divisions was not a groundless fear. In addition, he was afraid of alienating Britain, whose government was opposed to intervention; though this factor was not so important as has sometimes been argued.

The balance was thus tipped in favour of non-intervention. In the event, it appears that most Frenchmen were relieved to see their country stand aloof from the war, though the communists and some socialists agitated vociferously for action on behalf of the republic, and much of the Right was ardently pro-nationalist. The non-intervention policy was sustained in the Chamber of Deputies without undue difficulty, despite the fact that the Non-intervention Agreement was openly flouted by Germany, Italy, and the USSR. To abandon it would risk domestic difficulties, and perhaps also a confrontation with the Axis powers which France had good reason to avoid. It seemed better to pretend that the agreement was working, or could somehow be made to work better in future.

The position of the British government was very similar, though its motivation was different. The sympathies of the government lay mainly with the nationalists, who seemed more likely to protect British commercial interests and investments in Spain. For this purpose, a British diplomatic agent was appointed to Franco's government at an early stage, though formal recognition was only given (by Britain and France together) in February 1939. The main considerations behind British policy, however, were political and strategic. First, the British government was anxious that the war should not spread, and produce a general European conflict. Second, as a part of a wider policy, British sights were set from mid-1936 to 1939 on improving relations with Italy, and perhaps detaching her from Germany. Third, the British were anxious to ensure that whatever Spanish government emerged victorious from the Civil War should be at least benevolently neutral towards Britain. Put in crude terms, this meant a wish not to fall out with the likely winner, which the British government expected to be the nationalists. As a policy, it was perhaps ignoble, and it certainly required a great deal of pretence; but it was far from being unreasonable.

On these grounds, the British government seized eagerly on the proposal for a Non-intervention Agreement, and held on to it despite all adversities. Eden defended his course by analogy with a dam: a leaky dam, holding back at least some of the potential flow of arms to Spain, and preventing the war from spreading from Spain to the rest of Europe, was better than no dam at all. To keep up the pretence of the Non-intervention Agreement involved all kinds of shifts and expedients, smacking of hypocrisy and cowardice. For example, the German and Italian fleets were brought into the non-intervention patrol, even though their countries were blatantly interventionist. The government had to contend with the unease of some of its own supporters as well as the anger of the Labour opposition, which advocated allowing the republican government to purchase arms in Britain.

Only once did the British and French depart from their complaisant attitude towards Axis activities in Spain. In August 1937 there were several attacks on merchant ships heading for republican ports by so-called 'pirate' submarines, which were well known to be Italian. On 31 August a torpedo was fired at (but missed) the British destroyer *Havock*. At this point, the British and French governments called a conference of interested states (except Spain) at Nyon. Italy and Germany declined the invitation, and in their absence the conference (10–14 September) agreed that British and French warships should patrol the western Mediterranean and attack any unidentified submarine forthwith. The attacks ceased, but the moral effect of the Anglo-French show of strength was weakened by their agreement almost immediately afterwards to allow Italy to join in the anti-submarine patrol. As it happened, the Italian campaign had in any case been suspended on 4 September, before the conference met, so the effects of the conference were less clear-cut than they appeared at the time.

There was widespread apprehension that the Spanish Civil War might at any moment spill over and precipitate a general European conflict. The Italian submarine campaign and the attack on HMS *Havock* provided a sharp demonstration of how this might come about. What would have happened if the *Havock* had been hit, or if her depth-charges, dropped in retaliation, had sunk an Italian submarine? The same sort of thing might have happened in the land campaigns, where it was perfectly possible that Italian or German forces could have engaged Soviet tanks and their crews. War by the extension of some such incident in Spain or off the coast seemed a distinct possibility. Such fears were intensified by the emotions which gathered round the war. For anti-fascists all over Europe, the Spanish War, and in particular the siege of Madrid, became the symbol of their struggle against the enemy; and some men hoped rather than feared that the war would touch off a wider conflict. With so many people regarding the Civil War as a European war by proxy, there was always the possibility that it might turn into a European war in reality.

Much of this now appears exaggerated, even fanciful. The Spanish Civil War produced much high drama and emotion, but it did not precipitate a European war. Neither Germany nor the USSR had anything at stake in Spain that was worth fighting a European war about, and they made their contributions to the conflict in carefully measured doses. Italy was more deeply committed, because Mussolini's prestige was at stake, and he might have been willing to go to any lengths to maintain it. But Italy alone was unlikely to produce a European war out of the Spanish conflict; and in any case the Italian side never looked like losing. By the end of 1937 Spain was ceasing to be a major international issue – the Nyon conference of September 1937 was the last flurry of diplomatic activity on a Spanish question. As the serious movement towards a European war gained momentum in 1938 and 1939, Spain was only on the periphery of affairs, and the Civil War came to an anti-climactic end five months before hostilities began in Poland. In the European war that followed, the Axis powers received less help from Spain than they looked for. Franco had accepted their help, and paid for it when he had to, but he always sought to protect Spanish interests as he saw them. In the wider war, he gave help to the Axis powers in a limited fashion, but continued to put Spanish interests first.

Was the whole furore over Spain, then, merely much ado about nothing? In European terms, and if the issues could be reduced to cold fact, probably so. But beliefs are every bit as important as realities. War was a reality in Spain, and an atmosphere of war spread to much of Europe. Fears of general war emanating from Spain had their own weight, especially in France and Britain. This was not all. Spain made war respectable again. Many a formerly anti-militarist socialist felt that the defence of the republic was more important than pacifism. André Malraux, a French left-wing writer who fought for the republic, depicted in his novel *L'Espoir* (1937) anarchist troops making Homeric speeches before going out to certain death against Italian tanks. Heroism, and even heroics, were back in fashion. When a republican commander in Madrid was asked where his men should retreat if they had to, he replied 'To the cemetery', a phrase which was reported at the time, and has been remembered since, with admiration. They were brave words; but if they had come from Haig during the First World War they would have been treated differently. The spell cast by the war has not yet lost its power; there have been no anti-war novels or films about the Spanish Civil War.

At the more sober level of diplomacy, the Spanish War introduced a further element of discord. It was an obstacle to the improvement of relations between Italy and France or Britain. The prominent role of the International Brigades and the communist agitation about Spain throughout Europe revived the vision of international communism, to the exhilaration of some and the terror of others. The ill-scripted play-acting of the Non-intervention Committee, and the weakness, verging on cowardice, of the British government, inspired neither trust in potential friends nor fear in likely enemies. If at any time in the late 1930s an anti-German coalition might have been constructed – which is by no means certain – then events in Spain were quite sufficient to prevent it.

In the background to all these events lay the development of German policy and power in the first years of the nazi regime. The early stages of Hitler's foreign policy were cautious. On 3 February 1933, when he had just come to power, he told a meeting of generals that the first phase of rearmament would be dangerous: if France possessed real statesmen, she would not allow Germany time to recover her strength, but attack at once. To avoid such reaction, Hitler was prodigal in his public assurances of peaceful intentions, notably in speeches to the Reichstag on 23 March and 17 May 1933. He supported his words with ample evidence of a constructive policy. In May 1933 Germany renewed the Treaty of Berlin with the Soviet Union (originally signed in 1926) without fuss or delay. In July the government concluded a concordat with the Vatican, regulating the position of the Catholic Church in Germany – though the sceptical might have observed that it was signed three days after the Catholic Centre Party had been dissolved. In the summer of 1933 Germany took part in negotiations for a Four-Power Pact with Italy, France, and Britain. These did not come to fruition, but they allowed the nazi regime to demonstrate its goodwill and to be accepted among the powers of

Europe. The most spectacular development in German policy was the signature on 26 January 1934 of a non-aggression treaty with Poland. This was a bombshell, but of a peaceable kind. Previously, hardly a German politician could have been found who accepted the 1919 frontier with Poland. Stresemann and Bruening certainly meant to change it when they could. Yet Hitler confirmed it, and charmed away a persistent source of friction in European affairs. He was able to claim a brilliant success for direct diplomacy rather than the cumbrous workings of the League of Nations, and for some years he was able to point to the agreement with Poland as the way in which things should be done. That the treaty deprived the Franco-Polish alliance of much of its substance, and provided excellent cover for nazi activities in Danzig, were matters less remarked on at the time.

Against this list of constructive achievements were set two adventures of a potentially dangerous and disruptive kind. In October 1933 Germany announced its resignation from the League of Nations and departure from the Disarmament Conference. This appeared to involve some risk of retaliation from France or Britain, but Hitler rightly predicted that after some protests the western powers would renew their attempts to negotiate with Germany about armaments. The move was popular in Germany, and was confirmed by a plebiscite on 12 November. In theory, it should have diminished German respectability in the international community; but in practice it did not. The other adventure was in Austria. On 25 July 1934 Austrian nazis broke into the Chancellery in Vienna, shot the Chancellor, Dollfuss, and proclaimed over the radio that he had resigned. Other members of the government rallied, and the assassins had to surrender. Mussolini at once declared his support for Austrian independence, and had troops already on manoeuvres in the Alps to back up his point. The coup failed. No one doubted German complicity in these events. Bands of Austrian nazis were based in Bavaria; and when the assassins surrendered they unsuccessfully asked for safe conduct to the German border. Hitler strenuously declared his innocence, and it was doubtless true that strictly in terms of government activity Germany was not involved. But in terms of party conspiracy things were very different: German and Austrian nazis worked closely together, and the Germans were the senior partners. The attempted coup in Austria, with its use of violence and propaganda, was a portent of the nazi style in foreign policy; and if Europe had been alert, much might have been learned from this episode. Yet in the event Hitler managed to live down both the adventure and its failure. The respectable and aristocratic von Papen was sent as Ambassador to Vienna to soothe Austrian susceptibilities; and German policy settled down to attain the *Anschluss* by more patient methods.

Despite these two episodes, the nazi regime made an essentially cautious and peaceable start in its foreign policy. It became more daring and assertive in 1935 and 1936. In January 1935 Hitler secured the last advantage to be expected from the Versailles Treaty, when the plebiscite in the Saar prescribed in that instrument produced an overwhelming vote for reunion with Germany. There was nothing further to be gained from the treaty, and Hitler was free to discard it if he could do so with impunity. He proceeded to do so with boldness and rapidity, though always under the cover of professions of goodwill and offers of negotiation. In March 1935 Hitler proclaimed the introduction of conscription and the existence of the *Luftwaffe*, which enabled German rearmament to move ahead more rapidly, with no need for concealment. This step was accompanied by a meeting between Hitler and the British Foreign Secretary, Simon, in Berlin in March, and followed by the conclusion of the Anglo-German Naval Agreement in June 1935.[9] This was a striking success for German diplomacy, demonstrating that Germany, while having no truck with the Geneva approach to disarmament, was willing to make a specific agreement on arms limitation. The contrast with the pre-1914 Anglo-German naval race was made much of. Moreover, like the non-aggression pact with Poland in 1934, the Anglo-German Naval Treaty emphasized the isolation of France. In March 1936 there came the daring coup of the occupation of the Rhineland, covered by a smoke-screen of plausible diplomatic proposals; and later in the year Germany intervened in Spain, while virtuously adhering to the Non-Intervention Agreement. Both ventures were successful, though the German generals had thought they were too risky. Success breeds success, and the momentum of nazi foreign policy was building up.

In his writings, Hitler had looked to alliances with Italy and Britain to bring Germany out of isolation and prepare the way for an advance in eastern Europe. By the end of 1937 an alliance with Italy was in the making. The set-back of the failed coup in Austria in 1934 was made good by an Austro-German agreement in July 1936, in which Germany recognized Austrian sovereignty and Austria acknowledged that it was a German state – an imprecise but potentially far-reaching phrase. Italy accepted this agreement, and its support for Austria progressively diminished. In April 1937 the Austrian Chancellor, Schuschnigg, went to Rome to be told that Italy could no longer defend Austria by force, and his only hope lay in following a Germanic policy. Shortly before this, on 1 November 1936, Mussolini had spoken publicly about the existence of a Rome–Berlin Axis, and the tacit surrender of Austria to German influence showed where this alignment was leading.

German policy towards Britain was less clear-cut. Sometimes Hitler worked hard at building up relations with Britain. He met Eden in 1934 and Simon in 1935, and he angled for an invitation to go to London to see Baldwin. He also received a stream of unofficial visitors, including Lloyd George, Lord Allen of Hurtwood (a pacifist Labour peer), and

Ward Price, an influential journalist. After each visit, Hitler reaped a goodly harvest of praise for the qualities of his character and the peaceable nature of his intentions. Equally the British government showed itself eager to negotiate with Germany, especially on questions of armaments and economics. To all appearances, an agreement with Britain, if not an alliance, was there for Germany to take. But in the event Hitler never pressed his overtures beyond the stage reached in the Naval Agreement of 1935; and sometimes when the door to something further seemed open he made no move to go through it. In 1937 the German Foreign Minister, von Neurath, accepted an invitation to visit London; but it appears that the German government made no serious preparations for his visit, which was called off on the flimsy pretext of an almost certainly non-existent torpedo attack on a German cruiser off Spain. If an agreement with Britain was so firmly on Hitler's agenda as he himself had written earlier, such behaviour is hard to explain. However, in the short run this German hesitation had no serious consequences. British policy was favourable towards Germany, and played almost as much into German hands as if an alliance had existed.

During the whole of this period, and especially after March 1935, German military strength developed at a remarkable rate (see above, pp. 188–197). By the end of 1937 the army had achieved the first stage of its expansion, and the strength (and even more the reputation) of the *Luftwaffe* was formidable in relation to any of its possible opponents. Germany had become, in a mere four years, the strongest military power in Europe.

The rise of Germany was matched by the decline of France, which at the beginning of 1933 still retained a position of some strength, but by the end of 1937 had fallen into weakness and passivity. In part this was the result of internal problems – social and political conflicts, unstable governments, and a worsening economic situation. But in part the decline came from a failure to grapple with the problems presented by the rise of Germany. Only Louis Barthou, who was Foreign Minister from February to October 1934, made a determined effort to cope with these problems. Barthou had no doubt that the policy of conciliation practised by Briand and continued through most of the life of the Disarmament Conference must be abandoned. French security was at stake: it could no longer be attained through the League, so it must be sought by alliances. Barthou set himself to revive France's alliances with Poland, Czechoslovakia, Yugoslavia, and Rumania. He recognized that an alliance with Italy would be useful. Above all, he sought an alliance with the Soviet Union. Though sternly anti-communist within France, he would have no truck with the view that Germany was preferable to the USSR on grounds of ideology: power politics and geography were what counted for Barthou. He visited Warsaw in April

1934 to try to repair the Polish alliance, and to encourage the Poles to improve their relations with the Soviet Union. He toured other east European capitals to promote his idea of an eastern pact, which was designed to draw in the USSR as a guarantor in eastern Europe on the lines of the Locarno treaties in the west. It may well be that these efforts were foredoomed to failure because they sought to reconcile the irreconcilable: the states of eastern Europe had no wish to be guaranteed by the Soviet Union, a prospect which they regarded as somewhat akin to the sheep being guaranteed by the wolf. But at least Barthou knew his own mind, and tackled the problems with a courage and energy often lacking in others. He was also willing to treat the British with a brusqueness which had not been seen since Poincaré's time, and to disregard their tendency to obstruct any improvement in Franco-Soviet relations.

On 9 October 1934 King Alexander of Yugoslavia, on a visit to France, was assassinated by an agent of Croat terrorists. Barthou, who was riding in the same carriage, died of his wounds. His successor as Foreign Minister was Laval, who replaced Barthou's clear-cut policy with a series of half-measures. He reached agreements with Italy in January 1935 and the following months, but under pressure from Britain, he threw them overboard during the Abyssinian crisis. He signed a treaty with the Soviet Union in May 1935, but then took it through a long and unnecessary process of discussion by parliamentary committees and ratification by Chamber and Senate. He hoped to use his agreement with both countries not so much *against* Germany as to pave the way for an agreement *with* Germany. Moreover, he reaped the results which were almost bound to follow a treaty with the USSR: dismay and distrust on the part of eastern European states, with the exception of Czechoslovakia. The result was a confusion and uncertainty in which France was thrown back into dependence on Britain, with unhappy results.

From the French point of view, British foreign policy was at its worst in 1935. In March the Foreign Secretary, Simon, went ahead with a visit to Berlin immediately after Germany announced its open rearmament. In June Britain concluded the Naval Agreement with Germany without consulting France, even though French interests were directly involved. In October and November Britain led France into the fiasco of sanctions against Italy over Abyssinia. Laval was later to gain a reputation for being pro-German; but in 1935 it was the British who were far ahead of him in going to meet the Germans and playing into their hands. But however unreliable or ill-judged British policy might be, the French at this stage found their dependence on Britain inescapable. The alternative of throwing French policy into reverse, seeking the best available terms from Germany, and accepting the consequences, was a course which was not yet seriously contemplated.

The German remilitarization of the Rhineland in March 1936 marked both a strategic and a psychological surrender by France; and there was no recovery later in the year. The advent of Blum's Popular Front government placed a further, ideological, barrier in the way of restoring relations with Italy. An attempt to revive the Little Entente in eastern Europe found Yugoslavia and Rumania reluctant to offend the Germans or to court economic reprisals from them. Relations with the Soviet Union were not developed. The Soviets pressed hard for military conversations, and the French finally agreed in November 1936; but in practice they continued to stall by making sure that the talks contained little substance.

By 1937 France was reduced to almost complete passivity. The Foreign Ministry watched the growth of German power with a clear-sighted fascination, unwilling to accept but unable to prevent it. Old allies in eastern Europe were cool. Italian friendship had been thrown away, and that of the USSR had not been fully secured. The British were unreliable. The French knew they needed allies, but in practice they were grievously alone.

By the end of 1937 the state of Europe had changed profoundly from that of 1932. The balance of power and prestige had swung decisively away from the states which supported the status quo of 1919, and particularly France, towards those which sought change, notably Italy and Germany. Of these two powers, Italy was the more obviously active. Mussolini was positively happy to be seen using force, whether in Abyssinia or in Spain. After the Dollfuss crisis of 1934, when Italy acted for the last time to maintain the status quo in Austria, every Italian move was a blow to the stability of Europe: in particular, it was no small matter to outface and effectively destroy the League of Nations. The Italian role in these years, and the damage inflicted on Europe, was out of proportion to Italy's actual weight among the powers. But though Italy was the more active, Germany was by far the more formidable of the two revisionist states. By 1937 Germany had become in terms of land and air power the strongest country in Europe. The economy was booming. The nazi leaders were full of confidence, well justified by a record of almost unbroken success. In political, military, and psychological terms, Germany held the initiative in Europe, and the events of the next few years developed from what her rulers, and above all Hitler, chose to do with it.

REFERENCES AND NOTES

1.   J. Defrasne, 'L'événement du 7 mars 1936', in *Les Relations franco-*

allemandes, 1933–1939 (Paris 1976), pp. 251, 254–5.

2.   Figures from John F. Coverdale, *Italian Intervention in the Spanish Civil War* (Princeton 1975), pp. 115, 171, 176–7, 393, 417.

3.   Edward L. Homze, *Arming the Luftwaffe: the Reich Air Ministry and the German aircraft industry, 1919–39* (Lincoln, Nebraska 1976), pp. 170–4; Matthew Cooper, *The German Air Force, 1933–1945* (London 1981), p. 59; Hugh Thomas, *The Spanish Civil War*, 3rd edn (Harmondsworth 1977), pp. 977–8.

4.   Thomas, *The Spanish Civil War*, pp. 445–6, 980–2; P. Broué and E. Témime, *Revolution and Civil War in Spain* (London 1972), pp. 366–74.

5.   Thomas, *The Spanish Civil War*, pp. 982–4; cf. Broué and Témime, *Revolution and Civil War*, pp. 376–9, for rather lower figures.

6.   Thomas, *The Spanish Civil War*, pp. 448–50.

7.   This discussion of intervention has not mentioned the role of Portugal, which through its geographical position was in many ways crucial. The Portuguese government, under Salazar, took the side of the nationalists in Spain. This was of great importance for the outcome of the war, but of only marginal significance for international relations.

8.   Figures in Coverdale, *Italian Intervention*, pp. 91–2.

9.   The terms of this agreement fixed total naval tonnage at the ratio of Britain 100, Germany 35, and gave Germany the right to build up to equality in submarine tonnage, though she undertook not to exceed 45 per cent without giving notice.

Chapter 14

WAR POSTPONED, 1938

THE DISAPPEARANCE OF AUSTRIA

On 11 March 1938 the government of the Republic of Austria was taken over by nominees of Germany as a result of pressure from Berlin. The next day, German troops entered the country, with bands playing and bedecked with flowers. On the 13th, Hitler announced the annexation of Austria to Germany. Within two days, a sovereign state, guaranteed several times over by treaties and declarations, and previously supported by Italy, France, and Britain, disappeared from the map. Not a shot was fired: it was a parade, not an invasion. No one even thought of going to war. Yet by its circumstances, its methods, and its consequences, the German annexation of Austria marked an important step towards war in Europe.

The new Austria created in 1919 had never been sure of its identity. In 1919 the majority of its citizens had wished to join Germany, but were explicitly forbidden to do so by the Treaty of Versailles. After 1933 the settlement of 1919 was in decay, and *Anschluss* (union) with Germany looked increasingly possible. But it would now mean accepting nazism, and the two main Austrian political parties, the conservative Christian socials and the social democrats, both removed *Anschluss* from their programmes. Most Austrians, however, retained an ambivalent attitude towards Germany, and their sense of separate national identity remained uncertain.

Internally, the country was racked by ideological strife. In the early 1930s both the Christian socials and the social democrats maintained private armies, the *Heimwehr* and the *Schutzbund* respectively; and the *Heimwehr* developed into a form of Austrian fascism. In February 1934 the conservative Chancellor, Dollfuss, attacked the socialists in their strongholds in the blocks of workers' flats in Vienna, bombarding them with artillery in what amounted to a limited civil war. But the Austrian right wing was itself deeply divided, and in July 1934 the Austrian nazis assassinated Dollfuss in the course of an abortive *coup d'état*. After this, the new Chancellor, Kurt von Schuschnigg, sought to uphold his position against both nazis and socialists, both of whom looked abroad for support. The Austrian nazis had firm bases across the border in Germany. Socialists and communists in exile published news-sheets, and received rather amorphous support from left-wing opinion. To maintain its position in these circumstances, Schuschnigg's government depended heavily on Italian support, which had been powerfully demonstrated at the time of the Dollfuss coup. But in 1936 and 1937, with the development of the Rome–Berlin Axis, this support waned rapidly. In April 1937 Mussolini told Schuschnigg that he could no longer undertake to defend Austria by force. On 6 November 1937 the Duce told Ribbentrop, the German Foreign Minister, that he accepted that Austria was a German country; that the question would have to be resolved at some time; and that if a crisis arose Italy would take no action. With that declaration, Austria's external support was removed.

The Austrian government was thus left alone to face both internal discord and pressure from Germany. After the failure of the nazi coup in Vienna in July 1934, the official German policy became one of 'evolution' towards *Anschluss*. Von Papen was appointed Ambassador in Vienna to promote this policy, and in July 1936 an Austro-German agreement appeared to stabilize relations between the two countries. Germany recognized the full sovereignty of Austria; each government agreed not to intervene in the internal affairs of the other; and Austria agreed to be guided by the principle that it was a German state. Secret clauses included an amnesty for nazis in prison in Austria, and provided for the entry into Schuschnigg's Cabinet of Glaise-Horstenau and Guido Schmidt – neither of them nazis, but both acceptable to Hitler. It was an unusual start to a policy of non-intervention in internal affairs. In practice, the clandestine links between the German and Austrian Nazi Parties continued. In January 1938 the Austrian police discovered a plan for Austrian nazis to carry out acts of provocation (including the murder of the German Ambassador) so that when the situation seemed out of control the German government would intervene and impose a new government, in which the nazis would take a half-share. At the same time, the police collected 14 tons of propaganda printed in Germany for the Austrian nazis, and piled up at Salzburg railway station. The more formal organs of the German state were not necessarily informed of these activities – indeed, it would be necessary to keep the Ambassador in ignorance of his likely fate. It is not possible to tell how far Hitler was aware of the details, though he took a keen interest in Austrian affairs. But the whole conspiratorial scenario was characteristic of unofficial foreign policy under the nazi regime.

In the event, German pressure took a different form. On 7 January 1938 Schuschnigg was invited to visit Hitler at Berchtesgaden, where he eventually made his way on 12 February. There followed a remarkable display of Hitler's techniques of intimidation. Schuschnigg was subjected over several hours to verbal assault, psychological pressure, and threat of invasion. Hitler put ten demands, including the appointment as Minister of the Interior (and therefore in charge of the police) of the Austrian nazi Seyss-Inquart. Schuschnigg signed a protocol including these points, and was given three days to have them confirmed by the President of Austria. He left Berchtesgaden battered, dazed, and humiliated. When it is asserted (as it sometimes is) that at this stage Hitler was following an 'evolutionary' course, by which the *Anschluss* with Austria would come about gradually, it is necessary to remember the interview of 12 February 1938. Schuschnigg would have been glad to be spared this form of 'evolution', which in fact meant being bullied into sacrificing his country's independence.

At the last moment, the Austrian Chancellor tried to resist Hitler's pressure. On 9 March he announced a plebiscite, to be held on the 13th, asking Austrians to vote on whether they wanted 'a free and German, an independent and social, a Christian and united Austria'. Everything pointed to a massive 'Yes' vote. Socialist Party leaders, after an agony of doubt, instructed their members to vote 'Yes'; and in an extraordinary gesture of unity the former head of the socialist *Schutzbund* met the Catholic mayor of Vienna to discuss ways of resisting the nazis. It seemed at last that Austrian identity and independence were to be asserted, overriding the pull of internal discords.

Hitler had secret news of the plebiscite before it was announced in Austria. He thought briefly of trying to stop it, and then turned on 10 March to military action. The army had no plans ready for an attack on Austria, only a sketch for 'Operation Otto', prepared in case of a Habsburg restoration. But the staffs (including General Beck and other anti-nazis) set to work with a will to improvise a plan. In the event, no invasion was needed – telephone calls proved sufficient.

The single day of 11 March settled the issue. Hitler opened with a demand that the plebiscite be postponed. When this was yielded, Goering telephoned Vienna with the demand that Schuschnigg must resign and be replaced as Chancellor by Seyss-Inquart. This was resisted for a time, until Schuschnigg announced the resignation of his whole Cabinet except Seyss-Inquart, who remained as Minister of the Interior and the only minister still in office. On this, Goering issued a verbal order for German troops to cross the frontier, with Hitler signing the written instruction at 8.45 p.m. At 9.40 an invitation purporting to come from Seyss-Inquart in the name of a provisional government was received in Berlin, and treated as conferring legitimacy on the planned operation.

German forces entered Austria early on 12 March, in an ostentatiously friendly manner. Hitler followed later in the day, and was welcomed by cheering crowds at Linz, where as a boy he had gone to school. It appears to have been the heady atmosphere that decided Hitler to proclaim next day the annexation of Austria, rather than adopt some half-way house like a protectorate. There was a darker side to the occupation. Behind the army with its bands and flags there came the Gestapo. Himmler and Heydrich arrived in Vienna on 12 March. There were many arrests, ranging from Schuschnigg himself to Socialist Party members and Jews. The Defence Minister in Schuschnigg's Cabinet was murdered.

Austria's former protectors made no move. Mussolini was given no notice of events, but stood by his word and earned Hitler's heartfelt gratitude. France and Britain delivered separate protests in Berlin (France was actually without a government on 11 March); but they had long expected the *Anschluss*, which was thought to be inevitable and in principle right. In Britain in particular there was a widespread belief that the enforced separation of Germany and Austria had been among the errors of Versailles; and the Labour Party found it hard to sympathize with Schuschnigg's regime, the heir of those who had crushed the socialists in February 1934.

The danger of a European war arising out of the Austrian crisis was almost nil. Virtually the only possibility of conflict would have arisen from Austrian resistance to the German occupation: even a token struggle would have stripped away the veneer of legitimacy and the atmosphere generated by flowers and welcoming crowds. But it is hard to believe that brief and sporadic fighting would have provoked intervention by France, still less Britain; and the Austrians were in no real position to sacrifice themselves to awaken the rest of Europe.

War was therefore nowhere in sight; and yet the *Anschluss* was a long step towards it. German methods – subversion, the threat of force, the novel device of dictating orders to a foreign government by telephone – sank into the consciousness even of those who chose to ignore them at the time, and began the process by which nazi tactics finally became intolerable. Moreover, the appearances created by the *Anschluss* eventually overtook the reality, with far-reaching consequences. In reality, Hitler had not planned the events of 11 March 1938. He was certainly set on destroying Austrian independence, and was well on the way to doing so; but Schuschnigg's desperate call for a plebiscite produced a crisis which Hitler did not expect. He was compelled to improvise. In retrospect, however, the *Anschluss* became the first in a six-monthly series of crises, creating the impression of a plan and a programme, and so producing a view of nazi policy which in the long run did much to build up resistance to it. The effect of German actions was cumulative, and Austria began the process of accumulation.

THE CZECHOSLOVAKIAN CRISIS

The effects of the German occupation of Austria were felt at once in

Czechoslovakia, where the long-standing difficulties of this multi-national state were brought to a head and became a part of a great European crisis which in September 1938 brought the Continent to the brink of war.

The nationalities problem of Czechoslovakia may be illustrated by the census figures of 1930. These showed a total population of 14,730,000, made up as follows[1]:

Czechs	7,447,000
Germans	3,218,000
Slovaks	2,309,000
Magyars	720,000
Ruthenes	569,000
Poles	100,000
Others	266,000

The bulk of the German population lived in a horseshoe-shaped area along the frontiers with Germany and Austria, though there were also substantial concentrations in the cities of Prague, Brno, and Bratislava. The Magyars lived mainly in a long, thin zone along the Hungarian frontier, and the Poles were gathered round Teschen.

Conflicts between different nationalities were chronic, and in some cases acute. The Slovaks had developed a national consciousness during the nineteenth century, and found their position in the state anomalous. Technically, they shared with the Czechs the status of 'people of the state', as distinct from minorities. In practice, posts in the civil service and the professions tended to be taken by the better-educated Czechs, and the long-standing religious division between Protestant Bohemia and Catholic Slovakia remained sharp. A Slovak separatist movement, led by a Catholic priest, Andrew Hlinka, gained the support of up to about half of the Slovak electorate. Among the minorities, the Magyars and Poles looked to their national states across the border; but the main problems were associated with the Germans, who in 1919 had abruptly lost a position of predominance and become a subordinate minority, discriminated against in education, jobs, and the distribution of public funds. During the 1920s there were signs that they might absorb this sudden reversal of fortune and adapt to the new political system. Conservative Germans co-operated with the Czech Agrarian Party, and in 1929 German social democrats took office in a coalition government. The Weimar Republic in Germany assisted this process by advising Sudeten Germans to accept the new state, and giving no encouragement to those who rejected it.

This process of assimilation was checked in the early 1930s by the economic depression, in which the German industrial areas tended to blame the government in Prague for their misfortunes, and by the growth of ideological conflict. The nazi successes in Germany in 1932–

33 were welcomed by nationalists among the Sudeten Germans, and both the Nationalist and the Nazi Parties began to attract increasing support. These parties threatened both the parliamentary system and the internal cohesion of the state, but the Czechoslovak government proved insufficiently resolute to defeat them. In October 1933 both parties were suppressed, but shortly afterwards a new party, the Sudeten German *Heimatsfront*, was formed, under the leadership of Konrad Henlein. This was an obvious replacement for the former Nazi Party, but it was allowed to continue – the government had struck once, but did not continue the work of repression.

Henlein's new party was an immense success. In the parliamentary election of May 1935 it polled nearly 1.25 million votes, more than any other single party.[2] Henlein demanded the removal of all discrimination against the German population, and claimed that Germans should be appointed to the civil service in proportion to their numbers – he put the figure at 31,000 posts. The government, under President Benes, held that a democratic state could not entrust its administration to representatives of a totalitarian party. Early in 1937 Henlein began to demand autonomy for the German areas, which the government refused, partly because it was impossible to hand over parts of the country to an alien political system, and even more because any concessions to the Germans would be demanded by the Slovaks, Magyars, and Poles, and would end in the disintegration of the state.

The impasse was complete. The government had tried coercion but abandoned it. The only concessions which would meet the demands of Henlein's party would truncate the parliamentary system and threatened to dissolve the state. The *Anschluss* in Austria sharpened the conflict, providing a fillip for Henlein's party, whose membership rose from 550,000 to 1.31 million between February and May 1938.[3] The internal crisis of the Czechoslovakian state was coming to a head. Even as a domestic problem, it was hard to see how it could be resolved.

Why did the internal problems of Czechoslovakia bring about a European crisis and threaten general war? The main answer lay in the links between the Sudeten question and nazi Germany. From the early 1930s the Sudeten German nationalists and nazis were in contact with the German Nazi Party, and in 1935 the latter provided a large subsidy for Henlein's election expenses. On 28 March 1938 Henlein conferred with Hitler, and summarized his position (with Hitler's approval) as being that 'We must always demand so much that we can never be satisfied.'[4] Notably, Henlein agreed to keep in reserve a suggestion of Hitler's that he should ask for German regiments with German officers within the Czech Army – something which the Czech government was bound to refuse. On 24 April 1938 Henlein made a number of demands for autonomy in a speech at Karlsbad (including the right to practise and propagate nazi ideology): these demands had been prepared at a meeting in the German Foreign Ministry on 29 March. German influence on Henlein's party and its policy was thus significant, and was becoming predominant.

German (which in effect meant Hitler's) intentions towards Czechoslovakia early in 1938 were not absolutely clear-cut; but the degree of uncertainty amounted to no more than whether the state should be destroyed in the near or the rather more distant future, and whether this end should be attained by war or some lesser form of pressure. At a conference with his service commanders and Foreign Minister on 5 November 1937 (the so-called Hossbach conference), Hitler spent a good deal of time on Czechoslovakia. He asserted that Germany must go to war to solve her problems of living space no later than 1943–45; and that in favourable circumstances (the involvement of France in serious domestic strife or war with another power) Germany could act earlier to secure the overthrow of Czechoslovakia and Austria and so remove the threat to her flank in the event of war in the west. Hitler believed that Britain, and probably France too, had already tacitly abandoned Czechoslovakia and were reconciled to that question being 'cleared up' by Germany. Generals Blomberg and Fritsch were less certain, emphasizing that French and British enmity must not be incurred. Blomberg stressed the strength of the Czech fortifications, though Fritsch declared that he was already studying means of overcoming them.[5]

This conference was followed by the issuing of a new general directive (7 December 1937) by the High Command of the Armed Forces (OKW), giving Operation Green (an attack on Czechoslovakia) priority over defence in the west, and laying down that the main emphasis in mobilization planning was to be placed on this operation. No date, even approximate, was fixed. Planning for an attack on Czechoslovakia went forward, and on 21 April Hitler discussed the plan with General Keitel, rejecting the idea of an invasion with no shred of justification in favour of a lightning attack to take advantage of some incident, such as the assassination of the German Ambassador in Prague. (Ambassadors, as we have seen before, were considered expendable.) By August the General Staff had produced a plan to cut Czechoslovakia in two at its narrowest point, but Hitler criticized this on 3 September, emphasizing the political and psychological importance of a drive on Prague by all available armoured forces. The result was a somewhat unhappy compromise between these two concepts.

Were these plans meant to be carried out, or were they preparations for an eventuality which might or might not materialize? There are many indications that Hitler wanted war against Czechoslovakia in 1938, both to destroy the state in one blow and to demonstrate German power. He later expressed regret that he did not fight, and in 1939 was determined that no peacemaker should come along to deprive him of a war. General Beck, who was alarmed by the risk of war with the western powers, had no doubt that the plans were to be carried out. On the other hand, Hitler later boasted of the success of his war of nerves, which had given him a bloodless victory.

Whatever the exact state of Hitler's intentions (which may well have fluctuated), there can be no doubt that the ultimate German objective was the destruction of Czechoslovakia. From the meeting of 5 November 1937 onwards, Hitler repeatedly stated this intention: all that varied was the likely date. Beck himself did not oppose this aim; he was only dismayed by the risk of general war. Equally, there was an almost universal belief, in Germany and other countries, that Germany *would* go to war over Czechoslovakia.

In these circumstances, the prospect of European war seemed imminent. If Germany set out to destroy Czechoslovakia by force, using the Sudeten issue as a pretext, and the Czechs resisted, then other powers seemed bound to be drawn in. Czechoslovakia had an alliance with France dating back to 1924, reaffirmed by another treaty in October 1935, and supported by a military and air convention signed on 1 July 1935. She also had an alliance with the Soviet Union, signed in 1935, though this was to become operative only when the French treaty had already been activated. If France went to war, then it was likely that Britain, however reluctantly, would be drawn in. The Czechs had ample forces to act as a trigger for these alliances: an army of thirty divisions after mobilization, well equipped by a modern armaments industry, and with incomplete but substantial fortifications begun in 1936. Czech resistance to a German invasion might not be prolonged, but if it was determined there would be no walk-over.

This was the situation in principle, and the dangers of general war were obvious. In practice, there were many reasons to think that the scenario would not be played out according to this script. In a very real sense, there was only a crisis at all because French determination to support Czechoslovakia was known to have diminished to the point of vanishing. French military policy and organization made it virtually impossible for their army to move forward to the help of the Czechs. When the government consulted General Gamelin on the question, he said flatly that there could be no offensive at all until the covering forces were in position, and even after general mobilization there could be no strategic offensive for two years. Equally, the acceptance of German rearmament and of the occupation of the Rhineland had shown that the French lacked the political will to oppose Germany. France was effectively without a German policy. Daladier's ministry, which took office in April 1938, was divided between advocates of a strong anti-German stance (notably Reynaud and Mandel), those who were determined to find a solution even at the expense of Czechoslovakia, and those in between, notably Daladier himself, who often used firm words but finally looked desperately for a way to avoid war. Nearly all the senior French ambassadors and Foreign Office officials were, in varying degrees, in favour of concessions to Germany, largely because they believed that France would be completely isolated if she took any other line. Poland was hostile to Czechoslovakia, and on 22 May Beck (the Polish Foreign Minister) reserved his position in the event of war. Britain declined to commit herself to fight for Czechoslovakia, though accepting that she might be drawn in; and in any case could produce only two divisions for a land war. Only the Soviets claimed they would stand by their treaty with Czechoslovakia if France did so first; but they were not believed, and in any case the Red Army could only get into action through Poland or Rumania. The French faced the prospect of having to go to war with Germany virtually alone: the nightmare of French foreign policy since 1871. In these circumstances it is not surprising that the Foreign Minister, Bonnet, was determined to avoid a confrontation with Germany, and even to decline any initiative in negotiation, preferring to leave such ventures to the British.

With the paralysis of France, British policy attained a crucial importance which was unusual for a country which had for some years cultivated a detachment from European affairs in general and from eastern Europe in particular. The government, under the leadership of the Prime Minister, Neville Chamberlain, accepted its central role with remarkable energy and self-confidence. Chamberlain was a man of great ability, drive, and courage, determined to impart a sense of direction to British foreign policy which he rightly felt had been lacking under his predecessor, Baldwin. His policy was not in any strict sense personal – his views were shared by, rather than imposed on, his Cabinet, and despite later claims there was only scattered opposition within the Foreign Office, where the Permanent Under-Secretary, Cagodan, was in broad agreement with the Prime Minister.

The main lines of Chamberlain's policy were determined by the psychological, economic, and strategic considerations which have been discussed in earlier chapters. He shared in the widespread revulsion against war; he was acutely aware of Britain's financial and economic problems; and he was well aware of the state of the country's armaments. All these influences reinforced his personal desire to seek a negotiated solution for European difficulties, and specifically for the Czechoslovakian problem. In 1938 he wanted both to reach a general settlement with Germany and to resolve the specific Czechoslovakian crisis without war, because this was desirable in itself and because it seemed highly likely that if there was a war Britain would lose. As Cadogan wrote in his diary on 16 March 1938: 'We *must* not precipitate a conflict now – we shall be smashed.'[6]

The main lines of British policy on Czechoslovakia were laid down during 1937, while Eden was Foreign Secretary, starting before Chamberlain became Prime Minister in May of that year. Britain made repeated representations at Prague to urge the Czechs to remedy the grievances of the Sudeten Germans by meeting as many of Henlein's demands as possible. (Henlein himself visited London twice in 1935 and again in October 1937, making a favourable impression and being well received even by such anti-German figures as Vansittart and Churchill.) When the French Premier and Foreign Minister of the time (Chautemps and Delbos) visited London on 28–30 November 1937, Chamberlain told them that British public opinion was strongly opposed to being drawn into war over Czechoslovakia and believed that the Sudeten Germans had not been fairly treated. Eden hoped that Delbos would advise the Czechs to make concessions to the Sudeten Germans. Thus the policy which culminated in the Munich agreement of September 1938 was outlined nearly a year earlier, and was not associated solely with Chamberlain and Halifax.

When the Czechoslovakian crisis sharpened at the end of March 1938 British policy took on two main aspects: to continue to urge the Czech government to make concessions to Henlein, and later to Germany; and to warn the German government that if war arose out of the Sudeten issue, and France was involved, Britain might or would also be drawn in. The two aspects were far from being given equal weight. The pressure on Czechoslovakia was always strong and finally became intense, but the warnings to Germany were muted and lacking in conviction. As the British repeatedly said among themselves, it was unwise to threaten what you could not carry out, and they did not believe that they could fight Germany with any chance of success. At the same time, the British thought it necessary to restrain France from pursuing her obligations to Czechoslovakia, and from stiffening Czech opposition to the Sudetens. (In fact, such restraint was quite unnecessary, though Daladier often sounded bellicose.) The British were also determined to exclude the Soviet Union from the diplomacy of the crisis. Chamberlain believed that the USSR was trying to involve Britain in a war with Germany; and he was also convinced that to bring the Soviets into the negotiations would drive away Hitler, who was too anti-Bolshevik ever to deal with Stalin. The British aimed at a negotiated settlement, and therefore any co-operation with the Soviet Union must be avoided. Such calculations were added to the cumulative effects of twenty years of ideological conflict and distrust, and produced a firm determination to keep the Soviets at arm's length.[7] The preponderant line of British policy thus emerges as the search for a settlement by putting pressure on Czechoslovakia to meet first Henlein's and then Hitler's demands.

What of the Soviet Union, which like France was in formal alliance with Czechoslovakia? On 17 March 1938 the Commissar for Foreign Affairs, Litvinov, made a public proposal that interested powers should consult together about practical measures to preserve peace. This proposal was rejected by the British government, and not pursued even by the French, still technically in alliance with the Soviet Union. Thereafter, Litvinov affirmed from time to time that his country would in case of need carry out its obligations and aid Czechoslovakia, as long as France did so first. In May and June some Soviet aircraft were flown to Czechoslovakia through Rumanian (and sometimes Polish) airspace.

These assurances and actions enabled the Soviet Union to claim to have been Czechoslovakia's only true friend in the crisis. But the assurances were never put to the test, and to carry them out would have posed formidable problems. For the Red Army to reach Czechoslovakia, or to engage the Germans at all, it would have to pass through Poland. (The roads and railways across Rumania were quite inadequate.) The Red Army itself was in the throes of the purges, and most foreign military observers doubted its capacity for offensive action outside its own borders. In the Far East, the army was already (in July and August) fighting to protect Soviet territory against the Japanese. In all these circumstances, it seems certain that Stalin would only have gone to war over Czechoslovakia if he believed that that country represented an interest of crucial importance. Whether he held such a belief must remain doubtful: a substantial interest, but not vital, seems a realistic estimate. What was sure beyond a peradventure was that Stalin would not fight if the western powers stood aside; and in the event the USSR, like everyone else, stood aloof. One definite threat, made on 23 September, to denounce the Soviet–Polish Non-Aggression Pact of 1932 if Poland violated Czech territory, was not carried out when the Poles occupied Teschen. There would have been no point in such a gesture.

The policies and interests of France, Britain, and the Soviet Union therefore made it unlikely that they would in practice go to the help of Czechoslovakia. The Czech position was much weaker than its formal alliances indicated; and the likelihood of a European war arising out of the Czechoslovakian problem was correspondingly diminished. This seemed indeed to be the position during April 1938. Henlein, in a speech at Karlsbad on 24 April, set out eight demands for Sudeten German autonomy which stopped just short of a claim for complete separation, though if fully executed they seemed likely to lead to the disintegration of Czechoslovakia.[8] The British government believed what it wished to believe: that the speech offered a basis for settlement within Czechoslovakia. At a conference in London on 28–29 April the British and French leaders agreed that both countries should urge the Czechs to do their utmost to meet the demands of the Sudeten Germans, while Britain would also approach Berlin to find out exactly what the Germans wanted. All seemed set for a negotiated solution favourable to Henlein and Hitler.

But then, with pressure being exerted on Czechoslovakia but not yet producing any solid effect, there erupted the so-called 'May crisis', apparently revealing an immediate threat of war. On 19, 20, and 21 May there were widespread rumours of German troop movements in areas to the north of the Czech border. At that time, German plans for an invasion were not ready, and there was no intention of launching an attack, though some army units were engaged in manoeuvres. But the situation appeared critical. Local elections were in progress in Czechoslovakia, bringing out all the strains of the nationalities problem. Two Sudeten Germans were shot by a Czech officer near the border with Germany. On 21 May Ribbentrop told the British Ambassador in Berlin that there had been 100 German casualties in the Sudetenland, and that if such provocation continued the German people would intervene as one man. Only ten weeks earlier there had been German political pressure on Austria, and reports of German troop movements, and the *Anschluss* had come about within a couple of days. On 20 May the Czech government called up one class of reservists; though it was widely reported that they had mobilized two classes, and they were much condemned for being provocative.

In fact, there was no danger of a German attack, and therefore none of a European war. But the danger of war *appeared* to be real, and that was quite enough. Twice, on 21 and 22 May, Britain asked Germany to exercise patience, but also warned that if war arose over Czechoslovakia, France would stand by her obligations and there could be no certainty that Britain would not be drawn in. On 21 May Bonnet, the French Foreign Minister, stated publicly that France would act if German troops entered Czechoslovakia. When the alarm had subsided, Chamberlain wrote privately (on 28 May) that there was no doubt that Europe had been on the brink of war: Germany had made all preparations for a coup, and had only drawn back when warnings from Britain and France convinced her that the risk was too great. Despite all the French and British reservations, indeed their determination not to become involved in war over Czechoslovakia, they had suddenly, willy-nilly, come to the brink. From that time onwards, they redoubled their efforts to resolve the crisis, and increased their pressure on the Czechs to make concessions.

The May crisis had dramatic effects within Germany, which increased the likelihood of war. On 21 May, in the midst of the crisis, General Keitel submitted to Hitler a draft directive for Operation Green against Czechoslovakia, which opened: 'It is not my intention to smash Czechoslovakia by military action in the immediate future without provocation, unless an unavoidable development of the political conditions within Czechoslovakia forces the issue, or political events in Europe create a particularly favourable opportunity. . . .' But the events of the crisis infuriated Hitler, who had been accused of an aggression which he was not yet intending, and had been humiliated by appearing to yield to Anglo-French pressure. On 30 May a new directive was prepared: 'It is my unalterable decision to smash Czechoslovakia by military action in the near future. It is the business of the political leadership to bring about the suitable moment from a political and military point of view.' Support from Hungary and Poland was anticipated; French intervention was thought unlikely; Soviet air support for the Czechs appeared probable. The German military action must be speedy, energetic, and bold. The date for the execution of this directive was fixed at 1 October 1938 at the latest.[9]

The determination to crush Czechoslovakia was not new, but the setting of a date gave the situation a new aspect. Four months gave time for a diplomatic solution if one could be found or forced. Meanwhile, military preparations went ahead, with increased emphasis on speed and surprise. Events henceforth developed under the shadow of impending military action.

Negotiations continued between the Czech government and the Sudeten German Party, without success. The British and French grew impatient, and applied increased pressure on the Czechs. In July the British government forced upon the Czechs a so-called 'independent' mediator, in the shape of Lord Runciman, a former Liberal Cabinet minister, who arrived in Prague on 3 August to bring his persuasive powers to bear upon the Czech government. The French acted more forcefully. On 20 July Bonnet told the Czech Ambassador in Paris bluntly that France would not go to war over the Sudeten question. She would declare her support in public, to help the Czechs to negotiate; but on no account should the Czech government believe that France would stand by them if war broke out. German pressure continued to build up in rather a different fashion. Throughout August there were frequent reports (this time well founded) of German military preparations and troop movements. Divisions were brought up to a war footing, and work on the western defences (the Siegfried Line) was hastily pressed forward. By the end of the month, the French *Deuxième Bureau* was certain that the German Army was mobilizing in readiness for war against Czechoslovakia, with a thin covering force in the west.

The long drawn out crisis reached its climax in September, when in rapid succession war seemed imminent, was apparently averted, became once again all but inevitable, and finally was conjured away by the last-minute expedient of the Munich conference. This extraordinary switchback began on 5 September, when Benes, the Czech President, suddenly produced his 'Fourth Plan', which met nearly all the demands put by Henlein at Karlsbad. Rather than accept, the Sudeten Germans staged an incident in the town of Moravska-Ostrava, in which two of their parliamentary deputies were arrested, and then used this as a pretext to break off negotiations. The German Nazi Party rally in Nuremberg was in progress at the time. On 12 September Hitler addressed the rally, proclaiming his support for the Germans in Czechoslovakia, who would not be left defenceless. That night there were riots in the main towns of the Sudeten areas, giving the appearance of a general rising against the government. The Czech

Army restored order, and on the 15th Henlein fled to Germany.

The combination of Hitler's speech and the Sudeten German riots convinced Neville Chamberlain that war was imminent, and on 13 September he took the dramatic step of asking for a personal meeting with Hitler to find a solution before it was too late. He did not consult the French, but merely informed Daladier of what he was doing. Daladier too was convinced that the crux had come, and was desperately looking for something which would save France from being confronted with her obligations. He would have preferred a three-power meeting to an Anglo-German tête-à-tête, but had no option but to accept Chamberlain's decision. Chamberlain flew to meet Hitler at Berchtesgaden on 15 September. Hitler declared that he was ready to risk war to incorporate the Sudeten Germans into Germany, and Chamberlain rapidly expressed his willingness to agree in principle to the transfer of the Sudeten areas, though he would have to consult his Cabinet and the French. (The Czechs, whose territory was at stake, were not mentioned.) If this concession were carried through, the issue of principle was settled. All that remained to be worked out were the methods and timing of the transfer, and the limits of the territory concerned. It appeared that the issue had been reduced to whether the British and French Cabinets would agree to the cession of the Sudetenland to Germany (which was highly likely), and whether the Czechs could be coerced into acceptance (which was also likely). If so, then the corner was turned and peace was saved.

All went smoothly. Chamberlain carried his Cabinet with him. Daladier and Bonnet went to London on 18 September and agreed to the principle of the cession of the Sudetenland, in return for a reluctant British acceptance of an international guarantee for the remnant of Czechoslovakia. On the 19th the French Cabinet approved the proposals, which were then put to the Czechs. The Czech position was appalling. To accept meant, almost certainly, the dismemberment of their country, because it was clear that the Sudeten issue could not stand alone, but would be followed by Polish, Magyar, and Slovak demands. To reject the proposals meant war and invasion, to be faced without help from France or Britain. After a first impulse to refuse the terms, Benes virtually asked for the most extreme Franco-British pressure to be brought to bear, which was duly done in the shape of a statement that if the refusal were maintained France and Britain would leave the Czechs to their fate. On 21 September the Czech government yielded, and on the 22nd the Prime Minister, Hodza, resigned and was replaced by General Syrový, a change which symbolized acceptance of the new situation.

To all appearances, the situation was saved and the way was clear. Chamberlain had secured what Hitler had said he wanted, and on 22 September he returned to Germany with what he believed to be a settlement in his pocket. But the switchback suddenly took another plunge. Since the Berchtesgaden meeting, Hitler had taken steps to undermine any agreement. On 17 September he set up in Germany the so-called Sudeten German Free Corps, to make attacks and create incidents in Czechoslovakia. He encouraged Hungary and Poland to press the claims of their own minorities in Czechoslovakia – the Poles indeed had already claimed that any concessions made to the Sudeten Germans should automatically be extended to Teschen. The basis was thus laid for fresh complaints and fresh demands, which were at once produced when Hitler met Chamberlain at Godesberg on 22 September. Chamberlain arrived with his agreed concession: the Sudetenland was to be transferred to Germany. Hitler said at once that this was no longer enough. He brought out the Polish and Hungarian claims for territory, and Slovak demands for autonomy; and he used the pretext of unrest in Czechoslovakia to assert that Germany must occupy the Sudeten areas at once. He produced a prepared map with the zone of occupation marked on it. The next day, Hitler presented Chamberlain with a paper demanding German occupation of the area between 26 and 28 September, though as an apparent concession he agreed that the date should be put back to 1 October – the date set on 30 May for the invasion of Czechoslovakia.

Chamberlain agreed to pass on the new terms, and when he returned to London on 24 September he was prepared to advocate acceptance. But on 25 September Halifax came out against them, and the Cabinet in general supported him. On the 25th and 26th Daladier and Bonnet again came to London, and agreed to a proposal by Chamberlain to send an emissary to Berlin with a combined warning and last-minute appeal for a settlement. Chamberlain for his part undertook that Britain would go to war if France fought over Czechoslovakia. This remarkable departure showed how the situation had changed. Despite the deep reluctance of both the French and British governments, on 26 September war seemed imminent. The French began to mobilize, and on the 28th the British mobilized the fleet. The war crisis had come. Superficially, it arose over a question of the timing and method of the transfer of territory which had already been agreed on, but this was not the substantive issue. For the British and French, the question was not the ownership of a strip of land or the status of 3.5 million people, but Hitler's intentions. Was he aiming at limited objectives, which would allow a lasting settlement to be reached, or at something more far-reaching? Hitler's high-handed methods and sudden production of new demands at Godesberg had changed the situation, and made it seem that, despite deep Anglo-French reluctance, he must be resisted.

At this point, Hitler decided not to press on to his real objective, the destruction of Czechoslovakia, but to accept for the time being his stated aim of securing the Sudetenland. During 27 and 28 September proposals for a conference came from several directions, notably from Chamberlain, President Roosevelt, and Mussolini, who knew that

Italy was not ready for war and sought instead the laurels of a peace-maker. On the 28th Hitler agreed to a conference, which met at Munich on the 29th. The powers represented were Germany, France, Britain, and Italy. Czechoslovakia was excluded, and no one thought of inviting the Soviet Union. Mussolini, ostensibly acting as mediator, produced as a basis for discussion a set of terms drafted in Berlin; and by 2 a.m. on 30 September the conference reached an agreement. Sudeten German territories, depicted on an accompanying map, were to be ceded to Germany, with provision for plebiscites in doubtful areas. The final frontier was to be fixed by a committee representing the four Munich powers plus Czechoslovakia. German occupation was to begin on 1 October and be completed by the 10th. Polish and Hungarian claims were to be settled within a specified time. British and French guarantees of the new Czech frontiers were to be given at once, with German and Italian guarantees to follow. These terms were presented to the Czechs, who accepted them. In practice, the outcome was not in doubt after Hitler had agreed on a conference. War was averted.

How near did Europe come to war in September 1938, and why was it avoided? The imminence of war is a matter of assessing intentions. Did Hitler seriously intend, up to 27 September, to invade Czechoslovakia? Would France and Britain have fought rather than accept the Godesberg terms, or in face of a German attack? Neither question can be answered with absolute certainty. Up to 27 September the German military preparations were moving ahead with every sign of determination. Assault forces were moved up to the frontier that day; mobilization was fixed for the 28th; and the attack was to be launched on the 30th. The indications are that Hitler was not bluffing, but rather that he stepped back on 28 September. His generals were reluctant to fight; Goering was opposed to war; and Mussolini could not be relied upon. Armoured units passing through Berlin were watched by crowds in a dismal silence. The Czech Army had mobilized, making surprise unlikely and so diminishing the chance of a lightning victory. The mobilization of the Royal Navy made it appear that the British might go to war. All these considerations seem to have contributed to Hitler's change of mind. If he had pursued his earlier course, and launched the invasion, then it is hard to see that France and Britain would have been left with any alternative but to declare war. Their actions on 26 and 27 September pointed clearly in that direction: notably the French mobilized their army and, against all their inclinations, felt bound to fight. In all probability, therefore, war was very close indeed – two days away on 28 September.

That war came so close was primarily the result of German initiatives and actions. It is true that internal divisions and problems in Austria and Czechoslovakia were open to be exploited, but they only reached the point of the extinction of Austria and the disintegration of Czechoslovakia through German pressure, exerted from both without and within. The diplomatic initiative often lay with other powers, especially Britain, where Chamberlain worked ceaselessly to resolve the crisis without war; but the strategic initiative lay throughout with Germany, both in the general sense that everyone was reacting to German pressure and in the narrower sense that by September the German military preparations for an attack on Czechoslovakia were the most threatening element in the situation. 1938 was Hitler's year. By subversion, threat of force, and unorthodox diplomacy he secured a remarkable growth in German territory and power. Without his actions, there would have been no war crisis in 1938.

As Germany mainly created the crisis, so the avoidance of war was largely the result of a German decision. At the last minute, Hitler held back from an invasion of Czechoslovakia. In this he was greatly assisted by Chamberlain, who pursued his negotiations with the utmost energy and tenacity, determined to ensure that Hitler should secure what he said he wanted: the cession of the Sudetenland. France too played an important part, virtually abandoning her alliance with the Czechs and pressing them to surrender. In the final stages, Mussolini played a role which no one else could have filled: as a fellow-dictator he was acceptable to Hitler as an intermediary, and as an ally he was willing to stage-manage the Munich conference to Germany's advantage. Finally, the Czech government held a last choice in its own hands. If the Czechs had been prepared to be bloody, bold, and resolute, refused the terms produced at either Berchtesgaden or Munich, and then fought in self-defence, they might well have brought war down upon Europe, as the Poles did the following year. Instead they yielded: Europe had a year's respite, and Prague remained intact when Warsaw lay in ruins.

In September 1938, everyone stepped back in the last resort from the act of war. Britain and France shrank from war for all sorts of general reasons which have been sufficiently discussed, and also because they were afraid that they would lose, or at least sustain such damage as to make the effort self-defeating. This fear arose largely from their view of German air power. General Vuillemin believed that the French Air Force would be defeated within a fortnight – a view which he urged upon Daladier on the eve of the Premier's departure for Munich. In Britain the Air Staff produced estimates in September 1938 which roughly doubled the size of the effective German bomber force (1,019 instead of 582).[10] The *Luftwaffe* thus won one of its greatest victories without going into action.

The reluctance of the Czechs to opt for almost certain suicide by triggering off a general war may be readily understood. It was Hitler's last-minute refusal to take the risk of war, and to opt instead for the lesser gain from a conference, which was surprising. Counsels of caution, both from the professional soldiers and from Goering, prevailed. Hitler later came to regret his decision, and was determined not to repeat it over Poland in 1939.

This was a warning for the future. In avoiding war over Czechoslovakia, both Germany and the western powers made it more certain the next time. There would certainly be a next time. After Munich, Germany was stronger than before in power and self-confidence. Unless the German advance was checked by some extraordinary display of self-restraint, which was not to be expected and was certainly not forthcoming, it would simply be resumed with greater impetus than before. If opposed, Hitler would go to war with all the more determination because he had not done so in September 1938. On the other hand, for Britain, and to a lesser degree for France also, Munich represented the limit of the policy of concession. Peace at any price was never the policy of Chamberlain or his Cabinet, whatever impression they may have given and whatever intentions may have been attributed to them. They would not buy peace at the price of German domination of Europe and the threat to British interests and independence which that implied, nor would they accept for ever methods of unrestrained subversion, bullying, and coercion. Hitler's claim that he sought only territory inhabited by German-speaking peoples was accepted, but was regarded as setting a limit in terms of both power and morality. When that limit was overstepped, British policy, and with it the European situation, would change.

REFERENCES AND NOTES

1. *Bulletin of International News*, vol. XIII, p. 747 (figures rounded to the nearest thousand).
2. Ibid., p. 749. The next highest vote was 1,177,000 for the Agrarian Party.
3. Keith Robbins, *Munich 1938* (London 1968), p. 210.
4. *DGFP*, series D, vol. II, no. 107.
5. Ibid., vol. I, no. 19, the 'Hossbach Memorandum', 10 November 1937. Widely differing views have been taken of the significance of this document, from total acceptance as a plan for aggressive war to denial of any importance at all. See William Carr, *Arms, Autarky and Aggression* (London 1972), pp. 72–5, for a clear summary of the arguments. I follow the view taken in Gerhard L. Weinberg, *The Foreign Policy of Hitler's Germany: starting World War II, 1937–1939* (London 1980), pp. 34–42. The validity of the available copy of the memorandum is shown by Beck's point-by-point comments on another copy, written on 12 November 1937. Both Beck's criticisms and the revision of the general war directive by the Armed Forces Office (7 December) show that the meeting was taken seriously. As Weinberg points out, those who were at the meeting

or immediately involved in its consequences did not discuss its significance. They either got on with carrying out Hitler's wishes, or (in the
case of Beck) disputed them. There was no question of them not matter-
ing. The conference did not produce a blueprint for war; but it was a
serious meeting with practical results.

6. David Dilks (ed.), *The Diary of Sir Alexander Cadogan, 1938–1945*
(London 1971), p. 63.

7. It is often argued that British (or at any rate Chamberlain's) hostility to
the Soviet Union caused the government to adopt a deliberate policy of
turning Germany eastward in the hope that the two totalitarian powers
would fight one another and allow Britain to watch from the side-lines.
There were indeed speculations along these lines by individuals, but
Chamberlain seems to have been insufficiently ruthless or devious to
pursue such a policy. Shortly after the end of the Czechoslovakian crisis,
the British devoted their best efforts to restricting German expansion in
eastern Europe, though without abating their suspicions of the USSR.

8. The Karlsbad demands were: (1) full equality of rights and status for the
German and Czech peoples; (2) recognition of the German population
as a legal entity; (3) recognition of a specific German territory; (4) full
autonomy for that territory; (5) legal protection for Germans living
outside it; (6) the removal of injustices imposed since 1918; (7) German
officials to administer German territory; (8) the right to profess and
disseminate the nazi world outlook.

9. *DGFP*, series D, vol. II, nos 175, 221.

10. Edward L. Homze, *Arming the Luftwaffe: the Reich Air Ministry and the
German aircraft industry, 1919–39* (Lincoln, Nebraska 1976), p. 241.

Chapter 15

DECISIONS FOR WAR, 1939

The immediate results of the Munich agreement were disastrous for Czechoslovakia. The provisions which might have mitigated its severity were disregarded: the international committee supervising the execution of the terms accepted the German claim that the Austrian census of 1910 should be the basis for their calculations, and 51 per cent German population in that year should constitute preponderance. Thus Germany secured as much territory as possible. Then the claims of Poland and Hungary had to be met. During the whole crisis, Poland had insisted on the same concessions being extended to the Polish population in Teschen as were made to the Sudeten Germans. On 21 and 27 September 1938 the Polish government demanded the cession of territory round Teschen, and backed this up with an ultimatum on the 30th. Polish troops occupied Teschen between 2 and 12 October. Hungary laid claim to a long strip of territory on the southern frontier of Czechoslovakia, and also the whole province of Ruthenia. On 2 November 1938 the Axis powers ruled on these claims in the Vienna Award, which allotted the southern strip to Hungary but left Ruthenia in Czechoslovakia.

While these territorial changes were taking place, the structure of the state was being transformed. In November a new federal system of government was set up, with autonomous administrations in Bohemia-Moravia, Slovakia, and Ruthenia. In Slovakia, the National Front rapidly became the only political party, while the Ukrainian Rada controlled Ruthenia. Only in Bohemia-Moravia did the vestiges of parliamentary democracy remain briefly in existence. In the new hyphenated state of Czecho-Slovakia, German influence was predominant. Hitler received the new Foreign Minister, Chvalkovsky, on 14 October, and told him bluntly that he would destroy his country in twenty-four hours if it did not follow the German line. The Slovak National Front was under German influence, and Ruthenia had a tight economic agreement with Germany. The Vienna Award of 2 November was made without consultation with France or Britain, and without protest or comment from them, which indicated with apparent finality that the western powers had abandoned all interest in Czecho-

Slovakia, and probably in eastern Europe as a whole. The balance of power in eastern Europe had tilted decisively in Germany's favour.

The price paid to secure the Munich agreement was a heavy one. What did Britain and France hope for in return? They certainly sought a respite in which to gather their strength, and both countries pressed on with rearmament. But for a short time Chamberlain hoped for much more. At a private meeting with Hitler after the Munich conference, he had secured a joint declaration expressing the desire of their two peoples never to go to war with one another again. He believed that the Czechoslovakian settlement opened the way for further agreements with Germany, and so for a wider European settlement, though precisely what practical steps could be taken in this direction was unclear. Cadogan suggested going back to the question of colonies, which were Germany's only avowed territorial aim and apparently the only issue still outstanding between the two countries. In view of Hitler's earlier lack of interest in the matter, this did not seem hopeful; and in any case the predominant opinion in the Foreign Office was that Hitler would not be content with his recent gains in Europe. At the least he was expected to extend German economic predominance in south-east Europe and the Baltic states, while one gloomy and far-sighted official argued that Germany and Italy, with their dynamic ideologies, were not normal states with specific grievances but predators who would greet every concession with fresh demands.

The hopes for a wider agreement with Germany lacked substance from the start, and by mid-November they had faded away altogether. Relations between Germany and Britain, so far from improving, worsened rapidly after Munich. As early as 9 October Hitler made a violently anti-British speech, followed by others denouncing Churchill and Eden as warmongers who might yet control British policy. Fierce anti-Jewish riots in Germany on 9–10 November brought universal condemnation in the British press, with equally strident reaction from Hitler against interference in Germany's internal affairs. On 14 November Halifax told the Foreign Policy Committee of the Cabinet that he had secret information that Hitler regarded the Munich agreement as a disaster because it had prevented a display of German strength. He now regarded Britain as Germany's worst enemy, was trying to break up the Anglo-French alliance, and was using Japan to harry Britain in the Far East. On 16 November Chamberlain explained to the Cabinet that the colonial question could only be dealt with as part of a general settlement, which was clearly impossible in existing circumstances.

There remained from the post-Munich optimism only the prospect of improving relations with Italy. The Anglo-Italian agreement on Mediterranean affairs of 16 April 1938 was brought into effect on 16 November. (This was supposed to await the departure of Italian troops from Spain, but partial withdrawal was taken to be sufficient.) Chamberlain and Halifax visited Mussolini in Rome on 11–14 January 1939. Mussolini liked being courted, but was not impressed by his visitors – 'These . . . are the tired sons of a long line of rich men, and they will lose their empire', he remarked.[1] Chamberlain came home pleased with his welcome, and convinced that there was no great sympathy between Mussolini and Hitler. There were no practical results.

The relief afforded by Munich was thus short-lived, and early in 1939 the British government found the prospects steadily more alarming. In January and February they received a series of disturbing reports predicting German moves against Memel, Poland, Czechoslovakia, or the Ukraine, and, in the west, against the Netherlands and possibly Switzerland. These last were taken very seriously, and had far-reaching consequences. On 1 February 1939 the Cabinet agreed that Britain must go to war if Germany invaded either Holland or Switzerland: the Netherlands would pose a direct threat to British security, and Switzerland would be an unmistakable signal of an attempt to dominate Europe by force. There were also reports from Rome of the secret call-up of reserve officers, and the accumulation of alarms caused Chamberlain to declare in the House of Commons on 6 February that ' . . . any threat to the vital interests of France from whatever quarter it came must evoke the immediate co-operation of Great Britain'.[2]

This was the firmest statement of support for France made by a British government for a very long time, and it was accompanied by a reversal of British attitudes towards a military commitment in Europe. On 1 February the Cabinet agreed to open detailed staff talks with France. The proposal was made on 3 February, the first round took place between 29 March and 4 April, and the discussions continued at frequent intervals thereafter. Even more important, a paper by the Chiefs of Staff on 20 February argued that British security was bound up with that of France, and that home defence might have to include taking a share in the defence of French territory. The Cabinet accepted this proposition, and with it the principle that in the event of war Britain should create a large, Continental-style arm. It was the end of the doctrine of limited liability.

British policy was thus in the process of change in February 1939. The previous assumption had been that Hitler's aims were limited. It was now believed that the next German move against another state would signify that their aim was the domination of Europe – the phrase recurred more than once in discussion and correspondence. There was not the slightest hesitation in deciding that any such attempt must be opposed. The countries about which there was immediate alarm were in western Europe, but once accepted, the principle held good for the Continent as a whole. The policy of 'appeasement' had never meant peace at any price, but the acceptance of limited German advances. If German aims in fact knew no limits, then the British government would resist them, by war if necessary. This change in view was already under way in February 1939, though it did not become publicly apparent until March.

French policy after Munich continued to be uncertain and ambiguous. On 6–7 December 1938 Ribbentrop went to Paris to sign a Franco-German declaration, similar to that produced by Chamberlain after Munich, vaguely aspiring to good relations and consultation. Ribbentrop later maintained that during this visit Bonnet had agreed that eastern Europe was a German sphere of influence. Bonnet consistently denied this; but whatever was said, all recent French actions pointed to the *de facto* acceptance of German predominance in eastern Europe. This acceptance, however, was not unconditional. France still maintained economic interests in the Balkans, and an economic mission visited Rumania, Yugoslavia, and Bulgaria in November 1938. There was a tacit assumption that German predominance in eastern Europe should be exercised with restraint. And in the background the army command believed that war with Germany was virtually certain, and Gamelin set out to make up the loss of thirty Czech divisions, preferably by securing a firm commitment from the British and persuading them to introduce conscription.

Towards Italy, French policy was much firmer. On 30 November 1938 there was an organized demonstration in the Italian Chamber, with chants of 'Tunis, Corsica, Nice, Jibuti'. Daladier replied with a firm declaration that France was determined to maintain all her territory; and in January 1939 he made well-publicized visits to Corsica and Tunisia. British persuasion to find some concessions to sweeten relations with Italy was firmly rejected; and while Daladier allowed an unofficial mission by Baudouin, a director of the Bank of Indo-China, to go to Rome, he declined to follow it up.

In the five months after Munich, and before what is often seen as the turning point of March 1939, the British government lost hope of a general agreement with Germany, and moved instead towards a determination to resist a German attempt to dominate Europe by force, and towards a new position of support for France. France, though internally divided and conscious of her weakness, was firm in opposition to Italian claims and still nurtured an underlying conviction that the growth of German power must at some time be checked. It was already clear by February 1939 that Britain and France would be unlikely to repeat the pattern of 1938.

The key question after Munich concerned German policy. Would Germany be content to digest her recent gains, or seek further expansion? There was no serious doubt as to the answer, either in the long term or the short. In October 1938 Goering, under Hitler's instructions, set out a new armaments programme, including the impossible aim of quintupling the *Luftwaffe* by spring 1942. The development of the army was pressed forward, and in January 1939 the large-scale 'Z plan' for the navy was agreed on, to be completed by 1943–44. These preparations were directed towards large-scale war in three or four years' time, with Britain as a principal enemy. In the short term, German policy pursued two aims: the annexation or subjection of the remnants of Czecho-Slovakia, and negotiations with Poland to bring her into dependence on Germany.

Hitler privately declared his intention of annexing the rump of Czechoslovakia almost as soon as the Munich agreement was signed, and plans for an unopposed military occupation began to be worked out on 10 October 1938 and were completed by the 21st. In the same month Goering assured visiting Slovak politicians of German support for an independent Slovakia. On 12 February 1939 Hitler met Béla Tuka, leader of the Slovak National Party, and told him that the Slovaks should declare independence at once. German pressure was also at work in Ruthenia. Of the purpose of German policy there was no doubt, though in the event the final stages of the break-up of Czecho-Slovakia came so quickly that they took Hitler by surprise. As with Austria, the actual timing of the German take-over was decided by the victim. On 6 March President Hacha of Czecho-Slovakia dismissed the government of Ruthenia; on the night of the 9th/10th he did the same to the Slovakian government; and on the 10th he proclaimed martial law.

This convulsive attempt to preserve the unity of the state in fact precipitated its downfall. Hitler acted quickly. He invited the deposed Slovak Premier, Tiso, to Berlin, with the clear intimation that refusal would be met by immediate German invasion. Tiso arrived in Berlin on 13 March, and was presented with a declaration of Slovak independence which he agreed to put to the Slovak Parliament. It was accepted on the 14th, despite the doubts of some deputies. The Czechs were dealt with immediately afterwards. On 12–13 March the German press was full of stories of Czech attacks on the Germans still living in Bohemia. The Czech President and Foreign Minister asked for a meeting with Hitler to beg him to spare the existence of their state. Hitler received them in the small hours of 15 March, and told them that the German Army would enter their country at 6 a.m. the same day. (In fact, some units crossed the border during the night.) Their only choice, he explained, was between resistance which would be crushed at once and a peaceable occupation. Goering threatened to bomb Prague. President Hacha broke down under the threats, and signed a paper placing the fate of the Czech people in Hitler's hands.

On 15 March German forces occupied Bohemia and Moravia. On the 16th the provinces were declared a Protectorate of Germany, with the former Foreign Minister, von Neurath, as Protector. The SS moved in, responsible not to Neurath but to Himmler in Germany, a provision which spoke volumes as to the true nature of the new regime.

The newly 'independent' Slovakia signed a treaty accepting German protection, including the stationing of German troops in the country. As for Ruthenia, Hitler disregarded an appeal for German protection and instead allowed Hungary to occupy the province, fulfilling an aspiration which Hungarian governments had cherished since 1919. The Hungarian Army moved in on 15 March.

The remains of the former state of Czechoslovakia were thus removed from the map in the space of two days, 14–15 March 1939. Shortly afterwards, on 23 March, Germany annexed Memel, a German city seized by Lithuania in the far-distant days of 1923. Orders to prepare for this had been issued on 21 October 1938, and in December local elections had played into the hands of the nazis. The German ethnic claim to Memel was strong and its absorption into Germany had long seemed likely; but the impact of the occupation was still considerable. All over eastern Europe the disputes stored up after the First World War were flaring up, and the states created in the post-war settlement were crumbling away.

Between Czecho-Slovakia and Memel lay Poland, the other major object of German policy in the winter of 1938–39. Germany and Poland were divided by historic enmity, and after 1919 German resentment against the very existence of an independent Poland was strong. The new frontiers of 1919 cut East Prussia off from the rest of Germany, and placed about 800,000 Germans in Poland. The Free City of Danzig was overwhelmingly German in population (96 per cent in 1919), and after 1933 its internal administration was run by the Nazi Party, which won a majority in the Volkstag; but its foreign relations and customs regulations were controlled by Poland. This was a complicated arrangement, liable to create friction even with goodwill on all sides, which was rarely forthcoming. More important, Danzig represented a fundamental issue: for Germany, it was a matter of historic right and a German population; for Poland, it was a guarantee of access to the sea and a symbol of security.

These difficulties between the two countries were to some extent kept within bounds by the German–Polish agreement of 1934. On a number of occasions, notably in 1935 and 1937, Germany held out to the Poles the prospect of developing this agreement into an alliance against the Soviet Union, by which Poland might acquire territory in the Ukraine. More than once Hitler told the Polish Ambassador in Berlin, Lipski, that European solidarity ended at the Polish–Soviet border, where both Asia and Bolshevism began. Despite a hearty dislike of Bolshevik Russia, the Poles did not take up these suggestions, preferring to retain their independent position between their two great neighbours.

Between October 1938 and January 1939 the Germans took the matter up again in a number of conversations between Hitler and Ribbentrop on the one side and Lipski and Beck on the other. On 24

October 1938 Ribbentrop put to Lipski proposals for a new German–Polish agreement. Danzig should be incorporated in Germany, and a German-controlled road and rail link with East Prussia be established – a corridor across the Corridor. In return, Germany would guarantee her frontier with Poland, and extend the 1934 Non-Aggression Pact for twenty-five years. Finally, Poland should join the Anti-Comintern Pact, signed between Germany and Japan in 1936 and extended to Italy in 1937.[3] In Warsaw, Beck at once saw the crucial nature of this last proposal. To adhere to the Anti-Comintern Pact would mean a breach with the Soviet Union and the end of Poland's balanced position. It would signify unqualified entry into the German camp, which would quickly lead to subordination to Germany. Beck ruled this out totally. When the Polish reply to Ribbentrop's proposals was eventually delivered on 19 November, it rejected the annexation of Danzig, referred evasively to consultations on the road and rail link, and did not even mention the Anti-Comintern Pact. Hitler himself then repeated the proposals when Beck visited Berlin on 5–6 January 1939. He emphasized that a strong Poland was a necessity for Germany because every Polish division engaged against the Soviet Union saved a German division. (This was presumably not encouraging from Beck's point of view.) Beck was non-committal in his comments. Again, on 26 January, Ribbentrop went to Warsaw and pressed for a decision, but without success.

The Poles would never agree to be absorbed into the German sphere of influence, even if the only alternative was to become Germany's next victim. Nazi Germany had encountered a new and surprising phenomenon: a neighbouring state which could not be bullied. The Poles, unlike the Austrians or the Czechs, would fight for their territory, their independence, and their honour. Beck put the matter thus to a meeting of senior officials in the Foreign Ministry on 24 March 1939. Poland had established 'a straight and clear line. . . . Below this line comes our Polish *non possumus*. This is clear: we will fight.' The line comprised the territory of Poland, but also any imposed solution over Danzig, because Danzig was a symbol, and Poland would not join those other states which allowed themselves to be dictated to. Hitler had not yet met determined opposition. 'The mighty have been humble to him, and the weak have capitulated in advance. The Germans are marching all across Europe with nine divisions; with such strength Poland would not be overcome.'[4] Such confidence was in military terms reckless, and Poland's moral position was rendered dubious by her recent seizure of Teschen from Czechoslovakia. But even if Polish judgement and morality were open to question, their courage was not; and from Polish courage and self-confidence there arose a crucial element in the European situation in 1939. Under pressure from Germany, Poland would fight rather than yield.

In mid-March 1939 there were thus two crises in Europe. One was open: the break-up of Czecho-Slovakia. The other was largely concealed: the German demands upon Poland. Then, in the course of a frantic fortnight, the effects of the Czech crisis rebounded upon the Polish crisis, and a new European situation took shape.

News of the German occupation of Prague and the break-up of Czecho-Slovakia reached London in the morning of 15 March. The first British reaction was one of passive acceptance. The Cabinet agreed that there was no possibility of effective opposition, and that the Munich guarantee would not be carried out. Chamberlain observed, accurately if cynically, that the state to which the guarantee had been given no longer existed. In the House of Commons he expressed his regret, but added: 'do not let us on that account be deflected from our course. Let us remember that the desire of all the peoples of the world still remains concentrated on the hopes of peace.'[5] Yet another extension of German power was apparently to be accepted with only token protest.

Two days later Chamberlain gave another speech, in Birmingham. He still defended Munich, and the hope behind it, that with goodwill and understanding it was possible to resolve differences by discussion. But then the tone changed.

> The events which have taken place this week in complete disregard of the principles laid down by the German government itself seem to fall into a different category, and they must cause us all to be asking ourselves: 'Is this the end of an old adventure, or is it the beginning of a new? Is this the last attack upon a small State, or is it to be followed by others? Is this, in fact, a step in the direction of an attempt to dominate the world by force? . . . No greater mistake could be made than to suppose that, because it believes war to be a senseless and cruel thing, this nation has so lost its fibre that it will not take part to the utmost of its power in resisting such a challenge if it ever were made.[6]

The change was remarkable. What brought it about?

Part of the answer was that the change had been coming for some time, with the alarms of January and February which had caused the government to strengthen its commitment to France. It was already assumed that the issue was becoming one of the domination of Europe by force, though this had not yet emerged in public. The reaction of 15 March was thus more a reflex repetition of old formulae, while that of the 17th reflected the thinking of the last two months. Partly, too, Chamberlain was jolted into his forceful speech by a number of events between the 15th and 17th. There was a marked shift of opinion in the Conservative Party and press: constituency parties expressed dismay at the Prime Minister's speech in the Commons, and even *The Times*, previously a pace-maker for appeasement, was indignant about the Prague coup. Halifax urged on Chamberlain both the party political problems and the likely collapse of Britain's position in Europe if the coup were meekly accepted. There was also a sudden scare over Rumania on 16–17 March, when the Rumanian Minister in London, Tilea, produced an alarming story of a German near-ultimatum to his country over a demand for a monopoly on exports. Halifax had just seen Tilea when he helped Chamberlain make changes to his speech on 17 March. By the next day the story had been denied by the Rumanian government, and was thought dubious by the British intelligence services, but by then it had had its effect – the atmosphere after Prague was such that any reports of German aggression were bound to be taken seriously.

All these influences played their part. But the major explanation of Chamberlain's speech at Birmingham is probably the simplest: it had sunk in that he had been deceived. Hitler had departed from his declared principle of claiming only territories with German populations. Moreover, the blow was very personal: Chamberlain regarded the Munich agreement as above all his own achievement, and its repudiation struck home all the harder. This was not merely a matter of vanity, but of something very stern in Chamberlain's character. Churchill, who for so long opposed Chamberlain's policy towards Germany, wrote rightly that Hitler had misjudged his man: 'He did not realise that Neville Chamberlain had a very hard core, and that he did not like being cheated.'[7]

On 18 March Chamberlain showed this hard core when he spoke to the Cabinet. Up to a week ago, he said, the government had believed it was possible to get on better terms with the dictatorships, whose aims were believed to be limited. He had now concluded that Hitler's attitude made this impossible. 'No reliance could be placed on any of the assurances given by the Nazi leaders.' His speech at Birmingham was a challenge to Germany as to whether or not she intended to dominate Europe by force. In this explanation, he struck two notes which were to characterize British policy for the next twelve months and more: resistance to German domination of Europe, and the conviction that Hitler could no longer be trusted. The first represented a long-standing principle in British foreign policy, going back to the wars against Louis XIV. The second was a largely instinctive reaction, belated but profound, against the methods and tactics of the nazi regime, and of Hitler in particular. In this way the issues were simplified and personalized in a way which corresponded to an increasing feeling among the British people: something must be done to stop Hitler. During the next few days, and equally in the next few months, there was much in British policy that was hurried, muddled, and ill-conceived. Hope persisted that Germany would not go to war, and that some agreement might yet be reached. But if the worst came to the worst, the British would fight.

Principles and instincts were one thing; what to do was quite another. All attention was concentrated on eastern Europe, where it was not normally thought necessary for Britain to be involved. As the Rumanian scare died away, Poland seemed the most likely victim for the next German move, for which the pretexts in Danzig and the German minority were ready-made. The British also suffered from an acute, though hidden, fear that Poland might succumb to German influence: Beck had visited Berlin in January, and negotiations were known to be under way, which might well, so far as the British knew, succeed. To counter these dangers, some urgent British action seemed required. The first response, on 20 March, was a device which required only a low level of commitment: a proposal that Britain, France, Poland, and the Soviet Union should issue a joint declaration that if there were a threat to the independence of any European state they would consult immediately on the steps to be taken. This was unacceptable to the Poles, who refused any alignment with the USSR just as resolutely as they refused an alliance with Germany. In any case, it was too indefinite to meet the exigencies of the situation.

Something more definite was required, and the government considered the far-reaching step of a guarantee to Poland. Halifax put the arguments to the Foreign Policy Committee of Cabinet on 27 March:

> We were faced with the dilemma of doing nothing, or entering into a devastating war. If we did nothing this in itself would mean a great accession to Germany's strength and a great loss to ourselves of sympathy and support in the United States, in the Balkan countries, and in other parts of the world. In those circumstances if we had to choose between two great evils he favoured our going to war.

Chamberlain said specifically that if Poland declined to accept a conditional guarantee, 'we should be prepared to give her the unilateral assurance as regards the Eastern Front seeing that our object is to check and defeat Germany's attempt at world domination'.[8] The argument was clear and emphatic: to secure Britain's position in the world, and to check the German advance, there must be a firm guarantee to Poland, even at the risk of war. That there occurred at this point another scare of an imminent German attack on Poland hastened Britain into action, but did not fundamentally alter the position.

On 30 March Britain offered Poland a guarantee of her independence, which was at once accepted. Before it was announced, the Foreign Policy Committee considered but rejected a suggestion that it should be limited to cases of unprovoked aggression. It was thought that German techniques of aggression were such that Poland might be driven in self-defence to some action which could be construed as provocative: German tactics in Austria and Czechoslovakia had left their mark.

Chamberlain announced in the House of Commons on 31 March that, while consultations were going on with other governments:

In order to make perfectly clear the position of His Majesty's Government in the meantime before those consultations are concluded, I now have to iniorm the House that, during that period, in the event of any action which clearly threatened Polish independence, and which the Polish Government accordingly considered it vital to resist with their national forces, His Majesty's Government would feel themselves bound at once to lend the Polish ʿovernment all support in their power.[9]

The French government joined in this guarantee.

The precise significance of the guarantee has been much debated. It referred to Polish independence, not integrity, and thus left open the possibility of frontier changes; and in consequence it has been regarded as little more than appeasement under another name, with every chance of another Munich. On the other hand, it has been seen as making war virtu..lly inevitable, by throwing down a challenge which Germany was bound to take up. Its real significance lay between these two extremes, and was publicly explained by Chamberlain on 19 May. Britain was trying to create 'an assurance against forcible aggression, which may not, and we hope never will, arise'; or, in another phrase 'a peace front against aggression' which would avoid the outbreak of war.[10] The guarantee was designed as a deterrent, and if the deterrent worked, the guarantee would not have to be carried out. The trouble with this concept was that, after a prolonged series of concessions to Germany, the guarantee in itself carried little conviction and was an inadequate deterrent. Only the most determined military preparations by Britain and France (the introduction of conscription in Britain, and rapid supplies for the Polish Army and Air Force) might have conveyed a sufficient warning to check Hitler in his stride. As it was, the guarantee was enough to bring Britain and France into a war over Poland, but not enough to deter Hitler from launching one.

This weakness was demonstrated by the half-hearted way in which the guarantee was followed up. Beck visited London on 4–6 April, and offered to transform the one-sided guarantee into an Anglo-Polish alliance, but the r ʾgotiations on terms then dragged on until the end of August. At the en.. of April Poland asked Britain for a loan of £60 m. to purchase military equipment. The British offered a loan of £5 m. as long as France did the same, plus £8 m. in export credit guarantees – by July, only the latter had been agreed on. A British service mission went to Poland in May, and General Ironside, Inspector-General of Overseas Forces, followed in July; but nothing was done to follow up these contacts. The French behaved in a similar fashion. In May a draft agreement was prepared to bring the existing Franco-Polish alliance into line with the nev guarantee, but the signature of this agreement was delayed until 4 September. There were staff conversations in Paris on 15–17 May, and agreement was reached that in the event of a German attack on Poland or Danzig the bulk of the French Army would begin offensive action on the fifteenth day of hostilities. But Gamelin held that this agreement was subject to the conclusion of a political agreement – which was held up. The truth was, of course, as the French staff had just told their British counterparts, that France could not envisage a serious land attack on Germany without long preparation. The Poles were well enough informed to know this, and if they were deceived they closed their eyes to the deception. But the major point, for Britain and France alike, was that these were not the actions of states preparing urgently for certain war. The British and French both hoped that gestures of deterrence would suffice. They would not.

On 7 April 1939 Italy enlarged the area of tension by landing substantial forces to occupy Albania. This country had long been under Italian political and economic influence, and in some circumstances the action might have been seen as little more than consolidation. But three weeks after the Prague coup and a fortnight after the German occupation of Memel, with the air full of rumours of war, the event assumed a very different aspect. It indicated a degree of co-ordination between Germany and Italian plans far greater than was actually the case. It was a palpable breach of the Anglo-Italian agreement of April 1938, brought into operation only the previous November. It was accompanied by reports of an imminent Italian assault on the Greek island of Corfu. Altogether the situation was highly alarming, and not for the first time Mussolini had thrown in Italy's comparatively modest weight at a moment when it carried maximum significance.

The British and French response was far-reaching. British attention was fixed on Greece, while France insisted on extending any guarantees to Rumania, not because it was under threat from Italy but because it had been left out earlier. On 13 April Britain and France issued public guarantees to both Greece and Rumania, in the same terms as that to Poland. They thus extended their commitments in eastern Europe with astonishing prodigality. In the space of a fortnight (31 March–13 April) they had undertaken obligations in an area stretching from the Baltic to the Mediterranean, most of which they had apparently abandoned only a few months before. On the other side, Italy had taken a step towards war in the Mediterranean. The logical consequence was a tightening of links with Germany, and negotiations for an alliance were taken up in April 1939.

Vital lines had been drawn. German and Italian advances in Czecho-Slovakia, Memel, and Albania, accompanied by alarms about Holland, Switzerland, Rumania, Poland, and Greece, had pushed Britain and France into crucial commitments. In western Europe, they would certainly fight in the event of any German or Italian attack. In the east, they staked all on deterring Germany (and to a lesser degree Italy) from any further advance, in the hope that in the time thus gained the immediate problems might yet be resolved. If deterrence failed, here too they were committed to war. It was quite certain that the Poles at any rate would not let them out by yielding to German pressure.

The principal question, therefore, was whether Germany would be deterred. There was no sign that she would. On 3 April, four days after the British guarantee to Poland, a directive by Keitel instructed the German armed forces to prepare for an attack on that country at any time from 1 September. On 6 April the negotiations with Poland which had been going on since the previous October were broken off. In the directive for Operation White (11 April), Hitler emphasized that Poland was to be isolated before being attacked. On 23 May Hitler addressed the service commanders, partly on the long-term armaments programme, still aimed at completion by 1943–44, and partly about Poland. The real objective was not Danzig, but to secure living space and food supplies. There would certainly be war: 'We cannot expect a repetition of Czechia. There will be war.' Poland was to be isolated, and war with Britain and France avoided; though Britain, as Germany's main enemy, would have to be fought sooner or later.[11]

Preparations for an attack on Poland thus went ahead with the utmost speed. German diplomacy worked intensively to secure the help, or at least the neutrality, of small states which were politically or economically important in preparing for war: Sweden, Hungary, Rumania, Yugoslavia, Bulgaria, Turkey; and achieved much success. Among the great powers, Germany had worked in 1938 to create a triple alliance with Italy and Japan, which would paralyse Britain by pressure in Europe, the Mediterranean, and the Far East. Japan proved recalcitrant, insisting on an agreement directed solely against the Soviet Union, while Germany wanted it to be against all other powers; and in 1939 the Germans went instead for an alliance with Italy alone. After a rapid negotiation, the so-called Pact of Steel was signed in Berlin on 22 May. This alliance was not even nominally defensive in its terms, and represented a virtually complete Italian acceptance of a German draft. Ciano stressed in discussion that war should not break out before 1943, because Italy was not ready; but Ribbentrop was evasive on this point, and the text made no reference to the question at all. Germany secured the Italian alliance while retaining entire freedom of action.

With Italy secure (at least on paper), Germany moved to the next stage in the isolation of Poland and the undermining of the Anglo-French position by bidding for an agreement with the Soviet Union; but that belongs to a later stage in the narrative. Meanwhile, in May

1939 the German course was set for war with Poland, and its momentum was unchecked. The Anglo-French guarantees were failing to deter.

If anything was to add to their power, it would have to be the support of the Soviet Union. A firm military alliance between France, Britain, and the USSR offered the best, and perhaps the only, chance of confronting Hitler with circumstances in which he would not risk war. The negotiations for such an alliance between April and August 1939 therefore assumed a crucial importance. Their main lines were simple, though the details were sometimes complicated. The three powers started in April from widely different positions. Britain proposed that each should give separate, unilateral guarantees to Poland and Rumania. France suggested a Franco-Soviet treaty, binding both to go to the assistance of Poland and Rumania. The Soviet Union proposed (18 April) a three-power treaty of mutual assistance, binding all three to go to the help of the states on the eastern border of the USSR, and accompanied by a military convention. In the following months, the French moved with increasing urgency, and the British with painful slowness, towards the Soviet position, which the Soviets maintained, with the occasional addition of further demands.

The British began by rejecting the idea of a three-power treaty (8 May), and then accepted it in principle (24 May) – when it was at once agreed by France. The negotiations which followed encountered several obstacles. The British sought to introduce into the proposed treaty a reference to the moribund League of Nations, to which the Soviets successfully objected. There was dispute as to which states should be nominated for assistance, and whether they should be named publicly. It was eventually agreed to name, in a secret protocol, Finland, Estonia, Latvia, Poland, Rumania, Turkey, and Belgium; the USSR refused to include Holland and Switzerland. The British wished to conclude a political agreement first, and then proceed to a military convention; the Soviets insisted that the two should be signed and come into force simultaneously, and they gained their point. Finally, there was a problem over the definition of 'indirect aggression'. All agreed that states should be protected, not only against armed invasion, but against subversion and pressure on the Austrian model; but the British jibbed at granting the Soviets freedom to intervene in neighbouring states on conditions which the, hemselves laid down. No agreement had been reached on this matter when negotiations were broken off.

Such was the pattern of the political negotiations. It was not until 23 July that the British accepted that military talks should begin with a view to simultaneous signature of political and military agreements. The French nominated their delegation on the 24th, the British after a further ten days. The delegations then travelled to Moscow by ship and train, rather than by air. The French were instructed to secure the signature of a military convention in the minimum of time, the British to proceed slowly. Neither delegation was at first armed with plenipotentiary powers. Neither was over-eager to trust the Soviet General Staff with confidential military information, and so they sought to keep discussion on the plane of general principles, while the Soviets wanted to talk about precise intentions. The talks got off to a foreseeably difficult start, and rapidly came to a halt when the head of the Soviet delegation, Marshal Voroshilov, asked on 13 August whether Poland would accept the entry of Soviet troops before the event of a German attack. The Poles would not; and they declined to budge, despite urgent French persuasion, explaining simply that if the Red Army entered Polish territory it would stay there. In desperation, the French government on 21 August instructed its military delegation to agree that Soviet forces might enter Poland. Voroshilov asked whether Polish agreement had been secured. The answer could only be no, and the talks broke down.

Meanwhile, a parallel negotiation was in progress between Germany and the Soviet Union. This too moved slowly, until the final phase, when it suddenly careered along like an express train to a successful conclusion. The early stages of the German–Soviet *rapprochement* remain in some obscurity. On 10 March 1939 Stalin indicated to the Eighteenth Party Congress that he had no preference for either of the opposing blocs among the capitalist states; and it may be that Hitler responded to this hint when he handed Ruthenia to the Hungarians instead of occupying it himself, thus signalling that he did not intend to use the weapon of Ukrainian nationalism against the Soviet Union. If so, this diplomacy by sign-language led nowhere for some time.

The first definite move appears to have come from the Soviet side. On 17 April the Soviet Ambassador in Berlin told the permanent head of the German Foreign Ministry, Weizsaecker, that there was no reason why relations between their two countries should not be put on a normal footing and even improve further. On 3 May Litvinov, the Soviet Foreign Minister who had been associated with a policy of collective security against Germany, and was also a Jew, was removed from office and replaced by Molotov. At once the German press ceased its routine attacks on the Soviet Union and Bolshevism. On 30 May the Germans decided to reopen negotiations for an economic agreement, which had been tried without success earlier in the year. These continued into July, with no sign of haste on either side. The Germans then began to make the running, and switched the emphasis to political questions; at the end of July, Hitler and Ribbentrop prepared outline proposals for an agreement based on the partition of Poland and the Baltic states. As August went on, the Germans grew desperate. Hitler was then working to a deadline of 26 August for his attack on Poland (which was later changed), and needed an agreement before that date. On 12 August, under German pressure, the Soviets indicated that they were ready for political negotiations, to take place in Moscow. On 19 August an economic agreement was signed, and Molotov agreed to receive a visit by Ribbentrop on the 26th or 27th. This would not do, and on the 21st Hitler sent a personal message to Stalin that Ribbentrop must arrive in Moscow on the 23rd at the latest. This amounted to an ultimatum, and Stalin agreed within two hours.

Ribbentrop duly arrived, and on 23 August a non-aggression pact between Germany and the Soviet Union was signed. If either became involved in war, the other would give no help to the enemy; nor would either join any group directed against the other. A clause, customary in such treaties, allowing withdrawal if one signatory attacked a third country, was omitted; and the pact was to come into effect immediately upon signature. This allowed for the German attack on Poland which was by then imminent.

The published treaty was accompanied by a secret protocol providing, in the event of what was referred to as a territorial transformation taking place in Poland, for the partition of that country along the line of the rivers Pisa, Narew, Vistula, and San. This allocated to the Soviet Union all the Byelorussian and Ukrainian provinces of Poland, as well as the province of Lublin and part of that of Warsaw. Germany was to take the western part of the country, though the possibility of retaining a small remnant of a Polish state was kept open at this stage. Elsewhere, the USSR was to have a free hand in Finland, Estonia, and Latvia; and Germany in Lithuania. In Rumania, Soviet interest in the province of Bessarabia was recognized by Germany. Other Balkan matters were left vague.[12] Some of these territorial provisions were to be altered later, and important economic arrangements were also to follow.

The Nazi–Soviet Pact ended the Anglo-Franco-Soviet negotiations, and removed all possibility of a triple alliance which might have been strong enough to deter Hitler from an attack on Poland. In asking why one set of negotiations failed and the other succeeded, the two must be taken together.

In terms of method, the British conduct of their negotiations was so slow and inept as to invite failure. The French tried hard but without success to instil a sense of urgency. Behind the British attitude lay their long-standing distrust of the Soviet Union and Bolshevism, sentiments which were particularly strong in Chamberlain himself, who in May was virtually coerced by his Cabinet to take up negotiations for an alliance. The British were unconvinced of the value of a Soviet alliance in the aftermath of the purges, which had gravely weakened the Red Army. Moreover, they were rightly afraid that such an alliance would alienate most of the states in eastern Europe, and perhaps drive them into the arms of Germany: if they were to be eaten by the one or the other, most preferred to take their chance with Germany rather than the USSR. Above all, Poland would not enter an alliance with the Soviet Union at any price. When the British committed themselves to Poland, they to all intents and purposes ruled out an alliance with the USSR unless they threw the Poles overboard first. All this led the British to try to get the advantages of negotiations without the onus of an alliance, and to hope that Germany would be impressed by mere display. This was an illusion which the French, alarmed by news of German military preparations, did not share.

Delaying tactics were not the monopoly of the British, and the Soviets played the same game when it suited them. The Deputy Foreign Minister, Potemkin, was due to attend the Council of the League at Geneva on 15 May, and there to meet Halifax; he did not do so, even though the meeting was deferred until the 21st to suit his arrangements. In the military talks, if somehow the French could have done the impossible and delivered Polish acceptance of the Red Army, another condition about naval operations in the Baltic was ready to be produced. In their tactics, the Soviets were much assisted by good intelligence – it is likely that they knew of the main British negotiating positions before they were put forward, and they certainly knew of Hitler's timetable for war in August.

So much for methods and tactics; but the key to success and failure lay in the substance of the negotiations. The Soviets held a central position, and could judge which set of talks would better serve their interests. It is reasonable to assume that these were twofold: to keep out of a European war, especially when they were actually engaged in serious fighting with the Japanese in the Far East – they did not seek a war on two fronts; and to secure territory and a sphere of influence which would add to Soviet security, internal as well as external – it was advantageous to bring the Ukrainians in Poland under Stalin's control. The British and French offered nothing substantial under either heading. An alliance with them *might* deter Germany from going to war, but if it did not would certainly involve the Soviet Union in conflict at once. The British were not prepared to pay the price for this risk, and accept that the band of states from Finland to Rumania should become a Soviet sphere of influence. In 1938 they had sacrificed Czechoslovakia to Germany, but in 1939 they had too recently taken up the stance of guarantor of small states to hand over a whole batch to the Soviet Union. It is true that necessity knows no law, but in this case the necessity was not thought sufficiently pressing. Only the French were finally willing to pay part of the price, and offer to sacrifice the Poles; but the Poles proved unwilling victims, and in any case it was too late.

The Germans on the other hand were able to meet both Soviet interests. Instead of a risk of war, they could offer certain neutrality. In terms of territory and spheres of influence, they came bearing gifts, ready to carve up Poland and to yield at once when Stalin asked for the whole of Latvia to be in his sphere instead of only a part, as Ribbentrop at first proposed. Moreover, the Germans could deliver the goods forthwith, whereas the British and French could deliver nothing.

Beween the two sides, the Soviet choice could scarcely be in doubt. It is only surprising that so much obloquy has been heaped upon Stalin's head for making the best deal that he could get, and that so much criticism has been levelled at the British for their dilatoriness when nothing could have enabled them to match the German offers. The competition was decided on substance, not on method.

The Nazi–Soviet Pact was a decisive event. The Anglo-French deterrent against Germany, feeble from the start, was now completely undermined. The way was open for a German attack on Poland, for which preparations were being pressed ahead at breakneck speed. The haste with which the German negotiations with the Soviet Union were conducted showed the intense urgency of men working to a deadline. The invasion of Poland had to be launched before the autumn rains. On 14 August Hitler told senior officers that he meant to deal with Poland in a quick war. He was sure even then that the Soviets would stand aside, and he did not think that the British would fight; if they and the French did intervene, Germany would stand on the defensive in the west. On 22 August he addressed another conference of senior commanders in particularly brutal terms. The aim of the war against Poland was not to reach certain lines but the wholesale destruction of Poland.

Hitler confirmed in the afternoon of 25 August that the attack was to begin at 4.30 a.m. on the 26th, after propaganda preparations which were no longer thought to be important – no one would question the victors. At that point, he was surprised by two developments. Britain and Poland, undeterred by the Nazi–Soviet Pact, signed a treaty of alliance; and Mussolini went back on his obligations and announced that Italy would not go to war. In desperate haste, the orders for invasion were countermanded during the night of the 25th/26th. However, this was not cancellation but postponement: Hitler's aim was to gain a little time to detach Britain from Poland. On 25 August he made an extraordinary proposal to the British for a general settlement, and even an alliance, after the Polish problem was solved. But by now this overture was recognized by the British Cabinet as merely a divisive ploy, and it was disregarded. In the event, the German delay was only short. The last possible date to start the invasion of Poland in order to finish the campaign in good weather was set at 2 September, and Hitler did not wait until then. At 6.30 a.m. on 31 August the order was issued for attack on 1 September, to be carried through even if war with France and Britain resulted. The offensive opened at 4.45 a.m. on 1 September 1939.

Hitler was a man in a hurry, and was determined on war with Poland to a timetable which he set himself. The six-day delay from 26 August to 1 September was no more than a pause. Ciano grasped the reality of the situation when he met Ribbentrop at Salzburg on 11–12 August: the decision for war was certain, and the Germans would fight even if they were offered more than they asked for. What lay behind this driving haste? In personal terms, Hitler was much exercised by fear of an early death, whether by disease or assassination, and the necessity to accomplish his aims before he was struck down. Economic pressures were strong: the vicious circle in which armaments were built up to make conquests and then more conquests were necessary to expand armaments reached an explosive stage in 1939, when raw materials, labour, and food were all needed to sustain the pace. An economic agreement with the Soviet Union would do much to help; but so would war, not least by striking terror among those, like the Rumanians, who were being recalcitrant under other forms of pressure. The military situation was favourable, particularly in the air, so that even a general war could be risked. Hitler banked heavily on air power, and while the *Luftwaffe* of 1939 had serious limitations, and was still being built up for a general war in 1942, it was far superior to any other air force. Hitler drew his main impressions of air power from the ebullient Goering, and may well have been unaware of the *Luftwaffe*'s weaknesses; but even if he knew of them there was still a lead which offered an opportunity for war in favourable circumstances which might not recur.

For all these reasons Hitler pressed on towards war with Poland. He expected the British and French to remain neutral, and was momentarily shaken when the British stood firmly by their commitment to Poland, so that he found himself on the brink of a general war instead of the anticipated single combat with the Poles. His plan to isolate Poland, which seemed to have gone well, misfired at the last moment. But even this had to some extent been discounted in advance, and provision had been made for a defensive posture in the west. Hitler was set on war with Poland, and the only way in which such a war might have been avoided was for the Poles suddenly to cave in and accept all German demands without fighting. Polish determination was such that this was virtually impossible; and in any case there were indications that this time Hitler would not allow any peacemaker to deprive him of his war. A German–Polish war was as certain as anything can be in human affairs. Hitler was also prepared to risk war with the western powers, though this might have been avoided if Britain and France, contrary to their undertakings, had chosen to abandon Poland to her fate. Despite some appearances to the contrary, that was highly unlikely.

During the evening of 25 August some senior British officers were canvassing the odds for and against war. Lord Gort offered 5 to 4 against, and General Ironside 5 to 1 on. Neither was anywhere near right. The odds on war were by then overwhelming. It is true that there were flurries of last-minute activity. On 29 August Germany demanded that a Polish representative should come to Berlin within twenty-four hours to receive German terms relating to Danzig and the Corridor. A document setting out the German demands was prepared on 30 August. It comprised sixteen points, including the annexation of Danzig by Germany, a corridor across the Corridor, a plebiscite in the Corridor area to be held in twelve months' time, and a later exchange of populations. The port of Gdynia was to be recognized as Polish, thus leaving Poland with access to the sea. The substance of this was of little importance: it was never intended to be accepted, and it was not put to the Polish Ambassador until 1 September, when it was too late. It was intended to drive a wedge between Britain and Poland by demonstrating German reasonableness.

Nothing came of these proposals. The British were willing to go part-way down this road: Halifax thought there was something in the idea of an exchange of populations, and Chamberlain at one point thought mistakenly that the Poles might accept the annexation of Danzig by Germany. But the Poles had no intention of following the examples of Schuschnigg and Hacha and accepting a summons to be bullied by Hitler, and on this occasion the British did not try to coerce them to do so. In marked contrast with their conduct in 1938, the British did not apply to Beck the sort of pressure which they had brought to bear upon Benes.

There were other last-minute attempts at peacemaking. A Swedish businessman, Dahlerus, busied himself between Berlin and London, but he was no more than 'a fly which thinks it can stop the wheel'.[13] Probably the greatest significance of his activities was to confirm Hitler in his belief that the British would still give way. On 31 August Mussolini tried his hand and proposed a conference, to be held on 5 September; but in contrast to 1938 his role as peacemaker was no longer in the script. He persisted with the proposal even after the German attack on Poland had begun, and had some success with Bonnet; but the British insisted that a precondition for a conference must be the withdrawal of German forces from Poland, which was inconceivable.

The only significant question in these manoeuvres did not concern war between Germany and Poland, which was certain. It was whether Britain and France would stand by Poland. At the time, and for a long time afterwards, such was the suspicion that gathered round the motives and personality of Chamberlain that it was widely believed that he sought another Munich at the expense of Poland, and that he was propelled into war only by the wrath of the House of Commons. It is true that in July 1939 there were secret conversations in London between Wohlthat, an official of the German Economics Ministry, and British officials, including Sir Horace Wilson, who was a close confidant of the Prime Minister. These talks sought to revive the idea of a general Anglo-German settlement, and referred to the possibility of a peaceful settlement of the Danzig question. However, they were not pursued. It is also true that Chamberlain hoped to the last for peace, and that there was a long delay between the German attack on Poland and the British declaration of war, which seemed to indicate an attempt to evade British commitments. On 2 September, a day and a half after the German assault began, Britain had still not declared war or even sent an ultimatum to Berlin. The anger of the House of Commons broke round Chamberlain's head that evening, and even government ministers expressed their dismay in private. But the reason for the delay was not a search for another Munich, but the unavowable one of trying to keep in step with the French in going to war.

In France, Daladier had asked the Permanent Committee for National Defence on 23 August whether they could stand by and watch the disappearance of Poland and Rumania. The committee, made up of senior ministers and service chiefs, agreed that they could not. The French government as a whole did not move from this stance during the days that followed. They were certain that Britain intended to stand by her guarantee to Poland, and therefore that to negotiate with Germany would mean acting alone, which was out of the question. France had finally come to the end of the line of concessions, and had virtually no choice but to fight. A French fascist newspaper might ask rhetorically whether Frenchmen should die for Danzig, but the government knew that Danzig was not the issue. The choice, as Gamelin said, was between going to war now, at the side of Poland, and being attacked later when Poland had been eliminated. Bonnet, indeed, thought otherwise, and tried to pursue Mussolini's idea of a conference, asking as late as 3 September whether the Germans would not make a merely symbolic partial withdrawal in Poland and so allow the meeting to take place. But Bonnet's attitude was not widely shared. The Council of Ministers, meeting on 31 August, was firm in its support for Poland, and general mobilization was ordered on 1 September. The high command, however, was anxious to complete the process of mobilization before declaring war, and it was a combination of this desire with Bonnet's last-minute stalling in the hope of a conference which caused delay in a French declaration.

The hesitations on both sides of the Channel were only superficial. Both governments, however reluctantly, knew that they had no choice. The long line of concessions to Germany had come to an end, and they could go no further. On 3 September 1939 both Britain and France declared war on Germany, though they did not manage to do so together: the British declaration was at 11 a.m., the French at 5 p.m.

For the Poles, who had fought alone for two and a half days, this was rather late, but none the less welcome for that. Crowds took flowers to the British and French embassies in Warsaw – the only echo of the enthusiasm with which some had greeted the coming of war in 1914. Everywhere else, the mood was one of silent resignation. Even in Germany, where nazi propaganda had been hard at work on warlike themes for several years, the streets were quiet. Yet this resignation was accompanied by a profound determination. In France, the most commonly heard remark was 'Il faut en finir' – We've got to finish with it. In Britain, replies to a Gallup Poll question at the end of September showed 89 per cent in favour of fighting until Hitlerism was done away with – a remarkable figure, though the wording was vague. In Germany, events were to show that people would sustain the conflict with the utmost tenacity, in defeat as well as in victory. The war was nowhere welcome or popular in any gaudy or flag-waving sense, but it was widely felt to be inevitable. Countries where many still remembered the last great war accepted the burdens of another with something akin to fatalism.

War became increasingly inevitable as 1939 went on, and when it came it was a surprise to hardly anyone. It could only have been avoided in one of three ways. First, Germany might have chosen to settle for her gains of 1938 in Austria and Sudetenland, consolidate her new position, and allow Europe a period of calm, or at least of respite. Second, if Germany chose otherwise and continued to press for expansion (which was what happened) then her potential opponents in France, Poland, Britain, and the USSR might have combined together in a coalition so formidable and forbidding that Germany would have been deterred from further adventures by fear of the consequences. Peace might thus have been preserved by threats and the deployment of superior force. Third, those same potential opponents, individually or together, might have decided to accept German expansion, yield with as much grace as possible, and get the best terms they could for themselves. War might thus have been avoided by acquiescence in German demands. In the event, none of these things came about. Germany pressed on. The grand alliance against her never materialized. The Soviet Union struck a bargain with Germany, but Poland, Britain, and France did not. War was expected, and war came.

REFERENCES AND NOTES

1. *Ciano's Diary, 1939–1943* (London 1947), p. 10.
2. *House of Commons Debates*, 5th series, vol. 343, col. 623.
3. The Anti-Comintern Pact (November 1936) provided in its public clauses for co-operation against Comintern and its agents. A secret protocol bound the signatories not to sign any political treaty with the USSR.
4. W. Jedrzejewicz (ed.), *Diplomat in Berlin, 1933–1939: Josef Lipski*

(New York 1968), pp. 503–4.
5.   *House of Commons Debates*, 5th series, vol. 345, cols 437–40.
6.   Quoted in Roger Parkinson, *Peace for our Time* (London 1971), p. 116.
7.   W. S. Churchill, *The Second World War*, vol, I (London 1948), p. 269.
8.   Both quoted in Simon Newman, *March 1939: The British Guarantee to Poland* (Oxford 1976), pp. 152–3.
9.   *House of Commons Debates*, 5th series, vol. 345, col. 2415.
10. Ibid., vol. 347, cols 1833, 1839.
11. *DGFP*, series D, vol. VI, no. 433.
12. Ibid., vol. VII, nos 228 (Treaty), 229 (Secret Protocol).
13. L. B. Namier, *Diplomatic Prelude* (London 1950), p. 417.

Chapter 16

THE EXPANDING WAR, 1939–1940

Accounts of the origins of the Second World War in Europe usually end with the German invasion of Poland and the British and French declarations of war on Germany at the beginning of September 1939. Later developments are treated as being simply consequent upon these events, or as part of the war and therefore separate from its origins. This mode of presentation focuses attention sharply on the Polish–German conflict and the British and French reactions to it; and in this perspective theories of a European war arising largely by accident assume considerable plausibility. True, there was nothing accidental about Hitler's attack on Poland, which he pursued with single-minded determination. But when he began that war, he did not expect Britain and France to join in, and when they did so he found himself in a wider war at a time and in circumstances which he had not envisaged, and well before German military preparations for a general war were complete.

For the events of 1–3 September 1939, this interpretation holds good. But to narrow the focus of our attention in this way is misleading. In the simplest geographical sense, the four powers which went to war in September 1939 made up only a part of Europe and a minority of its population. Moreover, it seemed likely for a time that the conflict would remain localized between Germany and Poland, with Britain and France as little more than spectators, striking belligerent attitudes but abstaining from serious fighting. If this situation had persisted, then the events would not have constituted a Second World War, or indeed a European war of any significance. They might well have passed as a War of Polish Partition, another brief if bloody passage in the troubled history of eastern Europe. There was a long way to go before it became clear that there was indeed to be a major European war, with world-wide connotations. The question of why the German–Polish War was followed by other conflicts, merging to become what we call the Second World War, is a necessary part of our enquiry.

To end the story in September 1939 is to assume that Hitler's attack on Poland revealed the essence of his ambitions, rather than being an episode (albeit an important one) in a long process of German expansion. To stop in 1939 is to endow the actions of Britain and France with a greater and more active role in the coming of war than they actually deserve. The British and French declarations of war have given the date of 3 September 1939 a symbolic significance, but they represented only a brief seizure of the initiative by states which for the most part responded to the pressure of others. In Italian policy, abstention from the conflict of September 1939 was an isolated and uncharacteristic part of the whole story, which can only be fully understood if we take up the thread and follow it through to the events of 1940. In the vital matter of German–Soviet relations the events of August and September 1939 marked only a temporary halting-place; and the greatest single issue in European politics remained in suspense until the German attack on the Soviet Union in June 1941. In all these ways, to bring down the final curtain in September 1939 is to leave the play without its last act and its denouement.

There is another reason for pressing on with the enquiry. It is only between late 1939 and 1941 that it becomes possible to apply the test of events to the questions we have already raised about Germany's motives and intentions, which are crucial to any interpretation of the origins of the war. What sort of wars did the Germans wage, and what use did they make of their victories? This test is not infallible, because intentions are rarely carried out to the letter, and actions often have unforeseen consequences. But it is still important to see how far Germany under the nazis did what it had said it intended to do; and this involves looking well beyond September 1939.

The events of 1939–40 may be briefly described. The Germans won a rapid and overwhelming victory in Poland. Their armies reached the outskirts of Warsaw as early as 8 September, though the capital then held out until the 27th. On 17 September the Soviet Union joined in the conflict, and invaded Poland from the east. The Polish defence crumbled swiftly, and the last fighting ended on 5 October, only five weeks after the German attack began. On 6 October, in a speech to the Reichstag, Hitler made a vague 'peace offer', holding out the possibility of the restoration of a small Polish state and claiming that Britain and France had no reason to continue the war. Daladier rejected these proposals on 10 October, and Chamberlain on the 12th: neither would accept a peace based on a recognition of German conquests, with the certain prospect of more to come.

There followed a prolonged pause in military operations. Britain and France stood on the defensive in the west, though they toyed with various ideas for diverting the war to other parts of Europe, by opening a Balkan front, by bombing the Soviet oil-fields at Baku to reduce German oil supplies, or by launching a Scandinavian campaign to cut off German imports of iron ore from Sweden; but they pursued none of these speculations to the point of action. Hitler, for his part, sought no pause, but was compelled to accept one. As early as 27 September, before the fighting in Poland was over, he told the commanders of the three services that he intended to attack in the west at an early date, to smash France to pieces and bring England to her knees. On 18 October he signed a directive for Operation Yellow, an attack on France through Luxemburg, Belgium, and the Netherlands. His generals were reluctant, needing time to regroup after the Polish campaign and conscious of the deficiencies in their forces. They urged postponement until the spring, but Hitler would not allow it. On 25 October he set the date for the offensive at 12 November, and postponed it only because of adverse weather conditions. Throughout the autumn and winter new dates were repeatedly set, and fresh postponements imposed by the weather. The purpose never wavered: only the date was in doubt.

In the event, the winter imposed a pause even on Hitler. When operations resumed, they took the unexpected direction of a German invasion of Denmark and Norway on 8 April 1940. Denmark was occupied without resistance, but fighting went on in Norway for two months. The great German offensive in western Europe opened on 10 May, with astonishing success. The Panzer divisions moved with a speed and boldness which far outweighed deficiencies in their equipment, while the *Luftwaffe* worked closely with the army, and struck terror into soldiers and civilians alike. The whole campaign was a triumph for German military methods and enterprise, and was also a psychological success of a high order, in which the enemy was often demoralized by rumours of fifth-column activities and treachery from within – usually without foundation, but none the less effective for that.

The Dutch were defeated in less than a week, the army capitulating on 15 May, though the Queen and government went to Britain to continue the war. Belgium held out for just under three weeks. The army surrendered on 28 May; the King chose to remain with his people, but the government went to London. The greatest stroke was the defeat of France in a mere six weeks. The Germans entered Paris on 14 June. On 16 June the government headed by Paul Reynaud resigned, and a new government under Marshal Pétain asked for an armistice in the early hours of the 17th. By this time, Italy had entered the war (on 10 June), and the French signed armistices with Germany on 22 June and Italy on the 24th. The terms were severe but not catastrophic, leaving a French government in existence, about one-third of the country unoccupied, and the empire and the fleet intact. A new exchange rate between the mark and the French franc was fixed, highly favourable to Germany. By the end of June, all was over.

The nature of these campaigns and the uses to which the victories were put revealed much about German policy and objectives. The case of Poland was particularly instructive. For a brief period, Hitler appeared to contemplate the retention of a residual Polish state. The former German Ambassador in Warsaw, Moltke, prepared a scheme for a satellite state on 25 September; Hitler mentioned the possibility to Ciano on 2 October; and he referred to it publicly in his speech to the Reichstag on 6 October. But this idea was abandoned even while it was being discussed. On 27–28 September Ribbentrop made a second visit to Moscow, and agreed with the Soviet government on revisions of the lines of partition laid down in the agreement of 23 August. Lithuania was transferred from Germany to the Soviet sphere of influence, and in return the Polish province of Lublin and part of the province of Warsaw, previously allotted to the USSR, went to Germany. The new line through Poland gave the predominantly Polish areas to Germany, and the rest, with a large Polish minority among Ukrainian, Byelorussian, and Lithuanian populations, to the USSR.[1] Both the Germans and the Soviets agreed to suppress any Polish agitation directed against the other state; and with that agreement, any satellite Polish state under German control was effectively ruled out, because it might offer cover for anti-Soviet activities.

Hitler's true intentions for Poland emerged swiftly. Fighting ceased on 5 October, and on the 8th Hitler annexed to Germany northern and western areas of Poland which had been German territory in 1918.[2] On 12 October the rest of the territory occupied by Germany was organized as the Government-General of Poland, with Hans Frank as Governor of what was rapidly to become an SS state. In the territories annexed to Germany, a policy of total Germanization was begun at once. A list was drawn up of Germans resident in these former Polish territories, and a few Poles deemed capable of being Germanized. The remainder – the vast majority – were deprived of the normal rights of citizenship. They could not own property, form associations, receive education beyond the primary level, or be employed in any managerial capacity. At a conference on 2 October with Hans Frank and Martin Bormann, Hitler emphasized that the Poles must have only Germans as their masters. All Polish leaders and members of the intelligentsia were to be executed. There must be no mixture of blood between Germans and Poles. The elimination of the Polish élites began at once; and in the long term all Poles thought to be a threat to Germany or unfit for Germanization were to be deported to the Government-General or to Germany, for eventual extermination. The Government-General too was in the long run to be Germanized, and meanwhile was to serve as a reservoir of manpower for Germany, paid at cheap rates and fed on small rations. It was also used as a depository for Jews. From the beginning of October Jews in the annexed territories were rounded up and sent to the Government-General, and Hitler directed that the Jews of Vienna were to be treated in the same way. A decree of 26 January 1940 confined Jews in the Government-General to their places of residence – effectively, to their ghettos. Mass extermination followed from 1941 onwards.

These actions put into practice the proclaimed racial doctrines of nazism. In the 1920s Hitler had written of his intention to remove Poles from areas annexed to Germany and replace them with Germans. In August 1939 he told his service commanders that the object of war with Poland was not to reach certain lines but to destroy the people (see above, p. 262). This is exactly what he set out to do from the very beginning of October 1939, even before the fighting had ended in Poland and his 'peace offer' was made in the Reichstag. The war in Poland, and above all the occupation policy, was a racial conflict against the Poles and the Jews; and the driving force behind it was nazi ideology.

In the Soviet-occupied part of Poland, an elaborate charade of elections and petititions to enter the Soviet Union preceded formal annexation of the area in November 1939. The NKVD moved in to deport 'politically and socially dangerous' persons to Siberia or Central Asia; and it is probable that over a million people, most of them Poles, were forcibly removed. The Ukrainians and Byelorussians, on the other hand, were allowed the use of their languages for official purposes.

What of the policies pursued by Germany elsewhere? We have seen that Hitler was determined upon an attack in the west even before the Polish campaign was over, and pressed on with his plans despite the reluctance of his generals. His 'peace offer' of 6 October was fraudulent. He spoke of the restoration of a small Polish state when that had already been ruled out; and he emphasized that he had always wanted friendship with Britain and France at the same time as he said in private that his aim was a final military settlement with the western powers, amounting to their destruction. Certainly by this stage, and probably before, Hitler was firmly set on achieving predominance, not just in Poland, but in Europe as a whole.

The Scandinavian campaign of April–May 1940 was a side-show in this grand design, conceived as a riposte to Allied plans rather than undertaken on German initiative. The Germans were determined to secure their supplies of iron ore from Sweden, and at first sought to do so by means of a war-trade agreement with the Swedes, fixing the level of purchases at slightly under the total for 1938. During the winter of 1939–40 the western Allies considered various ideas for disrupting this traffic. During the Soviet war with Finland (November 1939–March 1940),[3] they prepared to send an expeditionary force to the ore-fields under the cover of helping the Finns. The British also considered mining the Norwegian coastal waters through which the ore trade passed in the winter months, when the direct route across the Gulf of Bothnia was frozen. Reports of these projects reached Germany, and in response plans for the occupation of Norway were put in hand during December 1939. In February 1940 the British destroyer

Cossack boarded a German vessel, the *Altmark*, in Norwegian territorial waters, and released British prisoners being clandestinely taken to Germany. At this, the Germans decided to move, and in March and early April 1940 German preparations for an invasion of Norway and British plans to sow mines in Norwegian waters went ahead simultaneously. The British began to lay mines on 5 April; the Germans launched their attack on Denmark and Norway during the night of the 8th/9th. The Germans occupied Norway, and were then able to apply irresistible pressure on Sweden. In July 1940 the Swedes had little choice but to allow German troops rights of transit across their country, and to accept a new trade agreement favourable to Germany. A campaign with a limited but important economic objective had been successfully concluded.

The German objectives in the west were on a different scale. Germany aimed at predominance in Europe, and victory over France secured it. To what end? What was Germany to do with the fruits of victory? One thing became clear at once: German policy was not following a 'blueprint'. The speed of the victories took everyone by surprise – the German high command, government ministries, even Hitler himself. So far from there being any detailed programme ready to be put into operation, nothing was prepared. As the surprise faded, however, some lines of approach quickly emerged.

The element of continuity with the German aims of 1914–18 was very strong in western Europe. What the German victories secured, this time with astonishing speed, was an opportunity to put into effect the western aspects of Chancellor Bethmann-Hollweg's programme of September 1914. The German Army occupied the Low Countries and most of France, and the economies of all these countries passed under German control. The old objectives of *Mitteleuropa* had been achieved. It remained to be seen how this great area should be organized and exploited.

At the end of May and the beginning of June 1940, papers prepared in the German Foreign Ministry envisaged a zone of very tight control, comprising the Netherlands, Belgium, Luxemburg, Norway, and Denmark. The Danubian states were thought to be already closely bound to Germany, and Sweden and Finland were to be drawn into the same position. These discussions were brought up short by Goering, who thought they were trespassing on his prerogatives in economic policy, and were followed by further proposals drawn up in the Economics Ministry. These envisaged an inner ring of states in western Europe and the Danube valley very closely bound to Germany; an outer ring, including Sweden, Finland, and Switzerland, treated separately but still associated with Germany; and others, including the USSR, Italy, France, and Britain, not belonging to the German bloc but in close relations with it. German industrialists working through the *Reichsgruppe Industrie* and the giant chemical firm of IG Farben also produced a number of proposals for the economic organization of Europe, concentrating on the advanced economies of western Europe and Scandinavia rather than upon the east or the Balkans, and seeking to suppress competition and secure markets. Hitler himself made no definite statement on the question of economic organization, but he frequently referred to it, especially when talking to visiting foreign statesmen, between autumn 1940 and spring 1941. His basic theme was that other countries should accept specialization of functions in the service of the German economy providing agricultural produce, raw materials, and fuel in return for German industrial goods. Rumania, for example, was to give up its own industries and concentrate on the production of cereals and oil, while Norway would supply not only Germany but much of Europe with hydroelectric power.

Countries occupied by Germany or under German influence were in fact compelled to accept trade agreements on German terms, as Denmark, Sweden, and Finland all did before the end of 1940. In France, occupation costs were set at 20 million marks per day, which was well above the actual cost of the operation, and the surplus was used to make purchases from the whole of France. The occupied countries were also used to provide labour, at cheap rates or without pay at all. This did not amount to a fully coherent economic policy, uniformly applied. In Lorraine, for example, German industrialists moved in to take over factories and amalgamate the area with the Saar and Ruhr for the profitable production of both iron and steel; but the government chose instead to concentrate on the production of iron ore, and deliberately ran down steel production to about one-third of its capacity by the end of the year. Eastern Europe brought out grave discrepancies between economic needs and nazi racial policy. Poland, and later the Ukraine and the Baltic states, should have provided Germany with large quantities of agricultural imports, especially cereals. In practice, nazi rule in these territories reduced them to ruin, and no attempt was made to encourage the population to sustain agricultural activity, so that food production fell drastically, and the chance of economic gain was thrown away. What might have happened in the long term, if the area had been systematically Germanized and colonized, remains unknown; but in the short run the economic and racial elements in nazi ideology came into conflict, and the racial element prevailed.

Over much of Europe, however, an outline economic organization took shape. It was accompanied by a new political order, partly provisional, but much of it intended to be permanent. By the end of 1940 the new Greater Germany had taken into full sovereignty Austria, the Sudetenland, a large part of Poland, Alsace-Lorraine, Luxemburg, and Eupen-Malmédy (formerly in Belgium). Germany exercised direct rule through Governors-General in Bohemia-Moravia and the Government-General of Poland. Slovakia was a Protectorate, with its government under close German control. The German Army occupied two-thirds of France, Belgium, the Netherlands, and Norway, pending political decisions as to their future. Denmark was also occupied, but with its own government still functioning. The German Empire, like most empires, was not wholly systematic in its administration; but it was of formidable strength, and in the Gestapo and SS it possessed a powerful binding force.

In the western and northern parts of the empire, the ideological element was much less prominent than in Poland. In France and the Low Countries the German Army was in charge, with the SS only in the background, and conduct towards the civilian population was correct and restrained. Only in Alsace-Lorraine, effectively annexed to Germany on 15 July 1940, was a policy of Germanization and deportation applied. Otherwise the peoples of western Europe were not at this stage subjugated, transported, or massacred in the same way as the Poles. There were, however, ideological aspects to the war, even in the west. In Norway, the Germans tried to install in power Vidkun Quisling, the Norwegian nazi with whom they had long been in touch. In the Netherlands, Belgium, and France the German victories brought a sharp revival in the fortunes of fascist or near-fascist parties which had been in decline since 1936. Many, of course, merely hastened to the help of the victor in the hope of a share in the spoils; but there were also those who genuinely believed that nazi Germany represented the wave of the future, and threw in their lot with it out of conviction. In France, the parliamentary regime of the Third Republic was widely discredited and held responsible for the country's defeat and disgrace. Pétain preached the need for national regeneration under an authoritarian form of government. Although the war in the west was far removed from the ruthless racial struggle waged in Poland, it still appeared inevitable that the German conquests must be followed by ideological adaptation.

While Europe was being organized, what was to be the next step in German policy? The first question was what to do about Britain; and on this Hitler displayed great uncertainty. One possibility was to make peace on compromise terms, leaving the British Empire, or most of it, intact. Several of Hitler's remarks, private and public, indicated that he expected the British to ask for terms. He told his entourage at the end of May 1940 that he would grant peace to England at the price of the colonies seized from Germany in the First World War, or perhaps simply in return for recognizing German predominance in Europe. He told an American journalist on 13 June that France was already beaten and he would soon reach an understanding with England. On 13 July he remarked to General Halder that a military victory over Britain would merely break up the British Empire for the benefit of Japan, the USA, and others; and there was no point in shedding German blood for that end. After the armistice with France, Hitler was apparently waiting for the British to approach him, and he was disappointed to hear nothing from London. He made a sightseeing visit to France, put off a speech scheduled for 8 July, and finally made a vague appeal for peace in a speech to the Reichstag on the 19th. He mentioned no terms, even in outline, but merely asserted, not for the first time, that he had never intended to harm the British Empire, and that he could see no reason why the war should go on.

There is no proof, but it may well be that at this point Hitler would have offered terms leaving the British Isles and most of the empire untouched; though the long-term prospects would have been a different matter. He seems to have been genuinely disappointed and baffled by the British determination to fight on, which faced him with the question of how they were to be defeated. The German staffs had no plan ready for an invasion of the British Isles, and Hitler did not order them to prepare one until 2 July. Even when under way, the planning was half-hearted. Hitler's directive for Operation Sealion (16 July) stated, with an unaccustomed note of uncertainty: 'I have decided to prepare a landing operation against England and, if necessary, to carry it out.'⁴ An opposed sea-borne landing was notoriously one of the most difficult of military operations, and one of which the German services had no experience. Counsels were divided and preparations uncertain. The one point on which all agreed was that the key lay in air superiority, which was never quite achieved. After prolonged hesitation, the plan was tacitly abandoned on 17 September by the face-saving device of postponing the date for fixing a date for the invasion.

As the prospects for an invasion receded, the Germans looked round for other means of defeating the British. One was a Mediterranean campaign, drawing Spain into the war and closing the straits of Gibraltar in the west, while reinforcing the Italians in Libya for an attack on the Suez Canal in the east. These projects were actively pursued between August 1940 and the end of the year, but were obstructed by evasiveness on the part of both Spain and Italy. In September Franco named his price for entry into the war as the whole of French Morocco, part of Algeria and the French Cameroons, and some territory in the Pyrenees. Hitler went personally to meet Franco at Hendaye on 23 October, and was presented with a long list of supplies and military equipment, clearly designed to be so extensive that it could not be met. Hitler's directive no. 18 of 12 November still referred to bringing Spain into the war and an attack on Gibraltar, but nothing materialized. Franco, to Hitler's disappointment, resolutely pursued Spanish interests as he saw them, and offered only limited assistance to the Axis powers. Meanwhile, Germany twice offered, in August and October, to send forces to help the Italians in Libya, but Mussolini prevaricated, and Hitler did not press the matter, though he instructed an armoured division to stand by for North Africa. This plan eventually took shape in the despatch of Rommel's Afrika Korps to Tripoli in February 1941; but the general plans for a full Mediterranean campaign were never followed up.

Another possibility was to bring together, in a grand diplomatic design, a combination of powers comprising Spain, Vichy France, the Soviet Union, and Japan, as well as the Axis powers, which would be so formidable as to compel a British surrender. Hitler had been at work off and on since 1938 to secure an alliance with Japan, and on 27 September 1940 a fresh bout of negotiations was brought to a successful conclusion with the signature of the Tripartite Pact between Germany, Italy, and Japan. The three participants recognized each other's spheres of influence in Europe and the Far East, and the treaty was openly designed to threaten both the USA and Britain. In October 1940 Hitler pursued his diplomatic efforts through meetings with Franco and Pétain, but with little tangible result. Franco, as we have seen, remained reticent, and though Pétain agreed in principle to collaboration with Germany (and so endowed the word with a new and pejorative meaning), the ways and means were left to be worked out in the future. The roles of Spain and France in the general coalition remained sketchy and insubstantial.

That left the Soviet Union. Molotov was invited to Berlin for talks with Hitler and Ribbentrop on 12–13 November 1940. Hitler talked sweepingly of the break-up of the British Empire – an estate in bankruptcy, as he put it; and Ribbentrop presented a draft agreement for the division of large parts of the world into German, Italian, Japanese, and Soviet spheres of influence. Molotov for his part was dismayingly precise, asking stern questions about Finland, Rumania, and Bulgaria, where Germany appeared to be trespassing on the Soviet sphere of influence already agreed on in 1939 (see below, pp. 288–90). However, he took Ribbentrop's proposals back to Moscow, and on 25 November produced a reply expressing agreement in principle, though requiring far-reaching conditions. German troops should be withdrawn from Finland at once; the Soviet Union was to negotiate a treaty with Bulgaria permitting the establishment of a Soviet base there; there should be another Soviet base in Turkey, at the straits into the Mediterranean; and Japan must renounce all claims to coal and oil concessions in northern Sakhalin. The proposed Soviet sphere in the grand partition of the world should be more clearly defined as lying between Batum, Baku, and the Persian Gulf. Many of these demands were to remain consistent elements in Soviet policy over the next five years, and there is no need to doubt the seriousness of the reply; but in the event the exchange stopped at that point. The Germans never answered the Soviet note, though the Soviet government reminded them of it a number of times.

With this, the negotiations for a grand coalition stretching from

Madrid to Tokyo by way of Moscow came to an end. They had not got very far, and even the Tripartite Pact with Japan, which was their most solid achievement, proved less effective than Hitler hoped. However, all these schemes for the defeat of Britain came to assume a secondary importance as 1940 came to an end. Hitler's mind had already moved to an attack on the Soviet Union, a project never far from his thoughts. He began talk of it to his generals in late July 1940, and he even thought of launching the attack that autumn, until he was persuaded that this was impossible. Planning and practical preparations went forward from August onwards, until in December all was sufficiently ready for Hitler to issue his directive for Operation Barbarossa. The significance of this will be examined in Chapter 17. It is enough to note here the speed with which Hitler turned towards an attack on the Soviet Union, long before other prospects had been exhausted, or even fully tried.

What emerges from German policies after the victories of summer 1940 to illuminate the origins of the war? There was no 'blueprint'. There were no plans ready for the invasion of Britain or for the organization of a conquered Europe. Hitler hesitated, uncertain what to do with his victory. Yet through the hesitation, and almost *because* there were no plans, the main impulses behind German policy emerged with great clarity. Economic demands had to be met: the supply of Swedish iron ore had to be secured. In the general economic and political organization of central and western Europe, the influence of ideas about *Mitteleuropa*, going back to the First World War and earlier, was strong. Hitler shared these ideas and began to put them into practice; but for him they were not enough. He had no clear idea about how to deal with the recalcitrant British, and his heart was never in a Mediterranean campaign. Always in the background there was the idea of an attack on the Soviet Union. The compass needle of nazi policy swung erratically in the summer and autumn of 1940, but it came to rest pointing east.

The forces behind the expansion of Germany stand out clearly in the light of that expansion itself in 1939–40. In Poland, the themes of race and living space were predominant, and the most extreme theories of nazi racial doctrines were unhesitatingly put into practice. In the west and north, the war was one which would have been easily recognizable to Bethmann-Hollweg and the German General Staff of 1914, fought to establish German political and economic domination. The new, nazi, elements in German policy marched side by side with the old; though with the growing success of the regime the nazi element grew steadily more powerful.

The German victories confronted almost every state in Europe with choices, and their responses both extended the scope of the war and further illuminated its nature. Of all the powers which had remained neutral in 1939, Italy was the only one to make a deliberate choice to enter the war. In September 1939 Mussolini declared Italy a 'non-belligerent', in the hope that this would sound better than being merely neutral. In practice, he recognized that his country, despite seventeen years of fascist rule, was not ready to fight. During the next few months Italy followed no fixed policy. Ciano thought that the war would be long and that the British would eventually win it, and he therefore tried to keep Italy out and to promote a negotiated peace. Mussolini lent some support to these efforts, and in a letter of 3 January 1940 tried to persuade Hitler that the restoration of a small Polish state under German tutelage would make a starting-point for peace. This made no headway, and the role of peacemaker proved both unproductive and humiliating – for two months Hitler did not even trouble to reply to Mussolini's letter. On the other hand, the prospects for war were still unpromising, and in January 1940 Marshal Badoglio advised Mussolini that Italy would not be ready for war that year, or fit to take the offensive until 1942.

Despite this advice, Mussolini now saw that there would be no compromise peace, and he did not believe that Italy could afford to stay out of the war until it ended. A reversal of alliances was impossible: as a fascist he could not join the democracies, and only the German alliance would enable Italy to attain her goals in the Mediterranean. In a memorandum of 31 March 1940 Mussolini concluded that Italy's only course was to wage a war parallel to that of Germany, and break free from her imprisonment in the Mediterranean. The problem was not whether to fight, but when and how. As to when, he set no date; as to how, he acknowledged that the main lines of strategy on land must be defensive in Europe and Libya, with local offensives from Abyssinia, but at sea the navy must launch an all-out attack. The comments on this memorandum from the service chiefs were not encouraging. Badoglio thought that action on *all* land fronts would have to be defensive, and the Chief of Naval Staff, Admiral Cavagnari, reported that the navy was not strong enough to take the offensive in either the eastern or western Mediterranean.

These counsels of caution were swept away by the German victories of April and May 1940. When Hitler wrote on 9 April with his rather belated announcement of the invasion of Norway, Mussolini said that he could not stand by with folded arms while others made history. On 13 May, three days after the Germans opened their offensive in the west, he told Ciano that the Allies had lost the war. Italy had already suffered enough dishonour, and he would declare war within a month. At a conference with service chiefs on 29 May he said that any date after 5 June would be suitable, and after consultation with Hitler 10 June was fixed upon. On that day, Italy declared war on France and Britain.

Mussolini's decision was a personal one. He refused to be restrained by the caution of Ciano, who had grown disillusioned with the German alliance, or by the pessimism of the generals and admirals. There was evidence in the police reports of the time that some sections of the Italian population favoured war, but at best the nation was divided on the issue. It is a clear example of a deliberate and individual choice for war, with no question of accident, or of war being forced upon Italy. Why did Mussolini make this choice?

His most prominent motive was an extremely simple opportunism. He remarked more than once in May and June 1940 that he needed a few thousand casualties to allow him to take his seat at the peace conference; and since the war, to all appearance, was almost over, he had to move quickly. But there was more to it than that. Mussolini had spoken repeatedly of Italy's need to break out of her imprisonment in the Mediterranean, and he had long sought a sphere of influence in the Balkans. War seemed to open the way to both objectives. Moreover, his own personal prestige and that of the fascist regime were at stake: to remain neutral would be to admit failure and accept humiliation. It is possible too that he sought in war a new impetus which would revive the regime at home and strengthen his hand against the monarchy. Mussolini's personal relations with Hitler also played some part – his meeting with the Fuehrer at the Brenner Pass on 18 March 1940 seems to have impelled him towards war. It cannot be said with certainty that a non-fascist Italy would not have gone to war for Mediterranean objectives; but it was clear that the nature of the fascist regime and Mussolini's personal role made war much more likely that not. In the long run, the fate of the regime indeed proved to be bound up with the war, though not in the way that Mussolini hoped.

The Italian declaration of war had far-reaching results. It extended the existing conflict to the Mediterranean, and resulted for a time in the waging of a separate and parallel war, as Mussolini claimed – a third war to follow the two in Poland and western Europe. It was the culminating point in a series of events through which Italy had played a considerable part in destabilizing Europe – Abyssinia, Spain, and Albania marked the earlier stages. It was almost the end of the road for Italian influence, which was at its greatest when Italy was courted on all sides and when her military strength was not too severely tested. Once at war, Italian weakness rapidly became apparent, and Italy sank to become merely a junior partner in the Axis.

On the other side of the conflict, a number of states made choices during 1939 and 1940 which brought out their views of the nature of the war and what was at stake in it. The first, and in many ways the most striking, case was that of Poland. As we have seen, Poland disappeared from the map, and the Polish people were ground between the upper and nether millstones of Germany and the Soviet Union. The Polish response was to continue the war. The government which began hostilities went to Rumania in September 1939, and its members were interned; but the President of the Republic delegated his powers, and on 30 September a new government was formed in Paris under General Sikorski. Warships had escaped, new army and air force units were formed, and Polish forces continued to fight, as they did for the next six years. In Poland itself, before the end of September, a clandestine resistance movement began to take shape in opposition to both the German and the Soviet occupations. For the Poles, in exile and at home, the issue at stake was nothing less than the existence of their nation, and the war was so important that it was not to be ended even by apparently total defeat. The pattern thus set of a government in exile continuing the war and an internal resistance movement maintaining opposition to an occupying power was later widely followed, and became a characteristic feature of the Second World War in Europe.

The German victories of April–June 1940 placed before several governments the choice of whether to leave their countries and continue the war from abroad, or to take the more usual course of staying at home, asking for terms, and continuing to administer the country, if necessary under foreign occupation. The crisis first came in Denmark, where in an extremely short time in the early hours of 9 April 1940 the government had to decide whether or not to resist the German attack. Seeing no chance of successful resistance, the government refused to declare war, and accepted German occupation. The possibility of going into exile was not considered. In Norway, invaded at the same time, events turned out differently. The Norwegian forces resisted from the start; and Hitler made what proved to be the capital error of trying to install Quisling, the Norwegian nazi leader, as the head of a new government. German parachute troops also tried but failed to capture King Haakon. Quisling's government proved a flop. The King remained at liberty; he and his government refused all negotiations with the Germans; and at the end of April they decided to go to Britain to continue the war. The ideological element, and perhaps the precedent of Austria in 1938, here led Hitler into a significant political failure. In the Netherlands, Queen Wilhelmina, who was determined that neither she nor her country should be bullied into submission, sailed for England on 13 May, followed by her ministers. When the Prime Minister later showed signs of wishing to seek a negotiated peace, he was speedily removed and replaced by a man of sterner stuff. In Belgium, counsels were divided. King Leopold saw it as his duty to stay with his army and his people, but the government went to London and pursued the war.

The most significant of all these decisions was made in France. By the middle of June 1940 it was clear that organized resistance to the German armies could no longer be maintained, and the French government had to choose between asking for an armistice and going abroad (to Algiers or London) to continue the struggle. On 16 June

Paul Reynaud, who advocated continued resistance, resigned as Premier, and was replaced by Marshal Pétain, who at once asked for an armistice and peace terms. In part his decision arose from a simple determination to remain on the soil of France and with the French people; but it also reflected a belief that it was possible to save something from the wreck and establish a place for France in a German-dominated Europe. Reynaud thought this was an illusion. They were not dealing with someone like the Kaiser in the previous war – 'Hitler is Gengis Khan', as Reynaud once exclaimed.

The division between Pétain and Reynaud reflected a profound difference of view on the nature of the war and the forces behind it; and the same question arose in each of the invaded countries. The governments which chose to accept defeat believed that the consequences would be tolerable. Those who chose exile believed on the contrary that occupation by Hitler's Germany represented a fundamental challenge which must be resisted to the end. That this latter view was so widely (though by no means universally) held and acted upon was an indication of the forces which lay behind the war, and especially their ideological element.

The British faced a similar choice, though in a less acute form. The likelihood that France would surrender was borne in upon the British government before the end of May 1940, and raised the question of whether Britain should also seek terms. The War Cabinet rejected the idea after long and tense discussions on 26, 27, and 28 May, and the question was not reopened at the actual time of the French armistice at the end of June, when it was largely taken for granted in the government, Parliament, and the press that the war should be continued. The pacific mood of the 1930s had vanished almost completely: when the Germans were at Calais, there were few who wished to see them at Dover. The coalition government under Churchill represented a unity of feeling based on a combination of instinctive self-defence, patriotism, and ideological opposition to nazism. In the disastrous circumstances of 1940, the British resolve to continue the war was a demonstration of the depth and significance of the reasons for which it had been begun, and for which it would be carried through.

The German victories of 1940, and above all the fall of France, also showed in a flash that the war was far more than merely European in its significance. In the Far East, Japan was presented with a tremendous opportunity. The defeat of France and the Netherlands left their Far Eastern possessions (Indo-China and the Dutch East Indies) open to attack; and the apparently impending collapse of Britain promised to offer even wider prospects. In the Atlantic, the USA faced dangers far more immediate and acute than most Americans had ever envisaged. The fall of France might well allow German influence to be extended to the French colonies in the Caribbean. If the Germans seized the French fleet, and if, worse still, the British surrendered and handed over the Royal Navy, the command of the Atlantic might pass into German hands. Many Americans, including President Roosevelt, also saw nazi ideology as a long-term challenge to American democracy. The USA, so long set on creating for itself an iron-clad neutrality, came increasingly to realize that its own interests and security were bound up with the fate of Europe, and extended its help to Britain as the first line of American self-defence.

The crisis of 1940 revealed much about the nature of the war, and therefore also about its origins. It was an ideological war, most plainly in Poland, though there were ideological elements also in the war in western Europe, which was more obviously a war about power and economic predominance. It was a war brought about by two expansionist powers, Germany and Italy, not working to detailed preconceived plans, but still pursuing long-held objectives. Mussolini could have remained neutral in 1940, but chose instead to make a bid for his Mediterranean aims. Hitler stood at the end of 1940 as the master of most of Europe, but this was still not enough. He was determined upon the invasion of the Soviet Union, which was to complete the process by which almost the whole of Europe was swept into war.

REFERENCES AND NOTES

1. The approximate population of the Soviet zone in September 1939 was 13.2 million including 5 million Poles, 4.4 million Ukrainians, and 1.2 million Byelorussians (Jan Ciechanowski, in R. F. Leslie (ed.), *Poland since 1863*, (Cambridge 1980) p. 214).
2. The population of those areas comprised 8.9 million Poles, 600,000 Germans, and 600,000 Jews (ibid.).
3. The Soviet Union demanded territorial concessions from Finland and the use of the Finnish base at Hangö, and attacked Finland in pursuit of these aims on 30 November 1939. The Finns resisted with unexpected tenacity and success, and did not surrender until 12 March 1940, when the Soviets imposed a harsher version of their original terms.
4. H. R. Trevor-Roper (ed.), *Hitler's War Directives 1939–1945* (London 1964), p. 34.

Chapter 17

GERMANY AND THE SOVIET UNION, 1940–1941

In the early hours of Sunday, 22 June 1941, Germany invaded the Soviet Union. The forces engaged on both sides were larger than in any previous campaign; the distances and areas involved were vaster; and the stake was nothing less than the existence of the two greatest European powers of the time. Alongside Germany fought her east European allies and satellites, Finland, Rumania, Hungary, and Slovakia, soon to be joined by three Italian divisions and the Spanish Blue Division. Hitler had said that when he attacked the USSR the world would hold its breath. It did. The climax of the long movement towards total European war had come.

These events obviously had the most profound effects upon the course and outcome of the Second World War. It is equally true, though rather less obvious, that they also have a fundamental bearing on the question of the origins of the war. Why did Hitler attack the Soviet Union? If it was the fulfilment of all his dreams and thoughts from at least the composition of *Mein Kampf* onwards, then all the events of the previous years must be seen in this perspective. The annexation of Austria and Czechoslovakia, the offers of alliance to Poland and then the attack upon her, appear as preparations to open the way to the ultimate goal. The offensive in the west and the defeat of France removed the threat to Germany's rear and allowed a concentration of forces in the east. All was part of a grand design, with improvisations and uncertainties here and there, but moving always in the same direction. If, on the other hand, the attack on the Soviet Union was largely a response to the pressures of war – an indirect means of defeating the British, or a response to Soviet obduracy in eastern Europe – then our perspective on the origins of the war is quite different. The grand design becomes less obvious or less influential, and may even be relegated to the status of mere talk.

Most of the questions raised in the different interpretations of the origins of the war – war by accident or war premeditated, an ideological war or war over power, Hitler's war or the continuation of the First World War – reach their logical conclusion in the events of 1941, which represent the final question mark over the origins and nature of the war. It is true that the questions involved cannot be answered with complete certainty or finality, turning as they do on interpretations of motive where we can only assess degrees of probability. But equally the bearing of the events of June 1941 on the origins of the war is such that to ignore them is to leave a whole area of explanation unexplored.

The military preparations for the offensive against the Soviet Union were lengthy. Planning began at the beginning of August 1940, and operational plans in different forms were prepared in September and November. The movement of troops to the east, and the preparation of supply depots and training camps, began that autumn. General Halder presented a completed plan to Hitler on 5 December 1940, and Hitler signed directive no. 21 for Operation Barbarossa on 18 December: 'The German Armed Forces must be prepared to crush Soviet Russia in a quick campaign even before the end of the war against England.' Preparations were to be completed by 15 May 1941.[1]

Not all plans are carried out – the directive of November 1940 for an attack on Gibraltar, for example, came to nothing. The absolute certainty of an attack on the Soviet Union cannot, therefore, be assumed on the basis of the military plans alone. But the scale of the military preparations, and the time and energy devoted to them, put the planning for Barbarossa in quite a different category from that for Gibraltar. Certainly from December 1940 onwards it was clear that this was no mere contingency plan, but, short of something extraordinary, would be put into effect. The question is why?

One answer is that it was the fulfilment of a long-formed intention. Alan Bullock concluded firmly in his biography of Hitler that: 'Hitler invaded Russia for the simple but sufficient reason that he had always meant to establish the foundation of his thousand-year Reich by the annexation of the territory between the Vistula and the Urals.'[2] Other motives, at the most, only reinforced a decision which he had already reached. This conclusion has been widely shared and the evidence for it may be found throughout Hitler's writings and talks to nazi and service leaders over a long period. His mind appeared to be firmly set in this mould by the 1920s, and the longer his dictatorship lasted the less open he was to new ways of thought.

By 1940 it is probable that the mould was unbreakable. Hitler took up other ideas – an invasion of Britain, a move through Spain, a Mediterranean campaign, a grand alliance to include the USSR – but he dropped them again. To an attack on the Soviet Union he constantly returned. Even when things went wrong, as in Mussolini's ill-judged and unsuccessful attack on Greece at the end of October 1940, Hitler's plans to cope with the problem went ahead alongside the plans for the USSR – his directive for the invasion of Greece, Operation Marita, was signed on 13 December 1940, and that for Barbarossa on the 18th. When other opportunities appeared, glittering and apparently within easy reach – as they did in the Middle East in February 1941, when the capture of the Suez Canal and an Arab revolt against the British were in the offing – Hitler was not interested in pursuing them. He insisted that there must be no large-scale operations in the Mediterranean until the USSR had been defeated. Hitler was often an opportunist, but he was only interested in certain opportunities, and a campaign in the Middle East was not among them.

German objectives in eastern Europe had obvious links with the victories of 1918, when the German armies had defeated Russia and occupied the Ukraine and the Caucasus. This continuity was not repudiated by the nazis, who were happy to share the mantle of Ludendorff. But by 1941 the impulse inherited from imperial Germany was far outweighed by current ideological concerns, to the grave detriment of German policy. During the First World War the Germans had made skilful and successful use of the grievances of the non-Russian nationalities, encouraging separatist movements and working closely with the government of a newly declared Ukrainian state. In 1941 the same opportunity was present, and was partially recognized. In western Europe in 1940–41 the Germans sought contacts with Flemish and Breton separatists. In the east, the *Abwehr* had long supported Ukrainian nationalists, and at least one staff paper during the planning for the attack on the USSR envisaged setting up a puppet government in the Ukraine. The extent of the opportunity was shown by the welcome frequently received by the German forces as they advanced into the Ukraine in the summer of 1941. But the Germans this time made no claims to come as liberators. When Ukrainian nationalists set up a provisional government in Lwow at the end of June 1941, the Germans at once suppressed it. They came as the master race, and in so doing they threw away a political weapon of the highest value.

Hitler insisted that the war with the Soviet Union would be one of ideology and race. He rejected the army's proposals for the military administration of conquered territory, laying down instead in a directive of 13 March 1941 that Himmler as head of the SS was to be responsible for 'special tasks' in the occupied zone. The SS, prosecuting the struggle between opposing systems of government and belief, were to liquidate the Jewish–Bolshevik intelligentsia and the Bolshevik commissars. On 31 March 1941 Hitler gave verbal orders that persons in these categories were to be placed outside the normal rules of war and shot on capture. On 6 June the so-called 'commissar order', that all Soviet military commissars captured on the eastern front were to be killed as soon as taken, was actually put in writing. It was freely accepted that millions of the people of the conquered territories would suffer the same fate as the commissars, by the more indirect means of famine. At a meeting of State Secretaries on 2 May 1941 it was agreed that all the German forces must be fed from the USSR by the third year of the war, and that the consequence of this was that millions of Russians would have to starve. A directive by Goering's economic staff on 23 May confirmed this: the food-producing areas of the USSR were to supply German needs, which would unavoidably mean famine for the urban populations normally fed from these sources.

When the campaign began, Hitler's absorption in it speedily became complete, and its visionary aims dominated his talk, in which he pictured a Soviet Union colonized with German towns, linked by great roads and separated from the native population, who would be kept in outer darkness. He hardly left his specially constructed headquarters in East Prussia, except to make forays to a command post in the Soviet Union itself. Germany, and even his old haunts in Bavaria, were rarely visited. It was the final sign of his obsession with the east.

Even in his obsession, it seems that Hitler was visited by doubts and hesitations. When he wrote to Mussolini to announce the invasion, Hitler referred to months of anxious pondering, and of winning through to a decision. He even seems to have had some premonition of ill-fortune, and on the night before the attack he said: 'I feel as if I am pushing open the door to a dark room never seen before, without knowing what lies behind the door.'[3] But despite such signs, it seems clear that Hitler moved against the USSR under the impulse of a long-cherished idea.

It may not, however, have been his only motive, and it was certainly not the sole explanation advanced by Hitler himself. In the summer of 1940 his most common argument was that it was necessary to attack the Soviet Union in order to defeat Britain. He told his senior commanders on 31 July 1940: 'England's hope is Russia and America. If hope on Russia is eliminated, America is also eliminated. . . . Russia the factor on which England is mainly betting. . . . Should Russia, however, be smashed, then England's last hope is extinguished.'[4] Hitler said much the same, in one form or another, to various foreign statesmen – to Teleki, the Hungarian Prime Minister, for example, on 20 November 1940. In March 1941, speaking to the commanders involved in Operation Barbarossa, he stretched the point so far as to claim the existence of a secret agreement between the USSR and Britain, which held the English back from making peace. Despite much repetition, however, the logic of the argument remained elusive, and Halder in particular seems to have been understandably uncertain as to how exactly the defeat of the Soviet Union would lead to a British surrender. The British had gone to war despite the signing of the Nazi–Soviet Pact: they had maintained their resistance in the summer of 1940 in the face of Soviet hostility; and there seemed no good reason for them to change their position. If it were the main German objective to strike at Britain, there were other more effective ways of doing so. To conquer the oil supplies of the Middle East was one way. To cut off all assistance from the USA (which meant far more to Britain than did the USSR) would have been more deadly still. But these objectives were not pursued. The argument is not decisive, for it remains possible that, however misguidedly, Hitler believed his own explanation. But it is reasonable to look elsewhere for more substantial motives.

In late 1940 and early 1941 there was increasing friction between Germany and the Soviet Union in eastern Europe, calling into question the working and advantages of the Nazi–Soviet Pact. In June and July 1940, in the aftermath of the fall of France, Stalin moved to secure his grip on the three Baltic states of Estonia, Latvia, and Lithuania, placed in the Soviet sphere of influence by the agreements of 1939. Soviet troops had been stationed on their territory since October 1939; in late June 1940 Soviet-controlled governments were imposed; and in July all three asked to be incorporated in the Soviet Union. Their request, needless to say, was granted. Hitler claimed to be shocked by this – perhaps he really was, because he did not like others to play his own game, and the Soviet move could have no adversary in view except Germany.

However, this move was not in breach of the 1939 agreements: Stalin was only annexing territory which had formerly been in his sphere of influence. But there then developed friction which directly impinged on the agreements. On 23 June, Molotov announced to the German Ambassador in Moscow that the Soviet Union proposed to occupy at once the Rumanian provinces of Bessarabia and Bukovina. The USSR had declared its interest in Bessarabia during the hasty negotiations of August 1939. Bukovina had not been mentioned though Ribbentrop had made vague remarks about the lack of German political interest in the Balkans generally. This was never in fact the case: German interest in Rumanian oil was strong, and an economic agreement of 27 May 1940 brought Rumania firmly under German influence. The Germans persuaded the Soviets to limit their occupation to the northern part of Bukovina, but then advised Rumania to accept a Soviet ultimatum of 26 June. But these events rankled in Berlin, and when on 30 August Hitler delivered a ruling (the Second Vienna Award) transferring most of Transylvania from Rumania to Hungary, he accompanied this further diminution of Rumanian territory with a guarantee of what remained. This guarantee was obviously directed against the Soviet Union, and Molotov protested about it, both at the time and during his visit to Berlin in November 1940.

The position of Rumania had been left vague in the German–Soviet negotiations of 1939; but there could be no doubt that Finland was placed in the Soviet sphere of influence. During the Soviet–Finnish War of November 1939–March 1940, Germany had respected this agreement, and had done nothing to impede, and something to assist, the Soviet campaign. By the summer of 1940, Germany was no longer content with this position. German conceptions of an attack on the

Soviet Union, from the end of July 1940 onwards, always included the participation of Finland on Germany's side, which meant that it was necessary to detach that country from the Soviet sphere. On 24 July a German–Finnish trade treaty was signed, and in September 1940 Germany negotiated an agreement for the passage of German troops through Finland to north Norway. The Soviets were not informed beforehand, and were understandably perturbed. Molotov pressed this matter hard on his visit to Berlin in November. Hitler agreed that Finland was the primary concern of the USSR from a political point of view, but he stressed Germany's economic interest in Finnish nickel and timber. He insisted that Finland was not occupied by German troops, who were only passing through. Molotov repeatedly pointed out that the existing German–Soviet agreements placed Finland in the Soviet sphere of influence, and remarked ominously that the Soviet government had the right to deal with the Finnish question. In the event, Finland continued to move into the German camp, and the Soviets did not make good this threat.

Further friction developed over Bulgaria, a country not specifically mentioned in the Nazi–Soviet agreements, though vaguely included in Ribbentrop's airy expressions of lack of interest. In November 1940 the Soviet Union proposed to issue a guarantee to Bulgaria, and warned the Bulgarian government against seeking German support. The Bulgarians refused the guarantee, only to be offered (25 November) a mutual assistance pact, which would include Bulgaria in the Soviet security zone. Again the Bulgarians refused, keeping Germany informed throughout and receiving her tacit support. On 25 November also, the Soviet note to Germany about proposed spheres of influence, following Molotov's conversations in Berlin, stipulated the establishment of a Soviet base in Bulgaria. The Soviet claims on Bulgaria were thus made absolutely clear; and yet on 28 February 1941 German troops entered the country, with the consent of the Bulgarian government. The challenge could not have been more direct.

At the same time, between November 1940 and March 1941, Germany made a series of diplomatic moves which emphasized her influence all over eastern Europe. On 20 November 1940 Hungary adhered to the Tripartite Pact between Germany, Italy, and Japan: Rumania followed on 23 November, and Slovakia on the 24th. The Tripartite Pact was openly directed against the USA, and its fifth Article declared that it did not affect the signatories' existing relations with the Soviet Union; but whatever the wording, there was no doubt that for east European countries to join the Pact was to declare for Germany rather than the USSR. In December 1940 there were staff conversations between Germany and Finland, and on 31 December the two countries signed a treaty of friendship. Finally, on 28 February 1941, having accepted the entry of German troops, Bulgaria too joined the Tripartite Pact. Of these moves, those involving Finland,

Rumania, and Bulgaria were of particular significance, and certain to be resented by the Soviet Union.

German–Soviet relations were thus under considerable strain, and it was open to question how long the pact between the two countries would survive. In these circumstances, the economic aspects of German–Soviet relations were also at risk. After a difficult start in the winter of 1939–40, when there was some very tough negotiating between the two sides, economic relations had been good, and had worked very favourably for Germany. A commercial agreement signed in February 1940 provided that the Soviet Union should supply Germany during the next year with 1 million tons of cereals, 900,000 tons of oil (including 100,000 tons of aviation spirit), and substantial quantities of cotton, phosphates, iron ore, and chrome ore. Almost as important, the Soviets agreed to make purchases in third countries on Germany's behalf, and to transport goods from the Far East along the Trans-Siberian railway. The supplies of rubber which reached Germany by this route were particularly valuable.[5] In return, the Soviet Union was to receive specimens of German industrial and military technology – tanks, aircraft, armour plate, mines, torpedoes, locomotives, and machinery for the oil industry. The chief German economic negotiator, Schnurre, noted that the Soviet Union had agreed to deliveries greater than were justified on economic grounds alone, and would have to provide them at the cost of her own economy.

The early Soviet deliveries of oil and raw materials under this agreement fell short of the required quantities, but they increased from May 1940 onwards. The agreement was renewed in 1941, and a further agreement signed in April 1941. The advantages to Germany were immense. She was largely freed from the pressure of the Allied naval blockade; most of her needs for raw materials and foodstuffs were met; and supplies of oil from Rumania were supplemented to an important degree. The question by early 1941 was whether to continue this arrangement, which was working well but involved the risk that at some time, if relations deteriorated too far, the Soviets could cut off supplies; or to conquer the Soviet Union and so bring the grain and raw materials of the Ukraine and the oil of the Caucasus directly under German control. If the Germans chose war, they would have to face the problem of how to prosecute it without the benefit of the supplies which they were accustomed to draw from the Soviet Union; to which the only answer was to ensure that the war would be short and victory swift. General Thomas warned that the oil installations of the Caucasus would have to be seized intact. The case for going to war to gain physical control of the supplies which so far had come by agreement was significant, but by no means overwhelming.

It is clear that there was friction between Germany and the Soviet Union over much of eastern Europe in late 1940 and early 1941. The initiative for this lay mostly on the German side, with the encroachment of German influence in Finland, Rumania, and Bulgaria. In a phrase borrowed from another context, the German–Soviet agreements had proved to be an uneasy alliance between the sand-dune and the sea – with Germany as the sea. But was this friction, and the questions which it raised for the long-term prospects of economic co-operation, the principal cause of the great German assault of June 1941? Of itself, it seemed more likely to produce further German demands, to reinforce their position and ensure their supplies; and it was demands of this kind that Stalin seems to have been expecting in June 1941. As a reason for all-out war, it only carries conviction if supported by other causes.

Hitler claimed when he went to war with the Soviet Union that Stalin had been preparing to attack Germany; and sometimes he added to this the assertion that the USSR entertained secret relations with Britain. For this claim there seems no evidence whatever. In the summer of 1940, though Stalin moved rapidly to establish his control over the Baltic states, Bessarabia, and northern Moldavia, his diplomatic demeanour towards Germany was impeccable. He offered his congratulations to Germany on the defeat of France, and issued an official communiqué (23 June) emphasizing the good relations between the USSR and Germany. When Britain sent a new Ambassador to Moscow, Sir Stafford Cripps, to improve Anglo-Soviet relations, he was received only formally by Stalin, who made sure that he passed on his account of the meeting to the Germans. Stalin even told Cripps that he saw no danger of the hegemony of any one country in Europe – which on 1 July 1940 implied either blindness or untruth. For the next months, Cripps tried in vain to see even Molotov.

Later, in November 1940, Molotov's visit to Berlin was not a success from the German point of view, and he was obstinately precise and difficult in asking questions about Finland and Rumania when Hitler wanted to talk sweepingly about the partition of the world. But the visit was not a complete failure: Molotov bore away the German proposals for the arrangement of vast spheres of influence, and returned a reply within a fortnight, stating conditions which were severe, but could have been a basis for discussion. It was the Germans who then broke off the exchange, despite a number of Soviet enquiries about a reply (see above, p. 277).

As 1941 advanced, the German Ambassador in Moscow, Schulenberg, was certain that the USSR had no intention of attacking Germany, and his view was confirmed by all Stalin's actions in May and June. Deliveries of goods under the economic agreements were stepped up in the weeks before the German attack. On 8 May the Soviet news agency Tass denied stories of Russian troop concentrations on the country's western border. On 9 May the Soviet government withdrew its recognition from the governments of Norway,

Belgium, and Yugoslavia, and expelled their representatives from Moscow. On 12 May they recognized the government set up by Rashid Ali, who had rebelled (with German support) against the British domination of Iraq. On 3 June Soviet recognition of the Greek government, recently defeated by Germany and now in exile, was withdrawn. Finally, on 14 June Tass put out another statement in the Soviet press, denying foreign newspaper allegations that Germany had presented territorial and economic demands to the Soviet Union. The statement went on to affirm that Germany was observing the 1939 agreement as fully as was the Soviet Union. Recent transfers of German forces to the east must be connected with other matters having nothing to do with Soviet–German relations. This was almost a plea to Germany to join in the denial, or to open negotiations if indeed there were demands to be made. Germany made no reply.

The Tass statement made it clear, if evidence were needed, that the German troop concentrations in the east had been observed. There was ample intelligence about the coming attack, and the efficient Soviet agent in the German embassy in Tokyo, Richard Sorge, provided the exact date (22 June) in a report of 15 May. It was in any case scarcely possible for over 3 million German soldiers to gather along the Soviet borders without being observed. If Stalin had wished to cry provocation, he could have found ample cause. But he did not, and all the warnings were disregarded. The Soviet forces, indeed, were unready for war. The reorganization of the armoured formations, begun after the German victories of 1940, was still in progress. The high command and officer corps had not recovered from the effects of the purges. Fortifications along the former boundary with Poland had been dismantled, and a plan to replace them along the new frontier was approved only in the summer of 1940, and was scheduled to take several years to carry out. Even the most elementary precautions against attack were not taken, and the Tass statement of 14 June, which did nothing to appease the Germans, seems to have lulled some Soviet units into a false sense of security.

As for an Anglo-Soviet agreement to attack Germany, the prospect was so distant as to exist only in the most fevered mind. The British tried hard to alert and alarm the Soviets about German intentions. As early as 14 June 1940 the new British Ambassador, Cripps, told Molotov that Germany would turn east if France collapsed, and in the same month Churchill tried to tell Stalin that Germany would prefer to attack the USSR that very autumn, but would be compelled to wait until the spring. At the end of February 1941 Cripps told a press conference that Germany would attack the Soviet Union before the end of June. At the end of March 1941 Churchill was convinced by intelligence reports that Hitler intended to invade the USSR in May – which was at that time correct, the date being later postponed to June. Churchill telegraphed to Stalin with the gist of this information on 3

April, and was displeased with Cripps for not transmitting the message until the 19th. Cripps held it back at least partly because he thought the Soviet government would think it an attempt at provocation, in which he was very likely correct. It is certain that Stalin dismissed all British and American warnings of a German attack. By his own lights, this was perfectly reasonable. There was no cause for him to place any particular confidence in those who were, after all, his enemies, seeking to embroil him in conflict with Germany. On the other hand, the extraordinary flight of the nazi leader Rudolf Hess to Britain in May 1941 appears to have made a marked impression on Stalin, filling him with suspicions of Anglo-German collusion. Either way, he had little reason to trust the British. Of Soviet–British co-operation there is not the slightest trace.

Stalin was so far from preparing to attack Germany that he was not even ready for Germany to attack him. The German blow fell on him, and – far worse – upon his soldiers and airmen, like a bolt from the blue. The Soviet forces were naked to their enemies, and were devastated in the first few days of the attack. There has been much speculation as to why Stalin was caught out in this way. It has been said that he was paralysed, seeing the danger but unable to think of anything to do except to try to placate Hitler by over-fulfilling his economic commitments and making every possible gesture of goodwill. Certainly his actions in May and June 1941 made the western appeasers look like men of granite. It may be that he believed that the pact of 1939 was still working, and that he could trust Hitler and Ribbentrop but not the German generals: war, therefore, could come about only through the actions of 'fascist militarists'. This would explain the orders which were given to the Red Army to guard against being provoked. Or Stalin may have been under a genuine misapprehension, arising from ideological miscalculation, as to the nature of nazism: if Hitler was only the tool of monopoly capitalists, then his ravings about race and living space could safely be disregarded. An explanation which fits in well with Stalin's practical, material approach to negotiation is that he believed that the German troop concentrations were designed to exert pressure on the Soviet Union in a bargaining process which had yet to start. He may well have been waiting for the Germans to send demands for territory or further economic aid, when in fact they sent tanks. Any combination of these explanations may be found plausible; but as to the result there can be no dispute. Whether Stalin acted out of cowardice or calculation, he did nothing to provoke a German attack.

Why did Hitler invade the Soviet Union? No final answer emerges. Too much depends upon the dubious enterprise of searching the murky depths of Hitler's mind and personality. To lay exclusive emphasis on preconceived ideas of race and living space may be to produce too rigid a theory of inevitability. On the other hand, to appeal to opportunism or to the undoubted friction in German–Soviet relations seems inadequate. 'Opportunism' by itself does not explain why some opportunities were taken and others were let slip; and the attack on the Soviet Union was prepared over too long a period of time to be properly described as opportunist. Friction with the Soviet Union, over Finland, Rumania, and Bulgaria, and generally over spheres of influence as defined in 1939, certainly existed, but so far Germany was having the best of it and under little pressure to take extreme action. The German sphere of influence in eastern Europe was being steadily enlarged, while the economic arrangements with the Soviet Union still held good and operated increasingly to Germany's benefit. In these circumstances, immediate self-interest would surely point to maintaining this advantageous relationship. If the war with Britain was dominant in German thinking, the economic agreement with the Soviet Union allowed Germany to nullify the effects of the British blockade, and offered more tangible advantages than the hazardous and uncertain prospects of war.

In this balance of probabilities, ideological motives and the long-established mould of Hitler's thought carry more weight than the immediate circumstances of 1940–41, which seem sufficient to confirm a mind already made up but inadequate in themselves as a basis for decision. This view is reinforced by what happened in the campaign, which was fought, in Robert Cecil's words, 'not in the way most likely to lead to victory, but in the manner most consistent with Hitler's ideological preconceptions'.[6]

If this is so, then the German invasion of the Soviet Union in June 1941 stands as the culminating point of two of the underlying forces making for war in the 1930s and early 1940s: ideology and economics. The racial obsessions of nazism, its hostility to Bolshevism, and its determination to conquer living space and sources of raw materials, were worked out over the whole period, and took final shape in the great war in the east. To these may be added the third underlying force: strategy and military thought. A misleading over-confidence in the German military machine, fed and bloated by the astonishing victories of 1940, was an important impulse behind the attack. Of course, particular decisions still had to be made at points all along the line; but the impulse of the underlying forces was such that for Germany to escape from them would have required very determined action indeed: nothing short of internal revolution and complete transformation in thought and action. This never looked like happening. The German attack on the Sovet Union was the culmination of the whole process leading the continent of Europe into war; and to understand that process properly it must be seen as a whole.

REFERENCES AND NOTES

1. Quoted in Alan Bullock, *Hitler: a study in tyranny* (London 1952), p. 625.
2. Ibid., p. 651.
3. Quoted in Joachim Fest, *Hitler*, (London: Penguin Books 1977), p. 961.
4. Halder's diary, in *DGFP*, Series D, vol. X, p. 373 (italics in the original).
5. Henri Michel, *La Seconde Guerre Mondiale*, vol. I (Paris 1968), pp. 46–7, 50–2; Nikolai Tolstoy, *Stalin's Secret War* (London 1981), pp. 108–9.
6. Robert Cecil, *Hitler's Decision to Invade Russia, 1941* (London 1975), p. 167.

CONCLUSION

. . . though I know it (writing history) is all very right and necessary, I have
often wondered at the person's courage that could sit down on purpose to
do it.

(Catherine Morland, in Jane Austen, *Northanger Abbey*)

To sit down on purpose to summarize the origins of the Second World
War in Europe requires all the temerity wondered at by Miss Morland.
The story is still unfolding, with new evidence constantly coming to
light, and historians skirmishing vigorously about the interpretation of
events. What seems firm ground today may be undermined tomorrow,
and the clearest of guiding lights may prove on close investigation to be
a will-o'-the-wisp. Even with the fullest evidence, the historian has
only a limited vision into the minds and motives of his fellow-men, and
the decisions reached by individuals must often remain difficult to
explain; while the links between such individual decisions and the
underlying forces at work in the background are even harder to
establish with any degree of certainty.

These difficulties are real enough, and it is more than merely a
cautious historian's ritual to say that all conclusions are provisional;
but it remains tempting to reflect on what emerges from this study.

We started by examining the view that between 1914 and 1945
Europe passed through a Thirty Years War, of which the so-called
Second World War was only the final phase. This interpretation carries
much weight, in two notable respects. First, eastern Europe emerged
from the wreckage of the First World War and the ensuing settlement
in a profoundly unstable condition, with potential conflicts lurking in
half a dozen different areas. Moreover, in the period between 1919 and
1922 the countries of eastern Europe made very different assessments
about the use of force from those then current in the war-weary west.
The Bolsheviks fought and won a civil war, and established their
authority by force over much (though not all) of the old Russian
Empire. The Poles defeated a Russian invasion at the battle of Warsaw
in 1920, and then reaped the fruits of victory by pushing their frontier
eastward at the Treaty of Riga in 1921. They also seized Vilna and held

it in defiance of Lithuania; while the Lithuanians for their part occupied Memel. Rumanian forces intervened in Hungary in 1919 to overthrow the Bolshevik government of Bela Kun and stake a claim to Transylvania. While in France and Britain men counted their dead and meditated on the futility of war, the peoples of eastern Europe counted their gains and losses and observed the efficacy of force. It is not wholly surprising that, some years later, war was resumed in eastern Europe.

The second, and even weightier, point in the Thirty Years War thesis is that in 1918–19 Germany was beaten but not destroyed. Despite military defeat and political revolution, the country retained much of its old identity, resources, and aspirations. Under the surface, and among important groups in the population, there persisted the will to try again for the dominance of Europe which was so nearly achieved in 1914–18.

In both these respects, the causes of a renewed (rather than a brand new) conflict were present in the consequences of the First World War and its aftermath. Here lay the origins of the later crises over Czechoslovakia, Danzig, and Poland. Here too lay one of the springs of German expansionism, and a likely cause of conflict. A war of some sort was a likely consequence of these conditions; but in themselves they did not provide a complete explanation of the war which engulfed Europe between 1939 and 1941, which was not simply a repetition or continuation of that of 1914–18. In the simplest sense, the sides were different, with Italy fighting alongside Germany rather than with the Allies, and the Soviet Union (until June 1941) practising a neutrality favourable to Germany instead of being one of her main opponents. In a more profound sense, the issues at stake in 1939–41 were more complicated and far-reaching than those of 1914–18, because the Continent itself had been transformed, politically and economically, in the intervening years.

The conflict which developed in Europe between 1939 and 1941 arose from three major elements: the expansionist urge of Germany and Italy; the willingness of other powers to accept their expansion for so long that it became impossible to check it without major war; and the eventual determination, on the part of these same powers, to resist that expansion even at the cost of war. All three elements may be largely explained by the underlying forces which were at work in Europe.

In Germany, the forces making for expansion were given an immense new impulse by the advent to power of Hitler and the Nazi Party, with an ideology based on ideas of racial superiority and the overriding demand for living space. Moreover, under the nazi regime Germany achieved both domestic economic recovery and a rapid rate of rearmament, which together generated a great demand for imports, and hence an acute balance of payments problem. Since Hitler rejected any pause in the headlong pace of rearmament, an immediate solution to this problem appeared to lie in conquest, to secure direct control over sources of food and raw materials and to impose favourable terms of trade on other countries. Considerations of ideology and economics thus combined to generate a powerful drive for territorial expansion, whose specific timing was largely determined by strategic issues. After starting from a position of marked inferiority, Germany rapidly built up an army and air force which by 1938 were capable of taking the offensive against her neighbours. But this advantage would probably be short-lived: in a few years her potential adversaries would catch up, so that if expansion were to be achieved a brief strategic opportunity, lying somewhere between 1938 and perhaps 1943, would have to be seized.

In Italy, the fascist regime brought a new drive and self-confidence to the pursuit of long-standing aspirations in the Mediterranean and Africa. Previous Italian policy had been limited in its aims and cautious in its methods, depending largely on skilful diplomacy and juggling with alliances. Under Mussolini, Italy took a much more adventurous course, pursuing prestige, great-power status, and territorial expansion, and courting direct confrontation with France and Britain, her former allies in the First World War. In this new course, the aims and spirit of fascism played an important part, generating a belligerence and self-confidence which eventually outstripped the limits of Italian strength. But, for a brief period in 1940, Italy too appeared to be presented with a strategic opportunity which had to be seized before it passed.

In France and Britain, on the other hand, the underlying forces tended strongly against war. Both the prevailing views of politicians and the popular mood were opposed to the use of force as an instrument of policy, and were often against the idea of war at all, except as a last resort. The economic difficulties of both countries, so far from providing any impulse towards conflict, enhanced the desire for peace. For Britain in particular, large-scale war seemed bound to lead rapidly to bankruptcy through inability to pay for the country's imports. In terms of strategy and military calculation, neither France nor Britain thought in terms of opportunities to be seized, but of calamities to be avoided. Neither was capable of taking the offensive in a European war, and both went in mortal fear of air attack by a *Luftwaffe* which they assumed to be all-powerful.

In the USSR the situation was different, in so far as both communist theory and Soviet practice fully accepted the idea of war and the use of force. During the 1930s, however, the internal effects of Stalinism (collectivization of agriculture, the great purges, and a forced march towards industrialization which was still far from being completed) made the Soviet Union very chary of becoming involved in a major war. The Soviet economy remained backward in comparison with that of Germany, and the armed forces, though strong in numbers, were only dubiously capable of taking the offensive outside the boundaries of the state. On all these counts, it seems highly likely that the USSR was disposed to avoid a large-scale conflict if it was at all possible.

The underlying forces at work in Europe thus combined to produce two markedly different groups of powers. Germany and Italy were active and adventurous, and sought to disrupt the status quo for their own advantage. France, Britain, and the Soviet Union were passive and cautious. France and Britain were whole-hearted supporters of the status quo: they possessed all the territory they could desire, and wished only to be left in peace to enjoy it. The Soviet Union had no attachment to the status quo as such, whether territorial or ideological, but for the time being it could afford no adventures. The initiative in international affairs, from at least 1935 onwards, thus lay with Germany and Italy, who exploited it with great energy, brutal methods, and considerable skill. For a long time, their potential opponents (and potential victims) acquiesced in the advance of German and Italian power, seeking agreements which they hoped would satisfy those ambitious states without serious damage to their own interests. The Anglo-German Naval Treaty of 1935, the Hoare–Laval proposals over Abyssinia. The Anglo–Italian Mediterranean agreement of April 1938, the Munich conference, and the Nazi–Soviet Pact of August 1939, all formed part of this pattern. The particular actions of the different states were separate and uncoordinated, but all were governed by the same guiding idea. While these events were taking place, it may be that opportunities were lost to check the German and Italian advance without war: by imposing oil sanctions against Italy in 1935, for example, or by the French Army advancing resolutely into the Rhineland in 1936. This may be so; or the result might merely have been to start a different kind of war at an earlier date. We cannot tell. What is certain is that, once the advance of the active powers had reached a certain point, it could only be checked – if at all – by a major war.

That the advance would at some stage be opposed admitted of no serious doubt. Even in France and Britain, the policy of 'appeasement' never meant the pursuit of peace at any price. When it came to the crunch, both countries would fight to preserve their vital interests, their status as great powers, and their long-established forms of government and social organization. In eastern Europe, the bold and determined Poles would yield neither territory nor independence; and no one could expect the Soviet Union to surrender either its land or its ideological identity without a struggle. If the drive of the expansionist powers, and especially Germany, was maintained, it was bound at some stage to be opposed; and from that opposition a great war would almost certainly arise.

The basic elements of an explosive international situation were thus present in Europe during the late 1930s. But the exact course of events was by no means predetermined. Different peoples and governments made widely varying assessments of the situation, and much depended on the decisions (and hesitations) of individual statesmen. Hitler, while showing a broad and powerful consistency of purpose, still drew back from attacking Czechoslovakia in September 1938 and hesitated briefly over going to war with Poland at the end of August 1939; while in the summer of 1940 he cast around for some months, uncertain what to do after his spectacular victories. In Italy, Mussolini wavered on the brink in August 1939 and during the winter of 1939–40, and then made his personal choice for war in May–June 1940. In Britain, Chamberlain and his government believed in 1938 that it was possible to meet Germany's ambitions while preserving British security; but by February–March 1939 they had concluded that Germany's real aim was the domination of Europe, which they could not accept. French governments, often short-lived and always conscious of the weakness and divisions of their country, suffered for a long time a paralysis of will; but were eventually driven, however reluctantly, to the same conclusion as the British. In the USSR, Stalin followed his own judgement as to the interests of his country and played for safety by means of the Nazi–Soviet Pact. He continued, to the last moment, to hope that security could be maintained by co-operation with Germany, before finding – almost too late – that it could not. Even among the smaller powers, the scope for varying responses to the developing crisis was repeatedly manifested. In September 1938, for example, Czechoslovakia yielded to the combined pressure of Germany, France, and Britain, and chose to accept the disastrous Munich settlement; but in 1939 Poland stood firm against all comers, and fought rather than yield to German threats. The underlying forces remained much the same over the period under examination; but evaluations of their significance, and responses to them, varied widely, so that no theory of inevitability holds good for all the different participants in these great events.

In one important respect – and despite the length of this book – the explanation of the war is extremely simple, and historians have been prone to weave too many mystifications about it. Of the two expansionist powers, Italy was not by herself strong enough to risk or embark on a great war. Germany was; and unless German expansion halted of its own accord without breaching the limits set by the vital interests of other strong and determined states, then war was bound to come. German expansion did not halt, and certain choices were therefore presented to other countries in straightforward terms. In 1939 the Poles fought because they were attacked, and they went on fighting rather than accept the destruction of their state and the enslavement of its people. Britain and France fought because they finally felt that Germany had gone too far, and also because the issues posed by the growth of German power had become sharply personalized. Hitler was out to dominate the Continent, and to impose upon it his own particular brand of tyranny. He had demonstrated beyond a peradventure that he could not be trusted, and that agreements with him were futile. He therefore had to be defeated and his regime overthrown: it was not clear how, but it had to be done. Later, in 1940 and 1941, in the continuing – indeed by then the headlong – advance of German power, one state after another faced the question of whether to yield or resist; until finally the Soviet Union was compelled to fight by the simplest and most brutal imperative – invasion.

In all this there is no mystery. But all depended on the fateful premiss that German expansion would not halt unless it was forcibly resisted. It is not surprising that most of the discussion on the origins of the Second World War in Europe continues to concentrate on the motives and forces behind the expansion of Germany. On those questions the last word has not been, and may never be, pronounced.

FURTHER READING

The following is a selection from the mass of material on the origins of the Second World War in Europe. It is related to the topics dealt with in this book, and is restricted to books available in English. The arrangement is inevitably somewhat arbitrary, so that, for example, a book dealing with nazi Germany may be placed under either 'Ideology' or 'Germany'.

1. GENERAL

Anthony P. Adamthwaite, *The Making of the Second World War* (2nd edn.). London 1979.

Maurice Baumont, *The Origins of the Second World War* (Eng. tr). New Haven, Conn. 1978.

Peter Calvocoressi and Guy Wint, *Total War. Causes and courses of the Second World War*. London 1972.

Hans W. Gatzke (ed.), *European Diplomacy between Two Wars, 1919–1939*. Chicago 1972.

Ruth Henig (ed.), *The League of Nations*. Edinburgh 1973.

Laurence Lafore, *The End of Glory. An Interpretation of the origins of World War II*. New York 1970.

W. Roger Louis (ed.), *The Origins of the Second World War. A. J. P. Taylor and his critics*. New York 1972.

Sally Marks, *The Illusion of Peace. International relations in Europe, 1918–1933*. London 1976.

Henri Michel, *The Second World War* (Eng. tr.). London 1974.

Joachim Remak, *The Origins of the Second World War*. Englewood Cliffs, N.J. 1976.

Esmonde M. Robertson (ed.), *The Origins of the Second World War. Historical Interpretations*. London 1971.

A. J. P. Taylor, *The Origins of the Second World War*. London 1961; reprinted with new preface, 1963.

2. IDEOLOGY

Pierre Ayçoberry, *The Nazi Question. An essay on the interpretations of National Socialism, 1922–1975* (Eng. tr.). London 1981.

David Caute, *Communism and the French Intellectuals, 1914–1960*. London 1964.

David Caute, *The Fellow Travellers*. London 1973.

Federico Chabod, *A History of Italian Fascism* (Eng. tr.). London 1963.

A. James Gregor, *Italian Fascism and Developmental Dictatorship*. Princeton 1979.

Richard Griffiths, *Fellow Travellers of the Right. British enthusiasts for Nazi Germany, 1933–39*. London 1980.

Alistair Hamilton, *The Appeal of Fascism, 1919–1945*. London 1971.

Adolf Hitler, *Mein Kampf* (Eng. tr., with introd. by D. C. Watt). London 1974.

Adolf Hitler, *Hitler's Secret Book* (Eng. tr. with introd. by Telford Taylor). New York 1961.

Michael Howard, *War and the Liberal Conscience*. Oxford 1981.

Eberhard Jaeckel, *Hitler's Weltanschauung. A blueprint for power* (Eng. tr.). Middletown, Conn. 1972.

H. R. Kedward, *Fascism in Western Europe, 1900–45*. London 1969.

Walter Laqueur (ed.), *Fascism: a reader's guide*. Harmondsworth 1979.

Michael A. Ledeen, *Universal Fascism. The theory and practice of the Fascist International, 1928–1936*. New York 1972.

Adrian Lyttelton (ed.), *Italian Fascisms from Pareto to Gentile*. London 1973.

Werner Maser, *Hitler's Mein Kampf. An analysis* (Eng. tr). London 1970.

Roy Medvedev, *Let History Judge*. London 1971.

Ernst Nolte, *Three Faces of Fascism* (Eng. tr.). New York, 1969.

Alec Nove, *Stalinism and After*. London 1975.

Hermann Rauschning, *Germany's Revolution of Destruction* (Eng. tr.). London 1939.

Hermann Rauschning, *Hitler Speaks* (Eng. tr.). London 1939.

Stuart Woolf (ed.), *European Fascism*. London 1968.

Stuart Woolf (ed.), *The Nature of Fascism*. London 1968.

3. ECONOMIC AFFAIRS

D. H. Aldcroft, *From Versailles to Wall Street, 1919–1929*. London 1977.

Berenice A. Carroll, *Design for Total War. Arms and economics in the Third Reich*. The Hague 1968.

Carlo M. Cipolla (ed.), *The Fontana Economic History of Europe: The twentieth century*. 2 vols, London 1976. *Contemporary Economies*. 2 vols, London 1976.

Shephard B. Clough, *The Economic History of Modern Italy*. New York 1964.

Martin Fritz, *German Steel and Swedish Iron Ore, 1939–1945* (Eng. tr.). Göteborg 1974.

David E. Kaiser, *Economic Diplomacy and the Origins of the Second World War*. Princeton 1980.

Charles P. Kindleberger, *The World in Depression, 1929–1939*. London 1973.

A. S. Milward, *War, Economy and Society, 1939–1945*. London 1977.

A. S. Milward, *The German Economy at War*. London 1965.

G. C. Peden, *British Rearmament and the Treasury, 1932–1939*. Edinburgh 1979.

R. J. Overy, *The Nazi Economic Recovery, 1932–1938*. London 1982.

Robert Paul Shay, *British Rearmament in the Thirties: politics and profits*. London, 1977.

Amos E. Simpson, *Hjalmar Schacht in Perspective*. The Hague 1969.

4. STRATEGY AND ARMED FORCES

Uri Bialer, *The Shadow of the Bomber*. London 1980.

Brian Bond, *British Military Policy Between the Two World Wars*. Oxford 1980.

Matthew Cooper, *The German Army, 1933–1945*. London 1978.

Matthew Cooper, *The German Air Force, 1933–1945*. London 1981.

Wilhelm Deist, *The Wehrmacht and German Rearmament*. London 1981.

P. J. Dennis, *Decision by Default. Peacetime conscription and British defence, 1919–1939*. London 1972.

Harold C. Deutsch, *Hitler and his Generals: the hidden crisis, January–June 1938*. Minneapolis 1974.

John Erickson, *The Soviet High Command. A military–political history, 1918–1941*. London 1962.

N. H. Gibbs, *Rearmament Policy*. London 1976. Vol. I in J. R. M. Butler (ed.), *Grand Strategy* in the military series of the British official history of the Second World War.)

John Gooch, *Armies in Europe*. London 1980.

Jeffery A. Gunsburg, *Divided and Conquered. The French High Command and the defeat of the west, 1940*. London 1980.

F. H. Hinsley *et al.*, *British Intelligence in the Second World War*, vol. I, London 1979.

Edward L. Homze, *Arming the Luftwaffe. The Reich Air Ministry and the German aircraft industry, 1919–39*. Lincoln, Nebraska 1976.

Michael Howard, *The Continental Commitment. The dilemma of British defence policy in the era of two world wars*. London 1972.

H. Montgomery Hyde, *British Air Policy between the Wars, 1918–1939*. London 1976.

Williamson Murray, *The Change in the European Balance of Power, 1938–1939*. Princeton 1984.

Robert J. O'Neill, *The German Army and the Nazi Party, 1933–1939* (2nd edn). London 1968.

Adrian Preston (ed.), *General Staffs and Diplomacy before the Second World War*. London 1978.

Stephen Roskill, *Naval Policy between the Wars*. 2 vols, London 1968, 1976.

Donald Cameron Watt, *Too Serious a Business. European armed forces and the approach to the Second World War*. London 1975.

J. W. Wheeler-Bennett, *The Nemesis of Power. The German Army in politics, 1918–1945*. London 1953.

Robert J. Young, *In Command of France. French foreign policy and military planning 1933–1940*. Cambridge, Mass. 1978.

5. THE COMING OF WAR, 1935–1941

Christopher Andrew and David Dilks (eds.), *The Missing Dimension. Governments and intelligence communities in the twentieth century*. London 1984.

Sidney Aster, *1939. The making of the Second World War*. London 1973.

G. W. Baer, *Test Case. Italy, Ethiopia and the League of Nations*. Stanford, Calif. 1977.

J. W. Breugel, *Czechoslovakia before Munich. The German minority problem and British appeasement policy*. Cambridge 1973.

Gordon Brook-Shepherd, *Anschluss. The rape of Austria*. London 1963.

P. Broué and E. Témime, *Revolution and Civil War in Spain* (Eng. tr.). London 1972.

William Carr, *Poland to Pearl Harbour. The making of the Second World War*. London 1985.

Robert Cecil, *Hitler's Decision to Invade Russia, 1941*. London 1975.

John F. Coverdale, *Italian Intervention in the Spanish Civil War*. Princeton 1975.

Martin van Creveld, *Hitler's Strategy, 1940–1941. The Balkan clue*. Cambridge 1973.

J. T. Emmerson, *The Rhineland Crisis, 7 March 1936*. London 1977.

J. Gehl, *Austria, Germany and the Anschluss, 1931–38*. Oxford 1963.

Frank Hardie, *The Abyssinian Crisis*. London 1974.

Walther Hofer, *War Premeditated, 1939* (Eng. tr.). London 1955.

Barry A. Leach, *German Strategy against Russia, 1939–1941. Oxford 1973*.

John Lukacs, *The Last European War, September 1939–December 1941*. London 1977.

J. M. Meskill, *Hitler and Japan. The hollow alliance*. New York 1966.

J. W. Morley (ed.), *Deterrent Diplomacy. Japan, Germany and the USSR, 1935–1940*. New York 1976.

L. B. Namier, *Diplomatic Prelude, 1938–1939*. London 1950.

E. L. Presseisen, *Germany and Japan. A study in totalitarian diplomacy*. The Hague 1958.

Keith Robbins, *Munich 1938*. London 1968.

Telford Taylor, *Munich. The price of peace*. London 1979.

Hugh Thomas, *The Spanish Civil War* (3rd edn). Harmondsworth 1977.

Christopher Thorne, *The Approach of War, 1938–1939*. London 1967.

Mario Toscano, *The Origins of the Pact of Steel* (Eng. tr.). Baltimore 1967.

Gerhard L. Weinberg, *The Foreign Policy of Hitler's Germany. Diplomatic revolution in Europe, 1933–1936*. Chicago 1970.

Gerhard L. Weinberg, *The Foreign Policy of Hitler's Germany. Starting World War II*. Chicago 1980.

Gerhard L. Weinberg, *Germany and the Soviet Union, 1939–1941*. Leiden 1954.

Elizabeth Wiskemann, *The Rome–Berlin Axis* (rev. edn). London 1960.

6. PARTICULAR COUNTRIES

BRITAIN

David Carlton, *Anthony Eden*. London 1981.

Winston S. Churchill, *The Second World War*, vol. I, *The Gathering Storm*. London 1948.

Martin Ceadel, *Pacifism in Britain, 1914–1945*. Oxford 1980.

David Dilks, (ed.), *Retreat from Power. Studies in Britain's foreign policy in the twentieth century*. 2 vols, London 1981.

Franklin Reid Gannon, *The British Press and Germany, 1936–1939*. Oxford 1971.

C. A. MacDonald, *The United States, Britain, and Appeasement, 1936–1939*. London 1981.

Keith Middlemas, *Diplomacy of Illusion. The British government and Germany, 1937–39*. London 1972.

John F. Naylor, *Labour's International Policy. The Labour Party in the 1930s*. London 1969.

Simon Newman, *March 1939. The British guarantee to Poland*. Oxford 1976.

David Reynolds, *The Creation of the Anglo-American Alliance, 1937–41*. London 1981.

William R. Rock, *British Appeasement in the 1930s*. London 1977.

FRANCE

Anthony P. Adamthwaite, *France and the Coming of the Second World War, 1936–1939*. London 1977.

Joel G. Colton, *Léon Blum. Humanist in politics*. New York 1966.

J. Néré, *The Foreign Policy of France from 1914 to 1945* (Eng. tr.). London 1975.

Neville Waites (ed.), *Troubled Neighbours. Franco-British relations in the twentieth century*. London 1971.

GERMANY

K. D. Bracher, *The German Dictatorship* (Eng. tr.). Harmondsworth 1973.

Alan Bullock, *Hitler. A study in tyranny* (rev. edn). Harmondsworth 1962.

William Carr, *Arms, Autarky and Aggression. A study in German foreign policy, 1933–1939*. London 1972.

William Carr, *Hitler. A study in personality and politics*. London 1978.

Gordon A. Craig, *Germany 1866–1945*. Oxford 1978.

Joachim Fest, *Hitler* (Eng. tr.). Harmondsworth 1977.

Milan Hauner, *Hitler. A chronology of his life and times*. London 1983.

Klaus Hildebrand, *The Foreign Policy of the Third Reich* (Eng. tr.). London 1973.

Norman Rich, *Hitler's War Aims*. 2 vols, London 1973–74.

E. M. Robertson, *Hitler's Pre-War Policy and Military Plans, 1933–1939*. London 1963.

Paul Seabury, *The Wilhelmstrasse. A study of German diplomats under the Nazi regime*. Berkeley 1954.

Norman Stone, *Hitler*. London 1980.

ITALY

A. Cassels, *Mussolini's Early Diplomacy*. Princeton 1971.

Galleazzo Ciano, *Ciano's Diary, 1937–1938* (Eng. tr., introd. by Malcolm Muggeridge). London 1952.

Galleazzo Ciano, *Ciano's Diary, 1939–1943* (Eng. tr., ed. with an introd. by Malcolm Muggeridge). London 1947.

Ivone Kirkpatrick, *Mussolini. Study of a demagogue*. London 1964.

MacGregor Knox, *Mussolini Unleashed, 1939–1941. Politics and strategy in Fascist Italy's last war*. Cambridge 1982.

C. J. Lowe and F. Marzari, *Italian Foreign Policy, 1870–1940*. London 1975.

Esmonde M. Robertson, *Mussolini as Empire-Builder. Europe and Africa, 1932–36*. London 1977.

Denis Mack Smith, *Mussolini*. London 1981.

Denis Mack Smith, *Mussolini's Roman Empire*. Harmondsworth 1979.

POLAND

B. B. Budurowycz, *Polish–Soviet Relations, 1932–1939*. New York 1963.

Anna M. Cienciala, *Poland and the Western Powers, 1938–39*. London 1968.

Roman Debicki, *The Foreign Policy of Poland, 1919–1939*. London 1963.

W. Jedrzewicz (ed.). *Diplomat in Berlin, 1933–1939. Papers and memoirs of Jozef Lipski*. New York 1968.

W. Jedrzewicz (ed.), *Diplomat in Paris, 1936–1939. Papers and memoirs of Juliuz Lukasiewicz*. New York 1970.

R. F. Leslie (ed.), *The History of Poland since 1863*. Cambridge 1980.

SOVIET UNION

Robert Conquest, *The Great Terror*. London 1968.

Ronald Hingley, *Joseph Stalin: man and legend*. London 1974.

George F. Kennan, *Russia and the West under Lenin and Stalin*. London 1961.

Vladimir Petrov, *June 22 1941. Soviet historians and the German Invasion*. Columbia, S. C. 1968.

B. N. Ponomaryov, A. A. Gromyko, and V. M. Kostov (eds.), *History of the Foreign Policy of the USSR* (4th edn), vol. I, *1917–1945*. Moscow 1981.

Adam B. Ulam, *Expansion and Co-existence. The history of Soviet foreign policy, 1918–67*. London 1968.

Adam B. Ulam, *Stalin*. London 1974.

USA

Robert A. Dallek, *Franklin D. Roosevelt and American Foreign Policy, 1932–1945*. Oxford 1979.

R. A. Divine, *The Illusion of Neutrality*. Chicago 1962.

W. L. Langer and S. E. Gleason, *The Challenge to Isolation*. New York 1952.

W. L. Langer and S. E. Gleason, *The Undeclared War, 1940–1941*. New York 1953.

A. A. Offner, *American Appeasement. United States foreign policy and Germany, 1933–1938*. Cambridge, Mass. 1969.

OTHER COUNTRIES

Elisabeth Barker, *Austria 1918–1972*. London 1973.

Josef Korbel, *Twentieth-century Czechoslovakia*. New York 1977.

C. A. Macartney and A. W. Palmer, *Independent Eastern Europe, 1919–1941*. London 1962.

Antony Polonsky, *The Little Dictators. The history of eastern Europe since 1918*. London 1975.

Joseph Rothschild, *East Central Europe Between the Two World Wars*. Seattle 1974.

W. V. Wallace, *Czechoslovakia*. London 1977.

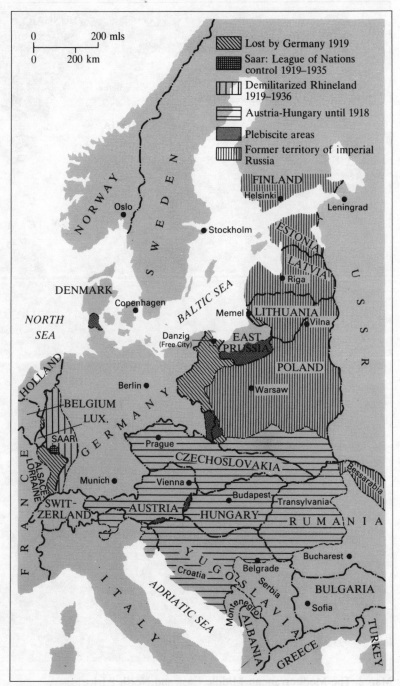

Map 1 European Peace Settlements, 1919–1920

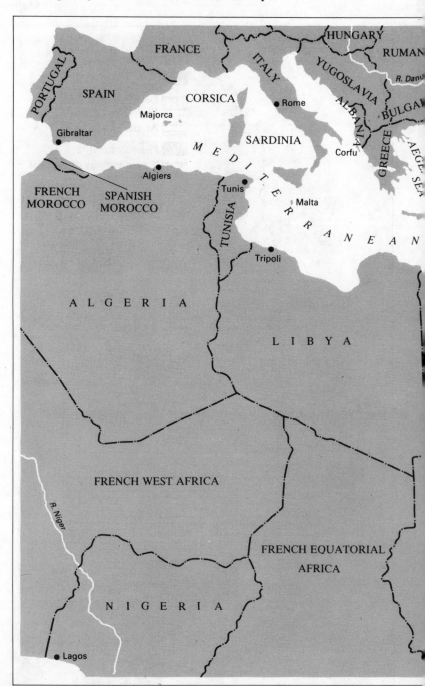

Map 2 The Mediterranean, Middle East, and North Africa

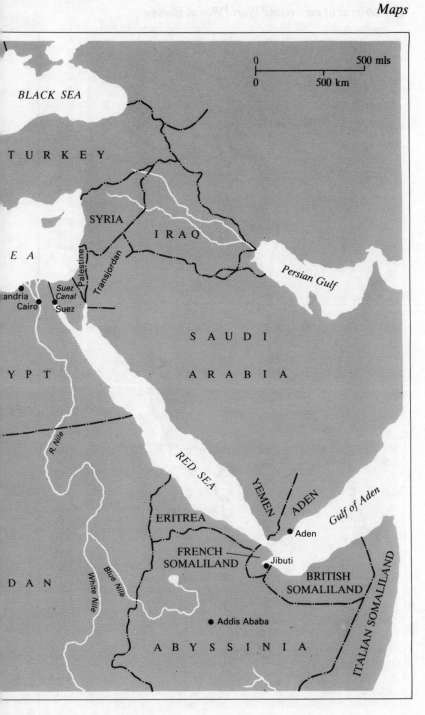

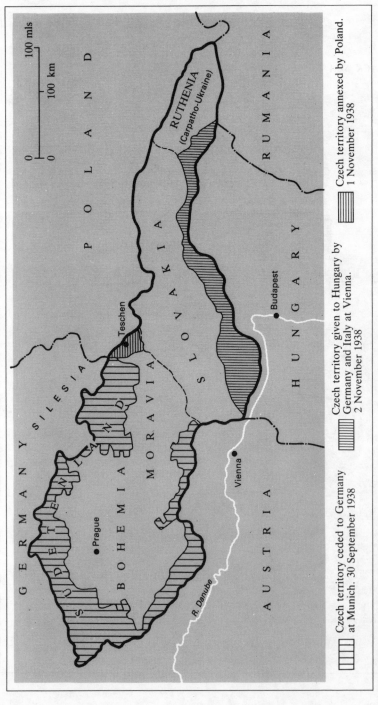

Map 3 Czechoslovakia, 1938

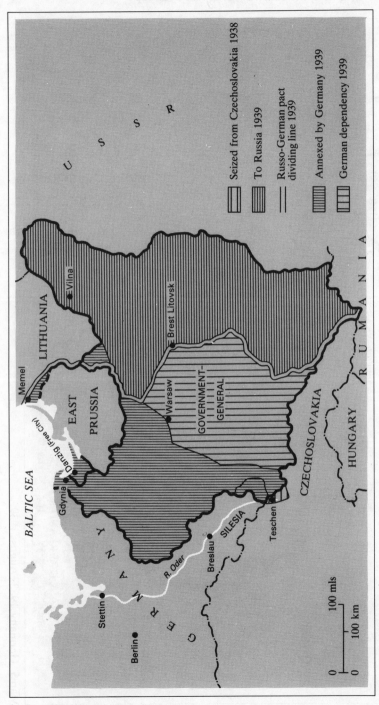

Legend:
- Seized from Czechoslovakia 1938
- To Russia 1939
- Russo-German pact dividing line 1939
- Annexed by Germany 1939
- German dependency 1939

U S S R

LITHUANIA

• Vilna

• Brest Litovsk

Memel

EAST PRUSSIA

Danzig (free city)

GOVERNMENT-GENERAL

Warsaw •

Gdynia •

BALTIC SEA

G E R M A N Y

R. Oder

Breslau •

SILESIA

Teschen •

CZECHOSLOVAKIA

R U M A N I A

HUNGARY

Stettin •

Berlin •

0 ——— 100 mls
0 ——— 100 km

Map 4 Poland, 1939

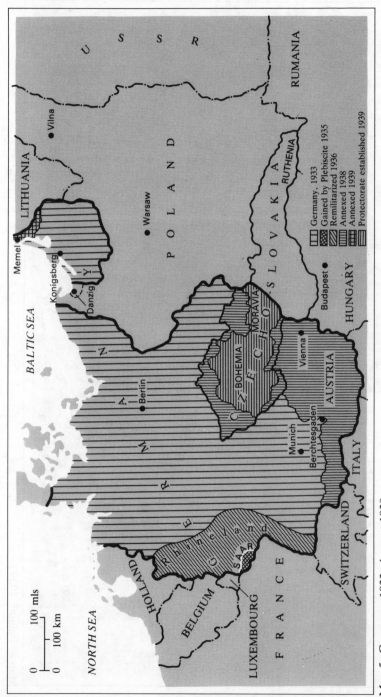

Map 5 Germany, 1933–August 1939

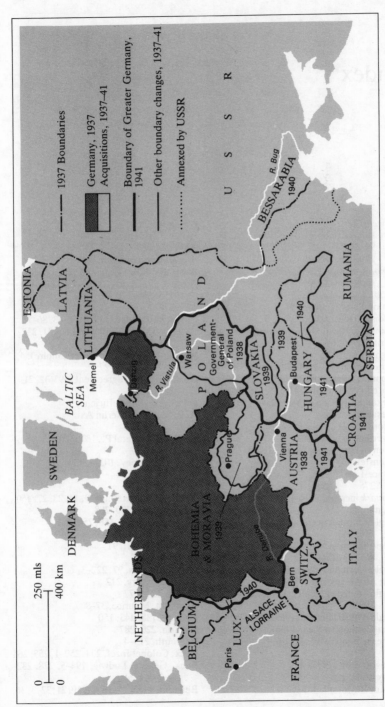

Map 6 Greater Germany, 1941

1937 Boundaries

Germany, 1937
Acquisitions, 1937–41

Boundary of Greater Germany, 1941

Other boundary changes, 1937–41

Annexed by USSR

315

Index